World religions and norms of war

World religions and norms of war

Edited by Vesselin Popovski, Gregory M. Reichberg and Nicholas Turner

United Nations
University Press

TOKYO · NEW YORK · PARIS

© United Nations University, 2009

The views expressed in this publication are those of the authors and do not necessarily reflect the views of the United Nations University.

United Nations University Press
United Nations University, 53–70, Jingumae 5-chome,
Shibuya-ku, Tokyo 150-8925, Japan
Tel: +81-3-5467-1212   Fax: +81-3-3406-7345
E-mail: sales@hq.unu.edu   general enquiries: press@hq.unu.edu
http://www.unu.edu

United Nations University Office at the United Nations, New York
2 United Nations Plaza, Room DC2-2062, New York, NY 10017, USA
Tel: +1-212-963-6387   Fax: +1-212-371-9454
E-mail: unuona@ony.unu.edu

United Nations University Press is the publishing division of the United Nations University.

Cover design by Mori Design Inc., Tokyo

Printed in the United States of America

ISBN 978-92-808-1163-6

Library of Congress Cataloging-in-Publication Data

World religions and norms of war / edited by Vesselin Popovski, Gregory M. Reichberg, and Nicholas Turner.
    p.   cm.
 Includes bibliographical references and index.
 ISBN 978-9280811636 (pbk.)
 1. War—Religious aspects. 2. Religions. I. Popovski, Vesselin. II. Reichberg, Gregory M. III. Turner, Nicholas.
BL65.W2W68 2009
205′.6242—dc22   2008055279

Endorsements

"As long as religious differences and religious doctrines remain significant sources of war and conflict, it will be vitally important for potential adversaries to achieve a greater mutual comprehension of the beliefs about the morality of war in their different religious traditions. But it is perhaps even more important for people to understand clearly the moral teachings about war in their own religion. This splendid new book provides a starting point for enhanced understanding in a series of concise, accessible, and historically informed expositions and analyses of diverse religious views of the morality of war. Among the book's many virtues is that it does not treat the dominant religions as monolithic but devotes a chapter to each major branch, thereby revealing both harmonies and differences not only between but within the different religions. There could hardly be a more timely or important book."
Jeff McMahan, *Professor of Philosophy, Rutgers University*

"All great religions hold life to be sacred; all profess peace; yet few are absolutely pacifist. The exploration of circumstances in which the use of force may be justified by religions offers rich potential to distil a universe of original wisdom and interpretive essays to shed light on an eternal question of philosophy, politics, law and morality. The chapters are full of insights into the contemporary human condition and offer a more nuanced and illuminating, not to say politically much needed, antidote to simplistic and self-fulfilling commentary on the clash of civilizations."
Ramesh Thakur, *Director, Balsillie School of International Affairs, Canada*

"This book is both timely and timeless: timely because of the surge of interest in the subject of religious perspectives on war and timeless because it covers millennia of human thought and principles that will remain with humanity for all time to come. The volume is incredibly rich: rich in historical description, rich in scriptural references and rich in illustrations of diversity within each religion. This magnificent collection demonstrates not only the wide divergences but also the many strong commonalities among religious traditions. The conclusions in the book come naturally from the depth of expert analysis, they reach beyond theology and make a powerful commentary on humanity's efforts to curtail and civilize the initiation and conduct of brutal wars."

Walter Dorn, *Professor, Royal Military College, Canada*

"This extraordinary edited volume should speak to those who are fed up with the use of religion to fuel conflicts. The original contributions in this volume represent the diversity of religious thinking about the variety of justifications for going to war (jus ad bellum) and ethical debates regarding methods of warfare (jus in bello). The discussion in this book is especially relevant and propitious at this moment in our history when the global hegemon seems to be signalling a potential policy shift from a 'clash of civilizations' to a 'dialogue among civilizations' framework. The content of this book is not just for theologians, historians and political scientists. Ordinary citizens from every civilization should read this book."

W. Andy Knight, *Professor of International Relations, University of Alberta, Canada*

Contents

Acknowledgements

This volume results from a joint project initiated and implemented by the United Nations University (UNU) and the International Peace Research Institute, Oslo (PRIO). The project depended upon the wide geographical and cultural spread of the contributors, which has resulted in a rich and unique volume. From the outset, the project has consciously striven to add perspectives from a range of disciplines including theology, history, philosophy and law.

Our limited funds were considerably supplemented by the generosity of our additional funders, whose assistance we gratefully acknowledge: the Norwegian Ministry of Foreign Affairs and the Research Council of Norway. Thanks are also due to PRIO's Cyprus Center, which helped host a workshop on the island where the volume chapters were first presented, to Ingeborg Haavardsson at PRIO and Yoshie Sawada at UNU, who have provided valuable administrative support for the project team, and to Dr Morteza Mirhashemi and Professor Mohammad Faghfoory, who translated Chapter 9 ("Norms of War in Shia Islam") from Farsi into English. Finally, we gratefully acknowledge the contribution of our two anonymous peer reviewers, whose detailed comments and suggestions did much to improve the volume, as well the invaluable editorial support of Robert Davis at UNU Press.

Vesselin Popovski
Gregory M. Reichberg
Nicholas Turner

Contributors

Rabbi Jack Bemporad has been Director of the Center for Interreligious Understanding since its inception in 1992. He is also Professor of Interreligious Studies at the Vatican's Angelicum University in Rome, as well as Senior Rabbinic Scholar at Chavurah Beth Shalom in Alpine, NJ. Promoting inter-faith dialogue for more than 30 years, he has met with world religious leaders from Pope John Paul II to the Dalai Lama and former Iranian president Mohammad Khatami. Author of *Our Age: The Historic New Era of Christian-Jewish Understanding*, Rabbi Bemporad has received the Luminosa award of the Focolare Movement and the Raoul Wallenberg Humanitarian Leadership Award of the Center for Holocaust and Genocide Studies at Ramapo College.

Mahinda Deegalle is Visiting Scholar in the Centre for the Study of World Religions at Harvard University,

and Senior Lecturer in the School of Historical and Cultural Studies at Bath Spa University, United Kingdom. He is the editor of the *Journal of Buddhist Christian Studies* and a committee member of the United Kingdom Association for Buddhist Studies. He serves as the Book Review Editor for *Buddhist Studies Review* and *H-Buddhism*. He is the author of *Popularizing Buddhism: Preaching as Performance in Sri Lanka* (State University of New York Press, 2006), the editor of *Dharma to the UK: A Centennial Celebration of Buddhist Legacy* (World Buddhist Foundation, 2008), *Buddhism, Conflict and Violence in Modern Sri Lanka* (Routledge, 2006), and the co-editor of *Pali Buddhism* (Curzon, 1996). His current research interests focus on the ethics of war and monastic politics in relation to armed conflict and violence in modern Sri Lanka.

Davood Feirahi is Associate Professor in the Political Science Department at the University of Tehran, Iran. He was born in Zanjan, Iran, in 1964 and educated at the Religious Seminary in Qom, and holds Political Science degrees (BA, MA and PhD) from the University of Tehran, where in 1997 he became Professor of Islamic Political Thought and Systems. Prof. Feirahi has written around fifty papers on Islamic political thought and Islamic contemporary political systems. His publications include *Power, Knowledge, and Legitimacy in Islam* [Qodrat, Dānesh, va Mashro'eyyat dar Islām] (Tehran: Ney Publication, seventh reprint, 2008), *Political System and State in Islam* [Nezām-e Siyāsi va Dowlat dar Eslān] (Tehran: SAMT Publication, sixth reprint, 2008), *History of Developments of State in Islam* [Tārikh-e Tahavvol-e Dowlat dar Eslām] (Qom: University of Mufid Press, second reprint, 2008), and *The Methodology of Political Knowledge in Islamic Civilization* [Ravesh shenasi-e Danesh-e Seyasi Dar Tamadon-e Islami] (Qom, 2008).

Robert Kisala holds a PhD in Religious Studies from Tokyo University, and his publications include *Prophets of Peace: Pacifism and Cultural Identity in Japan's New Religions* (University of Hawaii Press, 1999) and *Religion and Social Crisis in Japan: Understanding Japanese Society through the Aum Affair* (edited with Mark Mullins, Palgrave, 2001). He was formerly a professor at Nanzan University in Nagoya, Japan, and is currently a member of the General Council

of the Society of the Divine Word, a Roman Catholic religious missionary congregation, in Rome, Italy.

Valerie Ona Morkevicius (PhD, University of Chicago, Political Science, 2008; MA, University of Chicago, Committee on International Relations, 2000) recently completed her dissertation, which compares perspectives on just war in the Christian, Hindu and Islamic traditions, focusing on the relationship between theological views and political power. Her essay "Just war: an ethic of restraint or the defense of order?" was published in *Justice and Violence: Political Violence, Pacifism and Cultural Transformation* (Allan Eickelmann, Eric Nelson and Tom Lansford, eds, Ashgate Press, 2005). She is currently a visiting Assistant Professor at DePaul University in Chicago.

Vesselin Popovski is Senior Academic Programme Officer and Director of Studies on International Order and Justice in the Peace and Governance Programme of the United Nations University. He is a former diplomat, serving as a UN Desk Officer at the Bulgarian Foreign Ministry and later as First Secretary at the Bulgarian Embassy in London. He was Lecturer and Program Director at the Centre for European Studies, Exeter University, UK (1999–2002). He was a contributor to the ICISS Report *Responsibility to Protect* (2001) and co-author of the *Princeton Principles of Universal Jurisdiction* (2001). In 2002–4 he worked for the International Helsinki Federation for Human

Rights in Moscow, implementing the European Union Project "Legal Protection of Individual Rights in Russia". He has published on intervention, human rights, the International Criminal Court, and UN reforms. His most recent book is *International Criminal Accountability and the Rights of Children* (co-edited with K. Arts, Hague Academic Press, 2006).

Gregory M. Reichberg is Research Professor at the International Peace Research Institute, Oslo (PRIO). He holds adjunct positions at the Norwegian School of Theology (Oslo) and the Australian National University (Canberra). He has co-edited *The Ethics of War* (Blackwell, 2006) and *Ethics, Nationalism, and Just War* (Catholic University of America Press, 2007). Reichberg has published widely on historical aspects of just war theory, including, most recently, *"Jus ad Bellum" in War: Essays in Political Philosophy* (Cambridge University Press, 2008) and "Just War and Regular War: Competing Paradigms", in *Just and Unjust Warriors* (Oxford University Press, 2008).

Kaushik Roy specializes in South Asian warfare. He is Associate Researcher at the Centre for the Study of Civil War at the International Peace Research Institute, Oslo. He is also a Lecturer at the Department of History, in Presidency College, Kolkata. He has published six books and 30 articles in peer reviewed journals including the *Journal of Military History* and *War in History*. His most recent publications are *Brown Warriors of the Raj* (New Delhi: Manohar, 2008)

and *1857 Uprising* (London/Kolkata: Anthem, 2008). His book *The Oxford Companion to Military History of Modern India,* is forthcoming.

Amira Sonbol is Professor of Islamic History, Law and Society at Georgetown's School of Foreign Service. She specializes in the history of modern Egypt, Islamic history and law, women, gender and Islam and is the author of several books including *The New Mamluks: Egyptian Society and Modern Feudalism*; *Women, the Family and Divorce Laws in Islamic History*; *Women of the Jordan: Islam, Labor and Law*; *Beyond the Exotic: Muslim Women's Histories*. She is Editor-in-Chief of *HAWWA: the Journal of Women of the Middle East and the Islamic World* (published by E.J. Brill), and co-editor of *Islam and Christian-Muslim Relations*, a quarterly journal co-published with Selly Oak Colleges (UK).

Yuri Stoyanov graduated from the University of Sofia and obtained his MPhil and PhD from the University of London. A Fellow of the Royal Asiatic Society, he is based at SOAS, University of London, and is Associate Fellow of the American Albright Institute of Archaeological Research, Jerusalem. He has been a Visiting Research Fellow at St Edmund Hall, Oxford, an F. A. Yates Fellow at the Warburg Institute and a Lady Davis Fellow at the Hebrew University of Jerusalem. He was Director of the British Academy's Kenyon Institute, formerly the British School of Archaeology in Jerusalem (2006–2008). His books include *The*

Hidden Tradition in Europe (1994), *Christian Dualist Heresies in the Byzantine World c.650–c.1450* (assistant ed. and tr.), *The Other God. Dualist Religions from Antiquity to the Cathar Heresy* (2000).

Nicholas Turner is Academic Programme Associate in the Peace and Governance Programme of the United Nations University. He completed his MA in International Relations at the University of Kent in the UK, and previously worked for local government and charities there. He has taught at Aoyama Gakuin University and Hosei University in Tokyo, Japan. His specific research interests lie in human rights and ethics, focusing in particular on just war theory, the universalism/cultural relativism debate, the Responsibility to Protect, terrorism and justifications for derogations from human rights obligations. He is currently engaged in research into the implications for just war theory of the increased role of private military companies and other non-state actors in military conflict.

Introduction

Vesselin Popovski

War is a rational choice, but there is always a desire from all sides to look for a certain ideology behind the rationality of war – to couple the pragmatism of decisions with various beliefs, principles or dogmas. With the end of the East–West ideological confrontation, attempts have been made to review the sources and nature of conflicts. Samuel Huntington first proposed the idea of a "clash of civilizations",[1] arguing that, with the demise of Communism and the end of the Cold War, conflicts will emerge along the dividing lines of national, ethnic or religious groups, in effect bringing religion back as an ideological *causa belli*. Inter-religious or "holy" wars existed for centuries before Huntington. Scholars debated whether the Crusades were about religious supremacy, or whether the "holy" warriors used – or, rather, abused – the name of God for material interests, such as grabbing foreign land.[2] Some challenged Huntington for simplifying the causes of conflicts, and argued that civilizational identities are not necessarily solid foundations, that there could be official and unofficial, orthodox and unorthodox civilizations.[3]

Today, more people in more countries exercise individual freedom of expression and decide independently whether to identify themselves through ethnic or religious characteristics or to resist predetermined affiliations.[4] Yet many violent conflicts – Kashmir, Northern Ireland, Bosnia, Kosovo, Chechnya, Darfur and Iraq – have been presented as inter-religious conflicts, and have generated discussions about how religious traditions would justify wars between states, and rebellions within states. Recent terrorist attacks, carried out all over the world – in

World religions and norms of war, Popovski, Reichberg and Turner (eds),
United Nations University Press, 2009, ISBN 978-92-808-1163-6

Moscow, New York, Colombo, Bali, Madrid, Istanbul, London, Mumbai and Algiers, among others – by organizations claiming religious motivations, have raised further questions about religious attitudes to violence. To understand how religion and violence are connected, one must look at the original religious texts and at the subsequent teachings and interpretations within religious traditions. A fresh analysis of when and how world religions justify the use of force is necessary in order to avoid oversimplification in the explanation of recent conflicts, terrorism, asymmetric warfare, genocide, ethnic cleansing and crimes against humanity. The importance of examining such issues arises from the fact that religions continue to be the foundations of human civilization – the central anchors of human consciousness, motivation and behaviour.

This book results from a joint research project conducted by the United Nations University (UNU) in Tokyo and the International Peace Research Institute in Oslo (PRIO). It brings together theologians and historians with in-depth knowledge of religious traditions, who were approached and asked to research and write original chapters on how the world religious traditions address specifically the issues of justification of war (*jus ad bellum*) and methods of warfare (*jus in belli*). Many books on religion and war have been written by Western authors. A distinct feature of this book project is that it assembles scholars with deep roots in each tradition. We consciously aimed to create more direct access to the internal debates within the traditions and channel these debates towards *jus ad bellum* and *jus in bello* considerations. Our book is dedicated both to exploring the historical roots and interpretations of all the major traditions and to linking them to the challenges of modern warfare. An essential virtue of this book is that all the authors have profound expertise in their religions and they are both intellectually and emotionally engaged in the debates.

The book reflects on many historical texts and demonstrates how the world religions distinguish between offensive and defensive war, how they address principles such as necessity, proportionality, right cause and right purpose, and discrimination between combatants and non-combatants. The book avoids judgements; it does not apply labels such as "right" or "wrong", and it is not interested in generalizations about whether the modern world can be characterized as a "clash" or as an "alliance" of civilizations. The authors focus on each religion separately and avoid confrontational comparisons. Readers can obviously find similarities and analogies that manifest certain harmonies between the religious and ethical perspectives and also the distinctive features of particular religions, demonstrating their diversity. The book does not aim to classify which religion is more permissive or more prohibitive towards the resort to force, but rather aims to look at the variety of sources and interpretations of just causes and permissible instruments of warfare. Another challenge is that the chapters explore hundreds, and even thousands, of years of the evolution of each tradition, at various times subjected to splits and unifications, progressions and regressions. Sunni and Shia Islam; Catholic, Orthodox and Protestant Christianity; Theravada Buddhism; Japanese religion; and Hinduism all have historical connections and disconnections, dialogues and antagonisms. The authors re-emphasize both the pacifist and the belligerent messages of the religions, detailing various interpretations and misinterpretations, uncertainties and deliberate abuses of religious texts made for policy-driven purposes.

In addition to this comprehensive historical outlook, this book intends to illustrate how religions respond to modern developments – the creation of international regimes and organizations (such as the United Nations) – as well as to assess recent armed escalations (such as that in Lebanon in August 2006). As the chapters unfold, the realities of origin and interpretation, fairness and injustice, legitimacy and illegitimacy, among others, surface and lend reason to rethink the intertwined nature of religions and norms of war, to demonstrate and analyse how religious teachings engage in norm-making. Looking at the norms of war from the perspective of religious literature helps to understand modern threats to peace and security and the responses to these threats, including – *in extremis* – the use of military force. To summarize, the main objective of this book is to present the evolution of the norms of war in the world religions.

The order of the chapters is sequenced chronologically. The first religion to be featured is Hinduism, as its extant writings reach further back in time than the other traditions. The book then reflects the fact that Buddhism developed from Hinduism, and Christianity and Islam from Abraham/Judaism. To maintain this chronological approach strictly, one would have included Judaism second after Hinduism, but the order chosen also attempts to group together the religions of the same broad family: Hindu–Buddhist, Judaeo-Christian, and Islamic.

Kaushik Roy's chapter analyses the role of Hinduism in shaping the ethics and dynamics of organized violence in India and presents the Hindu religion as a key factor in the evolution of Indian military strategies. He examines the ambivalent relationship between religion and violence, arguing that, in comparison with the Western world's attempts to secularize warfare, religion is crucial in the understanding of the nature of warfare in many parts of Asia, where violence remains the moral essence of the warrior. His analysis challenges the view that Hinduism is a genuinely pacifist religion, showing that the rejection of warfare is only a marginal and comparatively recent trend, whereas the realist view of war has been highly respected for centuries. Apart from Gandhi, none of the major Hindu theorists spoke about non-violent resistance. Roy demonstrates that, in fact, in Hinduism the norms of war, not pacifism, have historically introduced humane principles, reducing the lethality of war and moderating the effect of warfare on non-combatants. The chapter is a model demonstration of how historical analysis can help to understand modern political options, and concludes that even today the Indian ruling elite's consciousness continues to be shaped by traditional philosophies. It is the Hindu religious texts, rather than the teachings of Hindu priests, that have influenced warfare.

Mahinda Deegalle's chapter offers a valuable comparative study of the teachings of Buddha, the Theravada traditions and those of their Mahayana alternative. It addresses the contradiction of being Buddhist and engaging in war, asking crucial questions such as: Can Buddhism justify a war? Can Buddhists join an army? If so, what happens to their Buddhist identity? How can states with a majority Buddhist population manage war situations? What is the role of Buddhism in such situations? Deegalle reveals the various sources of Buddhist traditions, and naturally focuses on identifying the conceptualization of war and the use of force in the Theravada Buddhist tradition of Sri Lanka, a country still ravaged by violence. The chapter offers additional value and relevance in understanding the contemporary conflict by asking whether violence is justified to protect the state. Deegalle explores both historical and contemporary interpretations and demonstrates how, both in theory and in practice, war is largely incompatible with Buddhist teachings and the Buddhist way of life, and how therefore the war in Sri Lanka is an enormous challenge to the way fundamental Buddhist teachings and practices have been developed and communicated.

Robert Kisala's chapter explores the influence of the Buddhist and Shinto traditions on war and peace in the context of Japanese history. Insofar as prior to the twentieth century Japan was involved in very few international armed conflicts, the most important influence on the premodern Japanese concept of peace was the experience of internal conflict and internal social order. The situation changed at the end of the Tokugawa era, when universal conscription was introduced by the Meiji regime and a national army created. Japan went to war with China in 1894 over spheres of influence, gained Taiwan as a colony, later fought Russia and was granted privileges and control of Manchuria. With the annexation of Korea in 1910 and by allying itself with European forces fighting Germany in World War I, Japan was able to expand its territorial control. It was in this context that Western pacifist and "just war" ideas entered the intellectual and public discourse in Japan, assisted largely by the activities of several Christian missionaries. Kisala shows how the defeat in World War II, the postwar occupation and, especially, the destructive use of atomic weapons have shaped Japanese attitudes towards "pacifism", in particular the presumption against the use of force and the renunciation of war in Article 9 of the Constitution. Along with pacifism, Kisala identifies a second characteristic of the Japanese religious concept of war and peace and calls it "civilizational morality" – a unique Japanese concept with a dual emphasis on individual moral cultivation and, at times, an oppositional schema derived from a sense of cultural superiority. The idea of "civilization" emphasizes the active pursuit of individual moral edification, leading to a refined, civilized state of the being. It can lead to a conceptual distinction between "civilized" and "uncivilized" regions, which in turn can result in a cultural mission aimed at spreading the benefits of "civilization" as they are enjoyed in one's own region. Kisala finds commonality between Japanese and Western usage of the "civilizational" mission to justify, or at least inspire, military and colonial conquest.

The book then turns to the three Abrahamic monotheistic traditions: a chapter on Judaism by Jack Bemporad; three chapters on Christianity – Gregory Reichberg's on Catholicism, Yuri Stoyanov's on the Orthodox tradition and Valerie Morkevicius' on Protestantism; and two chapters on Shia and Sunni Islam, respectively by Davood Feirahi and Amira Sonbol. Again, the order of these chapters follows the historical chronology, starting with the oldest tradition and finishing with the youngest.

Jack Bemporad recognizes that the Jewish tradition does not operate explicitly with the just war categories of *jus ad bellum* and *jus in bello*, but shows how many discussions in biblical and rabbinical sources engage in very similar considerations. One can categorize certain Jewish statements as contributing to right reasons for going to war and the right conduct of war. What is significantly different between these principles in Judaism and just war theory is the Jewish belief that war is not a natural condition and that universal peace can be a reality. The biblical and rabbinical sources are concerned with peace more than with war, even if the Old Testament contains stories of brutal mass slaying. Bemporad, similarly to the other authors, makes a brilliant cross-century historical voyage, arriving at the current state of affairs. He argues that Israel as a Jewish state cannot forsake the task of explaining its existence and behaviour in terms of Jewish tradition and heritage, and thereby in universal ethical categories. If Israel were a secular nation-state, it would respond in terms of realpolitik and ethics would apply secondarily, if at all. The dilemma becomes complicated with the issue of asymmetric war and with the post-Holocaust imperative of survival. Asymmetric warfare evolved gradually and the rift between political and religious factors deepened. The concepts of restraint and purity of arms, developed in the 1930s by what later became the State of Israel, were constantly under review, and the protection of enemy non-combatants in modern warfare has increasingly been called into question, owing to weapons of mass destruction, guerrilla warfare, terrorism and suicide bombing. Also important in the historical heritage is that many Holocaust survivors witnessed how millions of Jews, predominantly non-combatants, were marked for total extermination. The inhuman Nazi ideology – which not many could predict at the time – led to real and duly implemented genocidal policies, which the League of Nations and governments could not stop. As a result, Israel still lives with a "siege mentality" and the great challenge, as Bemporad ascertains, is how to preserve the original Jewish ethics when it comes to modern methods of warfare.

Gregory Reichberg presents the ethics of war in Catholic Christianity, where the substantive origins of the just war theory can be found. Reichberg describes four approaches – pacifism, just war, perpetual peace and regular war – and comprehensively analyses the changing tendencies and dynamics in different historical contexts over the centuries. He demonstrates that these four approaches have not developed in isolation and that various elements of them have frequently been integrated into the outlook of the same Catholic thinkers. This interconnectedness accounts for much of the complexity and richness of the just war theory within the tradition, adding an important element of right authority into the right causes and aims of war. Reichberg also shows how early Catholic convictions – such as those of Ambrose and Augustine – that war could be waged only for the maintenance of a just peace gradually developed into a main normative concept against which any resort to war was to be measured. As a result, motives of personal gain, power, territorial aggrandizement and economic reasons were explicitly excluded from the list of justifiable causes of war. Despite the richness of the early teachings, the actual just war theory did not arise until many centuries later, when the canon lawyers such as Gratian sought to organize early texts on war and violence – passages from the Bible, statements by Augustine, enunciations of church councils, formulations from ancient Roman law – into an articulated doctrine. Focusing on *jus ad bellum*, the chapter is comprehensive in both scope and time, exploring developments of the Catholic tradition up to the present day, discussing the role of the just war in shaping the prohibition on the use of force in the League of Nations and in the UN Charter, and examining recent messages from the Vatican, citing papal references to the humanitarian intervention in Kosovo.

Yuri Stoyanov's chapter undertakes a huge, almost impossible, task – to analyse attitudes of the Eastern Orthodox Church toward the use of armed force and methods of warfare. Most texts have remained unpublished or untranslated into English, but even those published have not received anything like the same degree of scholarly attention as parallel developments in Catholicism and Protestantism. Accordingly, this is an original and impressive chapter, assessing and bringing into the public knowledge many texts that have been largely unknown until now. The comprehensive historico-academic journey is structured, similarly to the previous two chapters, through the trichotomy of pacifism, just war and crusade as the main characteristics of Christian attitudes to warfare. Stoyanov discovers that the formation of religious-national ideologies in Orthodox Eastern Europe has led to the emergence of what can be defined as elements of crusading along with the traditional presence of pacifism and just war. The historically prevalent pacifist Eastern Orthodox stance has recently been categorically reiterated by Ecumenical Patriarch Bartholomew and a number of senior Orthodox ecclesiasts. Stoyanov makes some other significant findings – for example, that the 2000 Jubilee Council of Russian Bishops' Statement of Faith advances a rare exposition of a systematic Orthodox just war tradition. Although the Statement begins with an explicit emphasis on the Orthodox view of war as unconditionally evil, caused by hatred and human abuse of God-given freedom, it also identifies the cases in which war may be necessary, such as self-defence, defence of neighbours and "restoration of trampled justice". It alludes to cases in which national saints and churchmen have blessed defensive wars against invaders. To justify the resort to war in these instances, the Statement reproduces episodes of the church's high respect for the Christian virtues of soldiers who follow the precepts of a just war, and rewards them by canonizing them as saints. It also uses scriptural references to characterize the Orthodox teachings of *jus in bello* norms – a topic that was largely ignored in earlier Eastern Orthodox texts and speculations on justifiable warfare. Stoyanov also provides an in-depth exposition of the Orthodox concepts of peace, with the Russian Church's commitment to peace-making and its dedication to opposing propaganda of war and violence. He shows that the military conflicts in the former Yugoslavia, the former Soviet Union and the Middle East have compelled Orthodox clerical circles as well as theologians and historians to address the moral problems related to the justification of modern warfare more systematically. In a public statement from 1991 in relation to the first Gulf War, the Holy Synod of Bishops of the Orthodox Church in America declared that just war theory does not reflect the Orthodox theological tradition, which maintains that war can never be theologically justified. Accordingly, questions have been asked whether Western Christian-style just war systems can really be appropriate for the Orthodox Church. Stoyanov concludes that modern Orthodox thought can certainly draw on a rich heritage of theological and ethical views to stimulate such reconceptions.

Valerie Morkevicius' chapter follows naturally by describing how the

Protestant Christian tradition has contributed to the development of the norms of war. Morkevicius analyses five broad groups of historical origin: Lutheran, Calvinist, Anglican, Evangelical and Anabaptist. The first three and their successor churches, she affirms, uphold a traditional view of just war theory inherited from their Catholic predecessors. Morkevicius argues that these Protestant groups elevated the just war theory to an even higher position than under the Catholic tradition. It is important to note that within each of these divisions there are numerous independent groups, which in terms of practice may differ greatly and may not even recognize each other as members of the same family. Denominations associated with the first three traditions – Lutherans, Calvinists and Anglicans, as well as their daughter churches – have often been the main state churches or the most dominant forces within their societies. Evangelicals – a very loose grouping of denominations and sects – also often locate their historical roots in one or more of these three traditions. For this reason, their beliefs about war are as highly varied as their origins. The Anabaptists, with a few exceptions, primarily consist of denominations known as "peace churches", which uphold a pacifist doctrine. Morkevicius examines the evolution of three dominant approaches within Protestantism: pacifism, realism (or crusading) and just war. Of these three, she maintains that the just war approach has received the most attention. One explanation could be that the denominations that follow the just war approach have been more dominant in political, social and demographic terms, and more connected to the power of kings, emperors and colonizers.

Last, but not least, the two chapters on Islam by Davood Feirahi and Amira Sonbol present the views of Shia and Sunni Islam as a culmination of the monotheist Abrahamic traditions. Over many centuries, Islamic communities have developed norms and traditions pertaining to war and peace that can generally be referred to as Islamic ethics of war. The Qur'an and Hadith literature, the jurisprudence, politics and decisions necessitated by historical events, and the theological interpretations of war made by religious and political leaders have all contributed to Islamic war ethics.

Davood Feirahi offers a detailed assessment of the concept of *jihad* in the traditional Shiite jurisprudence, in which "offensive" war may be waged only at the command of an infallible (twelfth) Imam. The view that jihad cannot be conducted in the absence of instruction by an infallible Imam is in effect a prohibition on, or at least a suspension of, offensive warfare. In contrast, "defensive" jihad is permitted: if Muslims are attacked by an enemy or if the religion and lives of Muslims are in danger, the defensive war is a religious duty even under an unjust ruler. Feirahi outlines the various levels of self-defence in Shiite Islam, starting with non-violent opposition; then requesting help from others; and, if these are unsuccessful, the use of coercive sanctions, from simple, to more sophisticated, to confronting the enemy. These strategies aim to stop the aggression but, if the aggressor does not withdraw, then he, free or slave, Muslim or unbeliever, deserves death. The defenders shall be considered martyrs if they are killed in the process. These norms are valid only if the aggressor does not flee or cease fighting. If the aggressor stops and withdraws, any further harm should be avoided or compensated. This is in effect the genesis of the norm of protection of surrendered soldiers and prisoners of war. Feirahi also presents other norms of *jus in bello*: the prohibition on "cursing an enemy", and on the use of terror or deceit in warfare. Traditional Islam can be seen as the developer of the modern prohibition on weapons of mass destruction – it introduced the prohibition on poisoning water or the air. Even during defensive war, any use of weapons other than those absolutely vital is not permitted; if heavy weapons are used when there is no need, Islam demands punishment of the user.

Amira Sonbol undertakes a comprehensive overview of Islamic teachings on war with a special focus on the Sunni tradition. She argues that, notwithstanding the widespread belief among Muslims that key Sharia norms of war derive directly from the teaching of Prophet Muhammad, Islamic ethics have evolved significantly over 14 centuries of history since then. Even today, Islam continues to evolve in different directions. Sonbol makes the challenging argument that various groups, including the most radical, find fertile ground for their advancement by following the Islamic belief in an unchanging and absolutist framework for righteous war. She explains how deconstructing the discursive history of the ethics of just war in Islam is one way of illustrating the contradictions between what Islam is purported to say and how various political groups interpret Islam and act accordingly. Islam incorporates basic principles common among major religions, such as the protection of civilian life, respect for human dignity and opposition to aggression, from earlier traditions. Protecting human life is the first command of the Qur'an and the first lesson taught to Muslims; life is a valuable gift from God. A close second is protecting the vulnerable and the helpless; the Qur'an and Hadith demand that warriors feed orphans, take care of wayfarers, and protect them in every possible way. Sunni Islam also demands special care for the elderly, women, children and the disabled – in effect, all vulnerable people who may suffer during war. Among the latter group would also be non-Muslims who do not participate in war. The wounded among enemy warriors also fall within the category of the helpless; extending medical service to them, even if they previously participated in battle, is an essential part of Islamic war ethics and fits with its ultimate purpose of protecting life. Sunni Islam also advocates the fair treatment of prisoners who are unarmed and therefore rendered helpless. All these Islamic protections represent the source and the model for the later codification and development of international humanitarian law in the Hague and Geneva Conventions. In the same vein, the poisoning of water-wells is strongly forbidden in Sunni Islam, as is the poisoning of food supplies and the destruction of homes, animals or agriculture as methods of war. Also forbidden are outright massacres and punitive punishment meted out to the kin and tribes of enemies. Even a punitive war, or a war to take back what has been usurped, must be limited as precisely as possible and directed at the enemy who waged war against a peaceful community. Sonbol's assessment helps to orient and explain many contemporary issues, including the fact that Islam has nothing to do with al-Qaeda's pretences.

The book essentially documents how the world religions have developed various norms of war, but all the chapters, in addition to addressing this main task, maintain their own choice of historical texts, issues and specific focuses and can be read as independent individual assessments. Religions have often been ignored or reduced to stereotypes by social scientists and military strategists, who prefer to look at war as a rational, pragmatic exercise. This book comes as a necessary correction. It shows the richness of the cultural and religious parameters of war and argues that both the mind and the heart, both reason and emotion, are instrumental elements of when and how to fight.

Notes

1. Samuel P. Huntingdon, *The Clash of Civilizations and the Remaking of World Order.* New York: Simon & Schuster, 1996.
2. Christopher Tyerman, *God's War: A New History of the Crusades.* London: Allen Lane, 2006.
3. For example, Edward W. Said, "The Myth of the Clash of Civilizations", lecture delivered at the University of Massachusetts, 1998. Said advocated an alliance of civilizations and a coexistence of differences.
4. See Amartya Sen, *Identity and Violence: The Illusion of Destiny*, Issues of Our Time. New York: W.W. Norton, 2006.

1

Religion and war

Vesselin Popovski

"All armed prophets have been victorious. All unarmed prophets have been destroyed."

Machiavelli, *The Prince*[1]

Religion and war have always coexisted: loved or hated, studied or ignored – they are part of human life, part of human history, part of the past, the present and the future. The people of religion and the people of war are two clearly identifiable, uniform-wearing groups, characterized by high respect for hierarchy and discipline, adherence to rules and traditions, and compliance with the orders of superiors. Where necessary they can stoically endure hardships and sacrifice individual interests, material gains and even their own lives for higher purposes.

Religious attitudes to war

George Bernard Shaw once wrote that "there is only one religion though there are a hundred versions of it".[2] Indeed, different religions are based on similar beliefs: that there are issues beyond rational scientific explanation; that the material world is secondary to an idea, a design, made and driven by an omnipotent overarching Judge/Creator. Religions promote similar values, such as respect for human beings, ethical behaviour, modesty, hope, love and assisting people in need. They would normally reject and condemn acts of killing, raping, injuring or offending in another way

World religions and norms of war, Popovski, Reichberg and Turner (eds),
United Nations University Press, 2009, ISBN 978-92-808-1163-6

any innocent people. Accordingly, when states mobilize soldiers and declare wars, religious leaders are expected to advocate caution, tolerance and self-restraint.[3] In public opinion, wars are associated with extreme acts of violence, crimes against humanity and large-scale destruction of human life, and they cannot but seem repugnant to religions. Human death naturally challenges a key religious proposition – that life is given by God and only God can eliminate life. Issues such as the origin of the Earth and Man, the eternity of the human soul and life after death have deep roots in most religious traditions and influence considerations of all aspects of life, including the justification of the causes of war and the methods of warfare. Religions are normally precautionary; they would oppose military means, hatred or violence leading to large loss of human life. For churchmen who impart belief in God as the perfection of tolerance and goodwill, human life is sacred and should be always protected.

However, there are circumstances in which religions would find the use of armed force acceptable. The most obvious example would be self-defence – either individual defence of self and family, or the defence of the religion and its believers. With a few exceptions – such as Jainism or Baha'i teachings, known for their extreme pacifism – all traditions admit that war can be, in fact should be, a necessary and proportionate tool to stop an aggressor. Religious teachings, while generally condemning wars, find clear justifications for war when all other measures fail. Religions accept that war can be the lesser evil – the last resort to defeat a tyrant and restore peace and harmony.

The relationship between religion and war is therefore very complex. It is interesting to note that the only way to avoid military service in many countries that require compulsory military service is to gain the status of "conscientious objector", invoking religious convictions. Thus, religion can help people avoid unwanted military service. However, religion can also help recruit soldiers, which I will illustrate later in the chapter.

The complexity of the connection between religion and war arises from the ambiguity of religious attitudes towards war in the original scriptures. Religious statements commanding tolerance and love are interspersed with statements, sometimes on the same page, commanding the merciless destruction of the enemies of the faith. Tolerance and intolerance coexist in many religious texts. One can identify a few paragraphs from the Old or the New Testament, from the Qur'an or Hadith, and present the three Abrahamic traditions – Judaism, Christianity and Islam – as equally pacifist. But one can also select a few other paragraphs from the same original sources and present the same religions as ferociously belligerent. Moreover, there are thousands of interpretations of the original religious texts by apostles, teachers, preachers, historians, theologians, scholars and modern analysts that make both arguments – some saying that the religions are peaceful and others saying that the religions are intolerant. No classification of a particular religious teaching as advocating either "peace" or "war" could ever be possible without challenge.

Many religious leaders have been well-known advocates of peaceful protest and the rejection of war – Mahatma Gandhi, the Dalai Lama, Desmond Tutu, Ayatollah Sistani, Pope John Paul II, to name just a few. Martin Luther King, the leader of the campaign in the United States for civil rights and against racial discrimination, often linked his faith with the proclamation of non-violent resistance. Similarly, however, one can find reference to religion in statements by leaders who advocate or attempt to gather popular support for war – President George W. Bush invading Iraq in 2003 used to refer to the war as "crusading for freedom".

Because one cannot classify religions as either pacifist or bellicose, the focus should be on the context or the environment in which religions advocate peace; or, conversely, the context or the environment in which religions advocate war. One can analyse and compare these circumstantial differences and attempt to monitor the emergence of certain shared norms of war evolving from religious traditions. The main questions are when, and for what purpose, do religions justify the use of armed force, which is otherwise condemned generally as causing human death? What are the limits of the use of force? How did religions shape the development of the norms of war?

Religious traditions have been historically involved in and accused of intolerance or crusading, and the religions frequently defended themselves against such accusations by counterattacking other traditions for provoking wars. Accordingly, religious traditions over many centuries have experienced tensions, attempts for dominance, hostilities, assassinations and wars. The history of humankind is full of so-called "holy wars". In modern times, sectarian violence continues to erupt in many places around the world: it has shaped the armed conflicts between and within India and Pakistan, between Israel and Palestine, in Northern Ireland, Chechnya, the former Yugoslavia, Sri Lanka and Iraq, and elsewhere. Victims of inter-religious violence continue to die as we write this book. I will address later in the chapter the interesting debate about whether religions directly provoke wars, or whether religions only facilitate the wars that arise for other reasons.

Religion does matter a lot for many people. This is a reality not only in the Vatican or in Iran but in most secular countries. Religion is a powerful force and as such it has shaped the contours of all essential historical perceptions of war and peace. Samuel Huntington in *Clash of Civilizations* appeals for a greater focus on religions when examining the nature of the modern conflict.[4] One may agree or disagree with the conclusions of his book, but one lesson beyond dispute is that it is necessary to study and understand religious perspectives on conflicts and wars. Stephen Neff, in his book *War and the Law of Nations*, analyses the historical evolution of the theories of just wars and the development of the norms of the law of armed conflict.[5] Although a detailed examination of the religious perspectives was not a primary task of his book, one can easily verify how significantly religions influenced the setting and codification of the norms of war and of actual conduct during armed conflict. Religious teachings do matter before a war – *jus ad bellum* – to determine the right cause and purpose of military action; they matter during the war – *jus in belli* – to determine the right conduct in the treatment of civilians and captured soldiers, and the right weapons and tactics of warfare. Religion matters after conflict – *jus post bellum* – to determine the conditions of the just peace and to bring reconciliation and justice to the victims.

Religion does matter. However, it has also been underestimated. Jonathan Fox and Shmuel Sandler, in their book *Bringing Religion into International Relations*, identify an important gap: the "discipline of international relations was not ready for inclusion of the religious variable into the contending paradigms in the discipline".[6] They devote the book to the attempt to fill this gap, looking at how religions create political legitimacy and shape domestic and international policies, including when these result in armed conflicts. The authors demonstrate how religions have a significant say in the prerequisites of international relations, including when and how political violence is embraced and utilized. This is the case both in relation to the motivation and purposes of a particular territorial or ethnic conflict, and regarding the employment of specific tactics. It is important to recognize both that the emergence of the laws of war is founded upon religious theology and that such normative dynamism continues to evolve.

Religious traditions, apart from their similarities, described earlier, also have differences. They are based on different sources, memories, inspirations, priorities, symbols and messages. Prominent religious leaders have driven the evolution of the traditions over time through many phases and historical events (the rise and fall of empires, territorial conquests and wars for dominance). The contours of the norms of war stretch back 3,000 years and they originate from diverse religious traditions, as the particular chapters of this book will demonstrate. The norms of war have also evolved from humanitarian impulses, military doctrines and philosophers' ideas. Aristotle was among the first to write about "just war" when he explored acceptable forms of warfare.[7] For Aristotle, war is not an end in itself; it should have other ends that need to be justified – for example, to prevent a city's enslavement (an early notion of self-defence); to strengthen an empire to benefit all its inhabitants. Aristotle's famous expression "war must be for the sake of peace"[8] epitomizes the notion of the necessity of just war.

In modern times we can find similar parallels. Lev Tolstoy, a famous Russian writer and pacifist, presented the same dilemma in his classic opus *War and Peace*. Churchill often expressed the necessity of a "war to end all wars". From Aristotle to the present day, we see that war is often a political exercise, detached from religion – there is no necessary demand for religious approval or rejection of war. For many, the war is always a civic act, governed by states' necessities and rules. Athenians and Spartans may have believed in the same gods yet, despite their shared religious beliefs, they fought wars against one another. The religious beliefs of Nazi leaders were not determinant factors in the Reich's decisions to invade other countries or to exterminate the Jews. Nazism was a strong and comprehensive ideology and it did not need the support of a religion. There is little proof that the Holocaust resulted from the belief that Jesus Christ was sentenced to be crucified by a crowd of Jews 2,000 years ago. Even if some Christian preachers may have invoked anti-Semitic stories when blessing the extradition of Jews to Nazi Germany, such instances were too occasional and non-conclusive.

The first attempts to shape and systematically determine just war within religious traditions were undertaken by writers from the Catholic tradition, including Augustine, Aquinas and Vitoria. It is challenging to compare the ethics and norms of war in both pre-Christian and post-Christian traditions, to observe how they approach the justification of war and methods of warfare along similar or different lines of deliberation. Such a long historical voyage may lead to yet another challenge – are the norms of war cross-cultural and universal; are they faith neutral and secular? To turn the question around: is militancy inherent in religion, or has it been constructed as inherent? A third challenge would be to move beyond the strict military element of the use of force and address non-military forms of hostility – sanctions, non-recognition, blame, prohibitions, blasphemy, cartoons, and so on.

The relationship between religion and war is complex indeed. It is therefore important to develop research and knowledge and to understand how religious teachings approach and influence decisions concerning when and how to engage in armed conflict. It is also essential to investigate how the religious texts define and develop specific norms of war; to examine in what circumstances the major world religions would justify a resort to military force and, by the same token, what they would consider to be acceptable targets and weapons in war. Do the religious perspectives on *jus ad bellum* – right and wrong reasons for war – differ or agree? What do these traditions say, and teach, regarding *jus in bello*

– right and wrong methods of warfare? To what extent has faith developed norms of war and various elements of the use of force?

Religion and causes of war

The question is whether religious differences are the primary causes of violence, or whether these differences are exploited as a tool to recruit soldiers and supporters for wars that arise for other reasons and for other purposes, such as greed for power, appetite for land, water or other resources, desire for global strategic dominance, or to achieve domestic political gains. It is often recorded that suicide bombers blow themselves up and kill innocent people because they believe in post mortem rewards, such as saving them and their families from hell. Somebody manipulated the suicide bombers to believe in paradise after life; to believe that their suicidal actions serve some purpose of liberation or destruction of "enemies"; to believe that what they do is commanded by God. Suicide bombers with manipulated beliefs are instruments for war – they listen to preachers of hatred but do not attempt to find explicit verification in religious texts as to whether God commanded suicide with the parallel elimination of maximum innocent life.

I would argue that religious differences a priori do not cause violence as such. However, religious people are easier to manipulate and turn into fighters precisely because they more readily believe in the promises of the manipulators, who, ironically, would not themselves become martyrs in order to earn the rewards of paradise promised after their deaths. Religion per se does not cause violence, but it is a useful tool for recruiting people to commit violence, because believers can be incited to die for an idea. Certainly, not all soldiers have been manipulated by religions; many were sent to die by other ideologies – nationalism, communism, fascism. The wars had material, pragmatic causes, but ideologies (religions included) were used to facilitate the recruitment of soldiers. Sympathy and commemoration have always accompanied those who patriotically sacrifice their life for their country; war memorials are built as a tool to recruit more heroes for subsequent wars.

Religion is rarely the main cause of war. After reviewing hundreds of internal armed conflicts over the past 40 years, Paul Collier and Anke Hoeffler wrote *Greed and Grievance in Civil War*, arguing that "greed" outweighs "grievance" as a main cause of armed conflict.[9] The research is methodologically interesting, in that it does not approach the warlords for opinions. As the authors argue, the parties in conflict would obviously never declare that they are fighting for "greed"; rather, they will always try to find causes for "grievances". Collier and Hoeffler contend that economic motives and causality, rather than ethnic or religious injustices, comprise the origins of civil wars, at least during the period they looked at. The thesis is not beyond controversy: some left-wing observers criticized it as an attempt to undercut liberation struggles. I would support the view that, even if a conflict is based on grievances, these rarely originate in religious differences. Popular protests against dictators arise from social exclusion, misery, poverty and exploitation – i.e. mostly non-faith-based causes. The overthrowing of dictatorial regimes has little cultural or religious context; in fact, rebels may not be culturally different from dictators.

Alan Krueger, in his study of the causes of terrorism, *What Makes a Terrorist*, wrote: "We investigated whether being home to a population with a high percentage of Muslims or a high percentage of Christians, for instance, has an effect on the likelihood of a country also being home to perpetrators of terrorism. Our results showed no significant differences across major religions ... No religion has a monopoly on terrorism."[10] These studies by Collier and Hoeffler and by Krueger challenged a series of previous writings that considered religions to be major sources of discrimination and conflict.[11]

The complex correlation between religion and violence is addressed by R. Scott Appleby in *The Ambivalence of the Sacred: Religion, Violence, and Reconciliation*.[12] The book questions to what extent war is a sacred duty or a sacred privilege, and explores under what conditions certain religions justify violence. Appleby emphasizes religions' inherent internal pluralism and affirms that people normally have ambivalent approaches to the sacred. He examines both religious violence and religious peace-building, and shows that they flow from similar dynamics. Ambivalence is foundational for all religions. Christianity, Islam, Hinduism, Buddhism, Judaism and Sikhism have existed for long enough to produce various schools, orders and even different sets of daily practices, and, consequently, have perpetually contested their own original traditions. Religions maintain a recognized core identity, but their inherent pluralism also allows each tradition to be flexible and adaptable. Religions have core statements (commandments) regarding what is good or bad, what is authentic or not, what is permitted or prohibited, and what is sacred or profane. When they encounter differences, religions do not necessarily resist – they may adapt, interpret, rediscover or even re-identify themselves. There is a constant process of development in religions, which remains under-researched by those who simplify the causes of religious conflicts.[13] Even when it comes to antagonisms, the question is how many of these are religious. Do intolerance and violence result from an implicit denominational self-understanding? Or are they subordinate to a different ideology or identity, such as that of the nation-state or ethnic group?

Another book that follows the debate on whether religion, or its misuse, lies at the origin of conflicts is *Religion, Conflict and Reconciliation: Multifaith Ideals and Realities.*[14] The authors – Jerald Gort, Henry Jansen and Hendrik Vroom – criticize as one-sided both the view that religious exclusivity is a cause of conflict and the view that misuse of religion is a cause of conflict. The book concludes that it is "debatable whether the claim for uniqueness necessarily ends up in conflict, but as one of the main arguments of the critiques of religion, it should be taken seriously".[15]

To make people believe in any exclusivity – be it religious, ideological, ethnic or any other – may very well be the first step in the spread of intolerance, despite the fact that the bloodiest wars and genocides of the twentieth century in fact had little to do with religious beliefs. Examples may readily be found where nationalist and ethnic leaders actively "recruit" religion to legitimize their violent struggle for political and other purposes. Promoting martyrdom, sacrifice or compassion for fellow countrymen, co-religionists and families would certainly help to mobilize soldiers and present them with *causa belli.* One has to recognize that it is not easy to appeal for murderous violence as a human duty, and this explains why one of the ways to achieve such manipulation is to use – or, rather, to abuse – deep religious beliefs. It certainly helps when the militant appeal for the mass extermination of people is steered into the abstract world of the "sacred", where no necessity of proof exists. Promises of heaven, glory and post mortem gratification for the soldiers and their families, on the one hand, and cruel stigmatization of the infidel enemies, on the other, are the tools of such manipulation.

In summary, religions do not produce conflict directly, but they can easily be employed to prolong and deepen hostile attitudes. Implanted and sustained religious differences may protract conflicts. The Middle East conflict has always been over land and power, but both sides are constantly made to believe that "their God granted them the Holy Land", in what has become a very useful propaganda strategy to mobilize more fighters. Radical preachers can incite hatred and contribute to violence, as did some Catholic priests in Argentina during the Dirty War, some jihad-promoting imams and some Buddhist monks in Sri Lanka. Religious interventions may exacerbate and prolong conflict.

Religion may become the cause of extremism and violence if it acquires political power and serves political interests. The Muslim expansion after the death of the Prophet Muhammad could be attributed to a religious call for jihad, but de facto it was a politically uniting enterprise between otherwise warring Arab tribes, making them a successful fighting force. Religion was not even the vital driving force for the Crusades. It is the state that has the monopoly over the use of force and, accordingly, a religious state would be no less tempted to use force than a secular state.

Religious fundamentalists believe that the solutions to most societal problems lie exclusively in faith. This belief generates a platform to redefine and recreate religious states as opposed to secular states. A fundamentalist movement may win elections or forcibly remove a democratic secular government, and in any event it may sustain momentum over a long period of time. Fundamentalists may not only come to political power in one country; they can also act transnationally. Radical religious movements – similarly to nationalistic ideological movements – promote one vision, one version of the tradition, and declare this version to be the only answer to all societal shortcomings. A faith that embraces state power can impose its rule and use force to defend, promote and expand this rule. Wars are fought by states or political entities, and these can be religious states or religious entities. But religion as such is not a cause of wars.

Norms of war

The norms and ethics of war can be differentiated and grouped from three broad viewpoints. First, there is an argument that war is intrinsically wrong – that it can produce only death, destruction and suffering. "Pacifists" oppose any violence and all wars. Jainism as a religious tradition is an extreme pacifist example; even the murder of insects would be seen as wrong by Jainists. Apart from extreme pacifists, there are also moderate pacifists, who advocate non-military resistance to evil. They argue that, if aggressors are repeatedly presented with morally superior positive demonstrations and with mass non-violent protests, they will gradually acknowledge their wrongdoing. There have been some successes. The struggle for India's independence from British rule, led by Mahatma Gandhi, is one such example. Ibrahim Rugova, the popular leader of the Kosovo Albanians, attempted a similar non-violent approach. It did not deliver results and was brutally suppressed by the former Serbian President Milosevic. However, it gradually attracted the sympathy of the international community, which in 1998 adopted sanctions and in 1999 used military force to coerce Milosevic into withdrawing from Kosovo. But there is no guarantee of a happy ending. The non-violent protests by Buddhist monks in Myanmar have not yet achieved much of a change in a country where a brutal military junta has denied democracy and human rights for decades. These examples of non-violent resistance are in the context of people's struggles against tyrannical regimes. Some pacifists go further and argue that state-against-state aggressions could also have been prevented by massive popular resistance in both the aggressors' and the victims' countries.

A second school is the realists. Though acknowledging human suffering and war-related tragedies, they present war as a normal state of affairs, or even as a necessary element of international society.[16] In a famous expression, General von Clausewitz wrote that war is "a continuation of politics by other means".[17] The realists argue that states will never fully trust each other. They will endlessly maximize their military power to be always ready to engage in military combat to defend territorial boundaries and sustain national interests.

Interestingly, both pacifists and realists voice the same scepticism about the norms of war, expressed in the Latin maxim *inter arma silent leges* – in war the laws are silent. They agree that norms can do little to regulate war. Once armies engage in violence, both schools argue, no laws can exercise control. It is true that a substantive body of international humanitarian law has been developed and codified over the past century. Yet one is forced to recognize that this branch of international law has most often been ignored and deliberately violated. If international law is seen as the most fragile form of law, international humanitarian law can be seen as the most fragile form of international law.

A third concept – just war theory – challenges both the pacifist and the realist paradigms. It argues that war is neither wholly unacceptable nor always acceptable. There are just and unjust wars;[18] there is a middle ground between pacifism (war as always evil) and realism (war as a normal condition). Just war theory might have been born from the process of merging political and religious power, when the roots of pacifism in religion and the roots of realism in political science were intertwining in search of circumstances that can justify war. The pacifists condemned war whereas the generals accepted it, but above them the holders of political and religious power needed to justify aggressive wars, to find a moral imperative for the necessity of fighting and dying in wars. The power of the kings merged with the power of the church and religious teachings became instrumental in the justification of war: kings needed religion to solidify their power and inspire their soldiers. The political and religious leaderships united to find the line between "just" and "unjust" wars.

The just war theory distinguishes between just reasons for resort to armed force (*jus ad bellum*) and just methods (*jus in bello*) to be used on the battlefield. It seeks to answer two separate questions: When is it right to fight; and how is it right to fight?[19] Scholars of this orientation have developed criteria for when war may rightly be waged – for what purposes, by what authority and in what circumstances (such as a last resort). The just war theorists, in contrast to both the pacifists and the realists, reaffirm that in war it is possible to observe rules, such as the evacuation and protection of civilians, the reduction of non-combatant casualties, respect for wounded and surrendered soldiers, free passage for medical teams, care for agricultural land, animals, fruit-giving trees, and so on. Massacres of innocent populations or the poisoning of water sources are condemned, despite the fact that they may reduce the enemy's resistance, demoralize the enemy and serve a military purpose. The two parties at war can agree not to use weapons that may produce long-term damage to the land and the people. They can agree to exchange prisoners of war once the hostilities end. In short, the just war theory affirms that war can be subject to commonly accepted rules – like a chess game in which the two sides accept the rules of the game in advance.

Interestingly, the normative approach to war has not developed simply as an abstract appeal for ethical behaviour, as a result of sacred humanistic concern, or as a manifestation of the inviolability of the right of life. It has roots in the discipline of military strategy as well.[20] For example, the evacuation of civilians from a war zone may have become a rule not only owing to concerns about human innocence, but also because the military commanders on both sides prefer to facilitate the movement of their soldiers in the battlefield. Sparing the lives of enemy prisoners of war may have developed into a rule not only as a humane compulsion, but also with the expectation of exchanging the prisoners after the war and using them as already trained and experienced soldiers in the next war. It is well documented that disrespect for the norms of war – or international humanitarian law, once these norms were codified – tends to diminish public support for wars.

The establishment of the norms of war has been a historically long process, torn between advancements and challenges, full of steps forward and back. War has always been a very necessary instrument: firstly, to survive in a territorially limited space in the ancient world; secondly, to grab the land of disorderly neighbouring tribes and establish large and stable empires; thirdly, to enlarge a state's territory or acquire colonies when capitalism spurred the greed for profit but faced limited ownership of sufficient natural and human resources; and, finally, when the latecomers to the industrial revolution wanted to redistribute the already colonized and heavily exploited Asia and Africa. During all these stages, states always defined their interests in the best possible terms in order to justify war. They were thinking only about their own narrow selfish interests when presenting a "defensive" war argument but pursuing de facto aggressive goals. Religion was useful in this process, with its power to unite large numbers of people, to manoeuvre the masses behind ideas and goals (what comes from God does not need persuasion) and, most importantly, to mobilize soldiers. Religious texts are ambiguous enough to be manipulated – some could be interpreted as permitting the use of force, others (even within the same tradition) as prohibiting it. The first were needed to energize soldiers for fighting wars, the second to make people passive and obey the rulers. This is how religion was made to serve war. Kings and emperors appealed to preachers – the power of beliefs had to join the power of arms in a useful, even if later deadly, synergy.

Literature on religion and war

Many publications have addressed the connection between religion and war, covering various legal and political conceptions and addressing contrasts and similarities between the normative and the empirical aspects of war. Aggression, self-defence, reprisals, symmetric and asymmetric wars, and, more recently, humanitarian intervention and the "war on terror" are just a short list of the many issues covered by this literature. Various scholars have approached the religious perspectives on war from different angles, with different frames of reference, contributing to the understanding of the dimensions of the justification of the use of force. Although there is less variation in the conclusions arrived at, the differing approaches and contrasting analyses undertaken by the scholars broaden the horizons towards understanding the connections and disconnections between religion and war – a complex, challenging and dynamically evolving theme.

Stephen Neff's historically comprehensive and previously mentioned book *War and the Law of Nations* begins its analyses in ancient times and follows the evolution of the just war concept over the centuries, up to the present day.[21] The originality of the book is in the study of the use of force from the perspective of both international law and the religious teachings of the time. Focusing on legal conceptions, Neff explores the interplay between legal ideas on war and state practice in warfare. He demonstrates how international law provides the set of rules by which contests are conducted between nations. War is one of the institutions of international law; thus the winning side imposes peace terms on the losing side and alters the strategic balance. Neff explores the evolution of both aggressive and defensive doctrines and practices. From the just war doctrine of the Middle Ages, to war as an instrument of statecraft, to the evolution of war as a legal institution of the nineteenth century, and finally to war becoming a tool of self-defence and of collective humanitarian intervention, Neff offers an intellectual voyage of historical exploration of the legal and ethical underpinnings of the use of force. He provides an unparalleled investigation of the entire history of international law as viewed through different ethics of war.

Paul Robinson's marvellous collection of essays *Just War in Comparative Perspective* is more focused on the assessment of the links between war and religion.[22] This compilation of texts from distinguished religious experts highlights the dependence of military ethics on national, cultural and religious conditions. The texts explore the underlying themes advocating the use of force and conclude that the fundamental notions of "last resort", "right purpose", "necessity", "proportionality" and "protection of civilians" have been more equivalent than contradictory among various religions. The book is very wide in its historical grasp, covering teachings from as early as Confucius and Lao Tzu up to the present day, with reflections on the Gulf War and the 9/11 attacks. Accentuating the diversity of normative thinking about war and warfare while enhancing understanding of the motives of, and responses to, the terrorist campaigns of the Islamist fundamentalists or the atrocities of ethnic conflict in the former Soviet Union, the Asian subcontinent and Africa, among others, the book provides immensely valuable perspectives on the use of force in the context of various historical and geographical circumstances.

David Smock is another contributor to the literature on comparative religious knowledge on just war. His book *Religious Perspectives on War: Christian, Muslim, and Jewish Attitudes toward Force* concerns primarily the debates over the first Gulf War (1991). It explores diverse views and opinions, addressing various issues of the just war doctrine, explaining their differences and finding significant common ground among them.[23] One striking exploration that Smock undertakes concerns whether the just war theory is relevant in today's context, given the unceasing nature of low-intensity conflicts in the world. Are these conflicts "just" by origin or by nature, considering the difficulty in assessing when a conflict actually starts? Along similar lines, Smock searches for an explanation of whether modern warfare, given the irrelevance or the pardonable anachronism of the just war theory, can be morally justified. He discovers interesting and insightful parallels underlying and explaining the just war doctrine. The book is based on the accounts of 24 theologians and scholars, working with the United States Institute of Peace, who discuss and expound upon the relationship between religious ethics and the use of force and the classic doctrine of just war as a standard by which to judge the ethics of *jus ad bellum*.

An excellent study with even stronger comparative elements of various religious traditions' approaches to conflicts and wars is *The Ethics of War: Shared Problems in Different Traditions*, edited by Richard Sorabji and David Rodin.[24] It is unique in tracing how the main questions posed by contemporary events in Afghanistan and Iraq have been addressed in different cultures and in different periods. The book assembles both well-known traditions (Christianity, Judaism, Islam) and lesser-known traditions (Maimonides, Averroes) and goes further than its predecessors in cross-examining issues such as asymmetric responses, preventive strikes, innocent (collateral) damage and effects on human rights that are both contemporary and historically relevant.

Another valuable comparative contribution, with a major focus on Asian traditions – Judaism, Islam, Hinduism, Buddhism and Chinese and Japanese religions – is *The Ethics of War in Asian Civilizations*, edited by Torkel Brekke.[25] The book is an excellent attempt to respond to two fundamental research questions: are there universal standards of justification of war in the major ideologies of warfare; and are these shared by the major Asian religions? The Asian traditions are analysed with the objective of illuminating whether one can generalize a common ground for cross-cultural legitimization of the ethics of war, which have historically been more in line with the Western (Christian) just war tradition.

Peter Partner's *God of Battles: Holy Wars of Christianity and Islam* is an engaging study of the holy wars in these two monotheistic religions.[26] Partner challenges trends that equate Islam with fanaticism and terror and assume Islam to be a static entity, embracing the same beliefs and goals. Instead he offers an excellent overview of the shifting traditions of Islam in the past few centuries. Partner examines the origins of holy war and how it affects the modern world. He shows how the ideal of the Crusade came to permeate medieval Christendom, and how it later influenced Western societies, especially in their attitudes to colonialism. He also examines the reasons behind the fear of fundamentalism, placing the jihad of the East and the Crusade of the West in their historical context from the pre-Christian era to the Gulf War.

Two other volumes, *Arguing the Just War in Islam* by John Kelsay and *The Holy War Idea in Western and Islamic Traditions* by James Turner Johnson, also deal with the ethics of war in Islamic and Christian traditions.[27]

Religion and norms of war in international law

The literature listed in the previous section and many other sources – both theological and legal – demonstrate how religious attitudes towards war have become instrumental in the development of norms that were codified in the laws of war. An essential task for all religious traditions has been to examine in one way or another the justifiable and the unjustifiable rationales for resorting to war, including defence of self and allies, aid to the innocent, punishment for wrongdoing, revenge in the name of justice and national or religious honour. By justifying or condemning wars, in terms of both right motivation and right weapons and tactics, the religions contributed to the development of state practices and legal opinions. These practices and opinions gradually shaped first the customs and later the treaties of international humanitarian law – the 1899 and 1907 Hague Conventions and the 1949 Geneva Conventions.

The evolution of the universal prohibition on aggression and the unilateral use of force, short of self-defence, would be a good example. Today this prohibition is a central element in international law and in international relations, although it is by no means free from abuse. The use of force has always been permitted historically; moreover, it was seen as a normal continuation of politics by other means until the 1928 Pact of Paris (known also as the Kellogg–Briand Pact), which for the first time in history made the use of force unlawful as an instrument of national policy.[28] The principle of the non-use of force was then universalized by Article 2(4) of the UN Charter, which prohibited not only the use of force but also the threat of its use; and not only as a national policy instrument but also as an instrument for international dispute resolution.

There are two exceptions to this norm: the inherent right to self-defence (Art. 51) and collective military action authorized by the Security Council (Art. 42) to eliminate a threat to, or breach of, the peace. It is interesting to compare the two exceptions to the use of force in the UN Charter – self-defence and collective authorization – with the use of lethal force in domestic criminal law. One can kill in self-defence, but consequently will need to persuade a judge/jury that the threat to one's life was real, imminent and, to quote the famous expression from the *Caroline* case, "leaving no choice of means, and no moment for deliberation".[29] The other legal way to kill – the death penalty – is a decision made collectively, carefully scrutinized and applied if clemency, or right of superior veto, is not granted. Criminal law – old or modern – originates in what people believe to be correct or incorrect behaviour, and has been connected to the ethics of crime and punishment.

The emergence of laws regulating the use of force, and also of international institutions restricting the use of force, such as the League of Nations and the United Nations (relevant to *jus ad bellum*); the codification of international humanitarian law in the 1949 Geneva Conventions and their 1977 Protocols; treaties prohibiting weapons of mass destruction; and the 1998 Rome Statute of the International Criminal Court (relevant to *jus in bello*) are all significant milestones in the acknowledgement of the centrality of the international law of armed conflict and the use of force. The amount of attention given to the resort to force in the history of international relations has been growing. A similar centrality with regard to the norms of war exists in international legal studies.

Wars and the norms of war are significant themes in the evolution of each religious tradition, and they respond to the changing trends in warfare – the emergence of new varieties of weapons, new tactics and so on. A contemporary development, such as the destructiveness and anti-humanism of war resulting from nuclear and other weapons of mass destruction, is reflected in the renunciation of such weapons both by the state and by the church. It would be similarly interesting to look at martyrdom and the suicidal method of fighting and find its rejection or acceptance both in religious ethics and in state practice.

Decisions over the use of force are arguably the most significant and dangerous that leaders must take – legally, morally and in terms of achieving political goals. The question of reasons that can justify behaviour leading to the elimination of human life is as philosophical and ethical as it is political and legal. In the context of exponential increases in the destructiveness of war, particularly with the proliferation of nuclear and other weapons of mass destruction, these questions assume an even greater significance. In resolving moral and practical dilemmas, one may seek guidance from many sources, but arguably the most enduring and powerful of these are the religious traditions. Individuals, groups and societies are marked by the constant and powerful influence of religion on their thinking, discourse and actions. This has consequences in all aspects of human life, not least in situations of conflict and violence. It is widely acknowledged that most, if not all, religious traditions include ethical and practical teachings and guidance regarding the use of force. Such teachings concern both the resort to the use of force and the methods, instruments and limits of warfare.

Recent international armed conflicts such as those in Kosovo, Afghanistan and Iraq have further reignited the debates on the norms and laws of war and the methods of warfare. The concept of humanitarian intervention, or military intervention to protect human life at risk, has faced contradictory dilemmas and has been transformed into the concept of the "responsibility to protect", after in-depth research and several discussion meetings in different continents undertaken by the International Commission on Intervention and State Sovereignty, initiated by the Government of Canada and resulting in the issuing of the report *Responsibility to Protect* in 2001.[30] States gradually adopted the concept, though some of them regarded it as over-permissive and intrusive. Accordingly the concept was narrowed in the World Summit Outcome Document (adopted by the UN General Assembly in 2005) to apply only in extreme cases of war crimes, genocide, ethnic cleansing and crimes against humanity.[31] The concept is limited to the protection of victims; it does not include the prosecution of the perpetrators. The latter has developed in parallel with the establishment of the International Criminal Court and its practice.

New forms of warfare – terrorist strikes, suicide bombing and "martyrdom", particularly in their spread and increased impact on powerful nations – have reintroduced various questions regarding the ethics and norms of the use of force. The contemporary practice of asymmetric warfare represents a further challenge to existing ethical positions. Religious fundamentalism, intercommunal hatred, antagonism between individual rights and freedoms and societal security, terrorist ideologies and actions can all arise in societies where civil liberties are neglected, but they can also flourish in societies where civil liberties are respected.[32] One can look for answers in intercultural and inter-religious institutions and the values commonly espoused by them. The development of the norms of war is building a universal consensus that transcends cultural and regional differences and raises possibilities for understanding the justifications of the use of force and the methods of warfare.

It is necessary and timely to look for a better understanding of how just war concepts have been assessed within the world's leading religious traditions – Hinduism, Buddhism, Judaism, Christianity and Islam. These rich traditions, with their sects and factions, their continuous evolution and the powerful messages they produce, which can unite but can also split opinions, are central sources of understanding of the norms of war. There are many connections and disconnections between religions and wars, and the evolution of the norms of war would be one of the best possible illustrations.

I started this chapter with the coldly realist, and almost cynical, expression of Machiavelli – that all armed prophets were victorious and all unarmed prophets were destroyed. I would like to end the chapter with the reminder that there could be a war to end all wars. Perpetual peace, as dreamed of by many philosophers, is possible and all conflicts have solutions. But, for peace to materialize, one may need to go through just wars.

Notes

1. Niccolò Machiavelli, *The Prince*, 1532, Ch. 6; available at ⟨http://www.gutenberg.org/files/1232/1232-h/1232-h.htm⟩ (accessed 29 September 2008), translated by William K. Marriott.
2. George Bernard Shaw, "Arms and the Man", in *Plays: Pleasant and Unpleasant*. London: Richards, 1898, vol. II, preface.

3. An example would be the statements and efforts of Pope John Paul II before the Gulf War in 1991 to reach a negotiated solution, even if there was an almost universal consensus and a clear Security Council mandate for the coalition to intervene against Iraq.

4. Samuel Huntington, *The Clash of Civilizations and the Remaking of World Order*. New York: Simon & Schuster, 1996.

5. Stephen Neff, *War and the Law of Nations*. Cambridge: Cambridge University Press, 2005.

6. Jonathan Fox and Shmuel Sandler, *Bringing Religion into International Relations*. London: Palgrave, 2006, p. 1.

7. Aristotle, *Politics*, 350 BCE, I: 8; available at ⟨http://www.gutenberg.org/dirs/etext04/tgovt10.txt⟩ (accessed 29 September 2008), translated by William Ellis.

8. Ibid., VII: 14.

9. Paul Collier and Anke Hoeffler, *Greed and Grievance in Civil War*. Oxford: Oxford University Press, 2004.

10. Alan B. Krueger, *What Makes a Terrorist: Economics and the Roots of Terrorism*. Princeton, NJ: Princeton University Press, 2007, pp. 80–81.

11. See David Little, "Religious Militancy", in Chester A. Crocker and Fen Osler Hampson, with Pamela Aall (eds) *Managing Global Chaos: Sources of and Responses to International Conflict*. Washington, DC: United States Institute of Peace Press, 1996. See also David Rappoport, "Sacred Terror: A Contemporary Example from Islam", in Walter Reich (ed.) *Origins of Terrorism: Psychologies, Ideologies, Theologies, States of Mind*. Cambridge: Cambridge University Press, 1990.

12. R. Scott Appleby, *The Ambivalence of the Sacred: Religion, Violence, and Reconciliation*. Lanham, MD: Rowman & Littlefield, 2000.

13. Sam Harris, *The End of Faith: Religion, Terror, and the Future of Reason*. New York: W.W. Norton, 2005.

14. Jerald D. Gort, Henry Jansen and Hendrik M. Vroom (eds), *Religion, Conflict and Reconciliation: Multifaith Ideals and Realities*. New York: Rodopi, 2002.

15. Ibid., p. 25.

16. Hedley Bull discusses war as one of five conditions in international relations. Hedley Bull, *Anarchical Society*. New York: Columbia University Press, 1977.

17. Carl von Clausewitz, *On War*, 1832; available at ⟨http://www.gutenberg.org/etext/1946⟩ (accessed 29 September 2008).

18. See Michael Walzer, *Just and Unjust Wars: A Moral Argument with Historical Illustrations*. New York: Basic Books, 1977.

19. Apart from Michael Walzer's seminal book, see also Adam Roberts and Richard Guelff, *Documents on the Laws of War*, 3rd edn. Oxford: Oxford University Press, 2000; Yoram Dinstein, *War, Aggression and Self-Defence*, 4th edn. Cambridge: Cambridge University Press, 2001; Yoram Dinstein, *The Conduct of Hostilities under the Law of International Armed Conflict*. Cambridge: Cambridge University Press, 2004; and, most recently, Stephen Neff, *War and the Law of Nations*. Cambridge: Cambridge University Press, 2005.

20. See A. P. Rogers, *Law on the Battlefield*, 2nd edn. Huntington, NY: Juris Publishing, 2004.

21. Neff, *War and the Law of Nations*.

22. Paul Robinson (ed.), *Just War in Comparative Perspective*. Aldershot: Ashgate, 2003.

23. David Smock, *Religious Perspectives on War: Christian, Muslim, and Jewish Attitudes toward Force*. Washington, DC: United States Institute of Peace Press, 1992.

24. Richard Sorabji and David Rodin, *The Ethics of War: Shared Problems in Different Traditions*. Aldershot: Ashgate, 2006.

25. Torkel Brekke, *The Ethics of War in Asian Civilizations*. New York: Routledge, 2006.

26. Peter Partner, *God of Battles: Holy Wars of Christianity and Islam*. Princeton, NJ: Princeton University Press, 1999.

27. John Kelsay, *Arguing the Just War in Islam*. Cambridge, MA: Harvard University Press, 2007; James Turner Johnson, *The Holy War Idea in Western and Islamic Traditions*. University Park, PA: Pennsylvania State University Press, 1997.

28. See James Shotwell, *War as an Instrument of National Policy and Its Renunciation in the Pact of Paris*. New York: Harcourt, Brace, 1929. See also Robert Ferrell, *Peace in Their Time: The Origins of the Kellogg–Briand Pact*. New Haven, CT: Yale University Press, 1952.

29. See "Webster–Ashburton Treaty – The Caroline Case", in Hunter Miller (ed.), *Treaties and Other International Acts of the United States of America*, Vol. 4, Documents 80–121: 1836–1846. Washington, DC: Government Printing Office, 1934; available at ⟨http://www.yale.edu/lawweb/avalon/diplomacy/britain/br-1842d.htm⟩ (accessed 29 September 2008).

30. International Commission on Intervention and State Sovereignty, *The Responsibility to Protect*, ICISS, 2001; available at ⟨http://www.iciss.ca/report2-en.asp⟩ (accessed 29 September 2008).

31. United Nations General Assembly, *2005 World Summit Outcome*, UN Doc. A/RES/60/1, 24 October 2005.

32. See Krueger, *What Makes a Terrorist*.

2

Norms of war in Hinduism

Kaushik Roy

With the arrival of Aryans in the subcontinent around 1500 BCE, Hinduism took root and still continues to be the dominant religion of South Asia, where about one-fifth of the world's population resides. In this chapter, my objective is to analyse the role played by Hinduism in shaping the ethics of warfare and structuring the dynamics of organized violence in different contexts. Historical circumstances have shaped the evolution of Hindu religious theory and vice versa. Hence, while analysing the Hindu doctrine of warfare, I also attempt to historicize its evolution. This chapter suggests that religion is not the only determinant but is one of the key factors shaping India's strategic culture. As I will show, there is an intricate interrelationship between religion and violence.

Religion seems to be important for understanding the nature of warfare in the non-Western world. Christopher Coker asserts that the West is unique in secularizing warfare. Since the West has instrumentalized war, it has turned its back on the ritualized aspects of combat. However, for non-Western societies, violence remains the moral essence of the warrior. Taking the example of the *Bhagavad Gita*, Coker asserts that, for non-Western warriors, violence is existential. War for them is as much achieving one's humanity as achieving the objective of the state,[1] but this is not the case for modern Western soldiers.

Coker's view is dominant among Western military historians, the majority of whom assert that classical Greek civilization gave rise to the "Western Way of Warfare", which was further refined in Roman and medieval times. The Western tradition of warfare, characterized by tech-

World religions and norms of war, Popovski, Reichberg and Turner (eds),
United Nations University Press, 2009, ISBN 978-92-808-1163-6

nological innovations, rationality and the absence of religious and cultural ethics as regards the application of violence, gave the West global military superiority during the early modern era.[2] In recent times, the paradigm of a monolithic and homogeneous Western Way of Warfare has come under challenge.[3] Some scholars try to flesh out the effect of Christianity on the ethical aspects of warfare in the West. So, while studying the effects of Hinduism on warfare in India, one can also discern a role for religion in shaping the military culture of Western societies.

The twin opposing concepts of *dharmayuddha* (war against injustice) and *kutayuddha* (unjust war) shaped the dialectical interaction between Hinduism and warfare. This chapter chronologically charts the evolution of Hinduism and its relationship with the theory of warfare, enabling us to understand the contemporary political and strategic options open to the senior politicians and top-level civilian bureaucrats of the Indian republic. The first section covers the Epic and Vedic eras from 1500 BCE to 400 BCE and portrays the evolution of the theory of *dharmayuddha*. The second section concerns itself with the genesis of Kautilya's *kutayuddha* between 300 BCE and 100 BCE. The third section starts with the beginning of the Common Era and continues to the advent of the Muslims (Turks) in the subcontinent circa 900 CE. In this period, a watered-down version of *kutayuddha* emerged as a result of the influence of Manu's normative model of warfare. In the fourth section, we see how Hinduism adapted to Muslim political and military domination of South Asia between 900 and 1700 CE. The fifth section charts how Hinduism shaped resistance against British colonialism until 1947. The last section shows how a particular brand of Hinduism is used by India's strategic experts.

This chapter covers a span of more than 3,000 years of India's history. Throughout history, India has remained a multi-lingual, multi-ethnic and multi-religious society. Besides Hinduism, other religions such as Buddhism, Jainism, Sikhism, Islam and Christianity continue to exist side by side. In the 1990s, about 83 per cent of India's population was Hindu, 11 per cent Muslim, 2.6 per cent Christian and slightly over 3 per cent Sikhs, Jains, Parsis and Buddhists combined.[4] One Western scholar correctly asserts that Hinduism is not a religion but more a way of life. There is no single coherent body of beliefs.[5] Even within Hinduism, certain branches (Brahmanism, Vedantism, Vaishnavism, Shakti, Tantra, etc.) coexist.

So what is Hinduism? There is no single authoritative text or a single god in Hinduism. In fact, there are 33 *krores* of gods and goddesses in the Hindu pantheon. Broadly, Hinduism at different historical periods is based on certain texts. In the Vedic and Epic period, Hinduism evolved round the *Vedas* and the *Bhagavad Gita*. From the Common Era onwards, along with the *dharmasastra* literature (Sanskrit texts focusing on religious rituals and codes of individual and social behaviour), *Manusamhita* or *Manavadharmasastra* played an important role in the evolution of Hinduism. After 900 CE, the growth of Hinduism was mainly shaped by different commentaries on these texts. From the fifteenth century onwards, the two epics *Ramayana* and *Mahabharata* acquired religious significance. One can argue that Hinduism after 1500 BCE is the dominant religion of most of the people living between the River Indus and the Arakan Yomas. Hinduism is an amalgam of various strands of philosophies as well as a religion (based on certain rituals, beliefs and so on). Hence, Hinduism is best described as a culture, a way of life, i.e. *dharma*.

A comparative analysis with other religions that emerged both within and outside India is necessary because Hinduism reacted with other religious discourses as the historical context changed. Cross-cultural comparisons are necessary even when no apparent linkages are visible. For instance, in the Christian tradition, a trend towards restraint in the resort to war and limitations on the conduct of war evolved gradually.[6] Such a trend is also discernible in the case of Hinduism.

Most of the texts of Hindu literature in ancient India were written in Sanskrit. Unlike the Western tradition, a watertight compartmentalization between religious and secular texts cannot be applied in the case of Hindu literature. Even the *nitisastras* (works on statecraft) refer to *dharma*, a term to which I will return later. Since this chapter targets English-speaking readers, I use translated versions. Where my translation of particular terms varies from that of others, I refer to them.

Dharmayuddha and *kutayuddha* in the Vedic and Epic eras: 1500 BCE – 400 BCE

The word *dharma* is derived from the word *dhri*, which means to sustain or uphold. In the *Rig Veda*, *dharma* refers to the upholder or supporter of truth. In the *Yajur Veda*, *dharma* means firm and imperturbable. *Dharma* is considered a natural law for inanimate objects and natural phenomena. *Dharma* is regarded as an ethical and social standard of behaviour for people and a code of duties for the king. The moral content attached to the concept of *dharma* became more evident in the later religious literature. In the Vedic literature, the concept of *rita* stands for moral order, and violation of it requires penitence and prayer from the sinner. *Rita* is conceived as a regulating principle that runs through the whole realm of creation. Gradually, the moral sense of *rita* was absorbed into the concept of *dharma*.[7] This set the stage for the emergence of the concept of *dharmayuddha*.

Dharmayuddha depends on the ends (i.e. the objectives) of war. Any war undertaken against injustice becomes a *dharmayuddha*. *Dharmayud-*

dha also depends on the means and methods employed in war; i.e. combat techniques are regulated in accordance with certain laws.[8] *Dharmayuddha* is to an extent holy war, i.e. organized violence applied in accordance with certain codes and customs for the advancement or protection of the Hindu religion. The equivalent term in Western literature is "just war". The term *dharmayuddha* will be used in this chapter to differentiate the Indian notion from the Western concept of just war.

Dharmayuddha is war conducted in accordance with the principles of *dharma*, meaning *kshatradharma*, i.e. the laws of kings and warriors. *Kshatradharma* enjoins just and righteous warfare. It means *prakashyayuddha* (open battle) without indulging in any secretive techniques. Combat becomes a regulated frontal clash. The time and place of battle are to be settled by the warring parties beforehand, and war is to be declared with the blowing of conch shells. The warriors on chariots are then to fight each other with bows and arrows. By fighting courageously and dying on the battlefield, the warriors would achieve the status of heroes.[9] The *Bhagavad Gita* (composed by anonymous sages around 500 BCE) emphasizes that *dharmayuddha* is waged only by the Kshatriyas because only a Kshatriya has the qualities of courage, consistency, resourcefulness, generosity, leadership capability and a noble mind that are required for waging *dharmayuddha*. And it is the duty of the Kshatriyas to fight and, if necessary, to die. Killing in war is not considered illegal. In accordance with the laws of *dharmayuddha*, a warrior who kills not out of personal enmity but out of duty goes to heaven after death.[10] The concept of heaven in Hinduism is complicated. Attaining heaven in this context means *moksha*, or salvation, in a sense; it means freedom from the endless rebirths as enunciated in the *karma* doctrine. *Dharmayuddha* does not negate violence; Francis X. Clooney writes that it involves pain and suffering, with a necessary amount of violence applied in regulated doses.[11] The codes of *dharmayuddha*, which moderated the lethality inherent in warfare, says Manoj Kumar Sinha, gave rise to humanitarian laws of war in India, thereby reducing the destructive effects of warfare on society.[12]

Here it may be noted that in Judaism, too, war is subject to certain restraints. For example, during a siege food trees are not supposed to be cut down.[13] A version of just war emerged in China, writes Mark E. Lewis, around the fifth century BCE.[14] Strict rules of etiquette were followed during battles. The combatants fought only with opponents who were of the same social status.[15] The classical Greek warfare that evolved between 800 and 500 BCE developed certain conventions that circumscribed the lethality of fighting. Some of the rules were: that war should be officially declared; that non-combatants should not be harmed; that defeated foes are not to be pursued; that those who surrender are not to be killed and prisoners should be released after they offer ransom; that ambassadors should have diplomatic immunity.[16] These rules are similar to the laws of *dharmayuddha* developed by Manu at the beginning of the Common Era. In the Indian scenario, the later *Samhitas* emphasized that the drivers of chariots and diplomatic envoys are not to be harmed.[17] Besides moderation in the conduct of war, in the case of *dharmayuddha* the causes for war must be just. Similarly in the Western tradition, wars for self-defence or recovery of property are considered to be just.[18]

According to Sarva Daman Singh, the concept of *dharmayuddha* emerged in the context of the Aryan tribes fighting against each other. When the Aryans were fighting the Dravidians (the original inhabitants of India), the *Rig Veda* mentions the use of fire-tipped arrows. These arrows were probably dipped in flaming pitch before being fired towards the enemy. However, this weapon was banned in the later Epic literature, which formulated a code of conduct for fighting among the Aryans.[19] In contrast, Torkel Brekke asserts that in the epics there are no rules for conducting just war.[20] I shall discuss this later.

The *Rig Veda* – a collection of more than 1,000 hymns by unknown sages – was composed between 1200 and 900 BCE. One hymn says: "I stretch the bow for Rudra so that his arrow will strike down the hater of prayer."[21] The *Rig Veda* asserts that the Dravidians worship false gods. Hence, a war of extermination against them is acceptable.[22] *Agni* (the fire god) is invoked in the *Rig Veda* in order to destroy the Dravidians.[23] The *Sama Veda* also emphasizes that defeated foes should not be allowed to escape but must be crushed.[24] Here lies the core of the concept of *kutayuddha* (unjust war). The *Vedas* never refer to pacifism. Wendy Doniger and Brian K. Smith rightly argue that the worldview of the *Vedas* is similar to the martial values associated with the warrior class, i.e. the Kshatriyas. Self-aggrandizement and dominance are unabashedly embraced and displayed in the Vedic literature. Violence and power in the social realm are highlighted and portrayed as part and parcel of the natural order in the cosmos.[25] The brutal and materialistic worldview of the *Vedas* was shaped by historical circumstances. The Rig Vedic Aryans mostly engaged in cattle raids because cattle were of primary importance in the functioning of the pastoral economy of the Aryan tribes.[26] Further, the Aryans had to struggle continuously for survival against the Dravidians, who were outside the pale of Vedic culture.

The two epics *Ramayana* and *Mahabharata* provide us with some military details regarding warfare in India during the Epic age. Both these epics were composed around 400 BCE.[27] The *Mahabharata* (which is the longest poem in the world, with over 100,000 couplets) describes the struggle between the Aryan tribes regarding domination over north

India.[28] The *Ramayana* portrays Aryan expansion against the Dravidians of south India. From the *Ramayana* it is clear that, in order to defeat the numerically superior Dravidians, the Aryans resorted to the strategy of "divide and rule",[29] which later became *bheda* (encouraging internal dissension) for Kautilya and a principal component of his *kutayuddha*. Further, guile, treachery and viciousness characterized the Aryan conduct of warfare against the Dravidians.[30]

The *Mahabharata* depicts the struggle between two Aryan tribes – the Pandavas and the Kauravas. The Pandavas started *dharmayuddha* against the Kauravas only when the policies of *sama* (conciliation), *bheda* (fomenting internal dissension) and *dana* failed. *Dana* is not bribery, as Nick Allen translates it,[31] but means gift-giving out of generosity. In the *Mahabharata*, two military schools exist. The dominant school propagates *dharmayuddha*. This school argues that war must be fought between equals in accordance with the heroic ideals. But Lord Krishna, on the side of the Pandavas, and Aswathama, a Kaurava warlord, supported *kutayuddha*.[32] The *Mahabharata* emphasizes the importance of commanders for conducting *kutuyuddha* successfully. The Kaurava chief Duryodhana says that, without a good general, even a mighty army dissolves into a swarm of ants.[33]

Kautilya's *kutayuddha*: 300–100 BCE

According to one tradition, Kautilya (also known as Chanakya) was the principal minister of Chandragupta Maurya, who founded the Maurya empire in 319 BCE.[34] Kautilya's *Arthasastra*, composed around 300 BCE, is both a handbook for rulers on the management of their duties as well as a discussion on abstract politics.[35] Realism is defined as power politics shaped by political and military reasoning completely dissociated from religious morality.[36] Kautilya is a realist, but refers to *dharma* as the duties of the king. Brekke claims that the *Arthasastra* represents the ideal of prudence, which was opposite to the heroic ideal as espoused in the two Hindu epics.[37]

Kautilya writes that the object of a ruler is first to protect his territory and secondly to acquire more territory from other rulers. Kautilya portrays inter-state relations as a circle composed of various kingdoms. This is known as the *mandala* theory. The *mandala* is full of disorder, chaos and anarchy, a situation that is dangerous for everybody. The only security in such a dangerous, fluid situation is power. For Kautilya, strength is power and every state follows the policy of power politics. Hence, struggle between the various kingdoms is inevitable. The most successful ruler among the circle of kings is known as the *vijigishu*.[38] Kautilya's focus was on *chara* (espionage department), both for surveillance of subjects and for collecting military intelligence. As regards surveillance of civil society, the *Arthasastra* emphasizes watching the movements of state officials and the high castes,[39] probably because the high castes were economically powerful and literate and controlled the state bureaucracy. So Kautilya perceived a threat from them.

Brekke asserts that Kautilya in particular and the Hindu theoreticians in general failed to distinguish between internal sedition and external war.[40] One can argue that Brekke is interpreting Indian military philosophy from a European perspective. Carl von Clausewitz's bipolar, watertight compartmentalization of warfare into inter-state war and intra-state war is not universally applicable. For Kautilya and the later Hindu theorists, internal rebellions and external wars are interrelated. Kautilya declares that internal rebellions are often sponsored by external powers and, as a result, low-intensity war often escalates into inter-state war.[41]

Like Niccolò Machiavelli, Kautilya claims that the end justifies the means. The basic components of Kautilya's *kutayuddha* are intrigues, duplicity and fraud. Kautilya advocates the use of wine, women, poison and spies for achieving victory.[42] Interestingly, both Aristotle (384–322 BCE) and Kautilya said that tyrants employ female spies for gathering intelligence about their subjects.[43] For Kautilya, internal dangers are more important than external threats posed by neighbouring states. Kautilya warns the king that palace rebellions could occur owing to the participation of members of the royal families and of top officials such as generals and ministers in intrigues and sedition directed against the ruler. The leaders of the rebels should be won over. If that is not possible, then they must be assassinated. Kautilya continues by stating that continuous conflicts between various groups within the kingdom and among external neighbours would aid the *vijigishu* to maintain his power.[44] Instead of the overt application of military force, Kautilya focuses more on *bheda* (sowing dissent and disunity among the enemy).[45] In the paradigm of *dharmayuddha*, *bheda* is used to avert war; in the paradigm of *kutayuddha*, in contrast, *bheda* is used merely as a technique to weaken the enemy before initiating a regular attack. Only if subterfuges fail does the *vijigishu* have to resort to warfare with his army.[46]

Instead of a set-piece battle, Kautilya advocates an attrition strategy. He proposes the slow destruction of the enemy kingdom through harassment by the *vijigishu* and his allies.[47] When fighting a war, the *vijigishu*, instead of launching a frontal attack, should implement *kutayuddha-vikalpa*.[48] I translate this term as the use of alternative deception tactics. This concept is similar to the advocacy by the Chinese military theorist Sun Tzu (sixth century BCE) of the use of unorthodox techniques against the enemy.[49] Special commando units, says the *Arthasastra*, are to be stationed on the battlefield, whose duty is to kill the enemy commanders during combat.[50] For Kautilya, the use of a reserve force for winning a battle is a must.[51] One important component of *kutayuddha* is the preemptive strike.[52] The effective implementation of deceiving tactics, surprise attacks and the timely use of reserves, asserts Kautilya, requires drilling the troops with weapons in peacetime.[53]

Parallel with Kautilyan thought, an alternative philosophy evolved in north India within more or less the same time-frame. Gautama Buddha and Mahavira, the founders of Buddhism and Jainism, vigorously preached *ahimsa* (non-violence). The parallel figure in Chinese philosophy is Confucius (551–479 BCE), who emphasized public and private morality. Confucius declared that governments are maintained by the mandate of heaven, which could be gained by promoting the welfare of and justice for their subjects.[54] For Confucius, conflict is inappropriate for civilized men.[55] It is to be noted that in fourth-century BCE China, Mencius, a follower of Confucianism, argued in contrast to Sun Tzu that all those who advocate warfare and military expertise are criminals.[56] In the context of India, Chandragupta Maurya's grandson, Emperor Asoka (261–226 BCE), was influenced by Buddhism and was the greatest proponent of *ahimsa*. However, he did not disband his army. Though he focused on welfare measures to avert discontent among his subjects, the well-trained army under direct control of the emperor remained as a deterrent against internal uprising and external invasion.[57]

Post-Kautilyan synthesis: Common Era – 900 CE

S. K. Bhakari asserts that the tightening of the social system based on four *varnas* (castes) and the emphasis on stasis by the Hindu religious literature of the post-Kautilyan era obstructed intellectual innovations, especially in military affairs. The Hindu texts prohibited foreign travel, discourse with foreigners and overseas commerce. All these prohibitions resulted in the obstruction of the free flow of ideas and subsequent technological stagnation.[58] Jagadish Narayan Sarkar supports Bhakari's views and writes that both Kamandaka (who operated in the seventh century CE) and Somadeva Suri (a Jain saint who lived around the tenth century CE) emphasized the fourfold army comprising infantry, cavalry, elephants and chariots, though chariots had become useless several centuries earlier.[59] An analysis in a chronological manner of the texts generated by the Hindu theoreticians in the aftermath of the *Arthasastra* shows that the Hindu theoreticians attempted to blunt Kautilya's focus on *kutayuddha* and tried to integrate his teachings within the paradigm of *dharmayuddha*.

The greatest challenge to Kautilya's *kutayuddha* came from Manu's *Manusmriti* (*The Laws of Manu*), which sought to articulate an eternal science of politics. Manu was also responding to the challenge posed to Hinduism by the heterodox sects such as Buddhism and Jainism, and produced what could be termed "orthodox Brahmanical literature". We know next to nothing about the personal life of Manu. This is because *Manusmriti*, like all other Hindu religious texts, hides its true authorship in order to posit its own claim as transcendental and absolutely true. Religious discourse is assumed by Hindu teachers to express the "Words of God".[60]

Manu, like Kautilya, accepts that the *mandala* is composed of a circle of 12 kings and that a strong monarchical government is necessary for establishing order in the real world.[61] *Manusmriti* does not propagate antimilitarism. Manu, following Kautilya, writes that a kingdom is composed of seven interrelated constituents: ruler, ministers, capital, people, treasury, forts and army.[62] The duty of a righteous king is to rule and to punish transgressors in his realm. One of the principal components of proper rule is fear, and the instrument for projecting fear is the *danda* (force/coercion, i.e. the army). Victory favours the righteous; a king can be righteous only if he follows the ways of *dharma* and conducts warfare in accordance with the normative model of *dharmayuddha*. Manu built on the rules of *dharmayuddha*, which he had inherited from the *Vedas*. Manu wrote that, in *dharmayuddha*, the use of poisoned, barbed or burning arrows is not permitted. Further, enemy soldiers who are intent on surrender or have lost their weapons in combat are not to be killed. Enemy prisoners are to be protected and a retreating enemy army is not to be attacked.[63] Manu says that it is the duty of the Kshatriyas to take part in the defence of the realm.[64] This is necessary because Manu, influenced by the *Rig Veda*, asserts that only the Kshatriyas are capable of conducting *dharmayuddha*.

One of the characteristics of *dharmayuddha* is its defensive nature. Hence Manu, unlike Kautilya, overemphasizes the importance of forts. Strategic defence based on positional warfare is the credo of the strategic theorists of *dharmayuddha*. Forts for Manu are important for supplying the field army.[65] Even Kautilya, the most vigorous proponent of *kutayuddha*, argues against a strategic offensive policy. The *vijigishu* is advised to confine his activities within the subcontinent. This is probably because of the geographical insularity of India and also the vast size of the subcontinent.[66] In a just war, the strategic objectives of warfare must be limited. Similarly in the Bible and in the rabbinic tradition, asserts Norman Solomon, campaigns beyond the borders of Israel were not allowed during war against the idolaters.[67]

Banabhatta wrote the *Harsacharita* in the mid seventh century CE. It is a historical romantic fiction occurring in the reign of King Harshavard-hana of Kanauj (606–648 CE). Banabhatta accepts that the *vijigishu* should try to implement the policy of *digvijaya* (conquest of the subcontinent). He warns the *vijigishu* that he must be aware of his enemies, who might try to wage *kutayuddha*. The tactics of *kutayuddha* involve kidnapping the royal ladies of hostile kings, the assassination of enemy kings during diplomatic meetings, etc.[68]

Kamandaka's *Nitisara* (*Essence of Statesmanship*) was composed between the sixth and the seventh centuries CE. He attempts to establish a balance between *dharmayuddha* and *kutayuddha*. Like Kautilya and Manu, Kamandaka notes that a state is composed of seven interrelated elements. Kamandaka slightly modifies Manu's ideas by fusing capital and people into an element that he calls kingdom and introducing a new element, allies. Kamandaka, like Kautilya and Manu, accepts that the duty of a righteous king is to protect his subjects from both internal and external dangers. Military power is the product of three elements: forts, the treasury and the army. Kamandaka, probably influenced by Emperor Asoka's welfare measures, advises the ruler to depend on good governance, focusing especially on the economic prosperity of his subjects instead of military might for preventing internal rebellions. Kamandaka emphasizes self-restraint on the part of the *vijigishu* and discourages an overtly aggressive strategy. In contrast to Kautilya but like Manu, Kamandaka writes that a *vijigishu* must conduct *dharmayuddha*. Like Manu, Kamandaka says that the principal objective in war is not destruction of the enemy's army but capture of the enemy's forts.[69]

The *Panchatantra* is a collection of fables on *niti* (proper and wise conduct in life). Several tales in the *Panchatantra* focus on linkages between security and intelligence. In general, the *Panchatantra* provides a realist interpretation of society. The basic message is that what often seems superficially to be the reality is actually deceptive. Again, past experience and the study of history are considered important for gaining insights regarding the future conduct of policy. Like the writings of Kautilya, Manu and Kamandaka, the *Panchatantra* emphasizes the importance of winning and retaining intelligent allies.[70] One can see the influence of Kautilya in one of the verses of the *Panchatantra*, which notes that "intelligence is power".[71] The *Panchatantra* gives importance to loyal warriors with martial instincts. One verse notes: "One who finds in battle peace, Free from questionings, thinks of exile as of home, Is beloved of the kings."[72] Following Kautilya, the *Panchatantra* notes the importance of training for combat. One verse claims that the usefulness of the horse and sword depend on the quality of the user.[73] Finally, emphasizing *kutayuddha*, the *Panchatantra* concludes that when a soldier enters combat he should not think of right and wrong.[74]

Narayana, a worshipper of the god Shiva, was the court poet of Dhavala Chandra, who was a governor of the Pala empire in eastern India. Besides writing poetry, Narayana was also an erudite grammarian and philosopher, and composed the *Hitopadesa* sometime between 800 and 950 CE. The *Hitopadesa* contains extracts from the *Ramayana*, the *Mahabharata*, the *Puranas*, the *Panchatantra*, the *Arthasastra* and the *Nitisara*. The *Hitopadesa*, like the *Panchatantra*, is a collection of fables in prose, whose objective is to impart instruction in worldly wisdom and statecraft. The *Hitopadesa* offers a coda that includes elements of both *dharmayuddha* and *kutayuddha*. Following Kautilya, Manu and Kamandaka, Narayana emphasizes that the duty of the king is to protect the populace. In a tone similar to Kautilya, the *Hitopadesa* asserts that, before starting *vigraha* (war), spies should be sent to the enemy territory to gather military intelligence. The *Hitopadesa* tells us that, in cases of war between two groups with equal military power, victory will go to the side that resorts to cunning in order to get inside the enemy citadel. Here one finds the influence of *kutayuddha*. During combat, writes Narayana, a warrior should be as bold as a maiden who abandons all modesty while making love. However, following the normative model of *dharmayuddha*, Narayana enjoins that a diplomatic envoy from the enemy should never be harmed.[75]

The only voice of brutality imbued with an aggressive sense of realism among the post-Kautilyan theorists was Sukra, the author of *Sukraniti*, which was composed around 900 CE. He proclaims that for a weak king the only method of survival is to conduct *kutayuddha*, which involves attacking the enemy from the rear.[76] And if the weak king's regular army is too weak to engage in any sort of battle with the enemy force, then, says Sukra, the weak king should engage in guerrilla warfare. Influenced by Kautilya, Sukra writes that, like a robber, the king should suddenly attack the enemy and, after harassing the hostile force, should retreat. Here one finds the origins of the concept of mobile guerrilla warfare, which the Marathas (Hindus of west India) followed during the eighteenth century. Following the *Panchatantra*, Sukra claims that the enemy should be totally annihilated. A defeated enemy who is not annihilated is dangerous. Like an outstanding debt, it can grow and in future become a threat.[77] He argues that the army constitutes the principal strength of the government. Military power is the product of an amalgamation of weapons, military leadership and the physical strength of the soldiers. The only way an enemy can be subdued efficiently is by using the army. Sukra's realism is evident in the force structure he portrays for an efficient army; in contrast to most Hindu theoreticians, Sukra warns against over-dependence on elephants. He advocates an army composed of infantry and cavalry, with bulls and camels for logistical purposes. To raise the combat effectiveness of the army, Sukra, like Kautilya, emphasizes regular pay for the soldiers, intense pre-battle training, strict discipline and proper diet.[78]

In sum, even those authors who were advocates of *dharmayuddha* did not oppose inter-state warfare. Herein lies the basic difference between Hindu philosophy and Western theorists of perpetual peace. Whereas Jean-Jacques Rousseau and Immanuel Kant consider war to be a condition that can be expunged from international society (especially the society of democratic states),[79] the theorists of both *dharmayuddha* and *kutayuddha* agree on the inevitability of inter-state war. It remains true, however, that the supporters of *dharmayuddha* are keen to reduce the distressing effects of war on society. Hindu intellectuals after Kautilya are aware to a greater or lesser extent of the importance of *dharmayuddha* and *kutayuddha*. But most of them concentrate on power politics within the subcontinent. The Hindu texts show a lack of awareness regarding the nature of political and military power outside India, and this had disastrous consequences for the Rajputs, who had established numerous principalities in west and north India during early medieval times.

Hindu military theory in the Islamic era: 1000–1700 CE

From 900 CE onwards, the Turks, who had accepted Islam, started attacking India from Afghanistan. By 1200 CE they had conquered north India. The Muslim domination of South Asia continued until the rise of British power in the second half of the eighteenth century. Despite the Islamic Turkish versus Hindu confrontation being a case of a clash of civilizations, certain similarities as well as dissimilarities were present in the Islamic and Hindu philosophies of warfare.

One of the principal weaknesses of Hindu philosophy is that it emphasizes caste divisions, whereas Islam focuses on social solidarity and the equality of the faithful.[80] Hence, in Islamic philosophy every Muslim is a soldier, but according to Hindu philosophy not every Hindu can be a soldier. Only the Rajputs or Thakurs, i.e. Kshatriyas, who were India's hereditary class of warriors, were considered true soldiers by the Hindu theorists of ancient and medieval India. The exception was Kautilya, who advocated the recruitment of all castes in the army. The Turks who invaded India emphasized *al-harb khada*, which means deception in warfare. Interestingly, this concept is similar to the role of deception in warfare as highlighted by the theorists of *kutayuddha*.[81] Fakr-i-Mudabbir, a thirteenth-century Indian Muslim theorist, like Sukra refers to midnight raids on enemy camps.[82]

The Turks were opposed by the Rajputs. The Rajputs were somewhat similar to the *bushi*, an order of professional fighting men who emerged in medieval Japan.[83] In contrast to the Islamic Turkish culture of warfare, the Rajput code of warfare, which evolved from the code of *dharmayuddha*, was against launching surprise attacks. The principal component of Rajput military culture was chivalry, which was an essential element of *kshatradharma*. It emphasized the vanity of personal valour. This often resulted in battles degenerating into hand-to-hand combat. Occasionally, battles became a contest between champions or chosen warriors. The Rajput culture was geared to display individual bravery in battle. As enjoined in the *Rig Veda*, a warrior fulfilled his duty towards his master and acquired honour by becoming a martyr. Warfare was regarded as somewhat similar to sport. Practising intrigue was regarded as unacceptable for honourable and dignified warriors. Tactical retreat and nocturnal attacks, following *Manusmriti*, were looked down upon. A true Rajput when defeated was never supposed to leave the battlefield alive. Hence, during crisis situations, the Rajput warriors took opium and dressed in saffron coloured robes, because this colour represented death for them. Their aim was to sell their lives at the highest possible price to the enemy. It is to be noted that the medieval Japanese warriors' code of honour also dictated that, when defeated, the soldier should commit suicide by disembowelment. To sum up, the individualistic honour of the Rajputs prevented the development of large-scale, coordinated, bureaucratic warfare. Their Muslim adversaries commented that the Rajputs knew how to die but not how to fight.[84] The Rajput concept of chivalry was somewhat similar to the West European knights' chivalrous warfare. The medieval West European code of chivalry demanded that a defeated enemy be given quarter, and that prisoners were treated as gentlemen and later released for ransom.[85]

In 1192 CE, when Muhammad Ghori, the ruler of Ghur in Afghanistan, invaded India, the leader of the Rajput Confederacy was Prithviraj Chauhan, the ruler of Ajmir. Prithviraj, despite possessing numerical superiority, did not immediately attack Muhammad Ghori. Instead, in accordance with the creed of *dharmayuddha*, Prithviraj warned Ghori saying that, if he agreed to retreat, then the Ghorid army would be allowed safe passage. Ghori said that he would retreat and requested that Prithviraj suspend hostilities. The ruse was completely successful; Ghori launched a nocturnal attack on the unsuspecting Rajputs. The next morning Ghori launched a full-scale attack on the disordered Rajputs at Tarain and defeated them.[86]

The overemphasis on positional warfare by Kautilya and the later Hindu theoreticians also encouraged the Rajputs to opt for static defence based in forts. The *Panchatantra* notes that the forts were to be protected

with bushes, walls and moats. Further, the gates of the forts must be covered with catapults and the doors should have bolts, bars and panels.[87] A
belt of thick thorny bushes surrounded the fort of Ajmir. The fort of Mul-
tan had four gates and was surrounded by a moat, and the fort of Jalor
had gates protected by bastions.[88] *Manusmriti* considers hill forts as
being most effective. Many medieval Rajput forts such as Devagiri,
Asirgarh, Champanir and Raisen were built on hilltops.[89]

Certain similarities exist between *dharmayuddha* and jihad (holy war).
Dharmayuddha could be initiated only by the righteous king for establishing *dharma*. Similarly, just war in the Islamic tradition requires a just
cause, virtuous intent and a legitimate authority. *Dharmayuddha* allows
the righteous king to utilize force for the destruction of rebels within
Hindu society. Similarly, jihad could be conducted against Muslims challenging the policy of the established leadership.[90] Ziauddin Barani (a
Muslim intellectual of fourteenth-century India), like Sukra, says that
kingship is army and army is kingship.[91] Andre Wink asserts that both
the Hindus of ancient and early medieval India and the Muslim rulers
during the Middle Ages failed to develop strong centralized bureaucratic
states because both Hindu and Muslim political theories portray sovereignty not as unitary but as bifurcated. *Bheda* for Hindus and *fitna* (strife,
internal rebellions) for the Muslims were necessary components in the
rulers' expansionist policy for establishing a divisive sovereignty.[92] The
politics of *fitna* by the Muslim rulers of medieval India involved *bheda*
backed by *danda* (military power), which resulted in the absorption and
accommodation of potential rebels.[93] Only in the eighteenth century did
the British establish a centralized agrarian bureaucratic state in the subcontinent.

Hindu militarism and anti-militarism under the British empire: 1750–1947 CE

The Hindu religious tradition was not characterized by pacifism during
the eighteenth century. The large numbers of soldier monks in the service of regional polities in the eighteenth century point to the fact that
discipline, hierarchy and institutional loyalty, which were integral to monastic life, were easily transferred to military service.[94] In W. G. Orr's
view, warrior Hindu religious ascetics emerged in India in response to
the violence displayed by the armed Muslim faqirs against the Hindu ascetic orders.[95] The armed Hindu religious ascetics did not accept the doctrine of *ahimsa* (non-violence). They were known as Gosains and
Dasnamis, and worshipped Shiva and Vishnu. Asceticism for the Gosains
did not involve love for a distant forgiving god, but entailed becoming

god-men by acquiring political, financial and military power. They indulged freely in liquor and sex. They were attached to the *akharas* (monastic orders), which were ruled by the *mahants*. In the *akharas* thousands of retainers were inculcated from childhood in complete submission to the *mahants*. Hence, these ascetic recruits made disciplined soldiers. The rulers also employed Gosains as spies and secret assassins. Thus, they functioned as tools for conducting *kutayuddha*.[96] It is to be noted that Kautilya had recommended the use of ascetics as spies and secret assassins.[97] The self-abnegation of the Naga monks made them good soldiers, who functioned as shock troops. The Naga soldiers in the service of eighteenth-century Indian princes were adept at conducting nocturnal raids,[98] which constitute an element of *kutayuddha*.

The concept of war as shaped by Hinduism, and especially the *karma* theory, occasionally obstructed the adoption of new military technologies. During the seventeenth and eighteenth centuries CE, the Nayaka chieftains of Mysore were against the use of bows and guns. They considered the use of such weapons for long-distance killing to be unheroic and a variety of *kutayuddha*. Warriors indulging in *kutayuddha*, they believed, did not ascend to heaven after death. Righteous warfare, in their interpretation, involved a straight fight with swords and lances that resulted in heroic death.[99]

Toward the end of the nineteenth century, the British Raj was able to demilitarize the subcontinent. From the second decade of the twentieth century, a non-violent mass movement, led by Mohandas Karamchand Gandhi, challenged British rule in India. In order to sustain a nationalist struggle based on non-violent tactics (strikes, boycotts, etc.) against the British Raj, from the 1920s Gandhi emphasized the values of pacifism and tolerance. About the relationship between *ahimsa* and *himsa* (violence) in public affairs, Gandhi observed in 1942:

> I believe that non-violence is infinitely superior to violence, forgiveness is more manly than punishment.... The religion of non-violence is not meant merely for the *rishis* [ascetics] and saints. It is meant for the common people as well.... For *satyagraha* [force of truth] and its offshoots, non-cooperation and civil resistance are nothing but new names for the law of suffering. The *rishis*, who discovered the law of non-violence in the midst of violence, were greater geniuses than Newton. They were themselves greater warriors than Wellington. Having themselves known the use of arms, they realized their uselessness, and taught a weary world that its salvation lay not through violence but through non-violence.[100]

Gandhi's pacifism was derived from the Jain and Bhakti movements' aversion to sacrificial violence.[101] For conducting struggles against the colonial state, Gandhi used *satyagraha* and *ahimsa* for his civilizational

critique of Western culture based on military power.[102] Gandhi's negative view of pre-modern armed Hindu ascetics was shaped by the *bhakti*
or devotionalist culture that emerged in north India after 1400 CE. In accordance with the *bhakti* tradition, God is a distant loving entity who can
be reached only by praying.[103]

Despite the presence of a large number of goddesses in Hinduism, the
gods dominate the religious hierarchy. In the early Rig Vedic age,
Brahma (the god of fire) was the principal god and during the later Vedic
era Indra became the principal god. From the Common Era onwards,
Lord Shiva (the god of destruction) was the principal god. However,
from the sixteenth century onwards, a marginal strand within Hinduism,
flourishing in Bengal, accepted Durga (the Mother Goddess of supreme
power) as the most powerful among all the gods and goddesses. In the
works of all the principal Hindu military theorists, women are marginal
to the principal discourse. Sita and Draupadi play a marginal role in the
Ramayana and the *Mahabharata*. *Manusmriti* completely subordinates
women to men. However, from the second decade of the twentieth century, with the increasing participation of women in the nationalist movement led by the Indian National Congress, the political leaders had to
map out a strategy for integrating women in the anti-colonial struggle.
Within Gandhi's paradigm of non-violent Hinduism, women were subordinated to men. Whereas Gandhi conceived of a "Sita-like passive role"
for Indian women in the struggle against the British, the Bengali nationalist Subhas Chandra Bose visualized a violent role for Indian women,
modelled on Goddess Durga. With Japanese help, Bose set up the Rani
Jhansi Regiment (named after the Rani of Jhansi, who led an armed
struggle against the British during the 1857 Mutiny and subsequently became a nationalist icon and was compared to Goddess Durga) with Tamil
women in Singapore during 1943, to conduct an armed struggle against
the British in Burma.[104]

The early twentieth century also witnessed the emergence of militant
aggressive Hindu nationalism among certain religious reformers in Bengal. Swami (religious leader) Vivekananda urged the rejuvenation of Indian society on the basis of aggressive Hinduism. However, his message
had no overtly political objectives. *Rishi* Aurobindo was influenced by
the yogic tradition in Hinduism and for a time supported revolutionary
terrorism (throwing bombs at British officials, etc). It is to be noted that
most of the Hindu warrior ascetics of pre-modern India practised yoga.
The assumption was that yoga enabled them to discipline the mind (the
term yoga means mental exercise or a sort of meditation). The first reference to yoga was found in the *Upanishads*, which were composed between 800 and 500 BCE. The *Yogasutras*, probably composed by
Patanjali in the third century CE, state that through yogic practice one

attains mental steadiness and a refusal to be self-centred in a selfish world. The idea is to unite with the *atman* (self/soul) in order to ensure harmony between the mind and the body. The purpose is to attain calmness and cognitive insights.[105]

Hinduism and strategic cum military theory in the post-colonial scenario: 1947–2000 CE

What effect does traditional Hindu philosophy have on modern India's war leaders and strategic thinkers? George K. Tanham, an American policy analyst in the 1990s, argues that, owing to the caste system, which was first formulated in the *Rig Veda* more than three millennia ago, members of the Indian strategic elite continue to view the world in a hierarchical manner; they rank nations by size, culture and power. Tanham continues by suggesting that since 1947 India's foreign policy has been shaped by Kautilya's *mandala* doctrine. To an Indian foreign policy maker sitting in Delhi, the world appears as a series of circles. The first circle is India itself. The second circle includes India's South Asian neighbours such as Bhutan, Sikkim, Nepal and Bangladesh. The third circle comprises Pakistan, China and the former Soviet Union. The Indian Ocean region constitutes the fourth circle. And the last circle includes the distant great powers such as the United States. India's geopolitical interest declines as one moves away from the core, i.e. the inner circle. Following Kautilya, India's Ministry of External Affairs (Foreign Office) believes that India's enemy's enemy is its friend. Hence, to tackle its immediate neighbours Pakistan and China (which are bound to be hostile in the Kautilyan paradigm), Delhi has forged a relationship with Russia, which continues to experience border tensions with China and problems with Pakistan over the issue of Afghanistan.[106]

In a similar vein, C. Raja Mohan asserts that even Prime Minister Jawaharlal Nehru's so-called non-aligned policy could be traced back to the *Arthasastra*'s balance of power policy in the *mandala*. The Indian decision makers were steeped in the realist tradition and were influenced by Kautilya's *mandala* policy. For instance, India's treaties with Nepal and Bhutan were security alliances under which Delhi promised to protect these states from external threats. These states constitute the core of the Indian conception of *mandala*. In the next concentric circle, which encompasses India's extended neighbourhood (i.e. Pakistan and Bangladesh), New Delhi's policy is determined more by balance of power considerations than by any orthodox conservative ideological notions. The third circle includes China and Russia. India's policy until the break-up of the Soviet Union in 1991 had been to balance Beijing and

US-sponsored Pakistan with Moscow. In the new millennium, owing to the absence of a strong "bear", India is moving towards an alliance with the United States to balance China. Raja Mohan goes on to argue that India's shifting international alliances in accordance with the needs of its self-interest can be traced back to the assertion of the Kaurava warlord Bhisma, who in the *Mahabharata* says that in the sphere of politics there is no concept of permanent friends and enemies. Both friends and foes are determined by considerations of interest and gain. Friendship can become enmity with the passage of time and vice versa.[107] However, many Indian analysts are also suspicious about the degree of advantage New Delhi would derive from a strategic partnership with Washington. In 1999, one columnist on a famous Indian daily reminded its literate readership of the *Panchatantra*, emphasizing that there can be friendship only between equals.[108]

Besides grand strategy (national security policy, which is an amalgam of economic, foreign and military policies), Hinduism also shapes military strategy. In 1990, Lieutenant-Colonel G. D. Bakshi wrote that, despite technological progress, strategy and tactics continue to be shaped by timeless principles. Hence, the *Mahabharata* could teach the present generation of political and military leaders a lot. He asserts that, consciously and unconsciously, Indian warfare continues to be shaped by the heritage of the *Mahabharata*. For example, the *Mahabharata* speaks of short-duration high-intensity conflicts; the Mahabharata war lasted for only 18 days. Most of India's post-independence conflicts, such as the 1965 India–Pakistan war and the 1971 Bangladesh war, lasted for a short time – 22 days and 14 days, respectively. The *Mahabharata* asserts that the most suitable time for military campaigns is the period between November and March. Both the 1962 India–China war and the 1971 India–Pakistan war occurred in November and December.[109] Even in the medieval era, writes Jos J. L. Gommans, war started after the end of the monsoon in October and ceased with the beginning of summer in April.[110]

Waheguru Pal Singh Sidhu writes that, from the *Mahabharata*, one can derive the strategy of breaking into and out of enemy encirclement.[111] In accordance with the *dharmayuddha* school in the *Mahabharata*, symmetrical warfare remains the norm. Under this paradigm, chariots attacked chariots, elephants attacked elephants, and so on. Bakshi says that this concept continues to have a negative effect on the modern Indian Army. In accordance with the doctrine of symmetrical warfare as enshrined in *dharmayuddha*, the doctrine of Indian armoured formations continues to emphasize that the tank is the best weapon to use against enemy tanks. However, the use of tanks against the enemy's soft-skinned vehicles and infantry could have a greater effect on the opposing army. Bakshi warns that the very concept of *dharmayuddha* is preventing tactical innovations involving asymmetrical techniques.

Kutayuddha has remained marginal in modern India's military culture. Hence, in the Indian armed forces, the military officers look down upon covert operations. Even now, officers of the intelligence branch have very limited career opportunities vis-à-vis the other services. Bringing back the principles of *kutayuddha* is all the more important now, says Bakshi, because the Euro-centric distinction between war and peace is fast vanishing in the modern world. Bakshi is influenced by Kautilya and Sukra, who deny a clear-cut separation between high-intensity inter-state conventional battles and internal rebellions characterized by low-intensity warfare that are sponsored by foreign states. Further, from *Mahabharata* onwards, psychological warfare, which is a component of *kutayuddha*, reduces casualties on the side employing this form of warfare. Bakshi writes that India's military establishment must prepare for waging this sort of warfare against the enemy in the near future.[112]

Unconventional military strategy too is shaped both consciously and unconsciously by Hindu strategic thought. From the 1990s, Kashmir has witnessed considerable insurgency activity directed against the Indian state. Pakistan supports the insurgents financially and morally. Besides sending in its army, India's strategy is to encourage *bheda* (internal strife) among the militants, hoping that in the long run it will tire out the insurgents and bring them to the negotiating table.[113] Here we are back to Kautilya's policy of divide and rule vis-à-vis the internal enemies of the regime.

The Bharatiya Janata Party (BJP) is the most important political organization in present-day India as regards the policy of mixing Hinduism with modern statecraft. The BJP's policy is to create a Hindu India. Instead of a romantic and metaphysical interpretation of Hinduism, the BJP theoreticians promote a hard-line, realist interpretation of the Hindu texts. Rather than considering Hinduism as a peace-loving, pacifist culture, the BJP believes that Hinduism advocates domination of the non-Hindus (the others) in order to create a strong, aggressive state. In 1991, by gaining over 120 seats, the BJP emerged as the largest opposition party in the Indian parliament.[114] The BJP supports the pursuit of an aggressive foreign policy backed by strong military power, and it always promotes a policy of increasing military expenditure. It is to be noted that Sukra supported expenditure of 50 per cent of state revenue on defence. The BJP has always advocated a "blue water" navy, but India's economy cannot sustain such an ambitious programme.[115]

The Indian state is wary about the deployment of the American Fifth Fleet in the Persian Gulf region and further eastward. The Indian Navy also plans to utilize a sea denial strategy against the possible deployment of any extra-regional navy in the Indian Ocean.[116] Since the 1980s, the strategic administrators of India have viewed the United States as posing the principal long-term threat. In symmetrical war, the Indian armed forces would have no chance against the technologically advanced US armed forces. US planners believe that, taking their cue from the *Arthasastra*, the Indian armed forces would resort to asymmetric warfare in order to counter US military superiority. In 1988, the Office of the US Secretary of Defense concluded that India would seek to deny the US Navy total control over the Indian Ocean by using asymmetric techniques of warfare derived from the tradition of *kutayuddha*.[117]

To an extent, Hinduism structures the army–state relationship in India. In 1964, the American strategic analyst Stephen P. Cohen wrote an article in which he analysed civil–military relations in India through the prisms of the caste structure and the Brahmin–Kshatriya equation.[118] Cohen noted that the all-pervasive religiosity of ancient Hindu society limited the temporal power of the king (a representative of the Kshatriya class). In accordance with the Hindu division of labour, the Kshatriyas remained the group in charge of the military. Throughout history, the priestly class (the Brahmins) had defined the political objectives of the military.[119] The king (read the Kshatriyas) would conduct his own *dharma* (read policy) by waging righteous warfare as defined by the Brahmins.[120] In contrast, the Caliph was both the spiritual and temporal leader of the Muslims. Owing to the lack of a clear division between civil and military power, the Islamic states of the modern era continue to experience repeated military coups. Kautilyan philosophy also seems to be shaping civil–military relations in modern India. To prevent military coups, Kautilya opposes the appointment of a single *senapati* (general) over the armed forces.[121] This trend still continues and prevents the appointment of a Chief of Defence Staff in India. The Indian political establishment believes that a single unified armed forces commander might overturn the democratic framework by staging a military coup. In tune with Kautilya's policy of *bheda*, Indian politicians encourage civil servants to balance the uniformed men, and also encourage the Indian Air Force and the Indian Navy against the Indian Army. It is to be noted that both the Air Force and the Navy are suspicious that a Chief of Defence Staff might always be appointed from the Army, which dominates the other two services by virtue of its size and its budget.[122]

Hinduism and the nuclear issue

After conducting five underground nuclear tests on 11 and 13 May 1998, the Indian government, led by the BJP, officially declared itself a nuclear power.[123] In fact, the BJP and its antecedent, the Bharatiya Jan Sangh, had long been hawkish in terms of national security. In the 1980s, the BJP had promoted the idea of a "Hindu bomb" against Pakistan's "Islamic bomb".[124] Kanti Bajpai recently asserted that the BJP continues to be influenced by the ideas of M. S. Golwalker, a Hindu political theorist who at one time headed the nationalist Rashtriya Swayamsevak Sangh (National Volunteers' Organization). Golwalker's view of international relations is an extreme Hobbesian–Darwinian one. Golwalker is an arch-realist (and one could add that, in this sense, he is similar to Kautilya). In his writings, Golwalker claims that alliance with a superior power would result in enslavement (a similar message to that portrayed in the *Panchatantra*). China and Pakistan are the two enemies of India. Of them Pakistan, being Muslim, is more dangerous, because Muslims always strike first. In order to contain China, India needs to conscript all able-bodied males. India's security can be achieved only by the total destruction of Pakistan. And this will require, continues Golwalker, a total war on the part of India.[125] Interestingly, in 1999, Pakistan refused India's call to accept a "No First Strike" policy regarding the use of nuclear weapons. Furthermore, Pakistan's nuclear doctrine advocates the launching of pre-emptive strikes; this in turn has resulted in India developing a second-strike capability.

Hindu thought continues to shape India's nuclear policy. Swarna Rajagopalan claims that the *Mahabharata* focuses on the twin principles of good governance and collective cooperation with other powers to ensure security.[126] In other words, according to this interpretation, India should pursue nuclear disarmament. However, an alternative reading of ancient Hindu literature is put forward by the realist strategists of India. Raja Mohan asserts that India's strategic leaders are rediscovering *realpolitik* in place of *moralpolitik* from the *Mahabharata*, the *Arthasastra* and the *Panchatantra*, because all these texts appreciate the importance of power politics.[127]

To legitimize their aggressive stance, the nuclear strategists of India trying to construct a realist nuclear doctrine interpret ancient Hindu literature in a different manner from that of M. K. Gandhi. In 2002, Bharat Karnad wrote that pacifism and non-violence are not intrinsic to Hindu culture.[128] For him, Hindu religion is ultra-realist. The Hindu texts, claims Karnad, conceptualize a policy intolerant of any opposition. The texts preach that, if necessary, the goal of the state must be reached by fair means or foul, without any reference to morality. Whereas Jawaharlal Nehru's *moralpolitik* (the use of morality to gain space for political manoeuvring in the international arena) was influenced by the Gandhian ideal of non-violence, in Vedic literature one finds the existence of Hindu *machtpolitik*. Karnad's interpretation is that the basic message of the

Vedas is not the inculcation of passivity in external affairs but the advocation of adventure, daring, flamboyance and vigour and the uninhibited use of force to overcome any resistance, in order to achieve national greatness. The Vedic literature represents a "will to power" that is lacking among the power elite of modern-day India. The anti-nuclear lobby in India, led by Praful Bidwai and Achin Vanaik, claims that the message of Mahatma Gandhi demands that India renounce nuclear weapons and sign the Comprehensive Nuclear-Test-Ban Treaty (CTBT). Bidwai and Vanaik quote Gandhi to legitimize their stance, and also support the signing of the CTBT to avert the economic sanctions imposed on India by the G8 nations, under the leadership of the United States, in the aftermath of the Pokhran II Test. Karnad, in contrast, supports the ambitious plan of the hard-liners of New Delhi – to possess a robust arsenal of 400 intercontinental ballistic missiles equipped with megaton thermonuclear warheads in the near future. These weapons should be targeted against enemy cities because, after all, even the *Manusmriti* says, writes Karnad, that the enemy civilian population must be terrorized in order to hasten the surrender of the enemy state. These weapons should be used as the final alternative, because the *Mahabharata* says that *brahmastra* (ultimate weapons or weapons of mass destruction) are reserved as weapons of last resort.[129]

Karnad accepts the *Arthasastra*'s basic message that, in this world, power alone matters. Following Kautilya, Karnad interprets inter-state relationships and the amount of power wielded by a state within the theory of concentric circles. He says that a state's power can be interpreted on the basis of a series of concentric circles. The inner circle comprises the military power of the polity. Beyond it is the second circle, which represents the economic power of the state. Beyond that, the third circle represents the political power of the polity. And, finally, the outermost circle, the fourth circle, reflects the civilizational reach (i.e. the cultural power) of the state. These circles overlap with the equivalent concentric circles of neighbouring and distant states. Karnad asserts that, in the circle of states, India has to depend on brute force for its survival. In the immediate context, the threat is from China; in the long term, the United States might also present a threat. China is trying to surround India by supporting client states such as Pakistan and Myanmar. Following *mandala* policies, India should also surround China by following a friendly policy towards Vietnam and Taiwan. The assumption behind such a policy is the Kautilyan dictum: "my enemy's enemy is my friend." It is to be noted that, in the 1980s, Indira Gandhi's government was considering the idea of a strategic alliance with Israel for a strike against Pakistan's nuclear installations.[130]

Conclusion

This chapter supports Hans Kung's assertion that even those religions that are non-monotheistic encourage organized violence.[131] It is wrong to argue that Hinduism is a pacifist religion. Rejection of warfare is a marginal and recent trend in Hinduism. Except for Gandhi, none of the Hindu theorists in history spoke about disbanding the army. The concept of *dharmayuddha* is a double-edged sword. On the one hand, it introduces humane principles that somewhat reduce the lethality of war and moderate the effect of warfare on the combatants in particular and on society in general. On the other hand, the very concept of *dharmayuddha* prevents technological development and tactical innovations. This proved to be a serious weakness for the Hindu regimes practising *dharmayuddha* during the early medieval era. The realist interpretation of statecraft and organized violence has remained at the margins of Hindu philosophy until recent times. As far as the notion of *dharmayuddha* is concerned, Hinduism is not unique; concepts of just war are also present in other religions.

In post-colonial India, ancient Hindu texts and not Hindu priests remain important for the power elites and for the process of strategy-making. Nationalist Hindu priests organized under the umbrella organization Vishwa Hindu Parishad (VHP, or World Hindu Council) aim to spread the Hindu religion and to bring Hindus who have accepted other religions such as Islam and Christianity back into the fold of Hinduism. Their proselytizing activities have resulted in riots between Hindu and Muslim communities. The BJP uses the VHP for garnering Hindu votes during elections but never allows this body any say in strategic decision-making. In other words, in present-day India, the Hindu priests remain *persona non grata* as far as the formulation of grand strategy is concerned.

The yogic tradition is largely individualistic; it involves sacrificing the self for a greater cause. The ascetic Aurobindo argued that individuals might sacrifice themselves for a greater "good cause". This functioned as a motivation for Hindu youth to launch terrorist attacks on the colonial regime. The members of the strategic elite of the post-colonial state are uncomfortable with this line of thought, especially when independent India faces several religious-based insurgencies such as that of the Khalistanis in Punjab supported by Sikhism and the Islamic militants in Kashmir. Rather, the strategic decision makers and the Indian intelligentsia are more comfortable with the state-centric ancient Hindu texts. While one group advocates a realist reading of the texts, the other urges a more moderate pacifist interpretation of the strategic ideas embedded in the Hindu texts. Even for the second group, Gandhi remains unimportant. To conclude, a rigorous analysis of Hindu religion and its influence on warfare is necessary because the perceptions of India's ruling elite continue to be shaped by traditional philosophies.

Acknowledgements

My thanks to Dr Suhrita Saha and Professor Greg Reichberg for their comments on an earlier version of this chapter. The usual disclaimers apply.

Glossary

ahimsa: The creed of non-violence. The opposite of *hingsa/himsa* (jealousy, violence).

akhara: Hindu gymnasium, which at times also functioned as a centre for the individual training of armed Hindu monks.

Arthasastras: Texts on law and the polity. In this genre, the most famous is the text composed by Kautilya/Chanakya.

chara: Secret service/espionage department, as well as spies.

danda: Literal meaning: staff or rod. It means the science of government, especially focusing on punishment.

dhamma/dharma: The concept includes both the concrete and the abstract. At the broader level, it refers to the cosmic order, i.e. public order (disorder is *adharma*). At the lower level, *dharma* is *swadharma*, i.e. individual *dharma*. It actually refers to a code of conduct, i.e. living in a righteous way. The rules of *swadharma* are laid down in detail in the *dharmasastras* (treatises on *dharma*) composed around the second century BCE. Upholding *swadharma* by the public is necessary for the maintenance of cosmic as well as public order. In a sense, it means that both the king and his subjects have to behave properly to prevent the breakdown of public order. The king has to follow *rajadharma*, which constitutes the principles of politics.

dhammavijaya/dharmavijaya: Righteous conquest, which requires only obeisance and tribute from the defeated rulers. This is the opposite of the concept of *asuravijaya*, which entails the complete destruction of the defeated monarch and annexation of his kingdom by the *vijigishu*. Emperor Asoka was influenced by Buddhism and introduced a new concept of *dharmavijaya*, which means the propagation of *dharma* (i.e. religion) without using any form of coercion or the army.

dharmayuddha: War conducted in accordance with the principles of *dharma*. The Indian notion of just war.

digvijaya: Literal meaning: conquest of the four corners of the earth. It refers to wars of conquest undertaken by the *vijigishu*.

karma: Karma means action. It actually refers to the action–consequence cycle. The *Upanishads* record the idea of *karma* in which human beings are reborn repeatedly into circumstances conditioned by their actions in previous lives. One can break this cycle either through prayers or by participating in a *dharmayuddha*.

krore: A traditional Hindu unit of measurement. One *krore* is equivalent to 10 million.

kshatra: Refers to strength and power. To some extent it refers to physical strength. The concept of *kshatra* in the *Vedas* means the dominion of a ruler. In Hindu literature, *kshatra* is the power that belongs to the Kshatriyas (the warrior class), which is always subordinated to *brahma* (not to be confused with the fire god Brahma), the power of the Brahmins (the priestly class).

kutayuddha: Unjust war involving deception, treachery, etc. In such conflict, everything is free and fair. Night attacks, ambushes, tactical retreat and then launching a sudden counterattack, misinforming and disinforming the enemy, poisoning the enemy's leadership, and harming the non-combatants of the enemy country are some of the techniques of *kutayuddha*.

mahant: Leader of the Hindu religious institution and at times also of an *akhara*.

mandala: Circle of states, i.e. the international order.

nitisastras: Text focusing on politics and administrative laws. The most famous is by Kamandaka.

rishi: Hindu sage who emphasizes the power of asceticism through various yogic practices.

Upanishads: These texts were composed between 800 and 500 BCE. These texts treat the Vedic rituals as subordinate and aim to understand in a philosophical manner the relationship between the self, i.e. *atman* (one's soul), and the *brahman*, i.e. the universe.

Vedas: Technical meaning: knowledge. The most famous *Vedas* are the *Rig Veda*, the *Sama Veda*, the *Yajur Veda* and the *Atharva Veda*. These *Vedas* were composed between 1200 and 500 BCE.

vijigishu: The ideal would-be conqueror whose aim is to become the *chakravartin* (hegemon) of the *mandala*.

yoga: A generic term referring to mental exercises for achieving internal harmony. The objective of doing such exercises is to merge or unite one's soul with god, i.e. to merge the *atman* (self) with the *brahman* (the universal essence). The *Upanishads* refer to yoga. Around the fourth century CE, Buddhism also absorbed yoga. The grammarian Patanjali probably composed the *Yogasutras* in the third century CE. The *Yogasutras* present a detailed methodology for gaining liberating insight.

Notes

1. Christopher Coker, *Waging War without Warriors? The Changing Culture of Military Conflict*. London: Lynne Rienner, 2002, pp. 6–7.
2. Geoffrey Parker (ed.), *The Cambridge Illustrated History of Warfare: The Triumph of the West*. Cambridge: Cambridge University Press, 1995.
3. John A. Lynn, *Battle: A History of Combat and Culture*. Oxford: Westview, 2003.
4. Mark Jurgensmeyer, *Religious Nationalism Confronts the Secular State*. Reprint, Delhi: Oxford University Press, [1993] 1996, p. 81.
5. Coker, *Waging War without Warriors?*, p. 141.
6. Torkel Brekke, "Editor's Preface", in Torkel Brekke (ed.) *The Ethics of War in Asian Civilizations: A Comparative Perspective*. New York: Routledge, 2006, p. xi.
7. D. Devahuti, *Harsha: A Political Study*. Oxford: Clarendon Press, 1970, p. 113.
8. M. A. Mehendale, *Reflections on the Mahabharata War*. Shimla: Indian Institute of Advanced Studies, 1995, p. 2.
9. V. R. Ramachandra Dikshitar, *War in Ancient India*. Reprint, Delhi: Motilal Banarasidas, [1944] 1987, p. 59; *The Bhagavad Gita*, translated from the Sanskrit and with an Introduction by Juan Mascaro. New Delhi: Penguin, 1962, pp. 3–5.
10. Coker, *Waging War without Warriors?*, p. 135; *The Bhagavad Gita*, pp. xxiv, 80, 83.
11. Francis X. Clooney, SJ, "Pain But Not Harm: Some Classical Resources toward a Hindu Just War Theory", in Paul Robinson (ed.) *Just War in Comparative Perspective*. Aldershot: Ashgate, 2003, pp. 109, 114.

12. Manoj Kumar Sinha, "Hinduism and International Humanitarian Law", *International Review of the Red Cross*, 87(858), 2005: 285–286.
13. Norman Solomon, "The Ethics of War in Judaism", in Torkel Brekke (ed.) *The Ethics of War in Asian Civilizations*. New York: Routledge, 2006, p. 40.
14. Mark E. Lewis, "The Just War in Early China", in Torkel Brekke (ed.) *The Ethics of War in Asian Civilizations*. New York: Routledge, 2006, p. 185.
15. Robin D. S. Yates, "Early China", in Kurt Raaflaub and Nathan Rosenstein (eds) *War and Society in the Ancient and Medieval Worlds: Asia, The Mediterranean, Europe, and Mesoamerica*. Washington, DC: Center for Hellenic Studies; distributed by Harvard University Press, Cambridge, MA, 1999, p. 20.
16. Lynn, *Battle*, pp. 3–5; G. Scott Davis, "Introduction: Comparative Ethics and the Crucible of War", in Torkel Brekke (ed.) *The Ethics of War in Asian Civilizations*. New York: Routledge, 2006, p. 3.
17. Sarva Daman Singh, *Ancient Indian Warfare*. Reprint, Delhi: Motilal Banarasidas, [1965] 1989, p. 155.
18. Davis, "Introduction", p. 3.
19. Singh, *Ancient Indian Warfare*, p. 153; Gurcharn Singh Sandhu, *A Military History of Ancient India*. New Delhi: Vision Books, 2000, p. 68.
20. Torkel Brekke, "Between Prudence and Heroism: Ethics of War in the Hindu Tradition", in Torkel Brekke (ed.) *The Ethics of War in Asian Civilizations*. New York: Routledge, 2006, p. 115.
21. *The Rig Veda: An Anthology, One Hundred and Eight Hymns*, selected, translated and annotated by Wendy Doniger O'Flaherty. Reprint, New Delhi: Penguin, [1981] 1994, p. 63.
22. Sandhu, *A Military History of Ancient India*, p. 154.
23. Amal Sarkar, *A Study on the Ramayanas*. Calcutta: Rddhi-India, 1987, p. 23.
24. Sandhu, *A Military History of Ancient India*, p. 95.
25. *The Laws of Manu*, with an introduction and notes, translated by Wendy Doniger with Brian K. Smith. New Delhi: Penguin, 1991, p. xxiv.
26. Sandhu, *A Military History of Ancient India*, p. 73.
27. P. C. Chakravarti, *The Art of War in Ancient India*. Delhi: Low Price Publications, [1941] 1989, p. iv.
28. *The Bhagavad Gita*, p. xxi.
29. *Srimad Valmiki Ramayana*, with Sanskrit text and English translation, Part I. Reprint, Gorakhpur: Gita Press, [1969] 2001, pp. 947–948.
30. Sarkar, *A Study on the Ramayanas*, p. 15.
31. Nick Allen, "Just War in Mahabharata", in Richard Sorabji and David Rodin (eds) *The Ethics of War: Shared Problems in Different Tradition*. Aldershot: Ashgate, 2006, p. 140.
32. G. D. Bakshi, *Mahabharata: A Military Analysis*. New Delhi: Lancer, 1990, p. 73.
33. B. P. Sinha, "Art of War in Ancient India: 600 BCE–300 CE", in Guy S. Metraux and Francois Crouzet (eds) *Studies in the Cultural History of India*. Agra: Shiva Lal Agarwal and Co., 1965, p. 146.
34. *The Nitisara by Kamandaki*, edited by Rajendra Lal Mitra, revised with English translation by Sisir Kumar Mitra. Calcutta: The Asiatic Society, [1861] 1982, Preface, p. i.
35. Stephen Peter Rosen, *Societies and Military Power: India and Its Armies*. New Delhi: Oxford University Press, 1996, p. 67.
36. Henrik Syse, "Afterword: Ethics across Borders", in Torkel Brekke (ed.) *The Ethics of War in Asian Civilizations*. New York: Routledge, 2006, p. 202.
37. Brekke, "Between Prudence and Heroism", p. 113.
38. R. P. Kangle, *The Kautilya Arthasastra: A Study*, Part III. Reprint, Delhi: Motilal

Banarasidas, [1965] 2000, p. 2; Kautilya, *The Arthashastra*, edited, rearranged, translated and introduced by L. N. Rangarajan. Reprint, New Delhi: Penguin, [1987] 1992, p. 559.

39. Rosen, *Societies and Military Power*, p. 68.
40. Torkel Brekke, "Wielding the Rod of Punishment – War and Violence in the Political Science of Kautilya", *Journal of Military Ethics*, 3(1), 2004: 46.
41. Kangle, *The Kautilya Arthasastra*, Part III, pp. 262–3.
42. Chakravarti, *The Art of War in Ancient India*, p. vii.
43. Gregory M. Reichberg, Henrik Syse and Endre Begby (eds), *The Ethics of War: Classic and Contemporary Readings*. Oxford: Blackwell, 2006, p. 45.
44. Kautilya, *The Arthashastra*, pp. 132, 157.
45. Andre Wink, "Sovereignty and Universal Dominion in South Asia", in Jos J. L. Gommans and Dirk H. A. Kolff (eds) *Warfare and Weaponry in South Asia: 1000–1800*. New Delhi: Oxford University Press, 2001, p. 104.
46. Kangle, *The Kautilya Arthasastra*, Part III, p. 20.
47. Kautilya, *The Arthashastra*, p. 562.
48. Kangle, *The Kautilya Arthasastra*, Part III, p. 23.
49. *The Seven Military Classics of Ancient China*, translation and commentary by Ralph D. Sawyer with Mei-Chun Sawyer. Boulder, CO: Westview Press, 1993, p. 493.
50. *Kautilya Arthasastra*, translated by R. Shamasastry. Mysore: Wesleyan Mission Press, 1929, p. 418.
51. Chakravarti, *The Art of War in Ancient India*, p. vii.
52. Clooney, "Pain but Not Harm", p. 116.
53. Kangle, *The Kautilya Arthasastra*, Part III, pp. 41–42.
54. Lynn, *Battle*, pp. 41–42.
55. *The Seven Military Classics of Ancient China*, pp. 377–378.
56. Lewis, "The Just War in Early China", p. 187.
57. Gerard Fussman, "Central and Provincial Administration in Ancient India: The Problem of the Mauryan Empire", *Indian Historical Review*, 14(1–2), 1987/88: 49–55.
58. S. K. Bhakari, *Indian Warfare: An Appraisal of Strategy and Tactics of War in Early Medieval Period*. New Delhi: Munshiram Manoharlal, 1981, pp. 7, 9.
59. Jagadish Narayan Sarkar, *The Art of War in Medieval India*. New Delhi: Munshiram Manoharlal, 1984, p. 6.
60. *The Laws of Manu*, pp. xvii, xxii, xxxv, 133.
61. *The Laws of Manu*, p. 128; Kangle, *The Kautilya Arthasastra*, Part III, p. 15.
62. Sarkar, *The Art of War in Medieval India*, p. 5; Kautilya, *The Arthashastra*, p. 119.
63. *The Laws of Manu*, pp. xvii, 128–129, 137–138.
64. Dikshitar, *War in Ancient India*, p. 43.
65. *The Laws of Manu*, p. 136.
66. Kangle, *The Kautilya Arthasastra*, Part III, pp. 7–8.
67. Solomon, "The Ethics of War in Judaism", p. 41.
68. Devahuti, *Harsha*, p. 11; Banabhatta, *The Harsacharita*, translated by E. P. Cowell and P. W. Thomas, edited by R. P. Shastri. Delhi: Global Vision, 2004, pp. v–vii.
69. *The Nitisara by Kamandaki*, pp. i–iii, 6–7, 10, 33, 43.
70. *The Panchatantra*, translated from the Sanskrit by Arthur W. Ryder. Mumbai: Jaico, [1949] 2003, pp. 4–5, 7–8.
71. Ibid., p. 66.
72. Ibid., p. 28.
73. Ibid., p. 36.
74. Gustav Oppert, *On the Weapons, Army Organization, and Political Maxims of the Ancient Hindus with Special Reference to Gunpowder and Firearms*. Ahmedabad: New Order Book Co., [1880] 1967, p. 32.

75. Narayana, *The Hitopadesa*, translated from the Sanskrit with an introduction by A. N. D. Haksar. New Delhi: Penguin, 1998, pp. x–xi, 137–138, 140, 143, 152.
76. Sinha, "Art of War in Ancient India", p. 290.
77. Oppert, *On the Weapons, Army Organization, and Political Maxims of the Ancient Hindus*, p. 40; Jagadish Narayan Sarkar, *Some Aspects of Military Thinking and Practice in Medieval India*. Calcutta: Ratna Prakashan, 1974. p. 33.
78. Oppert, *On the Weapons, Army Organization, and Political Maxims of the Ancient Hindus*, pp. 83–86; Kangle, *The Kautilya Arthasastra*, Part III, pp. 28–29.
79. Julian Reid, "Foucault on Clausewitz: Conceptualizing the Relationship between War and Power", *Alternatives*, 28(1), 2003: 10.
80. Jadunath Sarkar, *Military History of India*. New Delhi: Orient Longman, [1960] 1970, p. 25.
81. Sarkar, *The Art of War in Medieval India*, p. 27.
82. Sarkar, *Some Aspects of Military Thinking and Practice in Medieval India*, pp. 33–34.
83. Karl Friday, "Might Makes Right: Just War and Just Warfare in Early Medieval Japan", in Torkel Brekke (ed.) *The Ethics of War in Asian Civilizations*. New York: Routledge, 2006, p. 159.
84. B. N. S. Yadava, "Chivalry and Warfare", in Jos J. L. Gommans and Dirk H. A. Kolff (eds) *Warfare and Weaponry in South Asia: 1000–1800*. New Delhi: Oxford University Press, 2001, pp. 66–69; Norman P. Ziegler, "Evolution of the Rathor State of Marvar: Horses, Structural Change and Warfare", in Karine Schomer, Joan L. Erdman, Deryck O. Lodrick and Lloyd I. Rudolph (eds) *The Idea of Rajasthan, Explorations in Regional Identity. Vol. 2, Institutions*. New Delhi: Manohar, 1994, pp. 195–213; Paul Varley, "Warfare in Japan: 1467–1600", in Jeremy Black (ed.) *War in the Early Modern World*. London: Routledge, [1999] 2004, pp. 55, 58.
85. Friday, "Might Makes Right", p. 171.
86. Sarkar, *Military History of India*, pp. 34–35.
87. *The Panchatantra*, p. 17.
88. Yadava, "Chivalry and Warfare", p. 81.
89. K. S. Lal, "The Striking Power of the Army of the Sultanate", *Journal of Indian History*, 55(2), 1977: 94; Bimal Kanti Majumdar, *The Military System in Ancient India*. Calcutta: Firma K.L.M., 1960, p. 43.
90. John Kelsay, "Islamic Tradition and the Justice of War", in Torkel Brekke (ed.) *The Ethics of War in Asian Civilizations*. New York: Routledge, 2006, pp. 86–88.
91. Lal, "The Striking Power of the Army of the Sultanate", p. 102.
92. Wink, "Sovereignty and Universal Dominion in South Asia", pp. 120–122.
93. Jos Gommans, "Warhorse and Gunpowder in India c. 1000–1850", in Jeremy Black (ed.) *War in the Early Modern World*. London: Routledge, [1999] 2004, p. 109.
94. William R. Pinch, "Soldier Monks and Militant Sadhus", in David Ludden (ed.) *Making India Hindu: Religion, Community, and the Politics of Democracy in India*. New Delhi: Oxford University Press, 1996, pp. 140–141.
95. W. G. Orr, "Armed Religious Ascetics in Northern India", in Jos J. L. Gommans and Dirk H. A. Kolff (eds) *Warfare and Weaponry in South Asia: 1000–1800*. New Delhi: Oxford University Press, 2001, pp. 186–187.
96. Ibid., pp. 187–197; William R. Pinch, *Warrior Ascetics and Indian Empires*. Cambridge: Cambridge University Press, 2006, pp. 116, 211.
97. Kautilya, *The Arthashastra*, p. 154.
98. William R. Pinch, "Who Was Himmat Bahadur? Gosains, Rajputs and the British in Bundelkhand, ca. 1800", *Indian Economic and Social History Review*, 35(3), 1998: 305.
99. V. Narayana Rao, David Shulman and Sanjay Subrahmanyam, "The Art of War under the Nayakas", in Jos J. L. Gommans and Dirk H. A. Kolff (eds) *Warfare and*

Weaponry in South Asia: 1000–1800. New Delhi: Oxford University Press, 2001, pp. 146–147.

100. *The Writings of Gandhi*, a selection edited and with an Introduction by Ronald Duncan. Calcutta: Rupa, [1971] 1990, pp. 48–49.

101. Pinch, "Soldier Monks and Militant Sadhus", p. 141.

102. Jurgensmeyer, *Religious Nationalism Confronts the Secular State*, p. 83.

103. Pinch, *Warrior Ascetics and Indian Empires*, p. 211.

104. Carol Hills and Daniel C. Silverman, "Nationalism and Feminism in Late Colonial India: The Rani of Jhansi Regiment, 1943–45", *Modern Asian Studies*, 27(4), 1993: 741–760.

105. Sue Hamilton, *Indian Philosophy: A Very Short Introduction*. New Delhi: Oxford University Press, [2001] 2006, pp. 107–110.

106. George K. Tanham, "Indian Strategic Thought: An Interpretative Essay", in Kanti P. Bajpai and Amitabh Mattoo (eds) *Securing India: Strategic Thought and Practice, Essays by George K. Tanham with Commentaries*. New Delhi: Manohar, 1996, pp. 42, 47–49.

107. C. Raja Mohan, *Impossible Allies: Nuclear India, United States and the Global Order*. New Delhi: India Research Press, 2006, pp. 267–268, 273, 283.

108. Raju G. C. Thomas, "India's Nuclear and Missile Programs: Strategy, Intentions, Capabilities", in Raju G. C. Thomas and Amit Gupta (eds) *India's Nuclear Security*. New Delhi: Vistaar, 2000, p. 101.

109. Bakshi, *Mahabharata*, pp. 72–73.

110. Gommans, "Warhorse and Gunpowder in India", p. 107.

111. Waheguru Pal Singh Sidhu, "Of Oral Traditions and Ethnocentric Judgements", in Kanti P. Bajpai and Amitabh Mattoo (eds) *Securing India: Strategic Thought and Practice, Essays by George K. Tanham with Commentaries*. New Delhi: Manohar, 1996, p. 175.

112. Bakshi, *Mahabharata*, pp. 73–76.

113. Kanti P. Bajpai, "State, Society, Strategy", in Kanti P. Bajpai and Amitabh Mattoo (eds) *Securing India: Strategic Thought and Practice, Essays by George K. Tanham with Commentaries*. New Delhi: Manohar, 1996, pp. 151–152.

114. Jurgensmeyer, *Religious Nationalism Confronts the Secular State*, p. 81.

115. Sandy Gordon, "Indian Security Policy and the Rise of the Hindu Right", *South Asia*, 17(Special Issue), 1994: 191–211; Nand Kishore Acharya, *The Polity in Sukranitisara*. Bikaner: Vagdevi Prakashan, 1987, p. 161.

116. Rahul Roy-Chaudhury, "The Limits to Naval Expansion", in Kanti P. Bajpai and Amitabh Mattoo (eds) *Securing India: Strategic Thought and Practice, Essays by George K. Tanham with Commentaries*. New Delhi: Manohar, 1996, pp. 191–200.

117. Coker, *Waging War without Warriors?*, pp. 142–143.

118. Stephen P. Cohen, "Rulers and Priests: A Study in Cultural Control", *Comparative Studies in Society and History*, January 1964: 199–216.

119. Swarna Rajagopalan, "Security Ideas in the Valmiki Ramayana", in Swarna Rajagopalan (ed.) *Security and South Asia: Ideas, Institutions and Initiatives*. London/New York/New Delhi: Routledge, 2006, p. 28.

120. Devahuti, *Harsha*, p. 116.

121. Kautilya, *The Arthashastra*, p. 161.

122. Varun Sahni, "Just Another Big Country", in Kanti P. Bajpai and Amitabh Mattoo (eds) *Securing India: Strategic Thought and Practice, Essays by George K. Tanham with Commentaries*. New Delhi: Manohar, 1996, pp. 164–166.

123. P. R. Chari, Sonika Gupta and Arpit Rajan (eds), *Nuclear Stability in Southern Asia*. New Delhi: Manohar, 2003, Appendix 1, p. 167.

124. Katherine K. Young, "Hinduism and the Ethics of Weapons of Mass Destruction", in Sohail H. Hashmi and Steven P. Lee (eds) *Ethics and Weapons of Mass Destruction: Religious and Secular Perspectives*. Cambridge: Cambridge University Press, 2004, p. 279.

125. Kanti Bajpai, "Hinduism and Weapons of Mass Destruction: Pacifist, Prudential, and Political", in Sohail H. Hashmi and Steven P. Lee (eds) *Ethics and Weapons of Mass Destruction: Religious and Secular Perspectives*. Cambridge: Cambridge University Press, 2004, pp. 313–317.

126. Rajagopalan, "Security Ideas in the Valmiki Ramayana", pp. 31–51.

127. Mohan, *Impossible Allies*, pp. 282–283.

128. Bharat Karnad, *Nuclear Weapons & Indian Security: The Realist Foundations of Strategy*. New Delhi: Macmillan, 2002.

129. Ibid., pp. xxi, xxii, xxvi, xxx, 17, 19.

130. Ibid., pp. xvii–xviii, xx, xxxi–xxxii.

131. Hans Kung, "Religion, Violence and 'Holy Wars'", *International Review of the Red Cross*, 87(858), 2005: 255.

3

Norms of war in Theravada Buddhism

Mahinda Deegalle

The use of force has become an important political and international issue among modern states. Recent events in Afghanistan and Iraq demonstrate that the use of force can trigger violent new wars. Over the centuries, wars fought nationally and internationally have caused immense destruction of property and loss of human life in all parts of the world. In the twenty-first century, the most pressing challenge for states is how to protect their citizens by countering the destruction inflicted by well-trained and highly coordinated terrorists who resort to violent means without any fear for their own lives. This is not only a serious security problem for the developed nations such as the United States and the European states but also an equally important concern for developing countries such as Sri Lanka,[1] where the majority of the population claim to be Buddhists. Reflection on the use of force from a Buddhist perspective will thus be immensely valuable for a comparative understanding of the issue at hand. Some questions for reflection are: Can Buddhists join an army? When one is a soldier what happens to one's Buddhist identity? Can a state that has a majority Buddhist population use force to manage a war situation? What is the role of Buddhism in a war-torn country? Can Buddhism justify a defensive war? Within the teachings of the Buddha, is there any consideration of the use of force? This chapter aims to answer some of these questions. Though the resources in other Buddhist traditions will be taken into account, the primary focus in this chapter will be identifying the conceptualization of war and the use of force as theorized in the Theravada Buddhist tradition of Sri Lanka.

World religions and norms of war, Popovski, Reichberg and Turner (eds),
United Nations University Press, 2009, ISBN 978-92-808-1163-6

War and peace: Buddhist approaches in dealing with violence

Peace is central to Buddhism, but war is not. Buddhism is praised by both insiders and outsiders for its doctrines of love and compassion. Some express the view that they have high expectations of Buddhism when it comes to issues of peace and violence in comparison with other world religions.[2] In the early Buddhist tradition, the concept of peace was expressed with the word "*santi*" (tranquillity, peace). It would be worthwhile to reflect here upon the example and words of the Buddha in order to understand the Buddhist approach to peace and war. One of the early Pali canonical texts, the *Dhammapada* (a representative text of the Theravada tradition), states: "There is no bliss higher than peace" [*natthi santiparam sukham*].[3] Highlighting the notion of peace, the Buddha is often identified with the epithet *santiraja* (king of peace).[4] The ultimate goal of the committed Buddhist practitioner is the attainment of perfect inner peace through leading a good life in this world. In their long history, Buddhists and Buddhist institutions attempted to follow the path of the Buddha aimed at achieving inner peace as well as peace in the social and cultural contexts in which they chose to live. The practice of a good life involved harmonious living with one's fellow beings. Texts denoted this aspect of life by using the Pali term "*sama-cariya*". Harmonious living, in turn, generated "inner peace" within the individual, which was identified as "*ajjhatta-santi*" (*Suttanipata*, verse 837).[5] In the Buddhist tradition, harmonious living (*sama-cariya*) has been identified very closely with the notion of righteous living (*dhamma-cariya*).[6] Righteousness and harmony must go hand in hand to achieve genuine peace within the individual and in the community at social levels.

In general, one can undoubtedly say that national and international peace are important concerns for Buddhists across the world. Like others, Buddhists witness the peaceful lives of ordinary people being destroyed by war and conflicts.

In many ways, Buddhism is realistic in its outlook, recognizing the existence of negative phenomena such as war. War was not an uncommon occurrence even in the Buddha's day in the sixth century BCE. Indian rulers who were around him, some of whom occasionally sought the Buddha's advice on governance and spirituality, nevertheless waged war against each other when such conditions suited them for achieving their political and selfish objectives. Throughout the history of Buddhism in Asia, in countries such as Sri Lanka, Japan, Korea, Thailand, Burma, China and Tibet, one can find plenty of examples of war situations. In relation to the use of force, however, an important question is to what extent Buddhism was an agent contributing to those wars.

In the context of military conquests by Japan and China, the peaceful history of Buddhism in Korea seems to have changed drastically during the Choson dynasty (1392–1910). In 1592 a Japanese army under General Toyotomi Hideyoshi (1537–1598) invaded Korea. Responding to that military conquest, Buddhist master Kihodang Yong-gyu, a disciple of Sosan Hyujong (1520–1604), gathered 600 monk soldiers and fought against the Japanese.[7] In 1636, when the army of Ch'ing invaded Choson, the monks Pyogam Kaksong (1575–1660) and Hobaek Myongjo were the leaders of the monks' army.[8] From a strictly doctrinal point of view, although the monks' active military engagement on the battlefield is a serious moral problem, the military success of the monks' army in Korea is viewed favourably today since their involvement safeguarded the integrity of the Korean nation in the face of foreign invasions:

> When the nation was in danger because of wars or invasions like the Hideyoshi and Ch'ing, Korean monks did not hesitate to sacrifice themselves to protect the nation and the people ... It was the monk-soldiers who rose up against the invaders all over the nation and, dealing fatal blows, played a major role in saving the nation. As a result of the active and independent participation of monks in both wars, the Buddhist community changed both its internal image and its public image. When the wars were over, the government did not disband the monks' army but had them join as members of the Choson army. The government also praised and rewarded the monks who had rendered distinguished service to the country during the wars.[9]

In medieval Japan, some powerful monasteries in the capital city, Kyoto, had their own armies to protect their own vested material and political interests. The Japanese word *sohei* refers to a monk-army or "warrior monks". Some of the major monasteries that had monk-armies were Enryakuji (the Tendai Buddhist headquarters on Mt Hiei), Onjoji (the Tendai-jimon headquarters in Shiga Prefecture) and Kofukuji (the Hosso headquarters in Nara). By the eleventh century, some of those armies began to attack rival monasteries. The monastic militias were eliminated from Japan by the warlords Oda Nobunaga (1534–1582) and Toyotomi Hideyoshi (1537–1598).[10]

In such war situations, the extent to which Buddhist teachings or Buddhist leadership contributed to war is an interesting and ethically worrying question. There have been varying degrees of involvement in war by some of those claiming to be Buddhists and those vowing to defend Buddhist interests or the national interests of countries that they aimed at protecting.

Both Buddhist traditions of South Asia and East Asia contain many classical teachings on war and violence. In analysing conflict situations, early Buddhism maintains that conflicts, intolerance and disharmony arise when human desire, hatred and ignorance are unlimited. According to the "Ratthapala Sutta" of the *Majjhima Nikaya*,[11] people seek riches and kings want to expand their territories: "A king, having forcibly conquered the earth, inhabiting a land with the ocean its confines, not satisfied with this side of the sea, hankers after the sea's further side too."[12] This is one of the classical explanations of the outbreak of war from a pragmatic religious point of view. Texts maintain that kings begin wars for such pragmatic purposes; unfortunately this has the inevitable result of hugely disrupting the daily lives of the common people, who are forced to live in disastrous and unhealthy situations. Their religious life or spirituality does not help them adequately to overcome the power of spreading violence when mighty states are determined to wage war against each other.

The historical Buddha Siddhartha Gautama (566–486 BCE) preached against war. But even the Gautama Buddha himself could not avoid the threat of war. Unfortunately, on two occasions the Buddha was forced to become directly involved in conflict resolution situations. The first was a dispute between his own relatives, the Sakyans and the Koliyans.[13] It was an argument over sharing the rights to the water of the Rohini River, which divided their two territories.[14] A dam was constructed across the Rohini River and the Sakyans and Koliyans used its water for agriculture. In a period of drought, a violent dispute arose between the Buddha's relatives over the use of the river water. This was a case of aggressive and competitive behaviour by two groups attempting to use force in order to gain possession of limited resources. They were ready to wage war against each other and to be annihilated in the war. At this point, the Buddha decided to intervene to bring harmony to the opposing relatives. After meeting the two sides, he asked them what was more precious for them: river water or their blood. By questioning their intention to wage war with each other, he demonstrated the futility of waging war for the sake of the River Rohini's water. Through his intervention, the Buddha was able to avert the imminent war. His intervention in the dispute was the compassionate action of a religious leader who cared about the lives of the innocent.

Even the historical Buddha failed to prevent war, as illustrated by the following narrative. While on a visit to his relatives in Kapilavatthu, at the age of 16, Prince Vidudabha, the son of King Pasenadi and Vasabhakhattiya, who later became the ruler of the Kosala and the Sakya, learnt from a contemptuous remark made by a slave woman in the Sakyan kingdom that his mother, who was given in marriage to his father King Pasenadi by the Sakyans, came from a low caste. The Sakyans were too proud to intermarry with King Pasenadi, and instead gave the slave woman to the king. Prince Vidudabha was furious with the Sakyans because of their deceit in cheating his father and the insult made to him by a slave woman on his first visit to see his mother's relatives. After King Pasenadi's death, King Vidudabha wanted take revenge on the Sakyans for the insult. The Buddha, knowing the danger to his relatives, stood three times on King Vidudabha's route to Kapilavatthu in order to prevent him from waging war against the Sakyans. Seeing the Buddha sitting under a tree with little shade on the boundaries of the Sakyan kingdom, after a brief conversation, King Vidudabha knew the Buddha's intention to protect his relatives from war and returned without waging war.[15] On the fourth occasion, the Buddha did not interfere with King Vidudabha's war effort since he saw that the *kamma* (negative previous action) of the Sakyans was severe. According to the narrative, their negative *karma* (deed) was that in a previous life the Sakyans had conspired to poison a river. In the absence of the Buddha to defend his relatives, King Vidudabha finally destroyed the Sakyans in the war. This karmic explanation and the Buddha's triple intervention demonstrate that even the Buddha had limitations in preventing a war that he witnessed in his lifetime.

Although the historical evidence shows that the Buddha did not encourage kings to go to war, there are also indications that the Buddha was not always especially proactive in taking steps to prevent wars taking place. This is illustrated by the story of Ajatasattu, the king of Magadha and son of Bimbisara, who was a casual visitor to the Buddha. The king wished to defeat the neighbouring Vajjians. Before going to war, Ajatasattu sent his chief minister Vassakara to ask the Buddha's advice about whether the Vajjians were likely to be defeated. In that conversation, the Buddha seems to have refrained from urging the king not to initiate war; instead the Buddha explained that it would be impossible for the king to defeat the Vajjians because they were strict practitioners of the *dhamma* (Sanskrit: *dharma*, righteous law), the seven conditions of welfare (*satta aparihaniya dhamma*), which they had learnt from the Buddha:

> So long ... as the Vajjians (i) foregather thus often, and frequent the public meetings of their clan ... (ii) meet together in concord and rise in concord, and carry out their undertakings in concord ... (iii) enact nothing not already established, abrogate nothing that has been already enacted, and act in accordance with the institutions of the Vajjians, as established in former days ... (iv) honour and esteem and revere and support the Vajjian elders, and hold it a point of duty to hearken to their words ... (v) no woman or girls belonging to their clans are detained among them by force or abduction ... (vi) honour and esteem and revere and support the Vajjian shrines in town or country, and allow not the proper offerings and rites, as formerly given and performed, to fall into desuetude (vii) so long as the rightful protection, defence, and support

shall be fully provided for the Arahants [religious persons] among them, so that the Arahants from a distance may enter the realm, and the Arahants therein may live at ease – so long may the Vajjians be expected not to decline, but to prosper.[16]

From this conversation on the statecraft of the Vajjians, we learn that righteous rule became the secret of the ruler's power. Another account suggests that, if the Vajjians became lax in their conduct of business, Ajatasattu would have a chance of defeating them.[17] Subsequently, Vassakara was successful in creating disunity among the Vajjians, which resulted in their defeat in war.

In the contemporary Buddhist world in South and Southeast Asia, one can find prescriptions for rulers and states as well as expectations of rulers derived from Buddhist teachings and classical practices. According to Buddhist conceptions of the ruler as found in the Pali canon of the Theravada tradition, the ideal ruler must govern the country with a modern policy and a just order, and maintain peace without invading neighbouring lands.

Buddhists have conceptualized a universal monarch (Pali *cakkavatti*; Sanskrit *cakravartin*) who rules the land with righteousness. Governance with non-violence is the universal monarch's trademark. One important scripture in the Pali canon, the *Cakkavattisihanada Sutta*, outlines the notion of an ideal king who rules the country on the basis of *dharma*.[18] It must be noted here, however, that even this universal monarch still has a fourfold army (*caturangabalakaya* – the elephant corps, the cavalry, the chariot corps and infantry), and wherever he travels in the country the fourfold army accompanies him. If the king is righteous and does not resort to violence, why does he have a fourfold army accompanying him? Does this suggest that the use of force is an inevitable feature of state power? Can a state run its own business without resorting to punishment and the use of force? By extension, the case of the universal monarch raises the question of whether Buddhist countries are still allowed to maintain armed forces, and whether such forces are merely for defensive purposes.

The concept of a universal monarch might to some extent undermine the necessity of the use of force. As portrayed in Buddhist texts, the universal monarch does not threaten people with force; instead, he forgoes the use of weapons and uses righteousness as the guiding principle. This rejection of weapons seems to empower him. People and local rulers under his power submit to him because of his righteous rule and in the belief that he will not resort to force. As a result of his righteous governance, other countries surrender to him and acknowledge his power without being forced to do so by means of weapons. Texts maintain that a pious and wise king should conquer the four quarters with virtues and fulfil his duties efficiently. Here emerges a notion of an ideal king who rules his territory without resorting to the use of force and weapons but who rules with the power of righteousness endowed in himself and in his statecraft.

The third ruler of the Mauryan dynasty in India, Emperor Asoka (268–232 BCE), who was probably a Buddhist, is often cited in the Buddhist literature as a model king. Asoka's inscriptions provide the first external evidence for the existence of Buddhist scriptures[19] and, in the tradition of Theravada Buddhism, Emperor Asoka is credited with sending Buddhist missions to countries such as Sri Lanka; he thereby did much to turn Buddhism into a civilizational religion.[20]

In popular Buddhist imagination, Asoka is an ideal king who demonstrated by example the attitudes that a ruler must cultivate towards one's subjects. His inscriptions demonstrate that he conceived his subjects as his own children: "All men [and women] are my children and as I desire for my children that they obtain every kind of welfare and happiness both in this world and the next world, so do I desire for all men [and women]."[21]

The Brahmanical term for the state's use of legitimate force is *danda* (stick). This can be rendered as the use of legitimate forms of violence for effective governance. The Buddhist tradition has not ignored various forms of violence practised in the Indian social milieu. Buddhist scriptures quite often mention punishments used by rulers at the time. What is striking is that, after Asoka's conquest, the tradition maintains that Emperor Asoka renounced the use of military force. At least, he had minimized the use of *danda* as a legitimate measure of governance. It is conceivable that this personal transformation within Asoka's life, which was translated into his public policy, may have occurred after conversion to Buddhism or encountering Buddhist teachings. Asoka's edict addressed to the Buddhist monastic community at Bairat gives the strongest indication of his connection to Buddhism. Asoka commends the Buddha's teachings as the *saddhamma* (good teaching) and mentions seven texts by name.[22]

After his victory in battle in Kalinga (present-day Orissa), a clear transformation is visible both in his change of heart and in the public policies that he adopted for his kingdom. In the battle, although he had enlarged his empire, he seems to have deliberately limited his military pursuit of conquest. Emperor Asoka publicly expressed his moral remorse in relation to the war in Kalinga. The Rock Edict XIII reveals his confession; it is an account of his remorse over the suffering and deaths which occurred in the battle. He dedicated himself to the propagation of *dharma*, and Buddhists believe that Emperor Asoka replaced the military drum with the drum of *dharma*. In the fourth Rock Edict of Kalsi, Asoka stated, "no more shall the drums of war (*bherighosa*) be heard in my territories, but the drums of *dhamma* (*dhammaghosa*) shall reverberate throughout the empire". Nowadays many believe that Emperor Asoka attempted to emulate the ideal of the universal monarch who rules the country righteously. By abandoning the pursuit of war and through personal transformation and the adoption of state policies of social welfare, Emperor Asoka became both a righteous king and the universal monarch that the Buddhist traditions envisioned.

The Buddha believed that it was possible to rule a country by adhering to the *dharma*, and without resorting to "harsh punitive measures or engaging in military conquests".[23] This situation, however, depends on many other factors. Buddhists would maintain that, when humanity is morally, spiritually and intellectually developed, it is possible for a universal monarch (*cakkavatti*) to rule a country without the use of force. This position, however, relies heavily on the belief that the world goes in cycles of births and deaths rather than in a linear fashion. In the cyclical worldview, human beings operate in a dependent relationship and have the capacity to develop both spiritually and morally.

There are also texts in East Asian Buddhism that are useful in understanding the notion of good governance and the efficacy of the use of force in handling crises. One of the Mahayana Buddhist texts, the *Dharmasamuccaya Sutra*, for example, suggests a technique to prevent war: "even if an army of another country should invade and plunder, a king should know first whether the soldiers are brave or cowardly and then conclude peace by means of expediency."[24] When the Indian monk Gunavarman (367–431 CE) visited China in 424 CE,[25] the Chinese emperor questioned him: "When foreign armies are going to invade my country, what should I do? If we fight there must be many casualties. If we do not repulse them, my country will be imperilled. O' master, please tell me what to do?" The monk answered: "just entertain a compassionate mind, do not have hurtful mind." The king applied his advice, and when the banners were going to be hoisted and the drums beaten, the enemies retreated.[26] This passage suggests that one should not fight against enemies and that the use of force is not the answer. On the contrary, it advises the practice of benevolence. From the Buddhist point of view, the ideal of benevolence has its own power to protect the righteous and prevent imminent danger from conquering enemies. This narrative highlights the importance of cultivating positive values and ethical qualities, which will eventually build trust and confidence and achieve harmony and tolerance.

But in a situation in which enemies are invading a country, what should the state do? As the ruler, the king has a duty to protect the country. If the king does not take action, the enemies may take advantage of his peaceful attitude. Alternatively, the subjects may rebel against the ruler. The Chinese Buddhist text in the *Taisho* collection explains the necessary expediency on the part of the ruler in detail.[27] Since the king's duty is to protect the country, he has to be ready to repulse the invading enemies. However, the text advises the king not to go to war but to negotiate and reach agreement in order to bring peace to both parties. It offers the king three strategies to safeguard the people and the kingdom. First, if the enemy is as powerful as the king's own army, warfare could inflict great damage on both parties and neither would benefit from it; many would inevitably lose their lives. If the enemy is more powerful than the king's army, then it is likely that the enemy forces would destroy many lives. In that case, the king should make peaceful negotiations and avoid possible war and the death of innocent people. Secondly, the king should try to solve the conflict by showing generosity and giving anything the enemy requires so that violence is prevented. Thirdly, if the enemy seems to be more powerful, the king should try to surprise the enemy king by pretending his own army is a more powerful force. If these three strategies fail, then the king is allowed to take up arms, taking into consideration the following points: owing to the lack of mercy on the part of the enemy, we engage in war and are forced to kill living beings; however, we hope that we will kill as few as possible.

In the case of Sri Lanka, one can cite the story of King Sirisanghabodhi (r. 247–249 CE), who followed the ideal of *bodhisattva* (one who aspires to enlightenment). This is a popular narrative that highlights the importance of the virtuous character of the ruler. *The Mahavamsa* ("The Great Chronicle"), a Pali chronicle written in sixth century CE, describes him as "rich in compassion" (Ch. 36, verse 94)[28] and full of "kindness to the other", and that he willingly went into solitary exile in the forest "since he would not bring harm to others" (36: 92).[29] *The Dipavamsa* refers to him as a "virtuous prince",[30] and *The Mahavamsa* mentions that he "reigned two years in Anuradhapura" observing the Five Precepts (36: 73).[31] According to the Sri Lankan tradition as recorded in the Pali chronicles, he was willing to give his head to his aggressive brother, Gothabhaya, who dethroned him. The dethroned King Sirisanghabodhi addressed the beggar who fed him lunch: "I am the king Samghabodhi; take thou my head and show it to Gothabhaya, he will give thee much gold" (36: 95–96). This episode has become a popular theme in temple paintings in Sri Lanka. The story of Sirisanghabodhi is an extreme case of passive resistance. During his reign, he often used *satyakriya* (an act of truth) to resolve difficult problems. On one occasion when there was a drought, "his heart shaken with pity" (36: 75) and with compassion for his people (36: 79), King Sirisanghabodhi lay down on the ground of the

Ratnamali Thupa in Anuradhapura with firm resolve: "Unless I be raised up by the water that the god shall rain down I will nevermore rise up from hence, even though I die here" (36: 76). Instead of punishing criminals by using force, King Sirisanghabodhi took rebels into custody, but "released them again secretly". Yet to cause terror among the public and to remove their fear of rebels, he replaced them secretly with the "bodies of dead men", which were subsequently set aflame (36: 80–81). When a red-eyed demon Ratakkhi began to devour his people, King Sirisanghabodhi was in distress and began fasting while observing the eight *uposatha* vows;[32] he resolved that "[t]ill I have seen the yakkha I will not rise up" (36: 82–85). By the king's power, the demon came to him and, instead of giving the life of his citizens, the king was willing to give up his own life: "No other can I give up to thee; take thou me and devour me" (36: 88). Finally, the demon agreed to accept an offering from every village. The life of Sirisanghabodhi illustrates that the notion of *ahimsa* (non-violence) was valued and that some inspired rulers who attempted to follow the Buddhist principles went out of their way to practise them and sacrificed themselves for a good cause that they believed in.

One of the most eminent scholars and Sri Lankan statesmen of the day, D. B. Jayatilaka (1868–1944), attempted in 1939 to explain the significance of Sirisanghabodhi's narrative for modern statecraft by combining the examples of both Vessantara and Sirisanghabodhi:

> The Great One [Buddha in his last life as Vessantara Bodhisattva] renounced a kingdom and a throne, wife and child, and all world comforts, and wandered as a beggar to serve those that suffer ... This was the spirit that pervaded ancient Lanka, and it was this spirit that King Sri Sangabo, of ancient lore, gave his head and died himself to save the lives of his countrymen.[33]

Sri Lankan kings such as Sirisanghabodhi tried to apply Buddhist principles to statecraft and occasionally were defeated when the aggressor was ruthless. The imperative of self-defence was hardly raised as an issue since, for Sirisanghabodhi and others like him, being righteous and truthful took precedence over worldly concerns. The stories of King Vessantara (*Jataka*, No. 547)[34] and King Sirisanghabodhi both illustrate a willingness to forgo violent resistance in circumstances of adversity. One could argue that they exhibited a fatalism that should not be followed in modern statecraft, because it would result in submission to intruders and enemies. Because of the extreme pacifist dimensions of Sirisanghabodhi's narrative, some insiders have criticized it. A modern author who wrote to a weekly newspaper about the widespread suicides in Sri Lanka lamented the negative interpretation and the adoption of the Sirisanghabodhi narrative and argued that "Sangabo's actions regrettably have led some

Buddhists to believe that suicide is laudable, a problem in a country that has the highest suicide rate in the world".[35]

Key sources in understanding the use of force in Buddhism

The approach that Buddhism takes to the use of force is rather different from that of other world religions. Because of its focus on the individual human being, discussions about the legitimacy of force concentrate on the obligations of individuals. One can generalize the Buddhist perspective on this issue as follows. Buddhist life involves the use of force inwardly rather than externally. The Buddha often advises his practitioners to "restrain the five senses" (*indiriya samvara*) in order to progress in the path.[36] This instruction is particularly important because it is a case of using force for self-cultivation. In religious practice, one is expected to be firm with oneself in putting oneself on the right path and becoming free from persuasions and enticements. For self-development, firm individual resolutions are essential, yet this should be done without treating oneself violently.

An important question requiring examination is the extent to which the Buddha resorted to the use of force. Various narratives support the view that the Buddha sometimes employed mild force in dealing with his disciples. On one occasion (as recounted in the *Vinaya Pitaka*, a collection of Buddhist monastic rules), the Buddha withheld signalling the beginning of the bi-monthly confession ceremony of reciting the rules given in the *patimokkha* text (2.236–7). After a long period of waiting, the Venerable Moggallana, his chief disciple, asked him about the delay. In response, the Buddha said that one monk in the gathered assembly was not fit to participate in the ceremony (owing to his impurity) and hence should leave. Three times the Venerable Moggallana called upon that person to leave the assembly and, upon receiving no response, Moggallana forced him out of the room. Only then did the *uposatha-kamma* (the recitation of the *vinaya* rules) resume. This episode illustrates that some direct use of force was needed to proceed with the recitation, and that the Buddha approved of Moggallana's intervention as a proper course of action. It also demonstrates that, even in a religious community, when other means of persuasion fail, some minor use of force is essential.

Another narrative, the *Abhayarajakumara Sutta* of the *Majjhima Nikaya* (M.1.391f.), indicates how harsh words could be put to effective use by the Buddha.[37] Pointing at the infant son on Prince Abhaya's lap, the Buddha said: "What do you think Prince? If, while you or your nurse were not attending to him, this child were to put a stick or a pebble in his mouth, what would you do to him?" The prince responded by saying: "Venerable Sir, I would take it out. If I could not take it out at once, I would take his head in my left hand and crooking a finger of my right hand, I would take it out even if it meant drawing blood. Why is that? Because I have compassion for the child."[38] The fact that the Buddha did not object to this response shows that he might allow for some harsh action, if it served a good purpose.

A classical account of defensive war

Over the centuries, Sri Lankan historiography, frequently written in Pali, has constructed an image of a distinct Sinhala Buddhist ethnic identity. It also has assigned to the Sinhala communities the historical role of protecting the "message" (*sasana*) of the Buddha (a collective term used nowadays in the meaning of Buddhism in Sri Lanka). Over the 2,300-year history of Sri Lanka, one can find many references to various types of war: internal battles, external conquests, coups and liberation struggles.

The most troubling question in relation to Buddhism is whether war can ever be justified within its doctrinal setting. In this connection, the most controversial historical episode was a battle between King Dutthagamani (r. 161–137 BCE) and King Elara in Anuradhapura, Sri Lanka, which is recorded in *The Mahavamsa*.[39] The chronicle shows King Dutthagamani, a patriotic Sinhala prince from southern Sri Lanka, defeating King Elara, an elderly Tamil from South India who had ruled Sri Lanka for four decades. This narrative of their battle presents a powerful myth that has contributed to what Tessa J. Bartholomeusz has identified as the foundation of the "just war ideology" in modern Sri Lanka: "The war exploits of Dutugemunu suggest that by the time *The Mahavamsa* took shape, Buddhist thinking had developed criteria that served as a framework for debates about which wars are justified and which are not."[40] Since "[t]he past inhabits the present in a variety of ways – in practices, things, and memory"[41] – there is no doubt the battle narrative of *The Mahavamsa* has had a formative influence on the imaginations of many in contemporary Sri Lanka.

The way the chronicler presents the battle narrative demonstrates an attempt to identify King Dutthagamani closely with Buddhism and the national interests of the majority Sinhalese community of modern Sri Lanka. This identification is reinforced by departing from the previous practices of kings; the chronicler records that King Dutthagamani invited Buddhist monks (*bhikkus*) to accompany him onto the battlefield:

I will go on to the land on the further side of the river to bring glory to the doctrine. Give us, that we may treat them with honour, bhikkhus who shall go on with us, since the sight of bhikkhus is blessing and protection for us. As a penance, the brotherhood allowed him five hundred ascetics; taking this company of bhikkhus with him the king marched forth. (25: 3)[42]

For a modern reader, this passage suggests that the political authorities at that time were using religious symbols, institutions and persons to further their war efforts. It is thus not difficult to read this passage as indicating a Buddhist involvement in war. This view is further strengthened when the chronicler mentions that King Dutthagamani himself had "a relic put into his spear" when he marched onto the battlefield (25: 1).[43]

In the passage quoted above, the reference to "bring glory to the doctrine" can be taken to mean safeguarding and protecting the Buddhist teachings, practices and institutions in Sri Lanka. "Brotherhood" refers to the Buddhist monastic community collectively known as the *sangha*. Having a company of *bhikkhus* with him while marching to war is perceived as an act of securing protection for Dutthagamani himself at the time of war. However, the monks themselves perceive it "as a penance" (25: 4). Placing a relic in the spear is an apotropaic action intended to ward off evil forces in times of trouble, as believed in many pre-modern societies.

Nevertheless, the task at hand for Dutthagamani was a rather difficult one since the text represents Elara as a righteous king. In a duel, Dutthagamani killed Elara (25: 67–70). After Elara's death, Dutthagamani honoured him by cremating him, marking the place with a monument and instituting worship there.

The remorse that Dutthagamani felt after the battle was quite severe, and similar to that Emperor Asoka had experienced after his battle in Kalinga. As in the case of Emperor Asoka, a transformation occurs, though not so dramatic, in the life of Dutthagamani through the intervention of the Buddhist monastic community. In removing Dutthagamani's remorse, their intervention can be seen as a "rehabilitation strategy" for an evil king who had caused a lot of suffering in pursuing a battle. In this case, the rehabilitation strategy is used to direct the king to Buddhist works. Though the "rehabilitation" of the king is noble, the justifications that the monks provided in consoling the king are controversial and problematic. They have serious implications for the issue of whether there are justifications for violence within Theravada Buddhism.

Though King Dutthagamani won the battle, there were many deaths in the battle. He was very unhappy about this. *The Mahavamsa* states (25: 104) that the *arahant*s (religious people) in Piyangudipa, knowing of Dutthagamani's remorse, sent a group of eight *arahant*s to comfort the king.

To them, the king confessed: "How shall there be any comfort for me, O venerable sirs, since by me was caused the slaughter of a great host numbering millions?" The *arahants*' response to Dutthagamani's confession has become severely problematic from the point of view of Buddhist doctrines:

> From this deed arises no hindrance in thy way to heaven. Only one and a half human beings have been slain here by thee, O lord of men. The one had come unto the (three) refuges; the other had taken on himself the five precepts. Unbelievers and men of evil life were the rest, not more to be esteemed than beasts. But as for thee, thou wilt bring glory to the doctrine of the Buddha in manifold ways; therefore cast away care from thy heart, O ruler of men! Thus exhorted by them the great king took comfort. (25: 109–112)[44]

Dutthagamani's remorse is eliminated when he is told that killing "evil unbelievers" carries no more weight than killing animals. It is important to note that the killing not only of human beings but even of animals is not encouraged in Buddhism.[45] As practitioners of "loving kindness" (*metta*), Buddhists have an obligation to protect all forms of life. Thus, when contrasted with canonical doctrines and early Buddhist practices, the position adopted in this fifth-century chronicle is rather controversial. This passage seems to suggest that certain forms of violence, such as killing during battle, can be allowed in certain circumstances, for example threats to the survival of Buddhism in Sri Lanka during the time of Dutthagamani. It is hard to justify this position either through Buddhist practice or from a doctrinal standpoint, as found in the Pali canon of the Theravada Buddhists.

This unusual statement, however, can be interpreted differently as an instance of Buddhist "skill-in-means". In the long run, keeping the victorious king remorseful or in a depressed condition would not help the Buddhist monastic community. Rather than aggravating these conditions, as spiritual advisers the monastic community had to make every effort to console the king. Up to that moment, whatever wrongs the king had committed became his own *karma*. The monastic community as a group could not change his past *karma* but, as a community who believed in free will and individual effort, it was possible for them to direct and channel the king in a positive direction. The unforeseen consequence of that strategy was a "gross calculation" of the victims of war as "only one and a half human beings" and "unbelievers and men of evil life".

Making the justification that killing Tamils during war is not a *papa* (unmeritorious action) is a grave mistake, even if it was used in *The Mahavamsa* as a skill-in-means. Such violations of the tolerant sensibilities found within post-canonical Pali chronicles cannot be justified or harmonized, since Buddhist scriptures do not maintain that the severity of one's negative acts may vary depending on one's caste, race or ethnic group.

This battle episode still shapes the thinking of some monks and lay people of Sri Lanka. The complexity in the way in which this single, controversial myth is interpreted, perpetuated and received as both an inspiration and a justification is well illustrated by a comment made in Ananda Wickremeratne's *Buddhism and Ethnicity in Sri Lanka*. Wickremeratne interviewed a Buddhist monk about the importance of this episode. He explained it as a historical document of self-righteousness:

> [I]t was King Dutthagamani who best exemplified the idea of self-imposed limits in the exercise of violence. The king gathered his forces to wage war against an enemy who had invaded the land, and threatened the secular order of things on which the very existence of Buddhism depended ... "He prevails over the Tamil invaders and kills their leader, Elara, in single combat. He honours the fallen foe and immediately stops his campaign, as he had achieved its purpose, waging a purely defensive war. He does not cross over to India to chastise the Tamils and refrains from wreaking vengeance on Tamils who were living in Sri Lanka, side by side with Sinhalese as its inhabitants."[46]

The myth of Dutthagamani and Elara is reinterpreted not only by Sinhala communities in Sri Lanka but also by Tamil communities, with different emphases. Tamil communities seem to have appropriated this myth in their own way by highlighting the role of the Dravidian King Elara for their own nationalistic ends.

Defensive war and the *dharma yuddhaya* discourse in modern Sri Lanka

In the recent publication "A 'Righteous War' in Buddhism", the Sri Lankan Buddhist academic P. D. Premasiri has outlined how Buddhist teachings on the conduct of defensive war can take into account the legitimate and pragmatic concerns of the current war situation in Sri Lanka. He draws attention to the righteous party's ethical conduct in a defensive war:

> Where one of the parties engaged in war is considered as righteous and the other as unrighteous, the Buddhist canonical accounts highlight the ethical qualities of the righteous party by showing that although they are compelled by circumstances to engage in war for the purpose of self-defence, they do not resort to unnecessary acts of cruelty even towards the defeated. The righteous party in war avoids harm to the innocent and is ready to pardon even the de-

feated enemy. Skilful methods are adopted in order to cause the least harm. Texts such as the *Ummagga Jataka* (J.IV.329ff) illustrate cases where the enemy could be defeated without injury to and destruction of life.[47]

Apart from Premasiri's exposition on ethical conduct in a defensive war, there are few systematic treatments of just war theory in the South Asian Buddhist tradition. Unlike Christian church fathers such as St Augustine (354–430 CE), who explicitly discussed just war and the grounds for declaring a holy war, Buddhist thinkers in Asia have rarely engaged in such an analysis. Though there are occasional arguments about war and self-defence issues in the modern period, South Asian Buddhist traditions still lack a systematic, philosophical reflection on the nature of war and its justifications.

There are military metaphors in the texts of the South Asian Theravada tradition. In explaining the spiritual achievements of individual practitioners, texts occasionally use military metaphors. The purpose is to compare a true Buddhist practitioner to a conqueror in the battlefield in terms of conquering defilement. Defilements that pollute the mental condition are seen as enemies. One popular text, the *Dhammapada*, comments: "One may conquer in battle a thousand times a thousand men, yet he is the best of conquerors who conquers himself" (verse 128). This emphasis on the inner transformation of the individual that runs through the military metaphor is relevant in discussing Buddhist views on war and its justifications.

It is very clear that early Buddhism and its followers disliked war and violence. Buddhist monks were prohibited from watching military parades and soldiers were not allowed to be ordained as monks. The Pali canon of Theravada Buddhists completely lacks any textual resource that could be used as the basis for developing a just war theory.

As mentioned above, however, one can nevertheless detect the seeds of justification of war in the particular unstable political context in Sri Lanka, as can be found in the post-canonical sixth-century chronicle *The Mahavamsa*. Owing to the disruptive political unrest in modern Sri Lanka, some nationalist thinkers, both lay and monastic (such as Nalin De Silva and Athureliye Rathana), have sought to justify the existence of military forces in primarily Buddhist countries and in particular have supported the prosecution of a defensive war against the Liberation Tigers of Tamil Eelam (LTTE).[48]

On the contemporary Buddhist discourse concerning defensive war, Tessa J. Bartholomeusz writes:

> For the monk, it does not logically follow that the Buddhist teaching of non-violence must always – in every case – lead to a conclusion of pacifism; real life

does not allow for such as an interpretation. The monk thereby distinguished between the ideal situation of the text and the situation "on the ground". Moreover, for the monk the CSS [*Cakkavattisihanada Sutta*] provides the contemporary Sri Lankan government with the Buddhist justification it needs to proceed with the war against the LTTE.[49]

In recent years, the Sanskrit term *dharma yuddhaya* (righteous, or religious, war) has gained currency in academic writings in the West and in popular writings in the East. The term and its related derivations do not have much history within Sri Lankan writings. Its first appearance was during the period of British colonial rule in the late nineteenth century, when Sri Lankan Buddhists sought to defend Buddhist ideas, values and practices vis-à-vis the widespread Christian (mainly Protestant) missions and cultural intrusions. In Sinhala publications, the term had two significations, one spiritual and the other political.

The spiritual signification referred to the inner victory over defilements that the Buddha had achieved when he conquered the Mara (the personification of death). *Dharma yuddhaya* was thus used figuratively to designate the mental struggle over negative mental conditions such as greed and hatred, as conceptualized in Buddhist doctrinal terms. In this way, military metaphors may be found both in monks' sermons and in popular Buddhist publications. For example, on 28 October 1898, *Sarasavi Sandarasa*, a Sinhala newspaper launched by the Buddhist Theosophical Society, published the following letter received from a reader. In the letter, the term *dharma yuddhaya* was mentioned and the war was spoken of figuratively:

> We, too, have a war to fight; but we do not need weapons such as guns. Our war is a "*dharma yuddhaya*". It is an opportunity to fight the demon of *mityadrsti* (false belief). Although we have been fighting this war for a while, victory is not yet ours because our weapons are old. We should get new weapons.[50]

In this period of revival under British colonialism and the Protestant Christian hegemony, ideas emerged for the necessity of an army and the permissibility of war with real weapons.[51]

According to its political signification, *dharma yuddhaya* refers to the struggle that one faces in attempting to protect Buddhism in an incompatible political and religious environment. Even then, and until the mid-twentieth century, it referred to non-violent social struggle. This usage of the term may be found for instance in the writings of Venerable Baddegama Wimalawansa (1912–1992), who was principal of Sri Lanka Vidyalaya, a monastic school in Colombo. A member of the monastic fraternity of Ramannanikaya, he was a monk of both nationalist and leftist political leanings. In the early 1950s Wimalawansa published a series of pamphlets under the title *Dharma Yuddhaya* that exposed the anti-Buddhist and anti-Sinhala activities of the Sri Lankan government and the Christian missionaries.[52] The first pamphlet in the series focused on "The Future of the Buddhist Monk". It argued that Christian missionaries had undermined the social significance of the Buddhist monk in Sri Lankan society. The second pamphlet was on "The Government and the Power of the Missionaries". The third one focused on "Buddhism Today". The seventh of the *Dharma Yuddhaya* series was on "The Activities of the Christian Clergy", who had immense power and influence over education and health services.[53]

In a similar vein, writing to a Sinhala publication, *Bauddha Lokaya* (Buddhist World), in 1951, the Pali scholar G. P. Malalasekera (1899–1973) used military metaphors to encourage people to get involved in social welfare activities:

> We should gather the weapons of *maitri* [loving-kindness], *karuna* [compassion] and *santi* [peace] and prepare for a *dharma yuddhaya* [righteous war]. We have to prepare for a religious fight, a long fight. This is not a revolution but an attempt to protect our ancestral religion – Buddhism. Thus, this is a *dharma yuddhaya*. This is not a war fought with the aid of weapons. We are fighting for the truth and the *dharma*. We have to start with loving-kindness and compassion. We have to fight to the end.[54]

In this quotation, it is clear that the term *dharma yuddhaya* is used in the sense of spiritual renewal rather than a war against another group or religion. Significantly, in the *English–Sinhalese Dictionary* that Malalasekera compiled and published in 1948 – a dictionary widely used today by students of English in Sri Lanka – the English term "holy war" is translated specifically with the term *agama udesa karana yuddhaya*, a war fought for the defence of religion. *Dharma yuddhaya* is not used in this context.[55] It might be noted that the dictionary contains no entries for "just" or "righteous" (Sin. *dharmistha*) war.

However, in Bartholomeusz's discussion of just war ideology in Sri Lanka, she attempts to show that there was a drastic shift in meaning from one sense of *dharma yuddhaya* to another:

> Significantly, the Sinhala writer's 1898 spelling of "war", transliterated as *yudhaya* [without the initial "d"], contains a Sinhala letter that is not used in contemporary spellings of the Sinhala term. The shift in spelling coincides with a shift in its expression: prior to the 1980s, when the literary spelling was commonplace, *dharma yuddhaya* most frequently referred to figurative war. In

other words, the literary spelling betrays the abstract referents of war, its mental and social dimensions in the Buddhist context. The vernacular spelling, *yuddhaya*, on the other hand, reinforces the concrete realities of military conflict.[56]

A close examination of the dictionary shows that Bartholomeusz had misread the Sinhala characters, since Malalasekera had accurately spelled the term in question. Her argument of a shift in meaning on the basis of a missing letter – "d" – is quite weak and stands in need of further investigation.

For Malalasekera, in the Buddhist case, spiritual renewal through the development of sublime qualities was essential and crucial to raise the profile of the Buddhists at the time. He used militaristic metaphors for that purpose; for him, non-violent engagement with Buddhism was essential for the Buddhist renewal in a colonial context.

In the political writings of Buddhist monks produced after the independence of Sri Lanka in 1948, one can detect quite frequent use of the term *dharma yuddhaya* and one can attribute violent dimensions to its usage as opposed to the spiritual and moral meanings that it contained earlier. A 1978 publication attempts to define *dharma yuddhaya* by outlining its spiritual dimensions: "Any battle that protects the truth is *dharma yuddhaya*. Fighting for a fair and just society is *dharma yuddhaya*."[57] In the Buddha Jayanthi year in 1956, *Bauddha Peramuna* (Buddhist Front) published an article in Sinhala entitled "Dharma Yuddhaya". It used the term *dharma yuddhaya* quite frequently, as follows: "Since he [the prime minister] has not obeyed the monks' pleas [not to hold elections in the Buddha Jayanthi year], they [the monks] are launching a *dharma yuddhaya*"; "To save this *dharmistha* [righteous] land we have to launch a *dharma yuddhaya*. Its leaders are Buddhists monks." The fact that the notion of defensive war gradually emerged in their writings is demonstrated in the following statement by a Buddhist monk on 27 April 1957: "Buddhism has always been a tolerant religion ... Although tolerance is advocated, at this time of emergency when it is attacked in various ways, Buddhists cannot be tolerant; ... Buddhists have to fight to save their lives."[58]

Likewise, by 1961, the use of force in defence of *dharma* came to be justified. An article published in *Bauddha Peramuna* on 11 March 1961 claims that, "[a]ccording to Buddhist principles, believers should always practice *maitri* [loving-kindness]; however, in order to protect the religion we have to peacefully fight our enemies. When Buddhism is threatened, we cannot merely practice *maitri*."[59] Finally, towards the middle of the 1980s, the notion of justified war emerged in the context of terrorism and the protracted civil war in Sri Lanka. Writing on "Terrorism and War", a Sri Lankan layman named D. G. Kulatunga comments:

Buddhism and war are a contradiction in terms. Like oil and water they do not mix ... No Government, however *dharmistha* [righteous] it may be, can afford to remain static and insensitive to an uprising against the State and cease to use fire-arms in highly explosive situations threatening the security of a country. It is the bounden duty of the State to protect at any cost the life and property of its citizens.[60]

This is a justification of the state-led use of the armed forces to bring peace in a war context. It allows defensive war when the state acts in the interest of the well-being of the majority of its citizens.

Most recently, at a conference in 2002, Athureliye Rathana, now the parliamentary leader of Jathika Hela Urumaya,[61] the political party of Buddhist monks, pointed to the potential inefficacy of some Buddhist doctrines, such as loving-kindness, for resolving war and other contemporary political problems. In presenting his paper "A Buddhist Analysis of 'The Ethnic Conflict'", Rathana stated: "There are two central concepts of Buddhism: compassion and wisdom. If compassion was [sic] a necessary and sufficient condition, then the Buddha would not have elaborated on wisdom or *prajna*. Hitler could not have been overcome by maitriya [loving-kindness] alone."[62]

Examining the notion of just war proposed by monks such as Rathana and closely examining Sinhala publications of the twentieth century, Tessa J. Bartholemeuz conclusively remarks:

Sinhala Buddhism is ambivalent about war, depending on the context (and depending on the Buddhist), the Buddhist tradition of Sri Lanka condemns, with as much frequency as it justifies, war and its violent legacies in defense of the *dharma* or the island.[63]

The agonies of the Sri Lankan ethnic war

There are two major parties to the current conflict in Sri Lanka: the LTTE militants and the armed forces of the Sri Lankan government. Both parties give justifying reasons for their engagement in the war. The LTTE presents its militancy as a "just" or "righteous" war against the oppression of the minority Tamil community by the Sinhala majority government. The government of Sri Lanka, drawn from all ethnic and religious groups, contains a Sinhala majority. The Sinhala majority controls the legislative and executive power of the state. For the best part of the last two decades, and even though some areas of the north and east of Sri Lanka have been under rebel control, public services such as education, health, transportation and the postal service have been provided by the central government in Colombo. Owing to the growing unrest and de-spondency, there is a Tamil claim that a separate state is the solution to the problem and that it can be achieved through armed struggle. This provides the ammunition for the Tamil terrorism and war that has re-sulted the death of nearly 70,000 people over the last two decades alone.[64]

War is a costly business. Disregarding the casualties from the Sri Lan-kan Air Force and Navy, the Sri Lankan Army alone lost 10,688 soldiers from 1983 to June 1999 in the Sri Lankan government's confrontation with the LTTE.[65] In addition, in the context of the protracted civil war and as a result of the revolts by the Janatha Vimukthi Peramuna in the late 1980s, a culture of disappearing people has emerged. A recent publi-cation, *An Exceptional Collapse of the Rule of Law*, has collected some of the narratives of the disappeared victims in the period 1987–1991.[66] The damage the war has done to human lives on both sides is immense and cannot be measured. For over two decades, since July 1983, Sri Lanka has experienced the agonies of a protracted war. The military expendi-ture of the Sri Lankan government is nearly Rs 100 billion although it was reduced to 4.0 per cent of GDP when the ceasefire agreement was signed in 2002.[67] The escalation of war again in November 2005 threat-ens to further increase the unbearable military expenditure. The cost of war for the Sri Lankan government is immense; in the ground attack on the Katunayake International Airport in July 2001, the LTTE destroyed 12 aircraft (half of the Sri Lankan Airlines fleet) and killed 21 people. Sri Lankan Airlines alone lost US$350 million.[68]

With the air strikes by the LTTE in March and April 2007, the war in Sri Lanka gained new momentum. For the first time, the Tamil Eelam Air Force (TAF) of the LTTE launched an air strike on the air base of the Sri Lankan Air Force (SLAF) at Katunayake International Airport on 26 March 2007, killing three Sri Lankan Air Force personnel and in-juring another 20 people. This terrorist attack and the air attack capabil-ities of the LTTE pose serious security threats to Sri Lanka as well as to neighbouring India.[69]

The war situation and the terrorism of the LTTE have paralysed pri-vate businesses in Sri Lanka. The air attack on the Shell company storage facilities at Kerwalapitiya, Colombo, on 29 April 2007 damaged almost all the fire-fighting equipment, costing Rs 700 million.[70]

Apart from the damage to the resources of the country, there are seri-ous implications for religion. When one considers the importance of reli-gion for all the ethnic and religious groups in Sri Lanka, and that Buddhists comprise nearly 70 per cent of the population, the use of force in a war situation becomes a problematic issue. When one conceptualizes the Buddhist tradition as a religious tradition that advocates pacifism and the cultivation of "loving-kindness" towards all sentient beings, a whole range of relevant questions emerge.

Contemporary poetic visions of war and peace

Modern Sri Lanka has been embroiled in an ethnic war for over two decades. It is appropriate to end this chapter with a discussion of war and peace. To demonstrate the moral crisis that has arisen in the context of the current war in Sri Lanka, I will analyse a popular Sinhala song (translated below),[71] which demonstrates that war as a theme has captured the creative imagination of modern artists. The song raises moral dilemmas that have arisen in the context of war and the absence of any visible and immediate solution to the problem. It also presents the challenges that have arisen to the Buddhist approach and the Buddhist way of life.

The Buddhist monk Rambukana Siddhartha composed the song "Bana Kiyana Ratak" ("A Country Where Buddhist Sermons are Preached") for the audio CD *Nasena Gi Rasa*.[72] The famous Sri Lankan vocalist Edward Jayakody sings the song accompanied by H. M. Jayawardhana.

A country where Buddhism is preached!
A country where Buddhist preaching is listened to!
How did it become a battlefield?
A path that can resolve it
A world full of blossoming flowers
When do we see it again?
A heart bent on accumulating merit
A hand that never committed misconduct
How did go to the battlefield?
An attempt to find out the reason
There is no sign of such an attempt
Thus became a battlefield.
A path to peace
Flower to battlefield
There is no one to take an initiative
An eye to see it
A path to heal hearts
Nothing remains; the entire country is cheated.

This Sinhala song demonstrates that recent literary and artistic works in the Sinhala language have attempted to capture the frustrations and dilemmas that prevail in a predominantly Buddhist society. The ongoing ethnic conflict has challenged the very existence and future survival of Buddhism in Sri Lanka.

Both in theory and in practice, war is incompatible with Buddhist teachings and the Buddhist way of life. The war situation in Sri Lanka endangers the peaceful existence of Buddhist communities and institutions, and since war is an extreme form of the expression of violence it needs an urgent and peaceful solution. The manifestations of war and conflicts have raised many questions and challenge the way the fundamental Buddhist teachings and practices are communicated in Buddhist society. This popular Sinhala song illustrates well the concerns of war and the growing public eagerness to seek peace.

In contemporary teachings and practices there is a range of views on war and violence, in particular with regard to the current protracted conflict with the LTTE. There are debates and arguments within Buddhist communities on the approaches that should be adopted. Since 2005, the permissibility of using armed force against the LTTE has received much public support. Some recognized politically motivated Buddhist groups, such as the Jathika Hela Urumaya, have made statements in support of the use of force to deal with the insurgents. On 26 April 2006, in the context of the attempted attack by a female LTTE suicide bomber on the Army Commander in Colombo, the Jathika Hela Urumaya (JHU) urged the government to place Sri Lanka on a war footing and to withdraw from the ceasefire agreement signed in 2002.[73] The leader of the JHU, Venerable Ellawala Medhananda, stated that patience and flexibility had proved to be a costly mistake and a new strategy should be put into effect. He urged the government to respond strongly to the LTTE violence.

There have been many accusations of human rights violations in Sri Lanka. For example, in 2005 the *UN Human Rights Committee Decisions on Communications from Sri Lanka* documented six well-known cases.[74] Another publication, *An Exceptional Collapse of the Rule of Law: Told Through Stories by Families of the Disappeared in Sri Lanka*, brings together 19 stories from surviving family members of disappeared victims during 1987–1991.[75] These violent incidents and episodes in Sri Lanka cannot be justified at all in light of the basic Buddhist principles.

In the past, Buddhist scholarship has been very keen to demonstrate the recognition of human rights and humanitarian laws by both the Sri Lanka government and Buddhist leaders and by Buddhist teachings. In 1991, L. P. N. Perera, a former professor at Sri Jayawardenepura University, published a very useful book entitled *Buddhism and Human Rights: A Buddhist Commentary on the Universal Declaration of Human Rights*, which attempts to interpret all the articles of the Universal Declaration of Human Rights from a Buddhist angle.[76] This demonstrates an eagerness to show the compatibility of Buddhist teachings with humanitarian and secular concerns raised in international contexts.

In today's world, it is common to resort to the use of force to settle territorial disputes. In many developing countries, one can witness groups asserting their rights to secure recognition for their ethnic, religious or national identities. Based on various rationalizations, threats to global peace are emerging rapidly. Particularly in developing countries, threats to peace are hindering the goals and strategies of development and thus denying the essential goods for life to a majority of the population. Those countries also have to bear an expensive war budget instead of developing the infrastructure of their societies. Countries such as Sri Lanka face a realistic choice: is war a viable option and can the state resolve existing conflicts by the use of force?

Notes

1. Here I am reminded of the terrorist attack by the Liberation Tigers of Tamil Eelam (LTTE) on Katunayake International Airport near Colombo on 24 July 2001. The 14 members of the LTTE Black Tiger suicide squad destroyed eight military aircraft on the tarmac and damaged another five K-8s and one MiG-27. They also destroyed two civilian aircraft (Airbus A340 and A330) and damaged two A320s and one A330. They were able to damage a significant portion of the Sri Lankan Airlines fleet of 12 aircraft. The airport was closed for 14 hours and flights were diverted to India. The cost of replacing the military aircraft was estimated at US$350 million, half of Sri Lanka's military budget. The terrorist attack caused a slowdown in the economy of Sri Lanka of about 2.5 per cent. On 26 March 2007, for the first time, using a light aircraft the LTTE launched an air strike on the Sri Lankan Air Force base adjoining Colombo's international airport.

2. Anthony Reid has said that people have high expectations of Buddhism when it comes to issues of violence such as suicide bombing. He expressed his opinion when presenting a response paper entitled "Religion, the State and Violence: Is Buddhism Different?" at the International Workshop on "Buddhism and the Crises of Nation-States in Asia" held at the National University of Singapore, 19–20 June 2008.

3. Narada Thera, *The Dhammapada*. Kuala Lumpur: Buddhist Missionary Society, 1978, verse 202.

4. K. N. Jayatilleke, *Buddhism and Peace*. Kandy: Buddhist Publication Society, 1983, p. 2.

5. D. Andersen and H. Smith (eds), *Sutta-nipata*. Oxford: Pali Text Society, 1990, p. 164.

6. Jayatilleke, *Buddhism and Peace*.

7. The Korean Buddhist Research Institute (ed.), *The History and Culture of Buddhism in Korea*. Seoul: Dongguk University Press, 1993, p. 192.

8. Ibid., p. 198. The premises of Dongguk University, Seoul, South Korea, contain a statue of the Son master Seo San. The bottom panel illustrates the master and his disciples with prayer beads as well as soldiers with weaponry.

9. Ibid., p. 200.

10. William M. Bodiford, "Monastic Militias", in Robert E. Buswell (ed.) *Encyclopedia of Buddhism*, vol. 2. New York: Macmillan Reference USA, 2003, pp. 560–561, p. 561.

11. R. Chalmers (ed.), *The Majjhimanikaya*, vol. II. London: Pali Text Society, 1898, p. 72.

12. I. B. Horner (trans.), *The Collection of the Middle Length Sayings*, vol. II. London: Pali Text Society, 1957, p. 265.
13. Jayatilleke, *Buddhism and Peace*, p. 6.
14. Helmer Smith (ed.), *Suttanipata Commentary*, vol. I. London: Pali Text Society, 1916.
15. F. L. Woodward (ed.), *Udana Commentary*. London: Pali Text Society, 1926; M. E. Lilley (ed.), *Apadana*. London: Pali Text Society, 1925.
16. See T. W. Rhys Davids and J. E. Carpenter (eds), *The Digha Nikaya*. London: The Pali Text Society, vol. 2, 1903, pp. 73–75. Quoted in Mahinda Deegalle, "Buddhist Principles of Democracy: An Exploration of Ethical and Philosophical Foundations?", *Buddhist Studies*, 26, 1997: 89–107, pp. 92–93.
17. *Samyuttanikaya*, ed. M. Léon Feer. London: Pali Text Society, 1888, vol. 2, p. 268.
18. See R. O. Franke (trans.), *Dighanikaya*. Gottingen and Leipzig: Vandenhoeck & Ruprecht and J. C. Hinrichs'sche, 1913, pp. 260–272.
19. Richard F. Gombrich, *Theravada Buddhism: A Social History from Ancient Benares to Modern Colombo*. London and New York: Routledge & Kegan Paul, 1988; revised edition, 2006, p. 20.
20. Frank E. Reynolds and Charles Hallisey, "Buddhist Religion, Culture and Civilization", in Joseph M. Kitagawa and Mark D. Cummings (eds) *Buddhism in Asian History*. New York: Macmillan, 1989, pp. 8–9.
21. Jayatilleke, *Buddhism and Peace*, p. 5.
22. Ibid.
23. *Samyuttanikaya*, vol. 1, p. 116.
24. *Taisho shinshu Daizokyo*. Tokyo: Daizokyo Kankokai, 1924–1935, vol. 50, p. 340b.
25. Gunavarman was a prince of Kashmir. He refused the throne, travelled and visited China in 424 CE and made 10 translations. He is said to have started the order of Buddhist nuns in China.
26. *Taisho shinshu Daizokyo*, vol. 50, p. 340b.
27. Ibid.
28. See Mahanama Thera, *Mahavamsa or The Great Chronicle of Ceylon*, translated by Wilhelm Geiger. Colombo: Ceylon Government Information Department, 1950, p. 263; available at ⟨http://lakdiva.org/mahavamsa/⟩ (accessed 9 October 2008).
29. Ibid., pp. 260–261.
30. Hermann Oldenberg (ed.), *The Dipavamsa: An Ancient Buddhist Historical Record*. New Delhi: Asian Educational Services, 1982, p. 219.
31. The Five Precepts that govern daily Buddhist life are: abstention from destroying life, from theft, from misuse of sex, from lying and from the use of intoxicating drinks.
32. These are the Eight Precepts that Buddhists observe on full moon days: abstinence from killing any living being, from taking what is not given, from the misuse of one's senses, from lying, from consuming intoxicating drinks, from taking meals at inappropriate times, from dancing, singing, playing instrumental music or watching comics, and from using comfortable bedding and seating.
33. D. B. Jayatilaka and V. de Silva, "Dawn of a Great Day", *The Buddhist*, 10(1), May 1939, p. 1.
34. V. Fausbooll (ed.), *Jataka with Commentary*, vol. 6. London: Pali Text Society, 1877–1896.
35. E. M. G. Edirisinghe, "Suicide in Sri Lanka: Incidence and Remedy", *The Island* (Saturday Magazine), 15 August 1998; Tessa J. Bartholomeusz, *In Defense of Dharma: Just-War Ideology in Buddhist Sri Lanka*. London: RoutledgeCurzon, 2002, p. 120.
36. "Indriya Sutta", *Samyuttanikaya*, vol. 4, p. 365.
37. V. Trenckner (ed.), *The Majjhimanikaya*. London: Pali Text Society, 1888, p. 392f.
38. Bhikkhu Nanamoli and Bhikkhu Bodhi (trans.), *The Middle Length Discourses of the Buddha*. Kandy: Buddhist Publication Society, 1995, p. 499.

39. See chapter 25 of Mahanama Thera's *Mahavamsa* (pp. 170–178) for this controversial episode. For the justifications of war within the Theravada Buddhist tradition, see Mahinda Deegalle, "Is Violence Justified in Theravada?", *Current Dialogue*, 39, 2002: 8–17.

40. Bartholomeusz, *In Defense of Dharma*, p. 53.

41. Steven Kemper, *The Presence of the Past: Chronicles, Politics, and Culture in Sinhala Life*. Ithaca, NY: Cornell University Press, 1991, p. 1.

42. Mahanama Thera, *Mahavamsa*.

43. Ibid.

44. Ibid.

45. Lambert Schmithausen, "Aspects of the Buddhist Attitude towards War", in Jan E. M. Houben and Karel R. van Kooij (eds) *Violence Defined: Violence, Non-violence and the Rationalization of Violence in South Asian Cultural History*. Leiden: E. J. Brill, 1999, pp. 57–58. Schmithausen has pointed out that it is possible that this adjustment of precepts for violence could have been influenced by certain Mahayana ideas developing two centuries earlier where the contravention of the precepts, including the killing of living beings, is allowed in certain exceptional circumstances.

46. Ananda Wickremeratne, *Buddhism and Ethnicity in Sri Lanka: A Historical Analysis*. Delhi: Vikas Publishing House, 1995, p. 294.

47. P. D. Premasiri, "A 'Righteous War' in Buddhism", in Mahinda Deegalle (ed.) *Buddhism, Conflict and Violence in Modern Sri Lanka*. London and New York: Routledge, 2006, pp. 78–85, p. 84.

48. The LTTE is a separatist movement that has waged civil war since the late 1970s for an independent state for Tamils in Sri Lanka. Details of the LTTE can be found in two recent works by M. R. Narayan Swamy: *Inside an Elusive Mind: The First Profile of the World's Most Ruthless Guerrilla Leader*. Colombo: Vijitha Yapa Publications, 2004; *Tigers of Lanka: From Boys to Guerrillas*. Colombo: Vijitha Yapa Publications, 2006.

49. Bartholomeusz, *In Defense of Dharma*, p. 40.

50. Quoted in Bartholomeusz, *In Defense of Dharma*, p. 70.

51. Ibid., p. 71.

52. The *Dharma Yuddhaya* pamphlets were printed at Sigiri Press in Colombo from 1953 to 1956.

53. K. N. O. Dharmadasa, "Buddhism and Politics in Modern Sri Lanka", in Maduluvave Sobhita et al. (eds) *Bhiksuva saha Lanka samajaya* [Buddhist monk and Sri Lankan society]. Colombo: Paravahara Sri Pannananda Nahimi Upahara Kamituva, 1997, pp. 259–260.

54. Quoted in Bartholomeusz, *In Defense of Dharma*, p. 76.

55. G. P. Malalasekera, *English Sinhalese Dictionary*. Colombo: M. D. Gunasena, 1978, p. 437.

56. Bartholomeusz, *In Defense of Dharma*, p. 71.

57. Quoted in Bartholomeusz, *In Defense of Dharma*, p. 83.

58. Ibid., p. 77.

59. Ibid., p. 82.

60. Ibid., p. 98.

61. For a detailed study of the political circumstances that led to the birth of the Buddhist monks' political party, Jathika Hela Urumaya, see Mahinda Deegalle, "JHU Politics for Peace and a Righteous State", in Mahinda Deegalle (ed.) *Buddhism, Conflict and Violence in Modern Sri Lanka*. London and New York: Routledge, 2006, pp. 233–254.

62. Athureliye Rathana, "A Buddhist Analysis of 'The Ethnic Conflict'", paper delivered at the "Buddhism and Conflict in Sri Lanka" International Conference, Bath Spa University, 28–30 June; see *Journal of Buddhist Ethics*, 10, 2003, available at ⟨http://www.buddhistethics.org/10/rathana-sri-lanka-conf.html⟩ (accessed 23 October 2008).

63. Bartholomeusz, *In Defense of Dharma*, p. 102.
64. Since the escalation of the war in November 2005, the number of casualties on both sides has increased dramatically (estimated at nearly 5,000 within a one-year period).
65. Bartholomeusz, *In Defense of Dharma*, p. xxi.
66. *An Exceptional Collapse of the Rule of Law: Told Through Stories by Families of the Disappeared in Sri Lanka*. Hong Kong: Asian Legal Resource Centre (ALRC) and Asian Human Rights Commission (AHRC), 2004.
67. Frederica Jansz, *The Consequences of Another War in Sri Lanka: February 27–May 5 2006*. Colombo: The Foundation for Co-Existence, 2006, p. 29.
68. "LTTE Terrorists Attack Colombo Airport", Sinhaya.com, 2007, ⟨http://www.sinhaya. com/airport.htm⟩ (accessed 9 October 2008).
69. See B. Raman, "LTTE's Air Strike: An Assessment", International Terrorism Monitor Paper No. 2185, 27 March 2007, ⟨http://www.southasiaanalysis.org/papers22/paper2185. html⟩ (accessed 9 October 2008).
70. "Shell Assess LTTE Air Strike", BBC Sinhala.com, 12 May 2007, ⟨http://www.bbc. co.uk/sinhala/news/story/2007/05/070512_shell.shtml⟩ (accessed 9 October 2008).
71. To aid English readers' comprehension, I have translated the song freely without limiting myself to a literal translation (the literal translation can become abstract and may not communicate fully the original intention of the composer of the song). For readers who are interested in the original Sinhala version of the song, I have given the transliteration below.

"Bana kiyana ratak"
bana ahana ratak
yuda bimak une kelesa
eya nivana mangak
mal pipuna lovak
api dakinu itin kavada
pin purana hitak
pav nodutu atak
yuda bimata giye kelesa
eya soyana bavak
nodanuya ivak
yuda bimak elesa
samayata mangak
yuda bimata malak
geni yanna kenek natuva
eya dakina asak
sit nivana mangak
notibuniya ratama ravata

72. Rambukana Siddhartha Thero, *Nasena Gi Rasa*. Nugegoda: Singlanka Ltd. Audio CD, song no. 14, "Bana Kiyana Ratak".
73. Wijeya Newspapers, "JHU Calls for War-footing", LankaNewspapers.com, 26 April 2006, ⟨http://www.lankanewspapers.com/news/2006/4/6618.html⟩ (accessed 9 October 2008).
74. *UN Human Rights Committee Decisions on Communications from Sri Lanka*. Hong Kong: Asian Legal Resource Centre, 2005.
75. *An Exceptional Collapse of the Rule of Law: Told Through Stories by Families of the Disappeared in Sri Lanka*. 2004.
76. L. P. N. Perera, *Buddhism and Human Rights: A Buddhist Commentary on the Universal Declaration of Human Rights*. Colombo: Karunaratne & Sons Ltd, 1991.

4

Norms of war in Japanese religion

Robert Kisala

One defining characteristic of the Japanese historical situation regarding war and peace is that, until the modern period, the country had been involved in very few conflicts with foreign powers. Until the nineteenth century its conflicts with groups outside Japan had been limited to a disastrous invasion of the Korean peninsula in the seventh century, some attacks by pirates on the southern island of Kyushu in the ninth century, two attempted invasions of Japan by the Mongols in the thirteenth century, and another invasion of Korea at the end of the fifteenth century. On the other hand, in the centuries leading up to the inauguration of the Tokugawa regime in 1603, Japan was racked by a series of internal conflicts among rival warlords, culminating in a century-long civil war that was brought to an end only with the institution of the new regime. Consequently, perhaps the most important influence on the pre-modern Japanese concept of peace was the experience of internal conflict and the consequent emphasis on stability and social order. As a result, pre-modern discourse on peace in Japan tends to emphasize internal social order, and there is little development of theories regarding international relations.

The situation changed dramatically, however, with the end of the Tokugawa policy of isolation and the opening of the country by the Meiji regime in 1868. As part of its policy to become a modern nation-state, on a par with the Western powers, in short order a national army was created and universal conscription introduced. Japan went to war with China in 1894 over spheres of influence on the Korean peninsula, and gained Taiwan as a colony as a result of that war. Ten years later, Japan

World religions and norms of war, Popovski, Reichberg and Turner (eds),
United Nations University Press, 2009, ISBN 978-92-808-1163-6

fought Russia, and with its victory was granted privileges in Manchuria. Korea was annexed in 1910 and, by allying itself with European forces fighting Germany in World War I, Japan was able to expand its control in China. It was in this context that Western pacifist and just war ideas entered intellectual and public discourse in Japan, largely through the activities of several influential Christians.

The experience of defeat in World War II and the postwar occupation of the country, and, especially, the experience of having been the only country to suffer the use of atomic weapons, have, of course, been decisive in forming postwar Japanese attitudes towards war and peace. *Heiwashugi* is the term used by most Japanese to describe their position, but while usually translated as "pacifism" it often refers to a presumption against the employment of force, rather than its absolute rejection.[1] Article 9 of the postwar Constitution "forever renounce[s] war as a sovereign right of the nation and the threat or use of force [as] a means of settling international disputes", but this is not normally interpreted as an absolute rejection of the use of force, and spending on the Self-Defense Forces is among the highest military spending in the world.

Along with this "pacifism", another characteristic of the Japanese religious concept of war and peace would be what I have identified in previous research as a "civilizational" element.[2] Civilization refers to a refined moral state of being, but it is often also used as a discriminating concept, to distinguish between areas where such a state exists and where it is absent. I propose the concept of civilization because I believe that the Japanese concept of peace encompasses both of these elements, namely an emphasis on individual moral cultivation and, at times, an oppositional schema derived from a sense of ethnic or cultural superiority. Therefore, the idea of peace based on the concept of civilization emphasizes the active pursuit of the moral cultivation of the individual, leading to a refined, civilized state of being that is identified as the foundation of a peaceful society. Furthermore, the idea of civilization can lead to a conceptual distinction between civilized regions and uncivilized regions, which in turn can result in a cultural sense of mission towards the spread of civilization as it is enjoyed in one's own region. Indeed, it was rhetoric reflecting this idea of mission that was used to justify, if not in fact inspire, Western colonialism as well as Japan's own military and colonial enterprises. Such rhetoric has also occasionally led to cases of extreme violence and atrocities, as seen in both Western and Japanese colonialism.

Japanese religion

Although Buddhism and Shinto are identified today as the major religious traditions of Japan, throughout much of Japanese history the two were so closely intertwined as to form a single religious complex with various expressions, and the forced separation of the two as the result of government policy at the beginning of the modern period in the mid-nineteenth century resulted in a great upheaval in Japanese religious practice that, some have argued, continues to have repercussions today.[3] In addition, these religious traditions have been combined with elements of Taoism and Confucianism from China, issuing in a kind of common or popular religiosity that is not easily contained in any one religious tradition. Christianity, introduced to Japan in the fifteenth century by the Catholic missionaries who accompanied the Spanish and Portuguese explorers, was actively persecuted throughout the early modern period (seventeenth century to mid-nineteenth century), and small groups of "hidden Christians" continue to preserve a secret faith tradition that they trace back to the time of persecution. Reintroduced in the modern period, Christianity has had little success in attracting members in Japan, with less than 1 per cent of the population belonging to one of the Christian churches. Christian influence is generally acknowledged as greater than those membership numbers would indicate, however, especially in the fields of education and social welfare, as well as the concept of war and peace.

The modern period has seen the proliferation of new religious movements in Japan. Some of the new religions trace their roots to the end of the early modern period in the first half of the nineteenth century. Groups from this period are often based on folk religious practices and the experiences of a charismatic founder, and they can be described as attempts to revitalize traditional cultural elements in the face of the influx of Western influences during that century. Another wave of new religious movements emerged in the immediate postwar period, attracting much media attention in Japan as well as abroad. These movements were often Buddhist-based lay movements, and some of them have been successful in attracting followers numbering in the millions. Part of the reason for their success is that they offered the increasingly urban population a means to perform traditional ancestor rites in the home, independent of the Buddhist clergy and temples that they left behind in the move to the cities. Finally, a third wave of new religions has emerged since the 1970s, mirroring religious developments predominantly seen in the West. These movements emphasize personal spiritual development and encourage the adoption of ideas and practices from a wide range of religions in order to contribute to that development.

The choice of these new religious movements as a window into the concept of war and peace in Japanese religion is perhaps problematic for some. These groups are often looked upon with suspicion, as at least a degenerate form of religion if not, in fact, dangerous either to their believers or to society at large – an impression that was reinforced by the poison-gas attack on the Tokyo subways by a new religious group on 20

March 1995. However, it would appear that nearly one-half of those who profess religious belief in Japan are members of one of these groups.[4] This would indicate that it is precisely these new religious groups that mediate the religious traditions of the country most effectively to the contemporary population, and reflect most clearly contemporary religious ideas of war and peace.

Pre-modern developments in religious concepts of war and peace

Although specifically Christian ideas on war and peace were introduced only in the nineteenth century, we can identify elements within the Buddhist tradition that correspond to pacifist and just war ideas as developed in the Christian West. For example, *fussesho*, the Buddhist proscription against the taking of life, provides the basis for the development of an ethical rejection of any use of force. However, similar to the case in the West, where the practice of pacifism becomes limited to certain individuals or small groups, the injunction of *fussesho* is, in practice, also seldom held to be absolute and is often limited to monastics. In his study of the social ethic of ancient Buddhism, Nakamura Hajime points out that sutras written in the Mahayana Buddhist tradition around the eighth century speak of a duty incumbent upon the sovereign to defend the state, even if this necessitates the use of force.[5] Nakamura goes on to indicate that injunctions to embark upon war only if there is a real chance of victory, to weigh the gains to be made by war against the destruction it will cause, to limit the extent of war, to engage in war only as a last resort, and to be prepared to take care of enemy wounded can be found in the Mahayana writings of this period.[6] All of these would correspond to elements of the just war theory as it developed in the West.

Nakamura also points out that the Mahayana Buddhist tradition places an emphasis on the wisdom and individual moral cultivation of the sovereign and the sovereign's subjects as the foundation for a peaceful society. For example, in the *Shiju Kegon* (c. fourth century), the following five conditions are given for a peaceful society: (1) that the sovereign lead a simple and thrifty life, (2) that the royal family lead a life of fidelity and not covet treasures, (3) that administrators be faithful to their positions and that there not be any unjust officials, (4) that all the people be righteous and deferent, and that there be no fear of theft, and (5) that the borders be at peace and that there be no fear of invasion.[7] It is significant that the final point dealing with secure borders is preceded by four points that emphasize the individual moral cultivation of the sovereign, the court and public officials, and the general populace.

The concept of the moral cultivation of the individual as the means to establishing peace was further developed and concretized during the period of relative stability that characterized pre-modern Japan, and it emphasized the virtues of stability and order. In recent years it has become commonplace to argue that rhetoric concerning the maintenance of proper relationships and harmony masks a considerable amount of dissent and conflict in Japanese society. The treatment of *bushido*, or the Way of the Warrior, in the intellectual history of Japan is one example of this phenomenon. Although modern tracts on *bushido*, beginning with the famous work by Nitobe Inazo,[8] emphasize loyalty as the foundation of the social order, the increasing emphasis on loyalty was in fact one of the results of the establishment of the Tokugawa order. The century-long period of civil strife that preceded the Tokugawa regime testifies to the presence of a more rough-and-tumble warrior ethic that marked this period of personal advancement through shifting loyalties. Indeed, some scholars argue that pragmatism and disloyalty were more the norm, contrary to the image portrayed in emerging rhetoric on the warrior ethic.[9]

For this reason, with the end of the so-called Warring States period and the establishment of the Tokugawa political order at the beginning of the seventeenth century, there was an understandable concern that the ideological underpinnings of this fragile new order be made secure. Herman Ooms argues that this was accomplished by a bricolage of ideological constructs, borrowing from the Buddhist, Shinto and Confucian traditions.[10] This ideology, as reflected for example in Tokugawa Ieyasu's *Testament*, published in the early seventeenth century, emphasizes the virtues of loyalty, benevolence and trust, and affirms the use of military power to preserve good order. In the *Bendo* and *Taiheisaku* treatises, written almost one hundred years later by the Confucian scholar Ogyu Sorai, the preservation of order is given an even more prominent place. According to Sorai, the duty of the sovereign is to ensure that the realm is at peace, and, indeed, it is the maintenance of order that is the true expression of benevolence. Furthermore, the use of military power for the sake of maintaining good order is positively encouraged, and Sorai argues that this imperative overrides all other moral duties, even that of the preservation of life.

Yasumaru Yoshio has argued that, in addition to the above values of loyalty and good order, hard work, thrift, filial piety and other common values were promoted in the latter half of the pre-modern period by popular preachers such as Ninomiya Sontoku (1787–1856), and thus became widely spread throughout Japanese society as a kind of popular morality.[11] Furthermore, Yasumaru points out that the cultivation of such virtues was used as the answer to the social problems caused by the economic upheavals of that time, contributing to an emphasis on individual moral cultivation that has remained prevalent in Japanese society until the present day.

Having sketched very briefly the outlines of the development of the concept of individual moral cultivation as the foundation of peace, let us now consider in turn the oppositional schema of "the civilized" and "the uncivilized" and the idea of national mission as it was developed in Japan.

The concept of a unique Japanese cultural identity has perhaps been expressed most clearly in the idea of Japan as *shinkoku*, the "Land of the Gods". Satomi Kishio outlines the development of this idea in his intellectual history of the concept of "national polity".[12] There he states that the first recorded use of this term can be found in the *Nihon Shoki* (The Chronicles of Japan), purportedly an early history of Japan compiled in the eighth century. The term further appears in records of prayers offered at Ise in 870 to protect the nation from pirate attacks on the southern island of Kyushu. The belief that Japan enjoys special protection as the Land of the Gods was strengthened by the unsuccessful Mongol invasion attempts in the thirteenth century. Furthermore, Satomi points out that around this time the concept of the Land of the Gods came to be connected with the idea of justice, resulting in the belief that Japan and its rulers embody justice by virtue of the fact that Japan is the Land of the Gods. By the time of the Muromachi Shogunate in the fourteenth century this concept had become connected with beliefs concerning the unbroken reign of the imperial family, an indication of order and stability that is both the result of the special favour of the gods and a proof of cultural superiority.[13] In the late sixteenth century this concept was used as justification for the invasion of the Korean peninsula. At that time, Toyotomi Hideyoshi, who had succeeded in subjugating most of the warlords in Japan, turned his sights on Korea, proclaiming it the duty of Japan as the Land of the Gods to extend the benevolence of good order to all of Asia.[14] The cruelty that accompanied that invasion – there are reports that the ears and noses of 30,000 decapitated Koreans were cut off and sent to Japan – indicates how such a concept of cultural superiority and the mission to "civilize" can lead to extreme violence, and foreshadowed the violence and atrocities that accompanied Japanese military action in the twentieth century, the acknowledgement of which remains a point of controversy today.

The above cluster of beliefs centring on the concept of Japan as the Land of the Gods was given a place of prominence in the writings of *kokugaku*, or the National Learning School, an awakening of Japanese nativism in the later half of the Tokugawa period. In this movement, Buddhist and Confucian influences were rejected as foreign and there was a search to identify what the origins and distinctive traits of native

Japanese culture might be. The concept of Japan as the Land of the Gods was, therefore, central to these nativist scholars, and the need to return to an initial pristine existence was emphasized.

The modern period

In the early part of the nineteenth century, as the Tokugawa policy of national isolation came under increasing threat by the appearance of Western and Russian ships in Japanese coastal waters, the two elements of an emphasis on moral cultivation and an oppositional schema based on a sense of cultural superiority were combined in the so-called "expel the barbarians" (*joi*) concept. Perhaps the clearest formulation of this concept is *The New Theses*, composed in 1825 by Aizawa Seishisai, a retainer of the Mito domain north of Tokyo. In this work Aizawa relies on the arguments of the National Learning scholars to explicate an original Japanese cultural identity, tied to the national creation myths and beliefs pertaining to the emperor. He asserts that this national consciousness is expressed above all in the virtues of loyalty and filial piety, and calls for the establishment of a national religion based on these beliefs and virtues, and the performance of national rituals in order to enhance the unity of the people. Although acknowledging the importance of military preparedness to repel incursions by foreign powers, Aizawa concludes that it is ultimately the awareness of the unique Japanese cultural identity and the adherence to the fundamental virtues of loyalty and filial piety that will provide peace and security for the nation.[15]

As Carol Gluck points out, in modern Japan this combination of individual moral cultivation with ideological elements that promoted a sense of ethnic superiority became a type of civic creed, through formulation in the Imperial Rescript on Education (signed by Emperor Meiji on 30 October 1890) and later commentaries on the Rescript.[16] Furthermore, as seen previously in Toyotomi Hideyoshi's justification of the invasion of the Korean peninsula in the sixteenth century, the extension of this peace and security, of the benefits of civilization, to the other countries of Asia could easily become the motivation for colonial exploits. Indeed, such rhetoric was used in the modern Japanese colonial expansion, which culminated in World War II.

Finally, Christian pacifist and just war concepts were introduced in the modern period through the influence of some prominent Christians, foremost among them Uchimura Kanzo. Although initially supportive of Japan's military intervention in Asia in the late nineteenth century as a "righteous war",[17] early in the next century he came to the resolution that "I am for the absolute abolition of all wars. War is murder, and murder is a crime."[18] As a reason for his conversion, he offers the following:

> The result of the Sino-Japanese War taught me that war is destructive and offers no benefits. Korean independence, the motivation for the war, is in fact less secure than ever; morality in Japan, the victor, has been immensely corrupted, and no one has been able to rein in marauders in China, the vanquished enemy.[19]

Postwar developments

A look at the doctrine and activities of some of the new religious movements will illustrate how the above elements have been developed in postwar Japanese society. I begin with three groups that can be identified as being within the Buddhist tradition – Nipponzan Myohoji, Soka Gakkai and Rissho Koseikai – to illustrate some of the complexities and ambiguities of postwar pacifism.

Nipponzan Myohoji

Nipponzan Myohoji is a small group of both lay and religious Nichiren Buddhists, numbering about 1,500 people. The first Nipponzan Myohoji temple was established by Fujii Nichidatsu in northern China in 1918. Fujii was born in 1885 in Kumamoto Prefecture, in the southern part of Japan. At the age of 19 he decided to become a Nichiren Buddhist monk and studied extensively in Tokyo and Kyoto before leaving on a missionary trip to China in 1917. Following the establishment of his first temple the following year, Nipponzan Myohoji temples were established in five other places in Manchuria within the next six years. In 1923, Fujii returned to Japan and in the following year a Nipponzan Myohoji temple was established at the foot of Mt Fuji. After Fujii's mother died in 1930 he embarked upon his next, and what he himself considered his most important, missionary endeavour – the return of Buddhism to India, the land of its birth. Perhaps the most important outcome of his activities in India was a series of audiences with Mahatma Gandhi. In later years Fujii often identified his own philosophy of non-violent activism with Gandhi's example.

Nipponzan Myohoji preaches an adherence to the principle of absolute non-violence, based on the Buddhist law of *fussesho*, which prohibits the taking of any life. In a sermon with that title given in 1950, just after the outbreak of the Korean War, Fujii called for steadfast perseverance in the path of non-violence, fully aware of the consequences such practice would engender in a world divided into two armed camps.

If disarmed Japan adheres to and practices persistent nonviolent resistance in light of the imminent international situation ruled by violence, the communist countries would seize the opportunity and give rise to a violent revolution and occupy Japan. At the same time, democratic countries would use Japan as their valuable strategic advanced base. At any rate, it is unlikely that we would be able to avoid being trampled, dishonored and killed at the will of today's violent civilization.[20]

There are indications in Fujii's writing, however, that the proscription against taking life fundamental to the pacifist position is not necessarily absolute. During the United States' participation in the Vietnam War, preference was given by Fujii to the Vietnamese nationalists fighting against the US troops, and their armed struggle was even offered as an example of non-violent resistance. His criticism of the United States, although directed at its reliance on military might in general, focuses on the manufacture and use of nuclear weapons, an issue of obvious importance in Japan, a point that I shall return to later. As the developer of nuclear weapons and the only nation to use them, the United States is condemned by Fujii as "an enemy of humankind" and "a criminal who destroys civilization".[21]

Soka Gakkai

Until its excommunication in November 1991, Soka Gakkai was officially a lay movement within the Nichiren Shoshu sect of Buddhism. The loss of approbation by its parent body, however, does not seem to have had a lasting adverse effect on this group, since it remains strong institutionally and its 8 million members make it the largest new religion movement in Japan. It is also remains the object of considerable controversy in Japan, largely as a result of its political activities.

Soka Gakkai was founded in 1930 by Makiguchi Tsunesaburo, an educator who stressed the role of creativity and personal experience in his educational philosophy. As its original name – Soka Kyoiku Gakkai, or Academic Society for Value-Creating Education – indicates, in its origins the group was primarily composed of educators interested in Makiguchi's philosophy. However, Makiguchi had become involved in the Nichiren Shoshu faith through an acquaintance in 1928, and from the mid-1930s the group gathered around him began to take on an increasingly religious character. Makiguchi and his leading disciple, Toda Josei, were imprisoned in 1943 as a result of their opposition to the religious policy of the wartime government, and Makiguchi died in prison in late 1944. As a result, it fell to Toda to rebuild Soka Gakkai following the war, and the fact that Soka Gakkai could claim a membership of over 800,000 families at the time of his death in 1958 attests to Toda's success in that task.

This phenomenal growth was at least in part the result of the intense proselytization activities of the Gakkai membership, activity centred on a method called *shaku-buku* that sought to wear down potential recruits through the employment of extreme polemics. It was also under Toda's leadership that Soka Gakkai initiated its political involvement, sponsoring more than 50 of its own candidates in local elections held in 1955. As a result of increasing involvement, and success, in both local and national election campaigns, Soka Gakkai founded its own independent political party, Komeito, in 1964. With a party constitution calling for the establishment of world peace based on a "global nationalism" and "human socialism", Komeito sought to steer a middle course between the conservative government and the socialist opposition. In elections held the following year, Komeito garnered over 5 million votes, making it the third-largest political party in Japan. Its successor, New Komeito, is currently the junior partner in the coalition government led by the Liberal Democrats.

Soka Gakkai professes to be a pacifist group, and it has long been engaged in drives against nuclear weapons and in peace education activities. Toda's successor, Ikeda Daisaku, has been prominent in international peace forums, addressing the United Nations General Assembly special sessions on disarmament and receiving the United Nations Peace Award in 1983. In his numerous proposals on peace and disarmament, Ikeda makes continual reference to the ideal of universal disarmament and resolution of conflict through negotiation. Any change to the post-war Peace Constitution, which renounces war as a sovereign right, is opposed, and the Constitution is held up as a model for all nations.[22] The lack of a Supreme Court decision on the constitutionality of the Japanese Self-Defense Forces is decried,[23] overseas deployment of those forces as part of the UN's Peacekeeping Operations is proscribed,[24] and the Japanese government is criticized for seeking protection under the United States' nuclear umbrella.[25] It would appear, however, that Soka Gakkai compromises on all of these principles in its continued support of New Komeito.

Ikeda himself recognizes the occasional need for the application of force in order to maintain order, although he would shift responsibility for the deployment of such force from the nation-state to an international body such as the United Nations. For example, although he disallows permanent membership for Japan on the UN Security Council – based on a perceived obligation for such members to participate in collective security activities, a requirement whose fulfilment he maintains is prohibited by the Japanese Constitution – this prohibition is apparently considered to be unique to Japan.[26] Specifically, the necessary use of force for the maintenance of collective security is recognized in the case of the Persian Gulf War.[27]

By choosing active involvement in the formation of public policy, Soka Gakkai and Ikeda have been forced to compromise their pacifist ideals. Rather than the strict pacifist option, which bans the use of force in any situation, their position is better characterized as calling for a limitation on the use of force. Indeed, even groups less politically involved tend towards this latter position, as indicated by the case of Rissho Koseikai.

Rissho Koseikai

Rissho Koseikai, which claims a membership of 6.5 million, rivals Soka Gakkai as a mass religious movement within the Buddhist tradition. Rissho Koseikai was also founded in the 1930s and enjoyed spectacular success in attracting members in postwar, urban Japan. Although following a path in some ways radically different from Soka Gakkai – remaining independent of any traditional Buddhist sect and pursuing a policy of cooperation with other religious groups – the rivalry between these two groups has, at times, been very public and very intense.

Rissho Koseikai was founded by Niwano Nikkyo and Naganuma Myoko in March 1938 and continued under their joint leadership until Naganuma's death 20 years later. While Niwano dabbled in various folk religious practices, some of which are still practised in Rissho Koseikai, it was Naganuma who possessed the charismatic power that allowed her to enjoy considerable influence over the direction of Koseikai's early development. After her death in 1957, authority was concentrated in Niwano's hands, and under his direction Koseikai has become a leader in the movement towards inter-religious dialogue and cooperative activities to promote peace.

Niwano was born into a large family in a farming village in northern Japan, an environment that by all accounts was a determining influence on his character and religious beliefs. Imbued with the traditional values of honesty, hard work and harmonious relationships, like many of his generation he left for Tokyo at the age of 17. There Niwano became interested in several forms of divination and folk religious practices before finally joining Reiyukai, a new religious movement in the Nichiren Buddhist tradition in 1935. It was from Reiyukai that Niwano developed an interest in the formal study of Buddhist doctrines, and it was the triple influences of traditional values, folk religious practices and Buddhist doctrine that contributed to the belief system of the group that he founded.

Like many other new religious groups, Rissho Koseikai became involved in politics in the early postwar period through its support of independent candidates. After the formation of the Komeito in the mid-
1960s, Koseikai increasingly threw its support behind the rival Liberal
Democratic Party (LDP) as part of its opposition to Soka Gakkai's political activity. The relationship with the LDP soured, however, owing to
the conservative party's efforts to provide official recognition and support
to Yasukuni Shrine, the Shinto establishment dedicated to Japan's war
dead, including convicted war criminals.

In addition to such political activity, Rissho Koseikai has chosen to
concentrate on the promotion of civic and inter-religious movements. In
1970, Niwano was instrumental in organizing the First World Conference
on Religion and Peace in Kyoto, and on both the national and international level Rissho Koseikai remains a central figure in the work of this
inter-religious body. In 1978 the Niwano Peace Foundation was established to provide funding for development projects, primarily in Asia,
and to promote peace research. That same year Niwano was also invited
to address the United Nations General Assembly First Special Session on
Disarmament.

Niwano and Rissho Koseikai do not advocate a strictly pacifist position. In his writings, the necessity of a Self-Defense Force is explained
by means of the analogy of public safety. Niwano points out that, although we would all like to live in a society where it is not necessary to
lock your door or to maintain a police department, humanity has not yet
reached the stage where that is possible. The challenge for humanity, and
especially for people of religion, is to make reality reflect the ideal, to
create a world where force or the threat of force is no longer necessary.
Until that ideal is achieved, however, the necessity of force is recognized.[28] However, Niwano displays a distrust of the concept of justice,
the ethical basis normally given as the criterion for judging when force is
necessary. The concept is criticized as lacking tolerance, and specifically
as devoid of meaning in the age of nuclear weapons. Although these arguments reflect broadly held contemporary opinions regarding just war
theories, alternative criteria for judging when force needs to be applied
are not provided.

The doctrine of these three groups mirrors public debate in contemporary Japan, where pacifist rhetoric dominates but there is little awareness
of the implications of this position. Although the use of force is to be
avoided if at all possible, there is at least a vague recognition that there
are certain extreme situations that might necessitate the employment of
force, but debate on what might concretely constitute such situations is
avoided, in fulfilment of the desire to maintain a "pacifist" position. We

turn now to postwar developments in the civilizational element of the concept of peace in Japanese religion.

Shuyodan Hoseikai

Shuyodan Hoseikai is a relatively small new religious group, comprising approximately 12,000 members. Its faith and practices reflect both the folk religious traditions and popular morality of Japan, as expressed by its founder, Idei Seitaro.

Idei Seitaro was born at the turn of the century in a poor farming community north of Tokyo. The already poor soil of the area was made largely unusable owing to pollution from local mining operations. Idei left for Tokyo at the age of 15, and he spent the next several years shining shoes, delivering papers and supporting himself with other odd jobs. After finishing his compulsory military service, he returned to Tokyo in 1923, just in time to suffer the effects of the Great Kanto Earthquake. There are indications that Idei began his own spiritual journey at about this time, as he recalls several experiences of receiving revelations while on pilgrimages in the area south of Tokyo. In the latter half of the 1920s Idei became an active member of the Tenri Kenkyukai, an offshoot of Tenrikyo, an early new religious group, which was critical of the contemporary social and political situation. In 1928, Idei was arrested, along with 500 other members of the Tenri Kenkyukai, for distributing leaflets critical of the government.

After his arrest, Idei temporarily ceased his religious activities and found employment in a munitions factory. In 1934, however, he quit his job and returned to religious work, this time acting independently as a kind of miraculous healer and preacher. In 1935 he was arrested once again, this time for promoting a contemporary theory that maintained that the emperor was merely an organ of the state, contrary to the official state doctrine, which exalted and deified the emperor. Upon his release from prison in 1938, Idei returned to his religious work and in 1941, with the aid of two retired army and navy officers who had become his followers, Idei was given permission to establish Shuyodan Hoseikai as a juridical foundation.

The collection of Idei's teaching during the war years, compiled by Hoseikai,[29] reflects the ambiguity of his position, namely a person with an arrest record for political crimes who nonetheless was able to obtain official permission to found a religious group in the most repressive of climates. Within this collection of teachings, although there are admonitions to love and respect all people, specifically including one's enemies, one can also find comments that seem to acknowledge the necessity of the war and call for renewed efforts to win the war. Furthermore, Idei actively employs concepts such as the "Land of the Gods", but frequently this concept is used as a standard to condemn injustice and corruption in contemporary society, calling for moral cultivation commensurate with this exalted position, rather than as an expression of cultural superiority.

With the end of the war, Idei began to call Shuyodan Hoseikai's facilities "Homelands of Peace" and proclaimed that the purpose of the organization would be to establish world peace. The practice of offering a prayer for peace every day at noon at Hoseikai's Tokyo headquarters was begun in 1952, and from 1958 Hoseikai began the erection of Peace Stone monuments in various locations at home and abroad. Since the mid-1970s an annual peace march can also be counted among this group's peace activities. There is no doubt, however, that Shuyodan Hoseikai's basic approach to peace is through the moral cultivation of its individual members.

By its very name this group proclaims its overriding interest in moral cultivation, for "shuyodan" means Association for the Cultivation of Morals. In the 10 Essential Points,[30] which summarize the teaching of this group, the followers are called upon to realize that they are children of God and to strive to learn the law of nature that they may live correctly. They are told to be thankful in all things, and to remember the value of labour. The head of the house is to be respected, children are to be loved and the harmony of the household should be maintained by striving for mutual understanding. They are to be aware of their words and actions and relate to others with a bright and warm heart. They are not to begrudge others their wealth or envy their virtue. They should not allow themselves to be discontent or to voice their displeasure, but instead should humble themselves, avoid conflict with all and cultivate a spirit that respects all people. They should take seriously their own responsibility, readily accept the instruction of their superiors and follow their direction unwaveringly.

Fujii Kenji has pointed out that this emphasis on relations within the family and with one's co-workers and neighbours, a so-called "ethic of daily life", is common to many of the new religions.[31] What is interesting here, however, is that Hoseikai explicitly makes this the foundation of its work to establish world peace. In the words of the founder, "Offering thanks to all things and aiming at friendly relations with all is the teaching of Shuyodan Hoseikai, and this is the road to world peace".[32] Furthermore, the fact that the facilities of this group are called "Homelands of Peace" indicates that, in the beliefs of Hoseikai, the various activities that take place there, in particular the interaction of the members with each other and the study of the group's teachings, are in themselves efficacious towards the establishment of world peace.

The civilizational divide

We have seen above how Nipponzan Myohoji's tendency towards a position of absolute pacifism under the influence of its founder, Fujii Nichidatsu, did not extend to his position regarding US involvement in the Vietnam War. His opposition to US involvement reveals most clearly how the oppositional element in the Japanese religious concept of war and peace has developed in the postwar period. To trace this development we can begin by looking at the contents of a letter that Fujii delivered to Gandhi during one of their meetings in the 1930s to explain his purpose on his mission to India.

Fujii begins by stating his belief that it is Indian Buddhism that is the true mother of Japanese civilization, and he goes on to express his regret that this same Buddhism finds no followers in the land of its birth. Moving on to the issue of Japan's military activities in Manchuria, which had already begun to attract the condemnation of various countries throughout the world, Fujii acknowledges that Japan has been forced into a position of isolation because of its actions in China, but states that, even if it should face the threat of armed coercion from the whole world, Japan should not sway from the course it believes is just. Fujii maintains that, although Japan might be a country small in area, the fact that in its 2,600-year history it has not once suffered invasion from a foreign power indicates strength out of proportion to its size. Furthermore, according to Fujii, aside from one or two wars fought to protect itself from destruction, in that 2,600-year history Japan for its part has not invaded any other country. Indeed, Fujii maintains that no other country in the world can boast such a peaceful history as Japan. Fujii goes on to state that it is religion, namely Buddhism, that has made Japan such a peaceful nation, and for that reason it is Japan's mission to spread that faith, so that other countries might enjoy the peace with which Japan has been blessed.[33] The contents of this letter clearly reflect the acceptance of some of the beliefs pertaining to Japanese ethnic or cultural superiority, connected in Fujii's case with belief in Buddhism as the foundation of that superiority.

After Japan's defeat in the war, Fujii returned to Kumamoto, the place of his birth, to contemplate what course of action he and Nipponzan Myohoji should take. He says that it occurred to him there that Japan had been most at peace during the early years of its history, just after Buddhism was introduced to the country. Of that golden age he writes: "The prime mover to the establishment of peace in that age undoubtedly was Buddhism. I naturally became convinced that a peaceful cultural nation was formed and a moral and orderly society emerged in those days thanks to nothing but Buddhism."[34] He goes on to state his belief that the centre of that Buddhist faith was the stupa, a memorial containing the relics of the Buddha. It is this belief that became the motivation for one of the primary postwar activities of Nipponzan Myohoji, the erection of stupas, or Peace Pagodas, throughout Japan and the rest of the world. Construction work on the first such stupa was begun in Kumamoto City that very year, and completed in 1954.

Since the mid-1950s Nipponzan Myohoji has also been active in opposing US military bases in Japan, which Fujii has described as tools for the United States' invasion of Asia.[35] In the 1970s, members of Nipponzan Myohoji participated in activities obstructing the construction of the New Tokyo International Airport at Narita, on the grounds that it could also be used for military purposes, specifically to support the US military intervention in Vietnam.

We have already seen how Fujii justified armed resistance to the US intervention, a judgement against the United States at least partly based on its use of atomic weapons against Japan. The nuclear threat in particular is used by Fujii to develop an oppositional schema of civilization, where the fault-line is identified as lying between science and faith, East and West, Buddhism and other religions. This is perhaps seen most clearly in a sermon of Fujii's entitled "Scientific Civilization and Religious Civilization". There he states that "scientific civilization", which has developed in the West since the sixteenth century, has led to ever more destructive wars in Europe and the European colonization of the world. Furthermore, this civilization has culminated in the development of weapons such as nuclear weapons that now threaten the destruction of humanity itself. In opposition to this, "religious civilization" teaches the value of life and promotes the development of trust among peoples. Fujii then goes on to echo his earlier claims concerning Japan's peaceful history, saying here that wars of aggression have been rare in the history of Asia, because of the influence of Buddhism.[36]

Thus, in Fujii's postwar thought the oppositional schema included in the concept of peace based on the idea of civilization has been shifted from one anchored in a specifically Japanese ethnocentrism to one that discriminates between science and religion, the West and the East, other religions and Buddhism. In this worldview, it is the spread of the culture of faith, specifically Buddhist faith, that is seen as the necessary condition for the establishment of peace in the world.

Fujii's take on the civilizational divide is perhaps more radical than most. More representative of the mainstream of current religious ideas in Japan would be that of Soka Gakkai. In its doctrine, Soka Gakkai tends towards an inclusivistic paradigm that goes beyond the divisions of East and West, towards a fusion that is described as a "third civilization".

In rhetoric reminiscent of Nipponzan Myohoji's Occidentalism, Soka Gakkai argues that the tide of history has turned against Western materialism and toward Eastern, Buddhist spiritualism. However, this will result not in the victory of one over the other but rather in a fusion of the two, and historical circumstances have determined that Japan is to play a central role in that fusion.

> At the present time, when the tragic contradictions and distortions of the Western materialistic emphasis have begun to appear, the course of history has focused on the importance of Eastern Buddhism ... It is clear that the unstoppable tide of history calls for a civilization founded on humanity's awakening to a higher dimension, transcending Western, rationalistic culture.... Here, let me say a word or two about the fusion of Eastern and Western civilization and Japan's mission. Since the Meiji Period, Japan has chosen the path of Europeanization, and has taken on Western sensibilities. Oriental traditions have also come to rest in Japan, as if it were the final stop on a train line.... Japan is the only country that has suffered an atomic bombing. In addition, geographically it is located as a bridge between East and West, a favorable place to contribute to world peace.... As the meeting point of Western and Eastern civilization, Japan possesses the call and responsibility to take the leadership in building a new civilization.[37]

Conclusion

Post–Cold War realities, and in particular the so-called war on terrorism, have brought the issue of Japanese pacifism to the forefront. The current effort on the part of the government to modify Article 9 of the Constitution will further intensify the debate. It remains to be seen, however, what criteria will eventually be adopted to clarify when the use of force is necessary or justified. Individual moral cultivation as the key to establishing a peaceful society will find a great deal of resonance with current trends that emphasize personal development and spirituality over organized religion, although notions of cultural superiority or national mission will remain problematic.

Notes

1. In a recent survey only 15 per cent said that in the event of war they would fight for their country, as opposed to 48 per cent who responded that they would not fight in any event and 26 per cent who said that it would depend on the circumstances. The survey was conducted in 2001, and a report on the results can be found in Robert Kisala, Nagai Mikiko and Yamada Mamoru (eds), *Shinrai shakai no yukue* [The Future of a Society Based on Trust]. Tokyo: Harvest-sha, 2007.

2. Robert Kisala, *Prophets of Peace: Pacifism and Cultural Identity in Japan's New Religions*. Honolulu: University of Hawaii Press, 1999.

3. For a discussion of this issue, see Robert Kisala, "Japanese Religions", in *Nanzan Guide to Japanese Religions*. Honolulu: University of Hawaii Press, 2006, pp. 3–13.

4. Figures regarding religious affiliation in Japan are notoriously unreliable. Almost every Japanese is nominally a member of one of the major Buddhist sects. Additionally, the entire population are automatically counted as parishioners of the local Shinto Shrine, resulting in a total religious membership of well over 200 million, nearly double the population of the country. Ministry of Education, *Shukyo Nenkan* [Religions Yearbook]. Tokyo: Ministry of Education, 1996.

   Membership figures for new religious groups are likewise based on the self-reporting of the groups, and wildly varying criteria for membership often lead to clearly inflated results. On the other hand, there is little dispute that several groups counted among the new religious movements can rightly claim a membership in the millions, so a total figure of 15 per cent of the population would not be unreasonable. In terms of people who identify themselves as belonging to a particular religion, total religious membership has remained at about 30 per cent throughout the postwar period, as measured in several independent social surveys – see, for example, Nihonjin no kokuminsei chosa Tokei Suri Kenkyujo Kokuminsei Chosa Iinkai (ed.), *Nihonjin no kokuminsei* [National Characteristics of the Japanese]. Tokyo: Idemitsu Shoten, 1991; and Nihonjin no shukyo ishiki chosa NHK Yoron Chosabu (ed.), *Nihonjin no shukyo ishiki* [Religious Awareness of the Japanese]. Tokyo: Nippon Hoso Shuppan Kyokai, 1984. Ishii Kenji provides a useful summary of postwar survey results: Ishii Kenji, *Gendai nihonjin no shukyo ishiki* [Religious Awareness in Contemporary Japan]. Tokyo: Shin'yosha, 1997.

5. In reference to the *Daijo Taishu Jizo Jurinkyo*, quoted in Nakamura Hajime, *Shukyo to shakai rinri* [Religion and Social Ethics]. Tokyo: Iwanami Shoten, 1959, p. 351.

6. Ibid., pp. 388–389.

7. Ibid., pp. 384–386.

8. Nitobe Inazo, *Bushido: The Soul of Japan*. Tokyo: Charles E. Tuttle Company, 1969.

9. William Farris, for example, argues against facile comparisons with the emergence of feudalism in Europe, precisely because "warriors acted more like mercenaries than vassals, repeatedly betraying their lords and switching their loyalties to the winning side". William Wayne Farris, *Heavenly Warriors: The Evolution of Japan's Military, 500–1300*. Cambridge, MA: Harvard University Press, 1992, p. 312.

10. Herman Ooms, *Tokugawa Ideology: Early Constructs, 1570–1680*. Princeton, NJ: Princeton University Press, 1985.

11. Yasumaru Yoshio, *Nihon no kindaika to minshu shiso* [Japanese Modernization and Popular Thought]. Tokyo: Aoki Shoten, 1974.

12. Satomi Kishio, *Kokutai Shisoshi* [A History of the Concept of National Polity]. Tokyo: Hentensha, 1992.

13. Ibid., pp. 217–219, 282–291.

14. Nakura Tetsuzo, "Hideyoshi no Chosen Shinryaku to Shinkoku" [Hideyoshi's Invasion of Korea and the Land of the Gods]. *Rekishi Hyoron*, 314, 1976.

15. For a translation of the *New Theses*, see Bob Tadashi Wakabayashi, *Anti-Foreignism and Western Learning in Early-Modern Japan: The New Theses of 1825*. Cambridge, MA: Harvard University Press, 1986.

16. Carol Gluck, *Japan's Modern Myths: Ideology in the Late Meiji Period*. Princeton, NJ: Princeton University Press, 1985, pp. 120–127.

17. Uchimura Kanzo, *Uchimura kanzo zenshu* [Complete Works of Uchimura Kanzo]. Tokyo: Iwanami Shoten, vol. 3, 1981, p. 39.

18. Ibid., vol. 11, p. 296.

19. Ibid., vol. 12, p. 425.
20. Fujii Nichidatsu, *Kill Not Life: Fusessho*, trans. Yumiko Miyazaki. Leverett, MA: Nipponzan Myohoji New England Sangha, 1985, p. 15. In this quote from Fujii's sermon I use the translation prepared by Nipponzan Myohoji.
21. Fujii Nichidatsu, *Buddhism for World Peace: Words of Nichidatsu Fujii*, trans. Yumiko Miyazaki. Tokyo: Japan-Bharat Sarvodaya Mitrata Sangha, 1980, p. 176.
22. Ikeda Daisaku, *Proposals on Peace and Disarmament: Toward the 21st Century*. Tokyo: Sōka Gakkai International, 1991, p. 66.
23. Ibid., p. 66.
24. Ibid., p. 132.
25. Ibid., p. 9.
26. Ibid., p. 132.
27. Ibid., p. 129.
28. Niwano Nikkyo, *Heiwa he no michi* [The Road to Peace]. Tokyo: Kosei Shuppansha, 1972, pp. 76–77.
29. This collection was published in three volumes as *Idei Seitaro Kunwashu* [*The Collected Moral Lectures of Idei Seitaro*] by Shuyodan Hoseikai between 1980 and 1982. *Idei Seitaro kunwashu*, vols 1–3. Tokyo: Shuyodan Hoseikai, 1980–1982.
30. "Shuyodan Hoseikai Koryo" [The Essential Points of Shuyodan Hoseikai's Teaching], reproduced in the members' handbook.
31. Fujii Kenji, *Seikatsu kiritsu to rinrikan* [Rules of Daily Life and Ethical View], in *Shinshukyo jiten* [New Religions Dictionary]. Tokyo: Kobundo, 1990, pp. 236–251.
32. Shuyodan Hoseikai Misesu no Tsudoi, *Mujoken jikko* [Unconditional Practice]. Tokyo: Shuyodan Hoseikai Misesu no Tsudoi, 1980, p. 306.
33. Fujii's letter, written in Japanese, was translated into English before being delivered to Gandhi by one of Fujii's disciples. However, I have been able to find only a copy of the Japanese original, reproduced in *Byakuju*, a collection of Fujii's sermons published in 1983. Fujii Nichidatsu, *Byakuju* [The Collected Sermons of the Reverend Fujii Nichidatsu]. Tokyo: Nipponzan Myohoji, 1983, pp. 74–83.
34. Fujii Nichidatsu, *My Non-Violence: An Autobiography of a Japanese Buddhist*, trans. Yamaori Tutsuo. Tokyo: Japan Buddha Sangha Press, 1975, p. 91.
35. Ibid., p. 118.
36. Fujii Nichidatsu, *Tenku* [The Sermons of Fujii Nichidatsu]. Tokyo: Nipponzan Myohoji, 1992, pp. 22–25.
37. Harashima Takeshi, *Soka Gakkai*. Tokyo: Seiki Shoten, 1969, pp. 88–89.

5

Norms of war in Judaism

Jack Bemporad

The discipline of ethics is concerned with applying norms to behaviour, so, when the capacity to act destructively in war rises exponentially or we encounter war-like and war situations that have little or no precedent, one can only enquire whether past discussion of war in the major religious traditions still has relevance today.

War in the contemporary world raises a number of ethical questions that cry out for discussion and resolution. These questions arise from nation-states' expanded power, which allows them to inflict lethal damage on adversaries. In nuclear war this damage may extend to the whole world – to all sentient life. Today, weapons of mass destruction (atomic, biological and chemical weapons) threaten civilian populations, and terrorist attacks concentrate on inflicting fear and terror on civilians. Modern warfare also seems to blur certain fundamental distinctions that have traditionally been recognized – the most significant of which is the distinction between combatants and non-combatants – through acts such as the saturation bombing of German cities and Tokyo; the atomic bombing of Nagasaki and Hiroshima; Germany's forced labour in conquered territories, and the killing of millions of civilians in death camps. If one were to chart the percentage of combatants killed as opposed to non-combatants it would be apparent that the trend in warfare is toward more noncombatant than combatant casualties.

Today, the very distinction between a state of war and one of peace has been blurred. Whereas the Cold War involved vast spheres of influence pitted against each other that could quickly turn the fragile peace

World religions and norms of war, Popovski, Reichberg and Turner (eds),
United Nations University Press, 2009, ISBN 978-92-808-1163-6

into seething war, the recent rise of terrorism and its continuing threat have created a twilight zone where it becomes hard to distinguish between conditions of peace and war.

Although the killing of civilians was not uncommon in pre-modern war, especially religious wars, the basic premise of conventional war and the foundation of all just war theories is the separation of combatants from non-combatants. It is the moral lynchpin of what makes a war a just war: extreme care must be taken to ensure that those killed in battle are soldiers – those fighting the war and not people who are not directly engaged in battle. The Geneva Conventions and organizations such as Human Rights Watch make this the essential factor in determining human rights violations in warfare.

This has been complicated by the way weapons themselves have changed and how they are used. Suicide bombers are the most recent and most effective weapons in the increasingly predominant form of post-modern war – asymmetric war, war that concentrates on the killing of civilians. Suicide bombers in asymmetric war can be considered the equivalent of the most destructive weapon in conventional warfare because they turn conventional warfare and its rules and ethics on their head.

Just war traditions arose for two main reasons. First, it was believed that there would always be war. Secondly, it was believed that civilized nations and individuals must impose moral standards with respect to what is proper and improper behaviour in warfare.

The two alternatives to just war traditions – realpolitik and pacifism – ultimately abandon any ethic of war. Realpolitik claims that moral categories simply do not apply to war, whereas pacifism claims that, since the deliberate killing of innocent human beings is immoral and no individual can act so as to do what is immoral, war, which by definition involves such killing, must be entirely disallowed on moral grounds. Proponents of the necessity for the category of just war claim that both of these alternatives are indefensible, and that a third alternative, a just war tradition, is necessary.

Although the Jewish tradition does not operate with the just war categories of *jus ad bellum* and *jus in bello*, many aspects of the discussions in biblical and rabbinical sources parallel these considerations. One can roughly categorize certain statements as contributing to right reasons for going to war as well as for engaging in war.

What is significantly different between Judaism and just war theory is the biblical and later Jewish belief that war is *not* a natural condition and that universal peace will become reality. Both biblical and rabbinical sources stress this point; the texts and Jewish tradition are much more concerned with peace and its importance than they are with war.

The Bible

In reviewing biblical texts, we must always keep in mind that the Bible did not create the reality it describes. Judaism emerged out of a tribal society that had its own rules and practices with respect to war. These practices often led to annihilation and enslavement, as evidenced in the historical books of the Bible. From the numerous descriptions of such biblical wars one might come to the conclusion that the Hebrew Bible endorses such practices. However, what is important in reading the texts is to see how the biblical authors tried to distinguish themselves from those ambient values and practices and introduced new ideas and ideals that are foundational for our understanding of society and humanity.

The most significant text related to war and peace in the Bible is Deuteronomy 20. In this chapter a number of the issues concerning war in the Jewish tradition are present. These include God as the Warrior for the Israelites:

1: When you take the field against your enemies, and see horses and chariots – forces larger than yours – have no fear of them; for the LORD your God, who brought thee up out of the land of Egypt is with you.
2: Before you join battle, the priest shall come forward and address the troops,
3: He shall say unto them: "Hear, O Israel, you are about to join battle with your enemy; let not your courage falter. Do not be in fear or in panic, or in dread of them;
4: for it is the LORD your God marches with you to do battle for you against your enemy, to bring you victory."

In essence, this passage states that God is the warrior in Jewish battle. He alone is the executor of warfare. This is brought out in the verses that follow listing all those exempted from military service. The list is so extensive that it becomes seemingly impossible to mount an army to make war and reinforces the belief that it is God who fights for Israel and not man.[1]

5: Then the officials shall address the troops as follows: "Is there anyone who has built a new house but has not dedicated it? Let him go back to his home lest he die in battle and another dedicate it."
6: "Is there anyone who has planted a vineyard but never harvested it? Let him go back to his home lest he die in battle and another harvest it."
7: "Is there anyone who has paid a bride-price for a wife, but who has not yet married her? Let him go home lest he die and another marry her."
8: The officials shall go on addressing the troops and say, "Is there anyone afraid and disheartened? Let him go back to his home, lest the courage of his comrades flags like his."

Those who built new houses, farmers (those who planted vineyards), bridegrooms, and those who were afraid or emotionally susceptible to compassion during battle were all exempt from going to war. In the Bible it thus appears that the primary need is to provide continuity of life even during war. These verses are then followed by the command to sue for peace before beginning hostilities. Verse 10 reads: "When you approach a town to attack it, you shall offer it terms of peace." Deuteronomy 20 then ends with a caution against wanton destruction:

> 19: When in your war against a city you have to besiege it a long time in order to capture it, you must not destroy its trees, wielding the axe against them. You may eat of them, but you must not cut them down. Are the trees of the field human to withdraw before you into the besieged city?

Weinfeld describes Deuteronomy 20 as "orations of an idealizing character", and states that much of Deuteronomy, including Deuteronomy 20, is the product of speculative thoughts that do not derive from cultic reality.[2] Boecker writes that an essential feature of Deuteronomy is "the theologization of older legal prescriptions".[3] Although modern biblical scholars such as Millard C. Lind, Martin Buber, Moshe Greenberg and Gerhard von Rad disagree about how much has been correctly attributed to the past in biblical narratives, they all agree that war is something God wages on behalf of Israel, and that Israel is, in the main, a passive recipient of God's wondrous deeds. As described in Joshua 23:3–13, "A single man of you put a thousand of them to flight, for it is YHWH your God who has fought for you."

The concept that everyone goes to war was not characteristic of the period of the judges, and going to war with soldiers and mercenaries happens only when a monarchy is established. Until the time of Samuel, the establishment of a monarchy was not in the Jewish tradition, for the biblical definition of God and His Law makes God the ultimate ruler, the ultimate king.

The Samuel narrative is clear in its description of the evils of kingship where a human king usurps the rule of God. I Samuel 8:19–20 reads, "Where they [the people] said, 'No, we will have a king over us that we may also be like all the nations, that our king will govern us and go out before us and fight our battles'", and Ezekiel 20:32 elaborates on this same point, maintaining that being like other people entails idolatry. When the prophet says "What is in your mind shall never happen – the thought, 'Let us be like the nations, like the tribes of the countries, and worship wood and stone,'" he is connecting the Israelites' desire for a monarch to pagan kingship and the temptation for hubris and idolatry, and the idea that idolatry, defined as self-aggrandizement and the rejection of God's will, inevitably leads to war.

As the years passed, however, and the threat of attack by the neigh-bouring Philistine nation increased, the people called for the coronation of a king to represent them in the halls of rulers (Assyria, Egypt) and to lead them in battle should there be a need. This loss of faith in God as Warrior would lead to their ultimate downfall. Under duress, God sanctioned the establishment of a Jewish monarch.

It is important to understand what it is about the kingship of the surrounding peoples that made the biblical authors contrast it with the kingship of God. Tsevat states:

> The meaning of the kingship according to the Bible is the denial to man of the concentration and permanence of power. Power in society is God's; He is the only source of might, authority, command, and ownership of the land; He is the author of morals, law, and judgment; He guarantees freedom and a measure of equality; He is the leader of journeys in the desert and campaigns in the towns. By the eighth century [BCE] the consequences of the idea of divine kingship had been ever more ignored by the rulers of the people, and reality had come ever more into conflict with it. It was then that the great prophets rose to adjust the reality of their day to the standards of the idea.[4]

Buber explains that the kingship of God archetype was decisive for biblical history. Everything is viewed through a theological lens that establishes God as the ultimate king and His law as the ultimate law. It is His law that is to predominate over the idolatrous practices of the surrounding peoples. Indeed, the justification that the Bible gives for the destruction of the Canaanites is to avoid Israel's falling into idolatry and practising its most horrendous aspect – child sacrifice. And Samuel clearly states (Chapter 12) that the people have done evil in rejecting God as their king and insisting on a human ruler, because a human king's ways will enlist them in war and open them to idolatrous temptation.

Why is this so crucial? Because the problem with idolatrous nations is that their gods engage in the very same injustices as their followers, and the logical consequence of such idolatrous action is war. This is why, for example, only God could bring judgement on the gods of Egypt. God waged war on Pharaoh, who was the embodiment of the worst elements of self-deification and pride (Exodus 12:12).

From the perspective of Psalm 82:6–7, it appears that the failure of the pagan gods was their intrinsic injustice and that the rule of the One God was needed to establish righteousness and justice in the world. War was seen as a horrendous evil most likely to occur when human rulers took on absolute unrestricted power. Knowing the devastation of war, the literary prophets (those who have books named for them) give us the vision of universal peace. Micah 4 repeats Isaiah's words (2:4): "And they shall beat their swords into ploughshares and their spears into pruning hooks; Nation shall not take up sword against nation; they shall never again know war." This is reaffirmed in Hosea 2:18–20, where the prophet quotes God: "And I will make for you a covenant on that day with the beasts of the field, the birds of the air and the creeping things of the ground; and I will abolish the bow and sword from the land and make you lie down in safety."

God also advises his people not to trust their weapons or alliances. Hosea 14:3 states it plainly: "Assyria will not save us, we will not ride upon horses; and we will say no more, 'Our God' to the work of our hands." God's rule will bring about a reign of peace: "In that day, Israel shall be a third partner with Egypt and Assyria as a blessing on earth, for the Lord will bless them, saying, 'Blessed be my people Egypt, my handi-work Assyria and my own people Israel.'" (Isaiah 19:25).

In light of the Hebrew Bible's emphasis on peace, why then does Deu-teronomy 20:16ff. contain an injunction to destroy the seven idolatrous nations?

> In the towns of the latter peoples, however, which the Lord your God is giving you as a heritage, you shall not let a soul remain alive ... lest they lead you into doing all the abhorrent things that they have done for their gods and you stand guilty before the Lord your God.

Many biblical texts illustrate that monotheism was superimposed on tribal practices that constituted the biblical environment and that, despite the passages that indicate the total murder of the Canaanites, historically that was not the case. Later biblical texts make it very clear that there was no genocide and the idolatrous tribes targeted for genocide conti-nued to exist after Joshua's war of conquest and later wars waged by the Israelite kings. Evidence is present in the first chapter of Judges and nu-merous other places, as checking a concordance clearly shows.[5]

It is therefore possible that even during biblical times the assertion of the murder of the Canaanites was a projection to the distant past, with the purpose of justifying the principle that all the Israelites at the time of the compilation of Deuteronomy and the Torah were descendants of those who had been present at Sinai with Moses. Furthermore, the Torah does not insist on perpetual holy war against the Philistines, the Phoeni-cians or other peoples in the immediate orbit of the Israelites – i.e. you were not to marry Moabites, etc., but you were also ordered not to de-stroy them. Witness the Book of Ruth; Ruth the Moabite even becomes the maternal ancestor of the Jewish Messiah.[6]

In the Bible, war is seen as an aberration and peace for all of human-kind is the ideal. As such, Israel has no special status and is judged by the same standards set for all others. If it does not reject the idolatrous practices of the Canaanites and if it does not abide by the covenant, it will suffer the same fate as other nations. This is illustrated when the prophet Amos states in 3:2, "You only have I known. Therefore I will punish you for all your iniquities", and in Hosea 13:9–11: "I will destroy you, O Israel, who can help you? Where now is your king, to save you? Where are all your princes, to defend you – those of whom you said, 'Give me a King and princes'? I have given you kings in my anger, and I have taken them away in my wrath."

This is because a Jewish sovereign, unlike pagan sovereigns, is bound by the Torah, the law of the One God. The laws of Deuteronomy 17:14–20 state:

[I]f after you have entered the land that the Lord your God has assigned you and taken possession of it and settled in it, you decide, "I will set a king over me as to all the nations about me", you shall be free to set a king over yourself, one of your own people; you must not set a foreigner over you, one who is not your kinsman. Moreover, he shall not keep many horses, or send people back to Egypt to add to his horses, since the Lord has warned you, "You may not go back that way again." And he shall not have many wives, lest his heart go astray; nor shall he amass silver and gold to excess. When he is seated on his royal throne, he shall have a copy of this teaching written for him on a scroll by the Levitical priests. Let it remain with him and let him read it all his life, so that he may learn to revere the Lord his God. To observe faithfully every word of this Teaching as well as these laws and not act haughtily toward his fellows or deviate from the Instruction to the right or to the left to the end that and his descendants will reign long in the midst of Israel.

Pagan rulers were not required to adhere to any moral or ethical codes that in any way resembled those in the Torah. For them, war was inevitable since the purpose of kingship is conquest. For the Israelites, according to the Torah, war was to be avoided. Israelite kings needed to be accountable to God. In rabbinic interpretation other elements were added – the Sanhedrin acted as the people's representatives and weighed in to maintain the system of checks and balances – to prevent any political or religious entity from running amok with power.[7]

Ravitzky summarizes the rabbinical belief that peace was the ultimate purpose of the Torah, quoting as his proof texts Tanhuma Shoftim 18 ("All that is written in the Torah was written for the sake of peace") and Bamidbar Rabah Naso 11, which says: "The prophets have planted in the mouth of all people naught so much as peace" and "God announceth to Jerusalem that they [Israel] will be redeemed only through peace."[8]

The rabbis and war

In order to gain a better understanding of the Talmudic and rabbinical discussions of war, it must first be noted that the two-fold law – the notion of a written and an oral tradition, the Mishnah and the Talmuds, – was codified after the destruction of the Temple and the devastation of Jerusalem by Rome, when the rabbis, in the course of transferring religious authority to themselves, had experienced the war and therefore had a horror of war. Solomon writes that, by the time the Mishnah and the Talmuds were compiled, the Jews had lost their political independence, and the legislation based on Deuteronomy 20 is a historical reconstruction of Messianic speculation, not operational law.[9]

The rabbis' thoughts and discussions were primarily directed to peace. "Sayings of the Fathers", a late tractate in the Mishnah, repeatedly discusses peace and its significance, and Leviticus Rabbah 9:9 contains a dictum of the rabbis on peace.

"And Grant you peace" – R. [Rabbi] Mani D'Sha'av and R. Yehoshua D'Sichnin in the name of R. Levi. Great is peace since all blessings, goodnesses and comfortings that the Holy One, Blessed Be He, brings upon Israel conclude with peace … Great is peace, for of all the commandments it is written … In relation to peace, "seek peace, and pursue it" – seek it in your own place, and pursue it even to another place as well.

The rabbis, who had religious authority but no sovereignty, did everything in their hermeneutic power to make the waging of war impossible. A parallel can be seen in their treatment of capital punishment – a sentence that is virtually impossible to carry out because the legal conditions can be met only in extraordinary circumstances.

The rabbis defined different kinds of war, using the rules of war in the Hebrew Bible as proof texts to create conditions that could never be met. These definitions of war, the exemptions and conditions are found in many rabbinical works that have been analysed and interpreted through the centuries.[10] Whereas many of the discussions in the rabbinical tractates deal with day-to-day existence, even down to the banalities of life, when it comes to the subject of war, all rabbinical discussion in the Talmud and the literature until the twentieth century is purely theoretical. We know this because the rabbis never published a tractate named "War".

The tractates of the Talmud are encompassing and contain a multitude of tangential materials on a multitude of subjects. Because of that, there are difficulties sorting out specific Halachot (rabbinic laws). Therefore Maimonides (1138–1204), trying to create some order out of the Talmud, wrote the Mishneh Torah, a codex that evolved into a premier reference for contemporary traditional Judaism and Jewish thought. Yet even he did not manage to present everything about war in one book or code – statements about war are scattered throughout his works.

Without a specific rabbinical code on how or why to fight a war, many issues are open to question. Nowhere are there detailed and minute discussions on war that compare to the tractates "Nashim" (women) or "Tohoroth" (purity and cleanliness). Instead, a variety of rabbinical writings and biblical texts are used for extrapolation. The discussion in both the Talmud and subsequent rabbinical writings is based on Mishnah "Sotah", Chapter 8, a tractate dealing with suspected adulteresses, not war. War is discussed there because it is part of a discussion on what laws need to be explained in Hebrew, the Holy Tongue (*Lashon Kodesh*), instead of the vernacular. In any event, the discussion there returns to the concept of God as Warrior for his people. The statement in Sotah 8 reads in part:

> "Let not your heart be faint at the neighing of the horses and the flashing of the swords; fear not at the clashing of shields and the rushing of the tramping shoes; nor tremble at the sound of the trumpets, neither be ye affrighted at the sound of the shouting; for the Lord your God is he that goeth with you. They come in the strength of flesh and blood, but ye come in the strength of the Almighty" reinforces the notion of war being fought by God on behalf of his people, who remain passive while He fights for them. The High Priest's battle cry, after all, is "Hear Oh Israel, Adonai is your God, Adonai is One."[11]

In declaring the One God, by praying, even twice a day, you will be delivered from the hand of the enemy. The Babylonian Talmud, in Sotah 42a, expands this:

> And [he, the high priest] shall say unto them, "Hear, O Israel." Why must he just [open with the words] "Hear, O Israel?" – R. Johanan said in the name of R. Simeon b. Yohai: The Holy One, blessed be He, said to Israel, Even if you only fulfilled morning and evening the commandment to recite the Shema' [ed. this also opens with "Hear, O Israel"], you will not be delivered into [the enemy's] hand.

> "Let not your heart faint; fear not" etc. Our Rabbis taught: He addresses them twice: once on the boundary [before marching into the enemy's territory] and once on the battle-field.

Sotah 8 describes two kinds of war: (1) obligatory war (*Milchemet Mitzvah*; also called in some instances *Milchemet Chova* – Hebrew for obligation), and (2) discretionary war (*Milchemet Reshut*). Wars of obligation are physical wars fought for the conquest of Canaan or fought in self-defence. Wars of free will (discretionary wars) are wars for the glory of the king and for the purposes of expansion.

Reading carefully one notices that, following Deuteronomy 20, the Mishnah in Sotah 8:2–7 exempts just about everyone from fighting in a discretionary war. In a later discussion in the Babylonian Talmud (500 CE), Sotah 42b–44b, these categories of exemption are expanded even further. This can be interpreted to mean that the wars the Mishnah considers – in addition to, or instead of, physical wars – were wars of persuasion for the Unity of the One God against idolatry. Rabbi Jose describes as exempt those who are afraid owing to the fact that they have sinned, and he makes that point a number of times. Are the sinners afraid they will die? Or are they afraid that they are not learned enough to persuade idolaters to believe in the One God? If they are not strong enough mentally to persuade, then they too are exempt from going to war,[12] for the rabbis were adamantly against wars of conversion.

In order for discretionary war to be declared they needed the existence of a Jewish sovereign state, a sovereign, the High Priest and his vestments (the Sanhedrin of 71 and the Urim and Thummim – the High Priest's oracle). The oracle of the Urim and Thummim, housed in the High Priest's breastplate, was of particular importance. Without it, war could not be declared. According to Kimelman, discretionary war requires the involvement of the Sanhedrin for its role as the legal embodiment of popular sovereignty, "understanding this to imply that the high court was the legal equivalent of 'the community of Israel as a whole'".[13]

Most rabbis maintain that to declare any war, obligatory or discretionary, *even in self-defence*, there needed to be a sovereign state for the Israelites, and in discretionary wars the High Priest is needed to declare war using the oracle, the Urim and Thummim. Rabbi Bleich takes this literally: "In the context of a discussion about discretionary war, the Gemarah Berachot 3B and Sanhedrin 16a declare that the king may not undertake military action other than upon the approval of the Urim ve [and] Thummim."[14]

Yet Josephus noted in Antiochus 3:218 that the oracle had not been used for at least 200 years. Ezra 2:63 and Nehemia 7:65 stated that those who returned from the first exile were disqualified from becoming priests and would not be able to "eat of the most holy things until a priest with Urim and Thummim should appear". In other words, to use the expression that the Urim and Thummim were required to deal with an issue really meant that discretionary war was inoperative. The Talmud notes that the oracle had not been used since the death of the pre-exilic prophets. So. when the rabbis say that you cannot declare a war without an Urim and Thummim, they mean any war.[15]

In continuity with the teaching of the Bible, the rabbinical literature, above all, demands the prerequisite to seek peace. As stated in Mishnah Shabbat 6:4:

> A man may not go out [on the Sabbath] with a sword or a bow or a shield or a club or a spear; and if he went out [with the like of these] he is liable to a sin-offering. R. Eliezer says these are his adornments. But the Sages say: They are naught save a reproach, for it is written, *And they shall beat their swords into plowshares and their spears into pruning-hooks/nation shall not lift up sword against nation, nor learn war anymore* [Isaiah 2:4].

In point of fact, no Jewish leaders encoding the law after the destruction of the temples and the exile dreamed that the issue of real war, defensive or otherwise, would come up. Their goal, perhaps for the safety of a people who were now dispersed among the nations, was to make peace paramount.

In consonance with this concept, Norman Solomon enumerates three ways in which the rabbis toned down Deuteronomy 20 so that it would not become a warrant for genocide. The rabbis concluded, "against the plain sense", that offers of peace were to be made to the enemy even as a siege was being laid. The Babylonian Talmud (Yoma 22b) and also Midrash Rabba (on Deuteronomy 5:12) describe Moses taking the initiative to seek peace with Sihon, a move confirmed and praised by God.[16]

Midrash Tehillim on Psalm 120:7 ascribes a similar initiative to the Messiah. The rabbis also ruled that, in wars other than those of the original conquest of Canaan, you must provide an escape route when you lay siege to a town (Rabbi Nathan, Sifre on Numbers 31:7). To reinforce how the genocidal implications of Deuteronomy 20 were very clearly viewed as inoperative by the rabbis, Solomon further proves this weakening of the injunction by quoting Joshua Ben Hananiah in Mishnah Yadayim, who noted that, since the time of Sennacherib, those nations had been dispersed and it was not possible to identify them, so that you could not kill them.[17] In a similar vein, Maimonides (in his chapter on "Kings" in the Mishneh Torah), referring explicitly to the injunction of Deuteronomy 20, reiterates that we do not know who the seven nations are, with the clear implication that for this very reason the injunction cannot apply.[18]

Everything we read about war in the Jewish tradition until the establishment of the Jewish settlements in Israel in the late nineteenth century is essentially theoretical, because the people of Israel had not been permitted or able to fight wars for almost two millennia. Elliot Dorff says that war is not oracular and that defensive war does not fall into either of the two categories of war as described in Deuteronomy 20 or in Sotah

8. Permission to conduct wars of self-defence is extrapolated from the criminal codes that state an individual is permitted to rise up and kill his attackers – *sheh ba aleichem* (those that are coming at you)[19] – before they get a chance to kill him. Dorff describes Rabbi Judah's discussion of what happens when foreigners besiege Israelite towns on the Sabbath, and asks whether or not one can bear arms to defend oneself. Not if these attackers come only to plunder, say the rabbis. But if they come to kill you, rise up and defend yourself, even if it is Shabbat – and if your town is on the border, you can defend yourself on Shabbat, even if they come only to plunder.[20]

Norman Solomon notes it is the duty of the sovereign state to protect its citizens from destruction: "A war of self-defence is designed to defend society as a whole or its most cherished values, for a crime within a society is subject to government control, whereas in war there is no overriding sovereign state to adjudicate conflicts." In other words, a nation has a right to protect itself from attack, but again, as Maimonides makes patently clear, the nation of Israel must, above all, pursue peace first, as referred to above.[21]

Maimonides is a rationalist in his discussions of war and peace. In the tractate "Kings", he reiterates that (i) violence is not a means of convincing anyone to change their religion, (ii) wars are really fought for ideological reasons, and (iii) peace is the ultimate goal. He reinforces the points already made in the Torah and the Talmud; one must sue for peace first [*jus ad bellum*], a siege must leave one side of the city open [*jus in bello*], and exemptions from service are made. In the Mishneh Torah tractate on Kings (6:1), Maimonides is concerned that nations that make peace with the Israelites accept the seven commandments of the sons of Noah and become "tributary to the king". Maimonides makes it very clear that the severity of these assertions is mitigated by noting that "before he [Joshua] entered the land, he said whoever wants to make peace should leave first", implying that the making of peace is the most important result [*jus post bellum*].[22]

Maimonides concludes his chapter on kings and war with a description of the Messiah and peace. The arrival of the Messiah is in different ways a universal dream of all the Abrahamic faiths – a dream we must all strive for as we live in the world God created for us. He writes that peace is the penultimate wish of the Jewish people. The goal that is yearned for is the end to all war and a reign of global prosperity and peace, where the lion shall lie down with the lamb and swords will be beaten into ploughshares – in other words, the true peace of Messianic times. Perhaps the most interesting part is what he says the Messiah will bring and how he will bring it. Jewish tradition is filled with stories of the coming of the Messiah – how he will arrive to the sound of the ram's horn; how he will be preceded by Elijah the prophet, with signs and wonders; and how all the Jews will be gathered on a flying carpet from the far-flung corners of the earth and brought to Zion. But what does Maimonides say?

> One should not entertain the notion that the King Messiah must work miracles and wonders, bring about new phenomena within the world, resurrect the dead, or perform other similar deeds. This is [definitely] not true ... He will then perfect the entire world, [motivating all the nations] to serve God together, as it is written [Zephaniah, 3:9], "I will make the peoples pure of speech so that they will all call upon the Name of God and serve Him with one purpose." ... The world will continue according to its pattern. He will not come [in order] to declare the pure, impure, nor to declare the impure, pure; ... Rather, [he will come in order] to establish peace in the world ... In that [the Messianic] Era there will be neither famine nor war, neither envy nor competition, for good things will flow in abundance and all the delights will be as freely available as dust. The occupation of the entire world will be solely to know God.[23]

Modern Israel

Hitherto, all Judaic conceptualization of war was derivative and hypothetical, since there was no Jewish nation or Jewish military to actually engage in a war. With the creation of the State of Israel in 1948, however, engaging in war was no longer a subject solely for intellectual debate. Yaron made the point: "The moral question of waging war is not a new problem for states and peoples, *but it is new and revolutionary for the Jewish nation.*"[24] Therefore, whatever Jewish factors are to be involved in thinking about war, they must primarily be those of ethical Judaism, since there is no framework that applies Halachic principles to modern warfare or the wars engaged in by the state of Israel.

And this is the dilemma of the modern state of Israel. Forged in a tradition where peace was the Messianic ideal toward which the faithful strove, constantly at the mercy of a world that readily used them as scapegoats and that forced Jewish acquiescence on all issues as an existential survival tactic, the creation of a homeland suddenly confronted the Jewish people with problems never before experienced. "Throughout the many centuries of Diaspora life, Jews were not faced with the necessity to decide in matters of state. The fundamental question is therefore how the traditional ethical teachings of Judaism can guide Jews in deciding upon the new state problems."[25]

For millennia, Jews have been subjected to discrimination, persecution and, most recently with the rise of Nazism, extermination.

Walzer describes a realpolitik attitude toward war: "War is a world apart, where life itself is at stake, where human nature is reduced to its elemental forms, where self-interest and necessity prevail. Here men and women do what they must to save themselves and their communities, and morality and law have no place."[26] Despite this acknowledgement that war is cruel and destructive – and in reality devoid of morality – Walzer and others believe that rules and morality must be applied to war. Civilized humankind has sought to rationalize the behaviour of men going to war (*jus ad bellum*) and the behaviour of those in war (*jus in bello*). We would add the necessity of planning for peace (*jus post bellum*) – meaning that we must establish conditions that would preserve peace once the fighting stops.

Essentially, the fundamental construct for justifying war has been:

1. There exists an international society of independent states ...
2. This international society has a law that establishes the rights of its members – above all, the rights of territorial integrity and political sovereignty....
3. Any use of force or imminent threat of force by one state against the political sovereignty or territorial integrity of another constitutes aggression and is a criminal act....
4. Aggression justifies two kinds of violent response: a war of self-defence by the victim and a war of law enforcement by the victim and any other member of international society [against terrorist groups such as al-Qaeda, Hizbollah, and other non-sovereign entities that attack sovereign states]....
5. Nothing but aggression can justify war....
6. Once the aggressor state has been militarily repulsed, it can also be punished.[27]

Regardless of the conceptualizations concerning just war, a singular principle remains – that of self-defence. Rabbinic exegesis on the issue is derived from Exodus 22:1. "As the Talmud puts it, '[I]f someone comes to kill you, get up early in the morning to kill him first' (Berakhot 58a; Yoma 85b; Sanhedrin 72a). Because each individual has both the right and the obligation of self-defence, one might reasonably infer that the community does likewise."[28]

Richard Norman writes: "Self-defense, by the individual or the community, is justified as a defense of rights. The most fundamental rights of individuals are the right to life and the right to liberty. The collective analogues of these are the right to territorial integrity and the right to political sovereignty."[29] Other social critics concur: "The development of international law from Grotius onwards, and its institutionalization through the League of Nations and subsequently the United Nations, have established the position that the only permitted wars are defensive wars."[30] This is indeed codified by the United Nations in Article 51 of its Charter: "Nothing in the present Charter shall impair the inherent right of individual or collective self-defence if an armed attack occurs against a

Member of the United Nations."[31] Thus, essentially, "In international law, the doctrine of self-defence provides the state with a legal basis for actions taken in response to the illegal use of force by another state, in the absence of effective action by the international community."[32]

The Jewish people and the founding fathers of Israel and Zionism understood what it meant to be strangers in a strange land, and what it meant to be nationally homeless and unprotected. They knew what it felt like to be victims, and, with the creation of a sovereign Jewish nation, defensive war was, for the first time in millennia, a real issue. On the day of its birth Israel was already engaged in a defensive war for its survival – without benefit of the Sanhedrin or the Urim and Thummim. Obviously, ancient oracular formulas no longer pertained. Therefore, Zohar could claim:

> Facing the challenges of a renewed Jewish polity, we ought to steer clear of the moral pitfalls entailed by an oracular halakhic philosophy. If the halakhic tradition is to be a source of inspiration for political thought in contemporary Israel, it must be guided by the classical eschewal of heavenly voices in favor of reasoned deliberation. This by no means implies that the study of Torah ought to be abandoned in favor of pervasive Western norms. Rather, it requires that we avoid using the forms of halakhic discourse as a medium for promulgating mysterious decrees.[33]

Thus, based on an ethical system that incorporated the best of Western civilization coupled with traditional Jewish thought, the concept of purity of arms became the hallmark of the Israel Defense Forces (IDF). As Katznelson, one of the founders of modern Zionism announced in 1939, "[L]et our arms be pure. We are studying arms, bearing arms, we are facing up to those who attack us. But we do not want our weapons to be tainted with innocent blood."[34]

Purity of arms as defined by the IDF is this:

> The IDF servicemen and women will use their weapons and force only for the purpose of their mission, only to the necessary extent and will maintain their humanity even during combat. IDF soldiers will not use their weapons and force to harm human beings who are not combatants or prisoners of war, and will do all in their power to avoid causing harm to their lives, bodies, dignity and property.[35]

This ethic is rooted in both the Bible and Jewish tradition. As Israel's Chief Rabbi Shlomo Goren (1917–1994), who served in the IDF as a paratrooper and chief chaplain, reiterated: "Since we are enjoined to imitate the moral qualities of God, we too should not rejoice over the destruction of the enemies of Israel."[36]

Solomon describes the "purity of arms" concept as emerging back in the 1930s and lists the following rationales: the pan-denominational Jewish stress on the ethical and moral values of Judaism; taking the Jewish perspective on personal relationships and applying it to international relations; a search for approval and therefore political support from the rest of the world, combined with "the naïve belief that military restraint would attain these objectives". Solomon's discussion on the Jewish state traces the application of these ethical ideas in Jewish tradition to what eventually became the modus operandi of the IDF.[37]

In the late nineteenth century, a Zionist Orthodox rabbi, Zevi Hirsch Kalischer, suggested that the settlements protect themselves with militias when he witnessed the clash for independence among the nations being born in Europe. By the turn of the century, Vladimir Jabotinsky, a veteran of Jewish units in World War I, called for the creation of a Jewish Legion in Palestine as a guarantee against Arab attacks. This led to the formation of the Haganah in 1920 (which became the IDF).[38]

At the same time, the Chief Ashkenazic rabbi of Palestine prior to the establishment of Israel, Abraham Isaac Kook, and the Chazon Ish in Europe (Rabbi Avrohom Yeshaya Karelitz) called for the establishment of the Jewish state by peaceful means only (they both maintained that it must be peaceful because there was no Urim and Thummim and only purely defensive wars would be permitted). Their thinking led to the establishment of a religious peace movement. This was exemplified by Moshe Avigdor Amiel, who wrote in 1938: "Even if we knew for certain that we could bring about the Final Redemption [by killing Arabs] we should reject such a 'Redemption' with all our strength, and not be redeemed through blood."[39]

Kook's own son, Rabbi Tzvi Yehuda Kook, interpreted this principle differently, demanding that no land within the biblical boundaries of Israel be given up voluntarily once settled by Jews, though he did not advocate aggressive conquest. His followers became the settler movement, and until 1930 they were allowed to defend themselves only by using restraint (*havlagah*), even during the Arab riots in 1920, 1921, 1929 and 1936. In the 1930s, after massacres and murders set a pattern of terror by the indigenous population, a military policy was set that demanded minimum force in the attainment of military objectives and discrimination between combatants and non-combatants.[40]

However, such a stance has its consequences. "[T]o the extent that people have power, they have a responsibility to use it wisely and justly. Unfortunately, this moral stance does not get us very far."[41] What should one do when the conventional rules of war are rejected, when you have to cope with an aggressor whose norms are diametrically opposed to your own, who breaks the rules of engagement (the Geneva Conventions) and wages asymmetric war with an utter disregard for human life? As Hirsch-field notes:

> If only we could fight a war in a manner that targets with such precision that only the guilty are afflicted while the innocent are spared. But in war there is no way to maintain that kind of precision. We should be horrified by the horrors of war, but must not be so horrified at the horrors of war that we come to the conclusion that no war is worth fighting because some wars are, indeed, worth fighting. As *Genesis* 9 tells us, sometimes we must kill because murderers cannot be allowed to go unpunished.[42]

Proportionality

To preclude inordinate suffering, civilized society has determined that, when an aggression occurs, reciprocity is permitted but only within proportional levels.

> The principle of proportionality specifies the level of collateral harm to civilians that is acceptable in achieving a specific military objective. The legal formulation of proportionality is contained in Protocol 1 to the Geneva Conventions, which states that it is prohibited for soldiers to engage in any attack "which may be expected to cause incidental loss of civilian life, injury to civilians, damage to civilian objects, or a combination thereof which would be excessive in relation to the concrete and direct military advantage anticipated".[43]

However, military historian Sir John Keegan has stated, "'the experience of land war in two world wars must raise a question as to whether formal legal codification is necessarily superior to notions of custom, honour, professional standards, and natural law' in making for battlefield decencies.... There is no substitute for honour as a medium of enforcing decency on the battlefield, never has been and never will be."[44] But how can there be concerns for "honour" when present-day warfare does not recognize the term? As Solomon has stated:

> Standards can be adopted unilaterally or set by international agreement, but the moral dilemma arises of whether a party that ignores those standards can be allowed to gain ascendancy, by perpetrating evil, over the moral side complying with them.... Though the religious principles for engagement in and the conduct of war seem clear, their application in practice is hard to determine. The acute questions that arise in modern warfare tend to be about the assessment of particular situations.[45]

It has already been established that it is within Jewish law to fight back when attacked and to fight back to win, since all wars are essentially concerned with survival. For this reason, proportionality, though a consideration, must take into account not only the event at hand but contextual events as well. As IDF Major General Yaakov Amidror observed: "As a little country fighting terrorists, guerrilla organizations and other states, we cannot allow ourselves to react proportionally and that is a very important message to the people around us."[46]

Thus, as Walzer noted in referring to the war in Lebanon in 2006:

> A military response to the capture of the three Israeli soldiers wasn't, literally, necessary; in the past, Israel has negotiated instead of fighting and then exchanged prisoners. But, since Hamas and Hezbollah describe the captures as legitimate military operations – acts of war – they can hardly claim that further acts of war, in response, are illegitimate. The further acts have to be proportional, but Israel's goal is to prevent future raids, as well as to rescue the soldiers, so proportionality must be measured not only against what Hamas and Hezbollah have already done, but also against what they are (and what they say they are) trying to do.[47]

Asymmetric war

Asymmetric war has a single goal: the "erosion of popular support for the war within the society of the enemy".[48] The methodology of engagement is to demoralize the enemy to the point of creating personal and political dysfunction and disintegration of the enemy state. This involves using guerrilla warfare, human shields, mixing combatants with non-combatants – in short, any and all means to disrupt the tactical and ethical constructs of conventional military personnel and the populations that support them. Such tactics are morally reprehensible and in violation of all ethical standards. "Such sheltering among the civilian population (including sheltering by the use of human shields, voluntary or involuntary) for the purpose of rendering one's forces immune from attack is a violation of the laws of war."[49] Nevertheless, such tactics have proven enormously successful for those for whom there is no moral compunction against the killing of non-combatants. Given the "on-the-ground" factors, the question of ethical action vis-à-vis non-combatants becomes a dubious point.

> [T]here are few if any absolutes in the conduct of war. A document such as the 1949 Fourth Geneva Convention relative to the Protection of Civilian Persons in Time of War and the subsequent Protocols thereto may attempt to define categories of non-combatants, or may recommend that hospitals be situated as far as possible from military objectives (Article 18), but this is of little help where enemy combatants are targeting hospitals or deliberately siting their own military units in hospitals in order to use the sick as hostages.[50]

Though it is against "the law" to place non-combatants in jeopardy, those who engage in asymmetrical warfare do just that – for good reason. Whenever a conventional army kills human shields, it becomes a public relations nightmare for them and a positive factor for the "underdog" aggressor who placed the non-combatants in mortal peril in the first place. The media are incapable of distinguishing, or deliberately refuse to distinguish, between those who are justifiably attempting to destroy the enemy's weapons and command and control centres and those who deliberately use civilians as their main weapon – whether as shields on their side or as targets on the other. So the question becomes: how should the conventional forces of a "Jewish" state or any state be expected to defend themselves in such a war?

There is nothing in Jewish law or in the Geneva Conventions to answer this question. The primary directive is that life must be preserved, but how do you defend yourself in such circumstances? The answer is that appropriate responsibility must be assigned so that proselytizing through the media is removed as a weapon of asymmetric war. The responsibility for the fate of non-combatants must reside in the hands of the offending party that has placed them in their precarious position. What must be challenged are the outcries of propagandized media that accuse conventional armies and excuse the perpetrators of the original crimes, who claim they have no choice but to kill innocent non-combatants because it is the only way they can wage successful wars against their enemies.[51] In short, if the media become propagators of propaganda, as opposed to being impartial providers of fair and accurate perspectives on the fighting (in words and pictures), then perhaps it becomes necessary to treat the offending media as part of the combatant infrastructure and react accordingly. This is not to deny the media their reporting power, but it is a call to hold them responsible and culpable.

The warfare Israel faces today from its active enemies is a problem that all nations face. Rules of conventional warfare are not observed by groups that resort to terrorism; they are responsible only to their organizations, and are officially unrelated to sovereign states.

How can Israel protect its own sovereignty and its non-combatants, while minimizing the deaths of its enemies' non-combatants? The Israeli philosopher Asa Kasher tried to deal with this by creating a Code of Purity of Arms for the Israel Defense Forces. In a long and very legalistic rationale, he basically says that, in asymmetric warfare, when a nation is attacked by a non-sovereign element in someone else's backyard and then uses the local inhabitants as human shields (via persuasion or extortion), minimizing the deaths of non-combatants is a priority. However, a sovereign state's first priority is to its own non-combatants, not those of the enemy.[52]

The modern era's campaign of Jewish genocide also conditioned the mentality and psychology of how Israel wages its wars. Until the partisans in the ghettos and forests rebelled against the Nazis, it had been the Jewish practice to submit and suffer rather than contest those inflicting injury. The Holocaust convinced the Jews that, if their enemies say that they want to exterminate them and wipe them off the face of the Earth, it is usually not hyperbole. They believe it because the experience was real.

Nuclear warfare

Such is the concern for the priority of life in Judaic law that the use of weapons of mass destruction is clearly condemned.

> The World created by God was meant for life; it was given over to Man to rule, to preserve and cultivate, and not to destroy and mutilate. Man is committed to the construction of the world, and under no circumstances to its destruction. This founding principle is well established both in Halakhah and Aggadah ... The prophet Isaiah stresses this point clearly: The Creator of heaven Who alone is God, Who formed the earth and made it, Who alone established it, did not create it for a waste, but formed it for habitation. (Isaiah 45:18)

As Broyde indicates, Judaic law would sooner mandate surrender than the use of such weapons. But Jewish law is one thing and Israel's concern about self-preservation is another. The Israelis have resorted to nuclear weapons (though not officially) because they are afraid of total destruction and have developed them as a preventative. However, this has set a dangerous precedent, since Iran and Korea now follow similar policies.

> In a situation of Mutually Assured Destruction if weapons are used, it is clear that the Jewish tradition would prohibit the actual use of such weapons if such weapons were to cause the large scale destruction of human life on the earth as it currently exists. The Talmud explicitly prohibits the waging of war in a situation where the casualty rate exceeds a sixth of the population. Lord Jakobovits [the former Chief Rabbi of England], in an article written more than thirty years ago, summarized the Jewish law on this topic in his eloquent manner:

> In view of this vital limitation of the law of self-defense, it would appear that a defensive war likely to endanger the survival of the attacking and the defending nations alike, if not indeed the entire human race, can never be justified. On this assumption, then, that the choice posed by a threatened nuclear attack would be either complete destruction or surrender, only the second may be morally vindicated.[53]

As Walter Reich, the former director of the United States Holocaust Memorial Museum, indicates: "All countries have an obligation to minimize the loss of civilian life, both on their own side and on the other. But no country has an obligation to allow itself to be destroyed or its people killed. Demanding that of any country is a perversion not only of the ethics of war but also of the ethics of life."[54] This seems to be the rationale for the possible use of nuclear weapons.

Conclusion

We have seen that, in the Bible, any human king – unless he abides by God's law – will literally aggrandize himself, abuse his people, take them to war and lead them to idolatry, because this is what unbridled kingship entails. Such behaviour is the reason for the Torah's limitation on kings, so that the law is above the kings, and the concept of a just king is one who embodies God's virtues. The Messiah is the king who obeys God's will. We also know that Deuteronomy is sermonical and that, until modern times, nothing is found in Jewish teaching that is any way practical or functional as regards strategies or theories of war. There is simply nothing in the law codes or texts.

Experience was Israel's teacher. It was constantly invaded by Assyrians and Babylonians under Persian, Greek and Roman rule, and hundreds of thousands were killed and suffered greatly. Therefore, the rabbis had a horror of war and never had the authority to go to war. Instead, they interpreted stories about the leaders of Israel to make them students of the Torah.[55] However, upon close examination one finds that there is no applicable Halacha for war, so that when it comes to Israel, the modern Jewish state, there is a profound tension.

As a Jewish state, Israel cannot forsake the task of explaining its existence and behaviour in terms of Jewish tradition and heritage, and thereby in universal ethical categories. If Israel were a secular nation-state like other secular states, it would respond in terms of realpolitik, and ethics would apply secondarily – if at all – since all would be subsumed under the imperative of survival.

Israel's dilemma becomes acute when dealing with asymmetrical war. Because it is so complicated, the concepts of restraint and purity of arms (which are noble and correct and were developed in the 1930s by what later became the State of Israel) are continually under review. In modern warfare, especially asymmetric war, maintaining doctrines to safeguard enemy non-combatants is problematic owing to: atomic/biological/chemical weapons; long-range missiles; guerrilla warfare; and terrorism/suicide bombing. Each of these systems is directed at non-combatants.

So what can Israel do when its civilian population is especially vulnerable? Many Israelis are Holocaust survivors who witnessed something categorically different during World War II, when Jews, almost all of them non-combatants, were marked for total destruction. At that time, the world was presented with an ideology that targeted every single Jew for extinction, but no one believed it, while others were complicit in their murder. Yet such governmental policies were indeed implemented and not one government did much to stop it. As a result, the continuity of Jewish existence can no longer be taken for granted and Israel lives with a siege mentality that looms large in its foreign policy. The Jews did not believe what Hitler said, but now they believe threats from anyone – however remote the possibility of extinction might be.

Under these conditions, the great challenge is to preserve Israel's ethics when it comes to war and not to accept the realpolitik approach, although that approach admits that there is no such thing as a just war. This is true; war cannot be viewed as just. The problem with just war theory is that, as defined by Clausewitz, it is subject to the proper, fair and prim rules of the duel. These rules are inapplicable to modern warfare, as are those of the Geneva Conventions, which apply to "fair wars", as if they are possible. *At best, one must try to make war not unjust; war is an evil that is necessary to prevent a greater evil.*

We must also recognize that the problems we face in carrying out ethical acts are immensely magnified during warfare. In war, we act without knowledge of all the variables and without control over the unforeseen consequences of our actions – consequences that may prove irreversible. What we have learned is that we need to develop resources to establish conditions that make for peace. *Jus post bellum* must become the most important element of just war theory.

The real challenge for Israel, then, is to take a tradition rooted in peace that has no real foundation for any concept of war, except for scattered tangential material and the history of its ancient tribes, and come to a modus vivendi that it can use to defend itself and establish a Jewish concept for the use of force that is understandable and not heinous. Then one could discuss what the proper Jewish attitude toward the use of force in war should be.

The ethical burden becomes one of justification, because immoral consequences are certain. The risks of war today are higher than they have ever been for the reasons enumerated above and also because we are not dealing solely with sovereign states. War is so terrible that we need an overwhelming burden of proof from anyone who wages war, even in self-defence, that what they are doing is justified. This means war cannot be glorified and its true brutality must be understood.

We know enough about what has happened since World War II to see how wars are contrived and how leaders fool their people and even themselves into thinking they are fighting right, just and necessary wars, even when it simply is not the case. For war is too often exactly what the Bible says it is, the idolatrous actions of rulers. The media are manipulated by leaders and manipulate the public in turn – so what do the public really know? That is why we should be very suspicious of the reasons states offer for engaging in war and learn to distinguish between the reasons given for war and why governments actually engage in war.

Peace is the result of a lesson everyone has to learn and the State of Israel should be at the forefront of that effort. Israel and other nation-states must develop the resources and conditions to create peace. Peace is the reason the Bible was the first book to speak of the end of war and to insist that kings embody the virtue of peace. The rabbis overwhelmingly speak of seeking peace and pursuing peace; peace is the ultimate Jewish tradition and perhaps the most unattainable one – unless we all make it possible.

Appendix A: Sotah 8:2–7[56]

1. When the Anointed for the Battle speaks unto the people, he speaks in the Holy Language, for it is written[i] *And it shall be when ye draw nigh unto the battle, that the priest shall approach* (this is the priest anointed for the battle) *and shall speak unto the people* (in the Holy Language), *and shall say unto them, Hear, O Israel, ye draw nigh unto battle this day against your enemies* – and not against your brethren, not Judah against Simeon, and not Simeon against Benjamin, for if ye fall into their hands they will have mercy upon you, for it is written, *And the men which have been expressed by name rose up and took the captives and with the spoil clothed all that were naked among them, and arrayed them and shod them and gave them to eat and to drink and anointed them and carried all the feeble of them upon asses and brought them to Jericho, the city of palm trees, unto their brethren: then they returned to Samaria.*[ii] Against your enemies do ye go, therefore if ye fall into their hands they will not have mercy upon you. *Let not your heart be faint, fear not nor tremble, neither be ye affrighted ... Let not your heart be faint* at the neighing of the horses and the flashing of the swords; *fear not* at the clashing of shields and the rushing of the tramping shoes; *nor tremble* at the sound of the trumpets, *neither be ye affrighted* at the sound of the shouting; *for the Lord your God is he that goeth with you.* They come in the strength of flesh and blood, but ye come in the strength of the Almighty. The Philistines came in the strength of Goliath.[iii]

i. Deuteronomy 20:2 ff.
ii. 2 Chronicles 28:15.
iii. I Samuel 17:4.

What was his end? In the end he fell by the sword and they fell with him. The children of Ammon came in the strength of Shobach.[iv] What was his end? In the end he fell by the sword and they fell with him. But not so are *ye, for the Lord your God is he that goeth with you, to fight for you* ... This is the Camp of the Ark.

2. *And the officers shall speak unto the people, saying, What man is there that hath built a new house and hath not dedicated it, let him go and return to his house* ... It is all one whether he builds a house for straw, a house for cattle, a house for wood, or a house for stores; it is all one whether he builds or buys or inherits [a house] or whether it is given him as a gift. *And what man is there that hath planted a vineyard and hath not used the fruit thereof* ... It is all one whether he plants a vineyard or plants five fruit-trees, even if they are of five kinds. It is all one whether he plants vines or sinks them into the ground or grafts them; it is all one whether he buys a vineyard or inherits it or whether it is given him as a gift. *And what man is there that hath betrothed a wife* ... It is all one whether he betroths a virgin or a widow, or even one that awaits levirate marriage, or whether he hears that his brother has died in battle – let him return home. These all hearken to the words of the priest concerning the ordinances of battle; and they return home and provide water and food and repair the roads.

3. And these are they that may not return: he that builds a gate-house or portico or gallery, or plants but four fruit-trees, or five trees that do not bear fruit; or he that takes back his divorced wife; or[v] a High Priest that marries a widow, or a common priest that marries a woman that was divorced or that performed *halitzah*,[vi] *or* an Israelite that marries a bastard or a *Nethinah*, or a bastard or a *Nathin*[vii] that marries the daughter of an Israelite – these may not return. R. Judah says: He also that rebuilds his house as it was before may not return. R. Eliezer says: He also that builds a house of bricks in Sharon[viii] may not return.

4. And these are they that stir not from their place: he that built a house and dedicated it, he that planted a vineyard and used the fruits thereof, he that married his betrothed wife, or he that consummated his union with his deceased brother's wife, for it is written, *He shall be free for his house one year: for his house*[ix] – this applies to his house; *he shall be* – this is [to include also] his vineyard; *and shall cheer his wife* – this applies to his own wife; *whom he hath taken* – this is to include also his deceased brother's wife. These do not provide water and food and do not repair the roads.

iv. II Samuel 10:16.
v. Cf. Yeb. 2:4.
vi. App. I 12,
vii. App. I 29.
viii. Where bricks were unsubstantial and not suited for building houses.
ix. Deut. 24:5.

5. *And the officers shall speak further unto the people [and they shall say, What man is there that is fearful and fainthearted?]* R. Akiba says: *Fearful and fainthearted* is meant literally – he cannot endure the armies joined in battle or bear to see a drawn sword. R. Jose the Galilean says: *The fearful and fainthearted* is he that is afraid for the transgressions that he has committed; wherefore the Law has held his punishment in suspense [and included him] together with these others, so that he may return because of his transgressions. R. Jose says: If a widow is married to a High Priest, or a woman that was divorced or that had performed *halitzah* is married to a common priest, or a bastard or a *Nethinah* to an Israelite, or the daughter of an Israelite to a bastard or a *Nathfn* – such a one it is that is *fearful and fainthearted*.

6. *And it shall be when the officers have made an end of speaking unto the people that they shall appoint captains of hosts at the head of the people*, and at the rearward of the people; they stationed warriors in front of them and others behind them with axes of iron in their hands, and if any sought to turn back the warrior was empowered to break his legs, for with a beginning in flight comes defeat, as it is written, *Israel is fled before the Philistines, and there hath been also a great slaughter among the people.*[x] And there again it is written, *And the men of Israel fled from before the Philistines and fell down slain ...*[xi]

7. What has been said applies to a battle waged of free choice (Milchemet Reshut); but in a battle waged in a religious cause all go forth, even the bridegroom out of his chamber and the bride out of her bridechamber. R. Judah said: What has been said applies to a battle waged in a religious cause; but in a battle waged in duty bound all go forth, even the bridegroom out of his chamber and the bride out of her bridechamber.

Appendix B: Sotah 42b–44b[57]

Sotah 42b

"Hear the words of the war-regulations and return home."[i] What does he say to them on the battle-field? "Let not your heart faint; fear not, nor tremble, neither be ye affrighted." [These four expressions] correspond to the four means adopted by the nations of the world [to terrorise the enemy]: they crash [their shields], sound [trumpets], shout [battle-cries] and trample [with their horses].

---

x. I Samuel 4:17.
xi. I Samuel 31:1.
i. Viz., those who are qualified for exemption. V. ibid. 5ff.

Sotah 43a

WHAT MAN IS THERE THAT HATH BUILT A NEW HOUSE? etc. Our Rabbis taught: "That hath built" – I have here only the case where he built; whence is it [that the law applies also to a case where] he purchased, inherited or somebody gave it to him as a present? There is a text to state, What man is there that hath built a house.[ii] I have here only the case of a house; whence is it that it includes a barn for straw, a stable for cattle, a shed for wood and a storehouse? There is a text to state "that hath built" – i.e., whatever [structure be erected]. It is possible to imagine that I am also to include one who built a lodge, loggia or verandah; there is a text to state "a house" – as "house" implies a place suitable for habitation so every [building for which exemption may be claimed must be] suitable for habitation. R. Eliezer b. Jacob says: [The word] "house" [is to be interpreted] according to its usual definition; [and the fact that Scripture does not read] "and hath not dedicated" but and hath not dedicated it[iii] is to exclude a robber.[iv] Is this to say that [this teaching] is not in agreement with that of R. Jose the Galilean?[v] For if it agreed with R. Jose the Galilean, behold he has said: Fainthearted[vi] i.e., he who is afraid ...

Sotah 43b

... because of the transgressions he had committed![vii]

AND WHAT MAN IS THERE THAT HATH PLANTED A VINEYARD? etc. Our Rabbis taught: "That hath planted" – I have here only the case where he planted; whence is it [that the law applies also to a case where] he purchased, inherited or somebody gave it to him as a present? There is a text to state, And what man is there that hath planted a vineyard. I have here only the case of a vineyard; whence is it that it includes five fruit-trees and even of other kinds [of plantings]? There is a text to state "that hath planted". It is possible to think that I am also to include one who planted four fruit-trees or five trees which are not fruit-bearing; therefore there is a text to state "a vineyard". R. Eliezer says: [The word] "vineyard" [is to be interpreted] according to its usual definition; [and the fact that Scripture does not read] "one hath not used the fruit" but "and hath not used the fruit thereof["] is to exclude one who bends or grafts [the vine]. But we have the teaching: IT IS ALL ONE WHETHER HE PLANTED, BENT OR GRAFTED IT! – R. Zera said in

---

ii. This is understood as: whatever man built a new house, the present owner of it is exempt.
iii. The suffix is superfluous.
iv. A man who steals a new house is not exempt.
v. Who exempts a sinner; v. *supra* p. 222.
vi. Deut. XX, 8.
vii. Consequently a robber may return home.

the name of R. Hisda: There is no contradiction, the latter referring to a permitted grafting and the former to a prohibited grafting.[viii] What is an instance of this permitted grafting? If I say a young shoot on a young shoot, it follows that he ought to return home on account of [planting] the first young shoot! It must therefore be [grafting] a young shoot on an old stem. But R. Abbahu has said: If he grafted a young shoot on an old stem, the young shoot is annulled by the old stem and the law of *'orlah*[ix] does not apply to it! – R. Jeremiah said: It certainly refers to a young shoot on a young shoot, and [the case of a permitted grafting is where], e.g., he planted the first [stem] for a hedge or for timber; as we have learnt: He who plants for a hedge or for timber is exempt from the law of *'orlah*.[x]

What is the distinction that a young shoot is annulled [when grafted] on an old stem[xi] but not [when grafted] on a young shoot?[xii] – In the former case if he reconsiders his intention with regard to it, it is incapable of retraction;[xiii] but in the latter case if he reconsiders his intention with regard to it, it is capable of retraction[xiv] since it is then analogous to [plants which] grow of themselves;[xv] for we have learnt: When they grow of themselves they are liable to "*'orlah*." But let him explain [the Mishnah[xvi] as dealing with] the case of a vineyard belonging to two partners, where each returns home on account of his own [grafting]![xvii] – R. Papa declared: This is to say that in the case of a vineyard belonging to two partners, the war-regulations do not apply to it.[xviii] Why, then, is it different with five brothers, one of whom dies in battle,[xix] that they all return home? – In the latter illustration we apply the words "his wife" to

viii. Two different species.
ix. Lit., "circumcision", the Law of Lev. XIX, 23 forbidding the enjoyment of the fruit of a tree during the first three years of growth. Since this regulation does not apply to a young shoot grafted on an old stem, it is not regarded as a new planting.
x. And similarly he would not have to return on account of it.
xi. And its fruit is not subject to *'orlah*.
xii. [Since it has been stated that one returns on account of a young shoot grafted on to another which has been planted for timber.]
xiii. An old stem can never become young again, consequently the young shoot grafted to it becomes annulled.
xiv. The planter can change his mind within the first three years, and determine the purpose of the young shoot, originally grafted for timber, to be for fruit, so that it becomes itself subject to *'orlah*.
xv. And at the time of their plantation there was no definite purpose in the mind of the planter whether it was for fruit or timber.
xvi. Which rules that one returns on account of grafting
xvii. [Instead of the far-fetched circumstance where the first young shoot was planted for timber.]
xviii. Lit., "they do not return on account of it from the army". The partners do not have exemption for a new planting or grafting which belongs to them jointly, so that the Mishnah cannot deal with such a case.
xix. Leaving no offspring so that his wife is due to marry one of his brothers.

each one of them;[xx] but in the other we cannot apply the words "his vineyard" to each one of them.[xxi]

R. Nahman b. Isaac said: [The Mishnah deals with the] case where he grafted[xxii] a tree into vegetables, and this accords with the view of the teacher responsible for the following teaching: If one bends[xxiii] a tree into vegetables – Rabban Simeon b. Gamliel allows it in the name of R. Judah b. Gamda of Kefar Acco,[xxiv] but the Sages forbid it. When R. Dimi came [from Palestine to Babylon] he reported in the name of R. Johanan, Whose teaching is it?[xxv] It is that of R. Eliezer b. Jacob. Did not R. Eliezer b. Jacob declare above, The word "vineyard" [is to be interpreted] according to its usual definition? So here also "planted" [is to be interpreted] according to its usual definition; hence if he planted he does [return home], but if he bends or grafts he does not.[xxvi]

When R. Dimi came he reported that R. Johanan said in the name of R. Eliezer b. Jacob: A young shoot less than a handbreadth in height is liable for *'orlah* so long as it appears to be a year old;[xxvii] but this only applies where there are two plants with two other plants parallel to them and one in front.[xxviii] Should, however, the entire vineyard [consist of such shoots], then it is talked about.[xxix]

Sotah 44a

AND WHAT MAN IS THERE THAT HATH BETROTHED A WIFE? etc. Our Rabbis taught: "That hath betrothed" – it is all one whether he betrothed a virgin or a widow or a childless widow waiting for her brother-in-law; and even when there are five brothers, one of whom died in battle, they all return home.[xxx] [The fact that Scripture does not read] "and hath not taken" but "and hath not taken her" is to exclude a High Priest who married a widow, an ordinary priest who married a divorcee or a *Haluzah*, a lay Israelite who married an illegitimate or a Nethinah, or a daughter of an Israelite married to an illegitimate or a Nathin. Is this to say that [this teaching is] not in agreement with

---

   xx. Since it is not determined which one will marry her.
   xxi. Since it belongs to them jointly.
  xxii. [So Rashi. Rabina is answering the question in the Mishnah exempting one who grafts, cur. edd: "bent".]
 xxiii. [Tosef. Kil. I, has "grafts".]
 xxiv. [Being a permissible grafting it exempts the owner.]
  xxv. Viz., the statement above: is to exclude one who bends or grafts (the vine).
 xxvi. [Even in a permissible case of bending or grafting.]
xxvii. Because if he uses its fruit, it might seem to others that he was doing what was forbidden.
xxviii. Five plants so arranged are considered a vineyard, to which all agree that the law of *'orlah* applies, v. Ber. 35a.
 xxix. It is generally known that the vineyard has this peculiarity, and he may use the fruit.
  xxx. V. *supra* p. 214.

R. Jose the Galilean? For if it agreed with R. Jose the Galilean, behold he has said: "Fainthearted" i.e., he who is afraid because of the transgressions he had committed!xxxi – You may even say that it agrees with R. Jose the Galilean, and it is in accord with Rabbah; for Rabbah said: He is certainly not guilty until he has cohabited with her. For what is the reason [of the prohibition] shall he not take?xxxii So that he shall not profane [his seed].xxxiii Hence he does not receive the punishment of lashesxxxiv until he has cohabited with her.

Our Rabbis taught: [The order of the phrases is] "that hath built", "that hath planted", "that hath betrothed". The Torah has thus taught a rule of conduct: that a man should build a house, plant a vineyard and then marry a wife. Similarly declared Solomon in his wisdom, Prepare thy work without, and make it ready for thee in the field, and afterwards build thine housexxxv – "prepare thy work without", i.e., a dwelling place; "and make it ready for thee in the field", i.e., a vineyard; "and afterwards build thine house", i.e., a wife. Another interpretation is: "prepare thy work without", i.e., Scripture; "and make it ready for thee in the field", i.e., Mishnah; "and afterwards build thine house", i.e., Gemara. Another explanation is: "prepare thy work without", i.e., Scripture and Mishnah; "and make it ready for thee in the field", i.e., Gemara; "and afterwards build thine house", i.e., good deeds. R. Eliezer, son of R. Jose the Galilean says: "Prepare thy work without," i.e., Scripture: Mishnah and Gemara; "and make it ready for thee in the field," i.e., good deeds; "and afterwards build thine house["], i.e., make research [in the Torah] and receive the reward.

THE FOLLOWING DO NOT RETURN HOME: HE WHO BUILT A LODGE etc. A Tanna taught: If [when rebuilding the house] he adds a row [of fresh bricks] to it, he does return home.xxxvi

R. ELIEZER SAYS: ALSO HE WHO BUILT A BRICK-HOUSE IN SHARON DOES NOT RETURN HOME. A Tanna taught: [The reason is] because they have to renew it twice in a period of seven years.

THE FOLLOWING DO NOT MOVE FROM THEIR PLACE: HE WHO BUILT A NEW HOUSE AND DEDICATED IT etc. Our Rabbis taught: A new wifexxxvii – I have here only "a new wife"; whence is it [that the law applies also to] a widow and divorcee? There is a text to state "wife", i.e., in every case. Why, however, does the text state "a new wife?" [It means] one who is

---

xxxi. If that is so, the men who contracted an illegal marriage should return home.
xxxii. Lev. XXI, 14, referring to the women forbidden in marriage to a High Priest.
xxxiii. Ibid. 15.
xxxiv. And but for the verse "and hath not taken her", they would not be exempted where there was betrothal.
xxxv. Prov. XXIV, 27
xxxvi. It is then regarded as a new house.
xxxvii. Deuteronomy XXIV, 5.

new to him, thus excluding the case of a man who takes back his divorced wife, since she is not new to him.

Our Rabbis taught: He shall not go out in the host[xxxviii] – and it is possible to think that he does not go out in the host, but he supplies water and food and repairs the roads [for the army]; therefore there is a text to state, "Neither shall he be charged with any business." It is possible to think that I am also to include [among those who do not move from their place] the man who built a house but did not dedicate it, or planted a vineyard and did not use its fruit, or betrothed a wife but did not take her; therefore there is a text to state, "Neither shall he be charged" – but you may charge others.[xxxix] Since, however, it is written "Neither shall he be charged", what is the purpose of "He shall not go out in the host?"[xl] So that a transgression of the Law should involve two prohibitions.

Sotah 44b

GEMARA. What is the difference between R. Jose and R. Jose the Galilean?[xli] – The issue between them is the transgression of a Rabbinical ordinance.[xlii] With whom does the following teaching accord: He who speaks between [donning] one phylactery and the other[xliii] has committed a transgression and returns home under the war-regulations? With whom [does it accord]? With R. Jose the Galilean. Who is the Tanna of the following: Our Rabbis taught: If he heard the sound of trumpets and was terror-stricken, or the crash of shields and was terror-stricken, or [beheld] the brandishing of swords and the urine discharged itself upon his knees, he returns home? With whom [does it accord]? Are we to say that it is with R. Akiba and not R. Jose the Galilean?[xliv] – In such a circumstance even R. Jose the Galilean admits [that he returns home], because it is written: Lest his brethren's heart melt as his heart.[xlv]

AND IT SHALL BE, WHEN THE OFFICERS HAVE MADE AN END etc. The phrase, BECAUSE THE BEGINNING OF FLIGHT IS FALLING should be, "because falling is the beginning of flight"! Read [in the Mishnah]: Because falling is the beginning of flight.

xxxviii. Ibid.
  xxxix. E.g., who have built a house and not dedicated it or betrothed a woman and not taken her to wife.
     xl. The former surely includes the latter.
    xli. Since they agree in defining "fainthearted" as one afraid of his sins.
   xlii. R. Jose does not consider this sufficient to warrant exemption; therefore in the Mishnah he instances marriages forbidden by the Torah as the kind of transgression for which exemption may be claimed.
  xliii. Upon the arm and the forehead. It is forbidden to speak between the putting on of the two.
   xliv. Since the latter does not understand "fainthearted" as relating to physical fear.
    xlv. Deut. XX, 8.

Appendix C: "Warfare and Its Restrictions in Judaism"[58]

Intermediate wars such as preventive, anticipatory, or preemptive [ones] defy so neat a classification. Not only are the classifications debated in the Talmud, but commentators disagree on the categorization of the differing positions in the Talmud.

The major clash occurs between the eleventh century Franco-German scholar Rashi and the thirteenth century Franco-Provencal scholar Meiri. According to Rashi, the majority position considers preemptive action to be discretionary whereas the minority position expounded by Rabbi Judah considers it to be mandatory.

... National self-defense is as much a moral right as is personal self-preservation. Whereas it is clear that offensive war cannot be subsumed under the inalienable right of self-defense, the moral status of pre-emptive attacks is not as clear. Is the moral category of self-defense limited to an already launched attack? The majority talmudic position, according to Rashi, and that of Rabbi Judah, according to Meiri, would answer in the affirmative. Their position is seconded by Article 51 of the United Nations Charter, which states: "Nothing in the present Charter shall impair the inherent right of individual of [sic] collective self-defence if an armed attack occurs against a member."

The minority position of Rabbi Judah, according to Rashi, and the majority position, according to Meiri, however, hold that a preemptive strike against an enemy amassing for attack is close enough to a defensive counterattack to be categorized as mandatory. This position holds that to wait for an actual attack might so jeopardize national security as to make resistance impossible....

According to Meiri, a preemptive strike, against an enemy who it is feared might attack or who is already known to be preparing for war is deemed mandatory by the majority of the rabbis, but discretionary by Rabbi Judah. Accordingly, Rabbi Judah defines a counterattack as mandatory only in response to an already launched attack. A similar reading of Maimonides also limits the mandatory classification to a defensive war launched in response to an attack.

Further reading

Mitchell G. Bard, *Myths and Facts: QA Guide to the Arab-Israeli Conflict.* Chevy Chase, MD: America Israeli Cooperative Enterprise, 2001.

Geoffrey Best, *War and Law since 1945.* Oxford: Clarendon Press, 1997.

J. David Bleich, "Response to Noam Zohar", in Daniel H. Frank (ed.) *Commandment and Community: New Essays in Jewish Legal and Political Philosophy.* Albany, NY: SUNY Press, 1995.

Abraham J. Edelheit, *History of Zionism: A Handbook and Dictionary*. Boulder, CO: Westview Press, 2000.

David J. Forman, "Goodbye, 'Purity of Arms' – Goodbye, Morality", at ⟨http://www.rhr.israel.net/pencraft/goodbyepurityofarmsgoodbyemorality.shtml⟩ (accessed 7 October 2008).

Alan B. Gewirth, "The Moral Status of Israel", in Tomis Kapitan (ed.) *Philosophical Perspectives on the Israeli-Palestinian Conflict*. Armonk, NY: M. E. Sharpe, 1997.

Uriel Heilman, "The Ethics of War", *The Jewish Journal of Greater Los Angeles*, 17 October 2002, ⟨http://www.jewishjournal.com/home/preview.php?id=9441⟩.

John Kelsay, *Islam and War: A Study in Comparative Ethics*. Louisville, KY: Westminster/John Knox Press, 1993.

Daniel Landes, "A Vow of Death", in *Confronting Omnicide: Jewish Reflections on Weapons of Mass Destruction*. Northvale, NJ: Jason Aronson, 1991.

Hillel Neuer, "Human Bombs, Human Shields", *Daily Express*, 6 May 2002.

David Novak, *Covenantal Rights: A Study in Jewish Political Theory*. Princeton, NJ: Princeton University Press, 2000.

A. Roberts and R. Guelff, *Documents on the Laws of War*, 2nd edn. Oxford: Clarendon Press, 1989.

Martin Sicker, *Between Man and God: Issues in Judaic Thought*. Westport, CT: Greenwood Press, 2001.

Richard Sorabji, "Just War from Ancient Origins to the Conquistadors Debate and Its Modern Relevance", in Richard Sorabji and David Rodin (eds) *The Ethics of War: Shared Problems in Different Traditions*. Burlington, VT: Ashgate, 2006.

Daniel Statman, "Jus in Bello and the Intifada", in Tomis Kapitan (ed.) *Philosophical Perspectives on the Israeli-Palestinian Conflict*. Armonk, NY: M. E. Sharpe, 1997.

Shelby Steele, "Life and Death", *Wall Street Journal*, 22 August 2006, p. A12.

Jan Van Der Meulen and Joseph Soeters, "Considering Casualties: Risk and Loss during Peacekeeping and Warmaking", *Armed Forces & Society*, 31(4), 2005: 483–486.

Kenneth L. Vaux, *Ethics and the Gulf War: Religion, Rhetoric, and Righteousness*. Boulder, CO: Westview Press, 1992.

Notes

1. The term "holy war" itself never occurs in the Bible, but the basic concept is that it is God who conducts war, as clearly expressed in the book of Exodus, which refers to Yaweh as a "man of war". It is the Exodus narrative that is the biblical paradigm for the understanding of warfare. In his commentary on the book of Exodus, Umberto (Moshe David) Cassuto refers to it as a great epic that details the deeds of Yaweh as the source of freedom and the liberator of the people from Egyptian slavery. Millard Lind, who wrote *YWHW is a Man of War*, calls this the Exodus paradigm. The Septuagint (the Greek translation of the Jewish Scriptures 300–200 BCE), concerned with

anthropomorphism, translates the Lord as one who destroys war, and Onkelos, a nephew of the Roman emperor Titus, who converted to Judaism and wrote on the Bible, states the Lord is the victor over war.

2. Moshe Weinfeld, *Deuteronomy and the Deuteronomic School*. Winona Lake, IN: Eisenbraus, 1992, pp. 51–52.

3. Hans Jochen Boecker, *Law and the Administration of Justice in the Old Testament and the Ancient Near East*, translated by Jerry Mosier. Augsburg: Fortress, 1980, p. 183.

4. Matitiahu Tsevat, *The Meaning of the Book of Job and Other Biblical Studies*. New York: KTAV Publishing, 1980, p. 91.

5. Take, for example, the Hittites. They appear in Joshua, Judges, both books of Samuel, Kings, Chronicles, Ezra, Nechemia and Ezekiel, as do the other nations.

6. Personal communication with Robert Seltzer.

7. A Sanhedrin (Hebrew: יְרֹדהנס; Greek: συνέδριον, synedrion, "sitting together", hence "assembly" or "council") is an assembly of 23 judges biblically required in every city. The Great Sanhedrin is an assembly of 71 of the greatest Jewish judges, who constituted the supreme court and legislative body of ancient Israel. The Great Sanhedrin was made up of a chief justice (Nasi), a vice chief justice (Av Beit) and 69 general members, who all sat in the form of a semi-circle when in session. "The Sanhedrin" without qualifier normally refers to the Great Sanhedrin. When the Temple in Jerusalem was standing (prior to its destruction in 70 CE), the Great Sanhedrin would meet in the Hall of Hewn Stone in the Temple during the day, except before festivals and Shabbat.

8. Aviezer Ravitzky, "Shalom", posted 17 February 2007 on The Network of Spiritual Progressives; ⟨http://www.spiritualprogressives.org/article.php?story=20070218062058498⟩ (accessed 6 October 2008).

9. Norman Solomon, "The Ethics of War: Judaism", in Richard Sorabji and David Rodin (eds) *The Ethics of War: Shared Problems in Different Traditions*. Burlington, VT: Ashgate, 2006, pp. 108–110, p. 110.

10. See, for example, *The Babylonian Talmud*, London: Soncino, 1969. Tractate Sanhedrin, pages 16a–b (available at ⟨http://www.come-and-hear.com/talmud/index.html⟩, accessed 7 October 2008):

    WAR OF FREE CHOICE etc.

    Whence do we deduce this? – Said R. Abbahu: Scripture states, And he shall stand before Eleazar the Priest [who shall inquire for him by the judgment of the Urim before the Lord. At his word shall they go out and at his word they shall come in, both he and all the children of Israel with him even all the Congregation] {Num. XXVII, 21–22}. "He", refers to the King {Joshua, who had regal authority}; "And all the children of Israel with him," to the Priest anointed for the conduct of war {and whose call to war must be heeded by all Israelites}; and, "all the Congregation," means the Sanhedrin {V. p. 3, no. 4}. But perhaps it is the Sanhedrin whom the Divine Law instructs to inquire of the Urim and Tummim? {I.e., that none but the Sanhedrin (also the King and the Priest anointed for war) may enquire of the Urim and Tummim: but not because of any need to obtain their permission for the proclamation of war} – But [it may be deduced] from the story related by R. Aha b. Bizna in the name of R. Simeon the Pious: A harp hung over David's bed, and as soon as midnight arrived, a northerly wind blew upon its strings and caused it to play of its own accord. Immediately David arose and studied the Torah until the break of dawn. At the coming of dawn, the Sages of Israel entered into his presence and said unto him: "Our Sovereign King, thy people Israel need sustenance." "Go and support yourselves by mutual trading {lit., "one from another"}," David replied, "But," said they, "a handful does not satisfy the lion, nor can a pit be filled with its own clods" {a community cannot live on its own resources}. Whereupon David said to them: "Go and stretch forth your hands

with a troop [of soldiers] {invade foreign territory}." Immediately they held counsel
with Ahitophel and took advice from the Sanhedrin {hence the ruling in the Mishnah,
that the permission of the Sanhedrin was required for the proclamation of war} and
inquired of the Urim and Tumim. R. Joseph said: What passage [states this]?

– *And after Ahitophel was Benaiah the son of Jehoiada* {the Biblical version of the
verse is *Jehoiada the son of Benaiah.* Tosaf. Hananel and Aruk (art. [H] a.) base their
versions on this reading and comment accordingly. Rashi and this translation follow
the text of the printed editions of the Talmud which agree with II Sam. XX, 23,
and I Chron. XVIII, 17} *and Abiathar; and the Captain of the king's host was Joab*
{I Chron. XXVII, 34}. *"Ahitophel"* is the adviser, even as it is written, *And the coun-*
sel of Ahitophel which he counselled in those days, was as if a man inquired from
the word of God {II Sam. XVI, 23}. *"Benaiah the son of Jehoiada,"* refers to the
Sanhedrin, and *"Abiathar"* to the *Urim* and *Tummim.*

11. Herbert Danby, *The Mishnah.* Oxford: Oxford University Press, 1933, p. 302.
12. See Sotah 8:5.
13. Reuven Kimelman, "Warfare and Its Restrictions in Judaism", Brandeis University, at
    ⟨http://www.bc.edu/research/cjl/meta-elements/texts/current/forums/Isr-Hez/kimleman_
    war.htm⟩ (accessed 6 October 2008).
14. See Rabbi J. David Bleich, in *Tradition, Journal of Orthodox Jewish Thought*, 21(1),
    1983: 35, fn 9.
15. *Encyclopedia Judaica*, Vol. 16. Jerusalem: Keter, 1972, p. 8.
16. Solomon, "The Ethics of War: Judaism".
17. Ibid.
18. Moses Maimonides, "Kings", in *The Code of Maimonides.* New Haven, CT: Yale Uni-
    versity Press, 1949, pp. 220–224.
19. Elliot Dorff, "In Defense of Defense", *S'vara*, 2(1), 1991; excerpt available at
    ⟨http://www.myjewishlearning.com/ideas_belief/warpeace/War_TO_Combat/War_Types_
    Hartman/War_Defensive_Dorff.htm⟩ (accessed 6 October 2008).
20. Ibid.
21. Solomon, "The Ethics of War: Judaism", p. 112.
22. Maimonides, "Kings".
23. Ibid.
24. Zvi Yaron, "Religion and Morality in Israel and in the Dispersion", in Marvin Fox (ed.)
    Modern Jewish Ethics, Theory and Practice. Columbus, OH: Ohio State University
    Press, 1975, p. 237 (emphasis added).
25. Ibid., p. 237.
26. Michael Walzer, *Just and Unjust Wars: A Moral Argument with Historical Illustrations.*
    New York: Basic Books, 1992, p. 3.
27. Ibid., pp. 61–62.
28. Dorff, "In Defense of Defense".
29. Richard Norman, *Ethics, Killing & War.* Cambridge: Cambridge University Press, 1995,
    p. 133.
30. Norman Solomon, "Judaism and the Ethics of War", *International Review of the Red
    Cross*, 87(858), 2005: 302.
31. UN Charter, Chapter 7, at ⟨http://www.un.org/aboutun/charter/chapter7.htm⟩ (accessed
    7 October 2008).
32. John C. Bender, "Self-Defence and Cambodia: A Critical Appraisal", in Richard A.
    Falk (ed.) *The Vietnam War and International Law: The Widening Context*, Vol. 3.
    Princeton, NJ: Princeton University Press for the American Society of International
    Law, 1972, p. 139.
33. Noam J. Zohar, "Morality and War: A Critique of Bleich's Oracular Halakha", in

Daniel H. Frank (ed.) *Commandment and Community: New Essays in Jewish Legal and Political Philosophy*. Albany, NY: SUNY Press, 1995, p. 254.

34. Mira Schuarov, "Security Ethics and the Modern Military: The Case of the Israel Defence Forces", *Armed Forces & Society*, 31(4), 2005: 187.
35. Israel Defense Forces website, "Ethics", at ⟨http://dover.idf.il/IDF/English/about/doctrine/ethics.htm⟩ (accessed 7 October 2008).
36. Quoted in Solomon, "Judaism and the Ethics of War", p. 307.
37. Solomon, "The Ethics of War: Judaism", p. 124.
38. Ibid., pp. 122 ff.
39. Quoted in Solomon, "Judaism and the Ethics of War", pp. 305–306.
40. Solomon, "Judaism and the Ethics of War", p. 306.
41. Solomon, "The Ethics of War: Judaism", p. 127.
42. "War, Ethics and Values: An Interview with Brad Hirschfield", National Jewish Center for Learning and Leadership, available at ⟨http://www.clal.org/ss46.html⟩ (accessed 7 October 2008).
43. David Rodin, "The Ethics of Asymmetric War", in Richard Sorabji and David Rodin (eds) *The Ethics of War: Shared Problems in Different Traditions*. Burlington, VT: Ashgate, 2006, p. 162.
44. John Keegan (quoting Sir Adam Roberts), quoted in Kenneth Anderson, "Proportionality in jus in bello", Kenneth Anderson's Law of War and Just War Theory Blog, 2006; available at ⟨http://kennethandersonlawofwar.blogspot.com/2006/07/proportionality-in-jus-in-bello.html⟩ (accessed 7 October 2008).
45. Solomon, "Judaism and the Ethics of War", pp. 308–309.
46. Joshua Brilliant, "Gen. Amidror: Hizballah's Recovery Timetable", United Press International, 6 September 2006; cited at ⟨http://dailyalert.org/archive/2006-09/2006-09-08.html⟩ (accessed 23 October 2008).
47. Michael Walzer, "War Fair", *The New Republic*, 31 July 2006.
48. "The Changing Face of War", available at ⟨http://www.henciclopedia.org.uy/autores/Laguiadelmundo/GlobalWar.htm⟩ (accessed 7 October 2008).
49. Kenneth Anderson et al., "A Public Call for International Attention to Legal Obligations of Defending Forces as Well as Attacking Forces to Protect Civilians in Armed Conflict", 19 March 2003. Reproduced on Kenneth Anderson's Law of War and Just War Theory Blog, available at ⟨http://kennethandersonlawofwar.blogspot.com/2006/07/civilian-collateral-damage-and-law-of.html⟩ (accessed 7 October 2008).
50. Solomon, "Judaism and the Ethics of War", p. 308.
51. Reuters photographs manipulated by computer software were used to make damage in Beirut look worse than it was; doctored ambulances in Cana were used by Associated Press to report falsely that Israel targeted ambulances; captions in TIME about a direct Israeli hit on a bank of Hezbollah truck-mounted missile-launchers in a Lebanese army parking lot were altered to say that an Israeli jet was shot down over civilian territory; *New York Times* reporter Judith Miller was used to convince Americans that going to war in Iraq was vital; the Arutz7 media network in Israel agitates for the far right in Israel; ultra-orthodox Rabbi Ovadia Yosef broadcasts out of context into Arab lands and his extreme views have a tremendous effect on their hatred of Israel as a "Jewish State".
52. Asa Kasher and Amos Yadlin, "The Military Ethics of Fighting Terror: An Israeli Perspective", *Journal of Military Ethics*, 4(1), 2005: 3–32.
53. Michael J. Broyde, "Fighting the War and the Peace: Battlefield Ethics, Peace Talks, Treaties, and Pacifism in the Jewish Tradition", available on the *Jewish Law* website, ⟨http://www.jlaw.com/Articles/war3.html⟩ (accessed 7 October 2008).
54. Walter Reich, "Ethics of War", *New York Sun*, 10 August 2006 (OpEd).

55. David S. Shapiro, "The Jewish Attitude towards Peace and War", in N. Lamm (ed.) *Studies in Jewish Thought*, Vol. I. New York: Yeshiva University Press, 1975.
56. *The Babylonian Talmud*, London: Soncino, 1969. Tractate Sotah.
57. *The Babylonian Talmud*, Tractate Sotah, available at ⟨http://www.come-and-hear.com/talmud/index.html⟩ (accessed 7 October 2008).
58. Kimelman, "Warfare and Its Restrictions in Judaism".

6

Norms of war in Roman Catholic Christianity

Gregory M. Reichberg

Introduction: Four approaches to war and ethics

Over the course of two millennia, several different approaches to the ethics of war have been propounded within the confines of Catholic Christianity. At the risk of excessive generalization, these may be characterized as four in kind: pacifism, just war, perpetual peace and regular war.

Pacifism

Pacifism[1] appears to have been the dominant viewpoint within the Church in its first three centuries. It must be said, however, that during this period the renunciation of armed force was more of a lived reality than a theological position.[2] This renunciation had four main sources of inspiration:

(1) Statements by Jesus, for instance Matthew 5:39, "If anyone strikes you on the right cheek, turn to him the other also."
(2) The example of Jesus, who expressly forbade his disciples to use force in his defence (to Peter he said, "Put your sword into its sheath", Matthew 26:52), and thereby willingly endured a martyr's death. That Jesus *freely* went to his death and in so doing redeemed the world is a central truth for Catholic Christianity; this, combined with the example of the early Church martyrs, lent credence to the idea that evil could efficaciously be combated by the purely spiritual

World religions and norms of war, Popovski, Reichberg and Turner (eds),
United Nations University Press, 2009, ISBN 978-92-808-1163-6

"arms" of love and patient suffering. Within the developing tradition, this would serve as an important counterweight to the just war idea; sometimes it would be cited as an argument against any resort to armed force (principled pacifism), at other times it would be advanced as a method of resistance to evil that could be applied in tandem with armed force.[3]

(3) Detestation of the idolatrous practices associated with Roman military life.

(4) A belief that the end of the world was near, such that participation in worldly practices (soldiering, lawsuits, etc.) was deemed inappropriate for Christians intent on achieving salvation in the next world.

On this fourfold basis, strong reservations against things military were expressed by some early Christian writers, most notably Justin Martyr, Tertullian, Origen and Lactantius. With the end of the Roman empire and the rise of Christian civilization under Constantine, this early pacifism lost much of its appeal for the mainstream church. And indeed, up until very recently, pacifism would endure in Catholicism mainly as a foil against which the just war doctrine would be compared. With the exception of Catholic authors of the Reformation era such as Erasmus (1466–1536), few would adopt it as a viable alternative, and some would even characterize it as a heretical viewpoint, identified as it were with the "excesses" of Protestantism.[4]

Pacifism nevertheless saw something of a renewal in the second half of the twentieth century among Catholic thinkers and activists such as Dorothy Day, Gordon Zahn and James Douglas.[5] Moreover, the pacifist emphasis on the efficacy of non-violent resistance to injustice has received endorsement in Church documents, for instance the 1993 pastoral letter on war and peace issued by the US Catholic Bishops.[6] The Church has been particularly insistent on the importance of implementing non-violent strategies within the context of intra-state struggles against injustice and abusive authority. Although admitting that "armed struggle" may be permissible as "a last resort to put an end to an obvious and prolonged tyranny which is gravely damaging the fundamental rights of individuals and the common good", it has nonetheless asserted that *passive resistance* is "a way more conformable to moral principles and having no less prospects for success".[7] The downfall of Communist totalitarianism in Eastern Europe during the pontificate of John Paul II is often cited as evidence of the efficacy of non-violent means of resistance.

Just war

The just war idea emerged in Christianity at a time (the fourth century) when Christians began to assume positions of leadership within the temporal sphere. No longer could they view the political order solely from the standpoint of critical outsiders. The defence of homeland from attack, the repression of criminality and protection of the innocent were now contemplated as live issues for Christians in positions of power, thus requiring a reappraisal of Christ's example and teaching in the light of these changed historical circumstances.

Spearheading this reappraisal were two bishops who were keenly aware of the new political role that Christians had begun to assume in the waning years of the Roman empire: St Ambrose (c. 339–397) and St Augustine (354–430). Neither wrote a treatise or even a section of a treatise on the moral problem of war, but the theme was nevertheless addressed by them in numerous passages, including some quite long digressions, where the justifiability of engagement in war was clearly enunciated.

The emergent just war doctrine was oriented around two key presuppositions. On the one hand, peace, not war, was viewed as the normative, baseline condition of humanity. In line with the Christian belief in the inherent goodness of creation, Ambrose and Augustine held that God had intended human beings and their respective communities to live together harmoniously, bound together by ties of mutual assistance and friendship (first presupposition). This condition of harmony was represented by the biblical narration of the Garden of Eden (Genesis 2:8–25), where interhuman violence had no place.

Yet Ambrose and Augustine also worked from the complementary idea that God's original plan for humanity had been contravened by human sin (second presupposition). The biblical story of humanity's fall from grace (Genesis 3) was summed up in the dogma of "original sin", according to which the transgression of Adam and Eve has had an enduring effect on their descendants (the universality of human beings), all of whom are born with a susceptibility to evil. Although war is not specifically mentioned, Cain's killing of his brother Abel (Genesis 4:1–16) and related stories, such as the Tower of Babel (Genesis 11:1–9), were meant to illustrate how violence and related forms of evil are endemic to our "fallen" world.

Although it was believed that restoration was possible through the redemptive action of Jesus Christ, it was also recognized that evil would endure in this world until his "second coming" at the end of time. Baptism did not entirely remove the tendency to sin, which would persist in Christians as a result of the original fall. Nevertheless, as agents cooperating in God's governance of a fallen world, Christians, especially those charged with the duties of public authority, were expected to resist evil actively, especially when grave injustice was directed against the weak and defenceless. At the limit, this would entail using armed force against those, whether internal malefactors or external enemies, who had disrupted the peace. This was famously summed up by Augustine when he wrote that "[i]t is iniquity on the part of the adversary that forces a just war upon the wise man".[8] On this understanding, "just war" (*bellum iustum*) was derived from the more fundamental concept of "peace" (*pax*). Armed force could be viewed as having a positive value (thereby warranting the designation "just") insofar as it contributed toward restoring a peace that had been violated by prior wrongdoing. By extension, since injustice could be expected to occur on a regular basis, officers of the law (police and soldiers) were deemed necessary in order to hold it in check. In line with our postlapsarian condition, the preservation of peace thus required just war as its unavoidable counterpoint.

Quite familiar to us today, this conceptualization of war as a derivative concept was not the standard understanding in the ancient world, where war was often viewed as a primordial reality that required no special justification, no addition of the adjective "just", to be accepted as a legitimate practice.[9] It was not uncommon for war to be considered the more primordial reality, such that peace could be defined negatively as the absence of war.[10] In this vein, several ancient writings testify to what one might term an "agonistic conception of life",[11] as for example in Plato's *Laws*, where the character Clinias boldly states that "the peace of which most men talk ... is no more than a name; in real fact, the normal attitude of a city to all other cities is one of undeclared warfare".[12] Like the oscillation of day and night, or the change of seasons, endemic warfare was thought to have a vital role to play in the maintenance of cosmic and human order: "all things happen by strife and necessity," wrote Heraclitus (sixth century BCE), adding that "war is the father of all and the king of all", since it is from war that the differentiation of gods and humans, slaves and freemen arises.[13]

At the heart of the emerging Christian idea of *bellum iustum* was accordingly the conviction that war could be waged only for the maintenance of a just peace. Peace was viewed as the chief normative concept against which any resort to war would have to be measured. As a result, motives of personal gain, territorial aggrandizement and the like were vigorously excluded from the list of justifiable causes of war. But, despite the richness of this early teaching (articulated most fully by Ambrose and Augustine), it did not yet represent a theory of just war. Such a theory did not in fact arise until many centuries later, when the canon lawyers of the Middle Ages sought to organize earlier materials on war and violence – passages from the Bible, statements by Augustine and other Church fathers, enunciations of Church councils, and formulations from ancient Roman law – into an articulated body of thought, i.e. a *doctrine*. The key figure in this process was the early canonist Gratian (twelfth century), whose influence will be discussed below.

The dominant school of thought within Catholicism from the Middle Ages to the present,[14] the just war idea has undergone significant transformation and development over the course of its history. The main burden of this chapter will be to outline the parameters of this idea within Catholic teaching.

Perpetual peace

Alongside the idea of just war, two related but distinct normative approaches to war have found representation within the Catholic tradition, both with roots in the Middle Ages. In the twelfth century, reflection on the practice of papal arbitration, whereby the popes would seek to prevent war by mediating disputes between rival princes, led some authors to postulate that recourse to war could be altogether eliminated within Christendom if all princes were obliged to submit their disputes to the pope's binding mediation.[15] A different version of this idea was later proposed by Dante Alighieri (1265–1321) in his political treatise *Monarchia*, this time with an emphasis on the adjudicating power of a (hypothetical) universal emperor, who would function as the supreme early judge. Possessed of full enforcement powers, his decisions would be imposed without further appeal, thereby preventing serious disputes from disrupting the peace. Now designated under the heading of "perpetual peace", thinkers with this outlook "typically hold that the just war view is at once too optimistic in thinking that war can effectively be regulated by moral norms and values, and too pessimistic in presupposing that war is an inexpugnable part of the human condition. Instead, they advocate a new set of political structures (notably an international body to adjudicate disputes between states), which, if effectively implemented, will one day render war obsolete."[16] Resurfacing in the eighteenth century with secular writings by authors such as Abbé de Saint-Pierre, Rousseau and Kant, the perpetual peace idea would gain currency in twentieth-century Catholic thought. Expressions of the idea may be found in papal documents and pronouncements, as for instance when Pope Paul VI famously declared at the United Nations (4 October 1965), "Never again war!"[17]

Regular war

It has already been noted that just war was the dominant approach to the ethics of war in the Christian Middle Ages, and it has remained so in Catholicism generally. This account is founded on the notion of just cause, which signifies, in substance, that war is a proceeding whereby a belligerent is empowered to punish a wrong done to it by another party. Understood as a response to prior wrongdoing, the notion of just cause is *unilateral* in character, for, if one party is entitled to apply a sanction or to enforce its rightful claim, the other party must be in the wrong. Strictly conditioned by its underlying cause, the legal effects of a just war could benefit only the righteous belligerent. The unjust adversary had no right to fight or even to defend itself.

Yet alongside the unilateralist conception of the just war tradition another approach was followed by some late medieval Christian authors. Legal theorists (termed "Romanists" since their work focused on applying the civil laws of ancient Rome to the Christian culture of Europe) such as Raphaël Fulgosius (1367–1427) and Andreas Alciatus (1492–1550) viewed war as a contest between equal belligerents, which both, owing to their sovereign status, enjoyed a similar capacity to wage war, regardless of the cause that had prompted the conflict. The whole problematic of just cause was thereby set aside in favour of *bilateral* rights of war.[18] As in a lawsuit or a duel, the opposing belligerents could enforce the same legal prerogatives against each other and were expected to abide by the same *in bello* rules. Much of the chivalric literature, in authors such as Honoré Bonet (c. 1340–1410) and Christine de Pizan (c. 1364–1431), was written from this perspective (although usually set in conjunction with just war elements). To underscore how the same set of rules (rights and duties) would apply to all sovereign belligerents, regardless of the justice or injustice of their cause, this would later be referred to as the idea of *regular war* ("guerre réglée").[19]

Subsequently developed by Gentili, Wolff, Vattel and other Protestant thinkers, the regular war approach would later find expression in international law (e.g. the Hague Rules of Land Warfare). But it has also had proponents among twentieth-century Catholic thinkers. Openly endorsed by Carl Schmitt,[20] an echo of this conception may be found in some recent documents of the Catholic Magisterium, for instance the US Bishops, who add "comparative justice" to the traditional list of just war criteria.[21] Moreover, during some periods the regular war viewpoint was reflected in the diplomatic engagements of the Holy See. During World War II, for example, attempting to maintain a stance of official neutrality in the face of a conflict that had engaged Catholics on the two opposing sides, Allied and Axis, Pope Pius XII and other high Vatican officials often used language reminiscent of the regular war approach. The faithful on both sides were urged to remain obedient to their respective governments by serving in the military, regardless of which belligerent might be thought to possess the just cause. The pope's moral admonitions focused mainly on urging the parties to observe the international laws of armed conflict.[22]

As was noted above, the following elucidation of Roman Catholic teaching on the ethics of war will concentrate mainly on the just war approach. In proceeding thus, it must be borne in mind that this approach has not developed in isolation from the three other approaches mentioned above. Elements of pacifism, perpetual peace or regular war have frequently been integrated into the outlook of Catholic thinkers who proceed primarily from within the perspective of just war. In fact, it is this intermingling that accounts for much of the complexity (and richness) of the just war idea within the Catholic tradition.

Sources and historical phases of the Catholic teaching on just war

The Catholic teaching on just war is ordinarily traced to the seminal writings of St Augustine. Although this is doubtless true, it must nevertheless be emphasized that the tradition as it emerged in the Middle Ages did not result from a direct reading of Augustine's disparate passages on war in the original texts. The articulation of a just war theory in the thirteenth century was based rather on reading Augustinian passages that had been organized into compilations, the most famous of which was the *Decretum Gratiani* (c. 1140).[23] In this work, the Italian canon lawyer Gratian devoted an entire chapter (*causa* 23) to problems associated with force and armed coercion from a Christian perspective. Based almost entirely on citations, with brief interjectory comments by Gratian, *causa* 23 brought together the building blocks that succeeding generations of Church lawyers and theologians would use to erect their own theoretical constructions on the ethics and legality of war. In addition to passages from Augustine, the *causa* included numerous citations from scripture (both the Old and New Testaments), other early Church theologians, e.g. Ambrose and Isidore of Seville, as well as Church councils and papal statements.

Gratian himself engaged in little independent theorizing. However, having become the main textbook for the emerging law schools of the Latin West, his *Decretum* gave rise to commentaries in which important new views on war and coercion were put forward, usually by reference to Roman law. The thinkers who wrote these commentaries were called Decretists, and among their writings we find the first explicit normative theories on topics such as the scope of self-defence and legitimate war-making authority. Around the middle of the thirteenth century, the interest of Church lawyers shifted to the newly gathered collections of papal legislation (called "decretals"); hence those who commented upon them were termed Decretalists. Among the most famous of these commentators was Pope Innocent IV (1180–1254), who carefully distinguished war from other forms of licit violence (self-defence by private individuals and internal police action by princes), thereby carving out the *ius ad bellum* as a distinctive sphere of normative reflection. Alongside Innocent, another Decretalist, the Dominican Raymond of Peñafort (1180–1275), wrote a treatise (the *Summa de casibus poenitentiae*[24]) that was intended to serve as a guide for confessors. By virtue of their power to absolve penitents from their sins, confessors exercised a role akin to judges, and were expected to apply the law within a special jurisdiction: the inner domain of conscience. Since many of the individuals who came to confession had contact of one sort or another with problems relating to war, this theme would receive careful treatment within Raymond's work. We thereby find him offering significant comments on a wide range of topics, including the five conditions that cumulatively must be fulfilled if a war is to be considered just, legitimate self-defence, the seizure of booty and civilian immunity.

Concurrently with the work of the Decretalists, theologians in the thirteenth century also began to write on problems associated with war. Most famous among them was undoubtedly St Thomas Aquinas (c. 1224–1274), whose division of just war criteria into legitimate authority, just cause and right intention has served as the basic armature for Western moral reflection on war down to the present day. Aquinas elaborated his account of just and unjust war against the backdrop of a normative theory of peace, which could be achieved at different levels. Defining "war" as violence done by one independent nation against another (in contrast to "sedition, whereby violent acts are committed against the internal order of a single nation"), he brought into Western reflection the idea that the nations of the world together constitute a *community*, for which there is a corresponding condition of *inter*-national peace.[25]

From the sixteenth century onward, Aquinas's *Summa theologiae* became the main textbook for Catholic students of theology in the Latin West. His question 40 "De bello" (in the part of the work known as the *Secunda-secundae*) became the principal locus for theological discussions on war.[26] Several commentaries were written on the "De bello", but the most influential was produced by the Dominican Cardinal Thomas de Vio (1468–1534), who is better known by the name Cajetan.[27] Central to Cajetan's account was the distinction (not explicitly formulated by Aquinas) between two kinds of war, defensive and offensive. Defensive war required no special appeal to legitimate authority; political leaders of lower status, or even private individuals, were permitted by natural law to resort to such force in case of urgent need. Offensive war, by contrast, was more a matter of choice than of necessity. This mode of warfare Cajetan equated with the administration of punitive justice. No political community could be deemed self-sufficient (a "perfect commonwealth") if it did not possess the power to exact just retribution against its internal and external foes. The authority to wage war against *external* wrongdoers, in particular, he viewed as the distinctive mark of a fully independent commonwealth. Despite the medieval cast of his work, in it we can already detect a glimmer of the new European system of independent sovereign states. Cajetan's commentary represented one of the most detailed discussions up to its time on the issue of legitimate authority, and the distinction that he drew between defensive and offensive war (both of which were deemed legitimate) became a mainstay in the subsequent literature. The idea that offensive war requires permission from the highest level of legitimate authority is still with us today, albeit under a different vocabulary, when it is maintained for example that "enforcement action" may be carried out only by the Security Council of the United Nations, although defensive action still falls under the initiative of individual states.

Catholic reflection on war was dramatically stimulated by Spain's colonization of the Americas at the beginning of the sixteenth century. Reports of indiscriminate killing, forced labour and confiscation of land had raised doubts about the fast-growing colonies. Since it was by resort to arms that Spain had come to exercise dominion over the indigenous peoples of the Americas, the theologians who were then debating this involvement would have to assess, *inter alia*, whether religious motives – for instance, a desire to convert the Amerindians to Christianity – could provide moral warrant for the employment of these coercive measures. It was in this period that one of the first full-fledged theological treatises on the problem of war between nations appeared in the Latin West: the *Relectio de Indis* by Francisco de Vitoria (c. 1492–1546).[28]

Of particular importance in Vitoria's treatment of war was the establishment of a tight conceptual linkage between the moral problem of conquest and war, on the one hand, and the norms of natural law, on the other. The latter designated a set of unwritten moral imperatives that are rooted in a source antecedent to human deliberation and choice, namely God, yet which do not depend on a special religious revelation (a holy book) and thus are applicable to all men, in whatever culture they may find themselves. Vitoria's emphasis on natural law would have a formative influence on the development of the modern Catholic conception of resort to armed force, which henceforth would be framed in terms of secular ("natural") rather than specifically religious (revealed) principles. Moreover, Vitoria was one of the first Christian thinkers to discuss war and peace with explicit reference to the common good, not only of an individual nation or people but of "the whole world" (*bonum totius orbis*). In a famous passage he similarly suggested that just war was akin to an act of policing to be undertaken by the authority of the international community (*totius orbis auctoritate*).[29] His allusions to this effect would likewise inform later thought, as elaborated for instance by the US Bishops, who invoked the idea of a "global common good" as the main referent for any legitimate war-making authority.[30] And more generally, building on Vitoria's insight, twentieth-century Church documents would affirm that "[i]nternational solidarity is a necessity of the moral order.... World peace depends on this to a great extent."[31]

Vitoria's line of thought was further developed by two fellow Spaniards, both Jesuits. The first, Luis de Molina (1535–1600), was instrumental in reformulating the notion of just cause so that it no longer presupposed personal guilt on the part of the adversary.

This he termed "material injury". Such an injury would arise if the offender carried out a wrongful act while in a state of "invincible ignorance"[32]. If the injury was of sufficient gravity, the offended party could have just cause to seek redress through resort to armed force. This resort would count as an instance of offensive war, yet, since it was not predicated on the culpability of the adversary, it could not be waged in view of punishment.[33]

By distinguishing war from punishment, Molina thereby established one of the central premises on which the modern *ius in bello* came to be built.

The second of the two Jesuits, Francisco Suarez (1548–1617), wrote a systematic treatise, *De bello*, which covered in some detail (and with numerous original arguments of his own) many of the points earlier treated by Vitoria. In a famous passage, he asserted that human beings are not condemned to settle their disputes by war since God has provided us with other means – including arbitration – to resolve controversies between commonwealths.[34] He insisted, likewise, that political and military leaders have obligations not only toward the well-being of their own polity but vis-à-vis the enemy commonwealth as well. Before declaring war, such leaders must make their grievances known to the enemy commonwealth, providing it an opportunity to avoid war by offering satisfaction for the wrong done.[35] Suarez is also noteworthy for the very careful treatment that he gave to the problem of side-effect harm in war (collateral damage), which he applied by reference to what has since become known as the "principle of double effect".[36]

Despite its vigour and the new perspectives that it opened up, the "golden age" of Spanish theorizing on war came to a close toward the middle of the seventeenth century. During the next three centuries, the Catholic teaching on war would enter a period of sterility. Apart from a few bright spots, for example the work of Luigi Taparelli d'Azeglio (1793–1862), who updated just war theory to deal with problems such as preventive war, and whose strong endorsement of international society, arbitration and arms reduction would contribute toward the papacy's later embrace of these ideas, most authors merely repeated points made by earlier just war theorists such as Aquinas, with few attempting to apply these ideas to current events. This was the heyday of *raison d'état* (classical international law), when it was generally assumed that individual sovereign states had full discretion in waging war to serve their interests. Matters of ethics were relegated to the private conscience of political leaders, and were not thought to be a fit topic for public discourse.

The normative landscape began to change dramatically, however, when journalists began to report on the large casualties associated with the Crimean (1854–1856) and Franco-Prussian (1870–1871) wars.[37] A wave of pacifist sentiment rose, making inroads among some Catholic organizations. World War I, in particular, made abundantly manifest how the consequences of an unbridled *ius ad bellum* could be truly disastrous. The League of Nations Covenant (1920) sought to remedy this state of affairs by establishing a system of obligatory arbitration, with the aim of preventing states from resorting to force to resolve their differences.

The legal regime established by the League stood in a somewhat ambiguous relation to the just war outlook of the Catholic tradition. On the one hand, in its underlying supposition that "the normal state of international relations is one of peace, with war permitted only as an exceptional act requiring affirmative justification",[38] the League represented a rejection of *raison d'état* and a return to the classic just war point of view. Likewise, in its strong endorsement of arbitration as a method for limiting resort to war, the League renewed ties with an approach that had traditionally been advocated by the popes and leading theologians such as Suarez. On the other hand, the League showed discontinuity with the earlier tradition of just war to the extent that it largely excluded the problematic of just cause from its deliberations. Built up around a set of rules that dictated what *procedural* conditions (chief among them the submission of disputes to arbitration) had to be met before a resort to force could be deemed lawful, the League could side-step the question "as to which side had legal right on its side".[39]

This change in outlook from the just war idea to the legal regime of the Covenant presented an obvious challenge to Catholic thinkers, who engaged in two lines of response. Some sought to minimize the difference between the two outlooks by arguing that the normative conception underlying the League was in fundamental continuity with the outlook of the traditional just war theorists (Vitoria, etc.). This argument was typically made in historical studies,[40] where the main tenets of earlier just war thinking were explained in some detail. The other, more common, approach was to call for a reformulation of Catholic teaching on war and peace, to render it more consistent with the contemporary outlook.[41] Emphasis on arbitration, arms reduction, non-violent peace-making strat-

egies, proportionality, last resort and the global common good would out-
flank the earlier preoccupation with just cause and legitimate authority.

Pivotal to the new trend in Catholic just war thinking were the
speeches of Pius XII (pope from 1939 to 1958). Seeking to bring the traditional just war doctrine into continuity with the UN Charter and other
developments in international law, the pope emphasized two points that
would have a lasting effect on subsequent Catholic teaching.

First of all, in his various statements on war and peace Pius XII endorsed the long-term goal of establishing a system of governance for the
international society of states. Taking inspiration from his predecessor,
Benedict XV, who expressed the desire that "all States, putting aside
mutual suspicion, should unite in one league, or rather a sort of family
of peoples, calculated both to maintain their own independence and safeguard the order of human society",[42] Pius viewed such an organized
international community as constituting the ideal setting for decision-
making about resort to armed force. Recognizing that such a system of
governance (as reflected for instance in the UN Charter) was still embry-
onic, in continuity with the doctrine expounded a century earlier by
Taparelli,[43] he suggested that the establishment of a centralized international authority could be viewed as an exigency of the natural law.[44] The
guiding idea was that each individual state would possess the right to use
armed force as long as international society lacked a unified structure of
governance. But, with the inception of the requisite juridical and executive functions at the international level, resort to armed force (for the
maintenance of justice and peace) would become the prerogative of this
international body; just war would henceforth take the form of international police action.[45]

Secondly, the pope moved away from the classic distinction between
defensive and offensive wars, preferring instead to characterize just cause
exclusively in terms of "legitimate defence". This stood in contrast to the
earlier tradition, which had recognized three justifiable just causes of war:
defence from attack, recuperation of goods wrongly seized and punishment of wrongdoing. Although some have criticized the pope for unduly
restricting the scope of just cause to defence against ongoing attack,[46]
it would seem that his divergence from the earlier tradition is in some
respects more verbal than substantive. For instance, the pope's denial, in
the Christmas discourse of 1944, that recourse to armed force can be "a
legitimate solution for international controversies and a means for the
realization of national aspirations" was meant to target the idea of *raison
d'état*; as such it should not be read as a repudiation of the notion of
offensive war as it may be found in traditional Catholic authors such as
Cajetan, Vitoria and Suarez.[47]

Moreover, unlike the traditional nomenclature of offensive versus defensive war, wherein the latter term was conceptualized narrowly as a reaction to armed attack, Pius seems to have thought of defence in somewhat broader terms, as encompassing the protection of persons and society not only from a cross-border armed attack but from other forms of "grave injustice". Hence we can find in his teaching an opening for humanitarian intervention and other limited uses of armed force, which, in the traditional terminology, would have been placed under the heading of *bellum offensivum*.[48] It remains true, however, that Pius's transition away from the traditional terminology did have the effect of moving subsequent Catholic teaching toward a considerably more restrictive conception of justifiable armed force than had been articulated in earlier ages, especially since many did not grasp the hermeneutical context described above and simply took his statements at face value.

The spread of nuclear arms after World War II further intensified calls for a major revision of Church teaching on just war. Symptomatic of this trend was the claim, enunciated with vigour by Pope John XXIII in his Encyclical *Pacem in Terris* (1963), that, "in this age which boasts of its atomic power, it no longer makes sense to maintain that war is a fit instrument with which to repair the violation of justice".[49] In line with this, the US Catholic Bishops published a pastoral letter in 1983, *The Challenge of Peace: God's Promise and Our Response*, which dealt specifically with the morality of nuclear deterrence.[50] Widely read, in both religious circles and the secular policy community, the letter opened with a summary of principles in which the Catholic teaching was described as implying "a presumption against war". Particularly noteworthy was the rejection of any kind of offensive war, which signalled a significant departure from the traditional just war doctrine of Aquinas, Vitoria and Suarez.

Moreover, further complicating this historical picture was the increasing recourse to humanitarian interventions and other limited military engagements in the post–Cold War period. This led some Catholics to call into question the "presumption against war" view, as articulated by the US Bishops and the Catholic Magisterium generally, on the grounds that it would paralyse the will to engage in forcible military action in precisely those cases where such action was needed (e.g. to halt ethnic cleansing and other atrocities). In its place, they have argued for a return to the traditional just war view, which is founded on "a presumption against injustice".[51]

Religious rationales for resort to armed force

It is quite striking that some of the earliest Christian treatments of just war were set within the context of "holy war", namely an employment of armed force in relation to specifically religious ends. This surfaces for instance in Augustine's polemical writings against the Donatists, a schismatic sect, in which he asserts that, if loving persuasion fails to bring straying Church members back into the fold, they should be forcibly compelled "by fear of punishment or pain" to return to the true faith.[52] A similar approach may be found in Gratian, whose treatment of armed force in *causa* 23 takes as its point of departure "a case of heresy into which certain bishops had lapsed, and its repression by their Catholic counterparts, acting upon orders from the pope".[53] Gratian likewise considers, in question VI of the same *causa*, whether "the Church may compel the wicked to the good", to which he answers in the affirmative, and then, by extension, argues in question VII that heretics may rightly be despoiled of their goods.[54]

The above reasoning of Augustine and Gratian applied only to Christians who were deemed to have deviated from the authentic teaching of the faith – heretics, schismatics and apostates. It did not apply to Jews, Muslims and other unbelievers who had never been received, by baptism, into the Christian faith. The former, as baptized Christians, stood permanently under the Church's spiritual jurisdiction. Hence, it was believed that the Church had the legitimate power to administer penalties for their deviation from the acceptable line of belief. These penalties could include excommunication or removal from office. But, in circumstances where the civil order was thought to be threatened by religious dissent, coercive sanctions such as confiscation of property, imprisonment or even execution could result, as carried out by the relevant civil authorities. This employment of temporal sanctions by the Church (acting through the mediation of civil authorities) was largely abandoned by the eighteenth century, but in some isolated cases, such as Spain, persisted up until the nineteenth century. The practice depended on an understanding of Church–state relations whereby "the welfare of the Commonwealth came to be closely bound up with the cause of religious unity".[55] Such a view is no longer operative within Roman Catholic Christianity, as evidenced for instance by the current *Code of Canon Law*, which includes no provisions for the administration of coercive civil sanctions against persons deemed guilty of heresy and other grave "sins against the faith".[56] It is now recognized in the official Church teaching that no state, even one where there is a majority of Catholics, can require a profession of faith on the part of its citizens.[57] Religious plurality and religious freedom are now deemed fully acceptable conditions within the modern state.

Historically, and from the earliest times, "non-believers" (in this category would be placed Jews, Muslims and pagans) were accorded a status different from that of dissident Christians. The mainstream view, from

Augustine forward, was that, in the words of Pope Innocent IV (c. 1250), "infidels ought not to be forced to accept the faith, since everyone's free will ought to be respected, and this conversion should [come about] only by the grace of God".[58] A similar, even more emphatic formulation may be found some 20 years later in a text by Thomas Aquinas, when he wrote (c. 1270) that "unbelievers ... who have never received the faith, such as ... heathens and the Jews ... are by no means (*nullo modo*) to be compelled to the faith ... because to believe depends on [a free act of] the will".[59] Alternative views did, however, find voice within the Catholic tradition. The influential jurist Hostiensis (c. 1200–1271) famously held that true dominion (ownership of land and self-rule) could be exercised only by Christians; hence force could be used against infidels, to seize their lands or even, in some circumstances, to compel them to the faith.[60] Likewise, the medieval theologian Duns Scotus (c. 1266–1308) argued that under certain conditions the children of unbelievers (Jews and Muslims) might be forcibly baptized (for their own good) against the wishes of their parents, a view echoed by some later authors as well.[61] Nevertheless, what was described above as the "mainstream view" finally won the day and has been enshrined in major Church documents such as the Declaration on Religious Freedom (*Dignitatis Humanae*), promulgated by Pope Paul VI in 1965. That this is the Church's canonical teaching has been reaffirmed on numerous occasions, notably by Pope Benedict XVI in his (now famous) lecture at the University of Regensburg, where he asserted (quoting from a medieval source) that "spreading the faith through violence ... is incompatible with the nature of God and the nature of the soul".[62] Given the historical background of theological vacillation on the permissibility of using force to promote religion, an unequivocal statement, by the Church's highest authority, condemning any such practice is not without significance.

As the tradition evolved, normative treatments of war were progressively detached from an explicit reference to the propagation or protection of the Christian faith. For example, in Aquinas's famous discussion of just war in *Summa theologiae* II-II, q. 40, a. 1 (written circa 1270), no reference is made to either heresy or the Crusades, and the aims of war (described in terms of "just cause") were enunciated in terms that could be readily understandable and even endorsed by non-Christians. War, he wrote, can rightly be waged "to protect the common weal against external enemies", to "rescue the poor", to "avenge wrongs" or to "restore what has been unjustly seized". It is not that specifically religious rationales were entirely absent from Aquinas's comments on war, but that these arise not so much with respect to the reasons for waging war, but rather apropos of what persons might legitimately take part in armed fighting. Priests, for instance, were excluded, precisely because of their sacramental function. As ministers standing in the place of Christ during the celebration of the holy mass, they were meant to imitate, symbolically, his voluntary sacrifice on the cross. Hence, "it is unbecoming for them to slay or shed blood. And it is more fitting that they should be ready to shed their own blood for Christ, so as to imitate in deed what they portray in their ministry."[63] A similar reasoning may be found in many authors of the same period.

The process of detaching reasoning about war from premises of faith exclusively available to Christians was especially visible in the account given by Suarez in the early seventeenth century. Section IV of his *De bello* is entitled "What is a just title for war, on the basis of natural reason?" To dispel any doubt that specifically religious rationales should be excluded from the *ius ad bellum*, in the following section Suarez asks whether "Christian princes have any just title for war beyond that which natural reason dictates". In this context, "natural reason" designates an employment of the human mind that is not inherently dependent on data from positive divine revelation. In contrast to teachings such as the divinity of Jesus Christ or papal infallibility, which are wholly unknowable to human beings apart from a special divine instruction given in the New Testament, the truths of "natural reason" can be known by virtue of the mind's fundamental ("created") capacity.

In applying this teaching on "natural reason" to decision-making about armed force, Suarez excluded a number of rationales that had been advanced by earlier thinkers, but which by his time the mainstream tradition had set aside as inappropriate grounds for war: refusal to accept the "true", i.e. Christian, religion, offence given to God by idolatrous practices, the alleged incapacity of non-believers to exercise dominion (self-government or ownership of property), and the alleged universal jurisdiction of the pope or the Christian emperor. On this basis, Suarez concluded that "there is no title for war so exclusively reserved for Christian princes that it has not some basis in, or at least some due relation to, natural law, being therefore also applicable to princes who are unbelievers".[64]

Nevertheless, Suarez did recognize one notable exception to his general rejection of what today is termed "holy war". This was a case in which a people, subject to a non-Christian prince, wished to accept Christianity against his will. Should the prince forcibly prevent this acceptance, say by prohibiting the entry of missionaries, then Christian princes ruling over other lands would have the right to defend (*ius defendendi*) those innocent people against their prince, and even punish offences committed by his regime against them. Suarez will not concede, however, that this line of argumentation would be generally available to other religions: if a people wished "to submit to the law of unbelievers – for example the Mohammedan [law] – and its prince is opposed to this submission, then an infidel Turkish prince would not have a similar right of war against that other prince". To hinder the preaching of (or conversion to) Christianity – the "true law" in Suarez's eyes – would constitute a serious injustice, "whereas there is no injury at all in prohibiting the acceptance of another [religious] law".[65]

In thus according a special status to Christianity as the rationale for a religiously based right of humanitarian intervention, Suarez was merely following the well-worn path of his predecessors. Vitoria, Thomas Aquinas, Innocent IV and Gratian had each advanced similar arguments. Defence of fellow Christians against religious persecution was in fact one of two principal grounds on which theological and canon law arguments for the medieval Crusades had rested.[66] (The other ground was the belief that Muslims had unjustly seized Jerusalem and the surrounding "holy lands", which had previously belonged to Christians; as a result, Christians were entitled to use military force to get their lands back.[67])

Since the end of World War II, the Catholic Church has progressively detached its teaching on humanitarian military intervention from its original religious setting – the limited case of Christians under attack. One manifestation of this development was the 1948 Christmas message of Pope Pius XII, in which he spoke of "an obligation for the nations as a whole, who have a duty not to abandon a nation that is attacked".[68] No special mention was made of Christians; the supposition was that this obligation to defend victims of aggression would arise irrespective of their nationality or religious affiliation. This was reaffirmed by Pope John Paul II in his message of 1 January 2000: "Clearly, when a civilian population risks being overcome by the attacks of an unjust aggressor and political efforts and non-violent defence prove to be of no avail, it is legitimate and even obligatory to take concrete measures to disarm the aggressor."[69] This teaching had found concrete expression the year before when Cardinal Sodano, then the Vatican Secretary of State, justified as legitimate the use of force in Kosovo to protect civilians (the majority of whom were Muslims) from attack by Serb militias.[70] Despite some claims that John Paul had left entirely undefined the parameters of this duty of humanitarian intervention,[71] it may be noted that he did at least clarify how such measures "must be limited in time and precise in their aims. They must be carried out in full respect for international law, guaranteed by an authority that is internationally recognized."[72]

Conclusion

The preceding analysis of the ethics of war in the Roman Catholic tradition has mainly focused on the resort to armed force between states (*ius ad bellum*). It may be noted, in conclusion, that the tradition has seen important developments in other areas as well.

The normative issues raised by civil war have certainly not gone unstudied. John of Salisbury's twelfth-century discussion of tyrannicide, the treatment of insurrection (sedition) by Thomas Aquinas in the thirteenth century, and, in our own time, the articulation of liberation theologies, have had a significant impact. The involvement of Catholics in intra-state conflicts such as the Spanish Civil War, class struggle in Latin America or sectarian violence in Northern Ireland has further fuelled reflection on this topic. In response to these trends, an important Church document, written under the direction of Cardinal Ratzinger (now Pope Benedict XVI), took care to assert that "systematic recourse to violence put forward as the necessary path to liberation has to be condemned as a destructive illusion and one that opens the way to new forms of servitude".[73]

The rules to be observed in armed conflict (*ius in bello*) constitute another area in which the Catholic tradition has made important contributions. The medieval peace movements of the early Middle Ages (tenth to twelfth centuries), the penitential casuistry of the thirteenth century, the chivalric literature of the fourteenth and fifteenth centuries, and the work of Spanish theologians such as Vitoria and Suarez in the sixteenth and seventeenth centuries have produced an important body of literature on non-combatant immunity, proportionality and side-effect harm.[74] In our own day, this has been applied to problems as diverse as nuclear deterrence and arms control, force protection, terrorism,[75] and ethnic cleansing. Fundamental to this teaching is the conviction not only that a just social, political or international order is the goal toward which all armed struggle must be directed, but also in addition that "[j]ustice must already mark each stage of the establishment of this new order".[76] In other words, "there is a morality of means"[77] that must always be respected in even the most just of wars.

Notes

1. The term is here taken to designate the renunciation of armed force in the face of violent attack (non-resistance to evil), or, more generally, opposition to war or violence of any kind. It may be noted, however, that, during the late nineteenth and early twentieth centuries (up to World War I), "pacifism" had a somewhat different meaning in Catholic literature. It then designated "a firm belief in the obligation to resort first to all possible means of peaceful settlement of disputes", hence "advocacy of … arbitration, disarmament, and some kind of international organization to prevent war" (Robert John Araujo, S.J. and John A. Lucal, S.J., *Papal Diplomacy and the Quest for Peace*. Naples, FL: Sapientia Press, 2004). This latter sense of "pacifism" was in fact promoted by thinkers who situated themselves within the just war framework, for instance Alfred

Vanderpol, who in 1911 founded the International League of Catholic Pacifists. In his articulation of just war theory, Vanderpol sought to show how the tradition viewed armed force as a justifiable last resort that would be permissible only after non-violent means of conflict resolution (arbitration, etc.) had first been conscientiously attempted. See Alfred Vanderpol, *La doctrine scolastique du droit de la guerre*. Paris: Pedone, 1919.

2. See James Turner Johnson, "Christian Attitudes toward War and Military Service in the First Four Centuries", in James Turner Johnson, *The Quest for Peace*. Princeton, NJ: Princeton University Press, 1987, pp. 3–66. For a more recent discussion of this theme, see Alan Kreider, "Military Service in the Church Orders", *Journal of Religious Ethics*, 31(3), 2003: 415–442.

3. See Jacques Maritain, *Freedom in the Modern World*, trans. Richard O'Sullivan. New York: Gordian Press, 1971 [1936], pp. 168–188, "spiritual and secular means of warfare".

4. See, for example, Francisco de Vitoria, *Political Writings*, ed. Anthony Pagden and Jeremy Lawrance. Cambridge: Cambridge University Press, 1991, p. 296.

5. For a survey of these Catholic pacifists, and their break with the mainstream just war tradition, see George Weigel, *Tranquillitas Ordinis: The Present Failure and Future Promise of American Catholic Thought on War and Peace*. Oxford: Oxford University Press, 1987.

6. National Conference of Catholic Bishops, "The Harvest of Justice Sown in Peace", *Origins*, 23(26), 1993: 449–464; see especially section I.B, "Two Traditions, Nonviolence and Just War" (pp. 453–454).

7. Congregation for the Doctrine of the Faith, *Instruction on Christian Freedom and Liberation*. Washington, DC: United States Catholic Conference, 1986, pp. 47–48, §79.

8. *The City of God*, book 19, 7, in Augustine, *Political Writings*, trans. Michael W. Tkacz and Douglas Kries, ed. Ernest L. Fortin and Douglas Kries. Indianapolis: Hackett, 1994, p. 149.

9. See Martin Ostwald, "Peace and War in Plato and Aristotle", *Scripta Classica Israelica*, 15, 1996: 102–118.

10. See the pseudo-Platonic *Definitiones*, 413a6, cited by Ostwald, "Peace and War in Plato and Aristotle", p. 103, fn 7.

11. The agonistic conception of life does represent the sole orientation of the ancient world. Plato himself gave voice to a pacific orientation when, in a famous passage of the *Gorgias*, he has Socrates assert that "wise men ... say that the heavens and the earth, gods and men, are bound together by fellowship and friendship, and order and temperance and justice, and for this reason they call the sum of things the 'ordered' universe, my friend, not the world of disorder or riot" (507e–508a11); Plato, *The Collected Dialogues*, ed. E. Hamilton and H. Cairns. New York: Pantheon Books, 1963, p. 290. A similar orientation may also be found, even earlier, in the Confucian tradition of China, where the political implications were explicitly deduced. See Stephen C. Neff, *War and the Law of Nations*. Cambridge: Cambridge University Press, 2005, pp. 31–34.

12. *Laws*, I, 626a; translation in Plato, *The Collected Dialogues*, p. 1227.

13. Cited in G. S. Kirk, J. E. Raven and M. Schofield, *The Presocratic Philosophers*, 2nd edn. Cambridge: Cambridge University Press, 1983, p. 193.

14. The special place accorded to just war ethics in official Catholic teaching has recently been affirmed in the *Catechism of the Catholic Church* (promulgated by Pope John Paul II in 1993, revised edition 1997), which assesses the permissibility of armed force by reference to "the traditional elements of what is called the 'just war' doctrine". The Holy See, *Catechism of the Catholic Church. Corrigenda*. Oxford: Family Publications, 1997, §2309.

15. On this, see Araujo and Lucal, *Papal Diplomacy and the Quest for Peace*, pp. 20–22.

16. From the preface to Gregory Reichberg, Henrik Syse and Endre Begby (eds), *The Ethics of War: Classic and Contemporary Readings*. Oxford: Blackwell Publishing, 2006, p. xi.

17. For the full text of his speech, see "Discours du Pape Paul VI à l'organisation des Nations Unis à l'occasion du 20ème anniversaire de l'organisation", 4 October 1965; available at ⟨http://www.vatican.va/holy_father/paul_vi/speeches/1965/documents/hf_p-vi_spe_19651004_united-nations_fr.html⟩ (accessed 10 October 2008).

18. For a fuller account of the regular war view, see Gregory M. Reichberg, "Just War and Regular War: Competing Paradigms", in David Rodin and Henry Shue (eds) *Just and Unjust Warriors: The Moral and Legal Status of Soldiers*. Oxford: Oxford University Press, 2008, pp. 193–213.

19. The term was coined by Emer de Vattel in his treatise *The Law of Nations* (1758) – see Reichberg, Syse and Begby, *The Ethics of War*, pp. 514–516. In line with its French equivalent, the English adjective "regular" is here taken to designate what is "conformable to some accepted or adopted rule or standard; made or carried out in a prescribed manner; recognized as formally correct" (*OED*, 5th sense of *regular*). By extension it is said of a "properly and permanently organized" military force of a state (7th sense), as in "regular army" or "regular soldiers".

20. Carl Schmitt, *The Nomos of the Earth in the International Law of the Jus publicum Europaeum*, trans. G. L. Ulmen. New York: Telos Press, 2003.

21. National Conference of Catholic Bishops, *The Challenge of Peace: God's Promise and Our Response*, A Pastoral Letter on War and Peace. Washington, DC: Office of Publishing Services, United States Catholic Conference, 1983, p. 29, §92.

22. See Guenter Lewy, *The Catholic Church and Nazi Germany*. London: Weidenfeld & Nicolson, 1964, pp. 242–251, "Pope Pius XII: Dilemmas of Neutrality".

23. *Decretum Magistri Gratiani*, in E. Friedberg (ed.) *Corpus Iuris Canonici*, pars prior. Leipzig: Tauchnitz, 1879. For a translation of some passages on war, see Reichberg, Syse and Begby, *The Ethics of War*, pp. 104–124.

24. Raymundus de Pennafort, *Summa de poenitentia, et matrimonio, cum glossis Ioannis de Friburgo*. Rome, 1603. For a translation of some sections on war, see Reichberg, Syse and Begby, *The Ethics of War*, pp. 131–147.

25. See *Summa theologiae*, II-II, q. 42, a. 1, in Reichberg, Syse and Begby, *The Ethics of War*, pp. 183–185. The novelty of Aquinas's conception of international order is discussed by Peter Haggenmacher, *Grotius et la doctrine de la guerre juste*. Paris: Presses Universitaires de France, 1983, pp. 122–125.

26. In *Summa Theologica*, trans. Fathers of the English Dominican Province, 1920; revised edition, Benziger Bros., 1948; reprinted 1981 by Christian Classics, pp. 1353–1357.

27. In *Sancti Thomae Aquinatis Doctoris Angelici Opera Omnia iussu impensaque Leonis XIII, cum commentariis Thomae de Vio Caietani Ordinis Praedicatorum*, vol. 8. Rome: Editori di San Tommaso, 1895, pp. 313–314. For a translation, see Reichberg, Syse and Begby, *The Ethics of War*, pp. 131–147.

28. For a discussion of the main points covered in the work, see the texts and commentary in Reichberg, Syse and Begby, *The Ethics of War*, pp. 288–332.

29. Vitoria, *On the Law of War*, in Vitoria, *Political Writings*, pp. 304–306; see Peter Haggenmacher, "La place de Francisco de Vitoria parmi les fondateurs du droit international", in A. Truyol Serra et al. (eds) *Actualité de la pensée juridique de Francisco de Vitoria*. Brussels: Bruylant, 1988, pp. 27–80.

30. National Conference of Catholic Bishops, "The Harvest of Justice Sown in Peace".

31. Congregation for the Doctrine of the Faith, *Instruction on Christian Freedom and Liberation*, p. 53, §91.

32. The term is originally from Thomas Aquinas. It refers to an erroneous belief that results

from an interplay of factors that are beyond an agent's voluntary control (see Reichberg, Syse and Begby, *The Ethics of War*, p. 317).

33. Reichberg, Syse and Begby, *The Ethics of War*, p. 332.

34. Francisco Suarez, *De bello*, section VI, §5, in Reichberg, Syse and Begby, *The Ethics of War*, p. 358.

35. *De bello*, section VII, §3 ff, in Reichberg, Syse and Begby, *The Ethics of War*, pp. 361 ff.

36. *De bello*, section VII, §§15–19, in Reichberg, Syse and Begby, *The Ethics of War*, pp. 364–366. For a general treatment of double-effect reasoning in the context of war, see Gregory M. Reichberg and Henrik Syse, "The Idea of Double Effect – in War and Business", in Lene Bomann-Larsen and Oddny Wiggen (eds) *Responsibility in World Business: Managing Harmful Side-Effects of Corporate Activity*. Tokyo: United Nations University Press, 2004, pp. 17–38.

37. In 1870, the difficulty of "trying assess the 'mass-homicide' of modern war in nicely balanced terms of cause and intention and method … prompted forty Catholic Bishops … to petition the Pope himself" for a revision of the Church's teaching on just war. A. C. F. Beales, *The Catholic Church and International Order*. New York: Penguin Books, 1941, p. 108. It was hoped, in particular, that this revision could be carried out at the Vatican Council (being held that same year), but the issue was never formally taken up by the assembled bishops. For a historical account of this proposal, which appears to have been undertaken originally at the initiative of the Armenian Synod, see Joseph Joblin, *L'Église et la guerre*. Paris: Desclée de Brouwer, 1988, pp. 218–223.

38. Neff, *War and the Law of Nations*, p. 279.

39. Ibid., p. 293.

40. The two most notable works in this genre were Vanderpol, *La doctrine scolastique du droit de la guerre*, and Robert Regout, *La doctrine de la guerre juste de saint Augustin à nos jours d'après les théologiens et les canonists catholiques*. Paris: A. Pedone, 1935.

41. For a discussion of this trend in Catholic thought, see René Coste, *Le problème du droit de guerre dans la pensée de Pie XII*. Paris: Aubier, 1962, pp. 148–163, "Faut-il une révision de la doctrine traditionelle?"; and Joblin, *L'Église et la guerre*, pp. 207–263. See also the comments on Pope Benedict XV in Araujo and Lucal, *Papal Diplomacy and the Quest for Peace*, ch. 4, "The Holy See and the Founding of the League of Nations: 1940–1920", pp. 91–129.

42. "*Pacem, Dei Munus Pulcherrimum*: Encyclical of Pope Benedict XV on Peace and Christian Reconciliation", 23 May 1920, §17; available at ⟨http://www.vatican.va/holy_father/benedict_xv/encyclicals/documents/hf_ben-xv_enc_23051920_pacem-dei-munus-pulcherrimum_en.html⟩ (accessed 10 October 2008).

43. See Luigi Taparelli d'Azeglio, *Essai théorique de droit naturel base sur les faits*, translated from the original Italian. Tournai: H. Casterman, 1875 [1840–1843], vol. II, pp. 290–294 (book 8, ch. 6, propositions 12–18).

44. See, for example, Pius XII's Discourse of 6 November 1955, cited by Coste, *Le problème du droit de guerre*, p. 183. On the relationship between Catholic teaching on natural law and the establishment of world government, see Robert P. George, "Natural Law and International Order", in David R. Mapel and Terry Nardin (eds) *International Society: Diverse Ethical Perspectives*, Princeton, NJ: Princeton University Press, 1998, pp. 54–69.

45. See Coste, *Le problème du droit de guerre*, pp. 56–58, who indicates how Taparelli's conception of international society and armed force influenced Popes Benedict XV, Pius XI and Pius XII.

46. For instance, James Turner Johnson, "Toward Reconstructing the *Jus ad Bellum*", *The Monist*, 57, 1973: 461–488, p. 480.

47. See Coste, *Le problème du droit de guerre*, pp. 159–160.

48. See Charles Journet, *Church of the Word Incarnate*, vol. 1, *The Apostolic Hierarchy*, trans. A. H. C. Downes. London and New York: Sheed & Ward, 1955 [1941]; and Gregory M. Reichberg and Henrik Syse, "Humanitarian Intervention: A Case of Offensive Force?", *Security Dialogue*, 33, 2002: 220–233. Similarly, in National Conference of Catholic Bishops, "The Harvest of Justice Sown in Peace", it is asserted that "legitimate political authorities are permitted as a last resort to employ limited force to rescue the innocent and establish justice" (p. 453).

49. "*Pacem in Terris*: Encyclical of Pope John XXIII on Establishing Universal Peace in Truth, Justice, Charity, and Liberty", 11 April 1963, §127; available at ⟨http://www. vatican.va/holy_father/john_xxiii/encyclicals/documents/hf_j-xxiii_enc_11041963_pacem_ en.html⟩ (accessed 10 October 2008).

50. National Conference of Catholic Bishops, *The Challenge of Peace*.

51. The phrase is from James Turner Johnson, who has used it as a polemical point of contrast with the "presumption against war" view – see James Turner Johnson, "The Broken Tradition", *The National Interest*, No. 45, 1996: 27–36. Johnson is himself a Protestant, but his articulation of this theme has found support among influential Catholic thinkers ("theocons", to borrow a term coined by Damon Linker, *The Theocons*. New York: Doubleday, 2006) such as Michael Novak and George Weigel. On the debate between these two conceptions, see Gregory M. Reichberg, "Is There a 'Presumption against War' in Aquinas's Ethics?", in H. Syse and G. M. Reichberg, *Ethics, Nationalism, and Just War: Medieval and Contemporary Perspectives*. Washington, DC: Catholic University of America Press, 2007, pp. 72–98. For an application to contemporary Church teaching, see Drew Christiansen, "Peacemaking and the Use of Force: Behind the Pope's Stringent Just-War Teaching", *America Magazine*, 15 May 1999. This debate was reopened by the invasion of Iraq; see Gregory M. Reichberg, "Preemptive War: What Would Aquinas Say?", *Commonweal*, 131(2), 2004: 9–10, ⟨http:// www.commonwealmagazine.org/article.php?id_article=831⟩ (accessed 10 October 2008); and George Weigel, "Iraq, Then & Now", *First Things*, April 2006, available at ⟨http:// www.firstthings.com/article.php3?id_article=115⟩ (accessed 10 October 2008).

52. Augustine's letter 185 to Boniface, in Reichberg, Syse and Begby, *The Ethics of War*, p. 88. See Phillip W. Gray, "Just War, Schism, and Peace in St. Augustine", in H. Syse and G. M. Reichberg (eds) *Ethics, Nationalism, and Just War: Medieval and Contemporary Perspectives*. Washington, DC: The Catholic University of America Press, 2007, pp. 51–71.

53. Cited in Reichberg, Syse and Begby, *The Ethics of War*, p. 109.

54. Reichberg, Syse and Begby, *The Ethics of War*, pp. 121–122.

55. Joseph Blötzer, "Inquisition", *The Catholic Encyclopedia*, vol. VIII. New York: Robert Appleton Company, 1910; available at ⟨http://www.newadvent.org/cathen/08026a.htm⟩ (accessed 10 October 2008). For a more elaborate treatment, see Journet, *Church of the Word Incarnate*, pp. 193–330.

56. See *Code of Canon Law*. Vatican: Libreria Editrice Vaticana, 1983. Revised translation of *Codex Iuris Canonici*, prepared under the auspices of the Canon Law Society of America, 1999; available at ⟨http://www.vatican.va/archive/ENG1104/_INDEX.HTM#fonte⟩ (accessed 10 October 2008). Book VI, "Sanctions in the Church", Canon 1311, states: "The Church has the innate and proper right to coerce offending members of the Christian faithful with penal sanctions." Canon 1312, §2, adds: "The law can establish other expiatory penalties which deprive a member of the Christian faithful of some spiritual or temporal good and which are consistent with the supernatural purpose of the Church." Among the ecclesiastical sanctions mentioned are excommunication (Canon 1331), suspension or removal from power or office (Canons 1333 and 1336), or prohibition (of priests or members of religious orders) from residing in a certain place or

territory (Canon 1337). No provision is made for the administration of punishment by civil authorities as a sanction for offences against the faith (heresy, etc.).

57. See Pope Benedict XVI's comments to this effect in his discourse to the Roman Curia, 22 December 2005, section entitled "Le difficile dialogue entre Église et modernité". Benedict XVI, "Réflexions sur une année de la vie de l'Église et le monde", Discours à la Curie romaine (22 December 2005), in *La documentation catholique*, No. 2350, 15 January 2006, pp. 56–63, pp. 60–62.

58. From his commentary "On Vows and the Fulfilling of Vows" to the decretal *Quod super his*; text translated in Reichberg, Syse and Begby, *The Ethics of War*, p. 154.

59. *Summa theologiae* II-II, q. 10, a. 8; Reichberg, Syse and Begby, *The Ethics of War*, p. 193.

60. See John Muldoon, *Popes, Lawyers and Infidels: The Church and the Non-Christian World, 1250–1550*. College Park: University of Pennsylvania Press, 1979, pp. 5–18.

61. For discussion and references, see Journet, *Church of the Word Incarnate*, vol. 1, *The Apostolic Hierarchy*, pp. 228–231.

62. Benedict XVI, "Faith, Reason and the University: Memories and Reflections", lecture at the University of Regensburg, 12 September 2006; available at ⟨http://www.vatican.va/holy_father/benedict_xvi/speeches/2006/september/documents/hf_ben-xvi_spe_20060912_university-regensburg_en.html⟩ (accessed 10 October 2008), third paragraph.

63. *Summa theologiae* II-II, q. 40, a. 2; cited in Reichberg, Syse and Begby, *The Ethics of War*, p. 179.

64. *De bello*, section V, §6, cited in Reichberg, Syse and Begby, *The Ethics of War*, p. 355.

65. *De bello*, section VI, §7, in Reichberg, Syse and Begby, *The Ethics of War*, p. 356. Suarez attenuates this Christian exceptualism in the passage that follows, when he notes that the reasoning in question could even apply to infidels who wished to forgo idolatry, "worship the one God and observe the law of nature" but were impeded from doing so by their rulers. Should another infidel ruler, "guided solely by natural reason", come to their aid, his resort to armed force would constitute a "just defense of the innocent" (ibid.).

66. A selection of relevant passages from these authors may be found in Reichberg, Syse and Begby, *The Ethics of War*, pp. 114–115 and p. 124 (Gratian), pp. 154–155 (Innocent IV), pp. 191–193 (Thomas Aquinas), pp. 304–305 (Vitoria). For an analysis of rationales for the Crusades, see Benjamin Z. Kedar, *Crusade and Mission: European Approaches toward the Muslims*. Princeton. NJ: Princeton University Press, 1984.

67. See Innocent IV's juridical formulation of this position in "On Vows and the Fulfilling of Vows", in Reichberg, Syse and Begby, *The Ethics of War*, pp. 152–155. Pope Innocent gave two reasons for the Christian claim to ownership of the Holy Land: (i) this land was "consecrated" by the birth, life and death of Jesus Christ, such that Christians were entitled to worship there, not Muslims; (ii) this land was justly conquered by the Roman emperor after the death of Christ, a jurisdiction that passed to the later Christian emperors.

68. Text quoted by the National Conference of Catholic Bishops, *The Challenge of Peace*, p. 24, §76.

69. "Message of His Holiness Pope John Paul II for the Celebration of the World Day of Peace", 1 January 2000, §11; available at ⟨http://www.vatican.va/holy_father/john_paul_ii/messages/peace/documents/hf_jp-ii_mes_08121999_xxxiii-world-day-for-peace_en.html⟩ (accessed 10 October 2008). The obligation in question is of a piece with the more general obligation, enunciated clearly by the revised English edition of the *Catechism of the Catholic Church* (1997), that "legitimate defense can not only be a right but a grave duty for one who is responsible for the lives of others" (§2265, p. 16).

70. See Christiansen, "Peacemaking and the Use of Force".

71. George Weigel, "Pope John Paul II and the Dynamics of History", the 2000 Templeton Lecture on Religion and World Affairs, *Foreign Policy Research Institute Newsletter*, 1(6), April 2000, section III; available at ⟨http://www.fpri.org/ww/0106.200004.weigel.popehistory.html⟩ (accessed 10 October 2008).
72. "Message of His Holiness Pope John Paul II for the Celebration of the World Day of Peace", §11.
73. Congregation for the Doctrine of the Faith, *Instruction on Christian Freedom and Liberation*, p. 46, §76.
74. See, for instance, The Holy See, *Catechism of the Catholic Church*. Mahwah, NJ: Paulist Press, 1994, which affirms "the permanent validity of the moral law during armed conflict" (§2312). The same text also enunciates specific *in bello* prohibitions, for example: "the extermination of a people, nation, or ethnic minority must be condemned as a mortal sin. One is morally bound to resist orders that command genocide" (§2313).
75. For instance, the revised English edition of the *Catechism of the Catholic Church* (1997) includes an unambiguous condemnation of terrorist tactics: "*Terrorism* threatens, wounds and kills indiscriminately; it is gravely against justice and charity" (§2297, p. 18). For a summary of contemporary Catholic teaching on actions prohibited in war, see Pontifical Council of Justice and Peace, *Compendium of the Social Doctrine of the Church*. London and New York: Burns & Oats, 2005, ch. 11, part III, "The Failure of Peace: War", pp. 249–257.
76. Congregation for the Doctrine of the Faith, *Instruction on Christian Freedom and Liberation*, p. 47, §78.
77. Ibid.

7

Norms of war in Eastern Orthodox Christianity

Yuri Stoyanov

The attitudes of the Eastern Orthodox churches to the use of armed force and the means and methods of warfare have not received such exhaustive treatment as the corresponding attitudes to the same phenomena in Western Christianity – Roman Catholicism and the various denominations of Protestant Christianity. Yet lately a thought-provoking debate has developed among Eastern Orthodox theologians and scholars centred on the historical development and transformations of the notions of "justifiable war" and "just war" or the categorization of war as a "lesser good" or a "lesser evil" in Eastern Orthodox Christianity.[1] These debates, as well as the Eastern Orthodox Christian responses to modern developments in international humanitarian law and new weapons and tactics of mass destruction, need to be considered in the context of the historical development and transformations of the Eastern Orthodox perspectives on war and peace, their principal stages and figures, their scriptural and patristic basis and their reinterpretations in modern ideologized and reformist trends in Eastern Orthodox thought.

Eastern Orthodox attitudes to the problems of warfare, just war and the ethics of war offer important parallels to and differences from the respective Western Christian attitudes, which need a careful and balanced analysis. It is worth mentioning at this stage that it is still difficult to present a definitive reconstruction of the evolution of the notions of just and/or justifiable war in Eastern Orthodox thought and societies, because some of the main relevant works in its classical representative tradition, Byzantine Christianity, either have not been edited and published or,

World religions and norms of war, Popovski, Reichberg and Turner (eds),
United Nations University Press, 2009, ISBN 978-92-808-1163-6

when edited, have not been translated into modern West European languages and thus remain inaccessible to the larger scholarly audience.[2] With the present state of evidence and research in this field of study, it will be possible to introduce what seem to be the most important Eastern Orthodox perspectives on the use of military force and right conduct during warfare, while remaining conscious of the above problems and the amount of unpublished source material in this particular field.

Scriptural and patristic basis

As in Western Christianity, the roots of the prevalent attitudes to war and peace in Eastern Orthodoxy can be easily traced back to the New Testament and its well-known passages concerning the use of force, violence, Christ's moral teaching and its emphatic pacifistic perspective (for example, Matthew 5–7, 26:52, Luke 2:14, 3:14, 6:29). At the same time, Eastern Orthodoxy inherited the potential for a non-pacifistic and even militaristic exegesis of the New Testament passages containing military imagery (for example, 1 Thessalonians 5:8, Ephesians 6:10, 1 Corinthians 9:7, 2 Timothy 2:3–4), Jesus' "sword" allusions (Matthew 10:34, Luke 22:35–38) and the heavenly war imagery in Revelation 20, which, as in Western Christianity, in particular circumstances and through suitably literalist interpretations could be used to sanction the use of force. Eastern Orthodoxy also inherited the evident tensions between the ideas of war and peace respectively in the Old and New Testaments, which, despite the continuity between the notions of the ultimate universal eternal peace in some trends of Jewish prophetic and messianic thought and early Christian messianism, diverged substantially in other areas.

These divergences had already caused divisions and schisms in early Christianity, as many of the Gnostic groups came to attribute the Yahweh-inspired war and violence episodes in the Old Testament to a lower, often wicked, demiurge of the physical world, and Marcion's (c.85–c.160) dichotomy between the New Testament God of salvation and love and the Old Testament God of the law of vengeance and justice also proved influential until the early third century CE. Millenarian trends in early Christianity, Montanism, and other related apocalyptic currents, seeking to revive apostolic Christianity, characteristically professed passionate pacifism and a rejection of violence. These pacifistic preoccupations in early Christianity could be coupled both with apocalyptic expectations of forthcoming eschatological peace and with pronounced rejection and condemnation of Christian participation in (Roman) military service. Such anti-militarism and pacific views were shared and articulated with varying degrees of intensity and qualification by early Church Fathers such as St Justin Martyr (c.100–c.165), Clement of Alexandria (c.150–c.215), St Hippolytus (c.170–c.236), Tertullian (c.160–c.225), Origen (c.185–c.254), St Cyprian of Carthage (d.258), Arnobius (3rd–4th century) and Lactantius (c.250–c.325).[3] At the same time, an increasing amount of evidence suggests that Christians served in the army in the pre-Constantinian era, particularly from the late second century onwards, and were beginning to form Christian milieus within the Roman military.

Constantine's Edict of Milan in 313, his conversion to Christianity and the legitimization and institutionalization of the Church in the Roman empire inevitably led to various patterns of rapprochement between the state's and the Church's attitudes to war and war ethics. This rapprochement is exemplified by Eusebius of Caesarea (c.260–c.340) but occurred against the protests and opposition of anti-militarist Christian groups such as the Donatists. The newly evolving concord between secular and clerical authorities followed somewhat differing patterns in the West and East Roman empire, conditioned by the contrasting ways in which Church–state relations developed in the Latin West (which amid the "barbarian" invasions and the formation of the Germanic states were also able to provoke frequent secular–ecclesiastic rivalries) and the Greek East (in the framework of the crystallization of Byzantine political theology within a centralized imperial state).

In the specific political and religious conditions in the Latin West (where the very survival of the Christian empire, forced to wage defensive wars, was at stake), St Ambrose (c.339–397) and St Augustine (354–430) eventually laid the foundation of the medieval Western Christian just war tradition, which, through a process well explored in Western scholarship, was systematized in the commentaries/syntheses of, for example, Gratian (d. by c.1160) and Thomas Aquinas (c.1225–1274). Adhering to a different corpus of patristic writings and a different set of relationships with the East Roman (Byzantine) state and ideology, the Eastern Orthodox Church retained important elements from pre-Constantinian Christian attitudes to war and its morality, whereas the Byzantine state itself inherited and retained core elements of the secular just war tradition of the pre-Christian Roman empire and Greek antiquity. In the East Roman world, the pacific tendencies of pre-Constantinian Christianity were brought into the framework of the newly evolving Christian imperial ideology by figures such as Eusebius, St Cyril of Alexandria (376–444) and St John Chrysostom (345–407), who argued that the establishment of the Christian empire fulfilled a providential design to pacify the world and put an end to humanity's violent conflicts and strife. Such notions drew to a certain degree on some earlier patristic views that, even in the pre-Constantinian Pax Romana, had in effect provided favourable conditions for the dissemination and internationaliza-tion of Christianity. Such views may show some general indebtedness to earlier Stoic thinking about the pacifying role of the pre-Christian Ro-man empire.

Not all of the Eastern Christian Fathers of the late East Roman/early Byzantine period, however, were prepared unequivocally to identify the earthly Roman empire with the "empire of Christ". Coexistence between the pacific and pacifistic theological and social attitudes transmitted from early to Byzantine Christianity, on the one hand, and the political and military needs of an imperial state (which retained important features of pre-Christian Roman military structures, machinery and ethos), on the other, was not always easy and unproblematic. The most telling manifes-tations of this tension are to be found in Eastern Orthodox Christian canon law, as in the 13th Canon of St Basil the Great (c.330–379) from his first Canonical Epistle to Amphilochus, Bishop of Iconium (378), ac-cording to which the act of killing during war needs to be distinguished from voluntary murder, although it is advisable that the perpetrators should be refused communion for three years.[4] The text of the canon also contains an allusion to an earlier pronouncement by St Athanasius of Alexandria (c.296–373) made in his *Epistle to Ammoun the Monk*, which (when extracted as a separate statement) asserts that it is "praise-worthy" to destroy adversaries in war.[5] When, however, the pronounce-ment is seen in the overall context of the rhetoric and imagery of the epistle, this can allow for different readings,[6] which cast doubt on its interpretation as a rare and important Eastern Christian patristic en-dorsement of the lawfulness of killing in war.[7]

A succession of canons in the Apostolic Canons and those of the Ecu-menical and Local Councils that entered Eastern Orthodox canon law spell out explicitly the prohibitions on Christian clergy and monks on en-tering military service or receiving positions in the secular state adminis-tration and government.[8] Stipulating further the prerogatives of clerical and monastic non-resistance to violence, these canonical regulations de-lineate the phenomenon that has been aptly defined as a "stratification of pacifism"[9] in the early medieval Church, applicable in varying degrees to the different Church activities in both the Greek East and the Latin West. Consequently, both clergy and monks were expected to main-tain the pacific and pacifistic standards of the early Church and were pro-hibited from any military activity, which was strictly reserved for the laity.

The subsequent developments of the inherited canon law of the patris-tic and early medieval periods followed differing trajectories during the High Middle Ages in Western and Eastern Christendom. Between the eleventh and thirteenth centuries, Catholic canonists, theologians and clerics introduced various innovations in Catholic canon law to accommodate and specify the role of the Church in the evolving Catholic just war and holy war doctrines (based generally on selective exegesis of the scriptural sources, the principal notions in Augustine's Christian justification of warfare and definitions of just war as well as Roman law) and the juridical theory of the Crusade.

No comparable contemporary developments can be detected in Eastern Christian canon law, although there were attempts to soften the harshness of the 13th Canon of St Basil and to consider it as an advisory rather than a mandatory canonical requirement. The commentaries by the prominent twelfth-century Byzantine canonists John Zonaras and Theodore Balsamon on St Basil's 13th Canon define it, respectively, as "burdensome" and "unendurable" – if it were to be implemented systematically, Christian soldiers involved in regular or successive warfare would never be able to partake of the "holy mysteries" of the Body and Blood of Christ.[10] Both canonists argue that, because the excommunication of Christian soldiers from the mysteries for three years, as prescribed by the canon, was widely seen as an excessive punishment, they were not aware of any instance when the canon had actually been enforced by the Church. However, both canonists refer to the proceedings of a Church synod during the reign of ascetically minded warrior-Emperor Nikephoros II Phokas (963–969) during which Patriarch Polyeuktos (956–970) and the ecclesiastical hierarchy invoked the authority of St Basil's 13th Canon to deny the emperor's request that the Church should establish canonical regulations through which Byzantine soldiers who fell in warfare would begin to be honoured on a par with the holy martyrs and accordingly be celebrated with hymns and feast days.[11] Significantly, Nikephoros Phokas' request that fallen soldiers should be treated as martyrs occurred during the emperor's offensives against the Arabs in Asia Minor and Syria, re-conquests that witnessed a more pronounced use of religious rhetoric. It is also significant that the refusal of the Byzantine Church to treat fallen Christian soldiers as martyrs occurred after Pope Leo IV (847–855) and Pope John VIII (872–882) had already stated that those who died defending the Church and Christendom would be granted absolution and receive heavenly rewards – notions that in the second half of the eleventh century would crucially contribute to the development and eventual formalization of the Crusade idea and the sanctification of holy war by the Catholic Church.

Within the Eastern Orthodox tradition, comparable notions appear in the ninth-century *Vita* of the celebrated missionary to the Slavs, St Constantine–Cyril the Philosopher (826/7–869), which records his ambassadorial visit to the court of the Abbasid caliph al-Mutawakkil (847–861) in 851 and his debates with Muslim theologians there. He was asked by the Muslim theologians why Christians do not apply in practice the precepts in the well-known verses in Matthew 5:38–44 teaching non-violence, non-resistance to evil/evildoers and love and prayer for one's enemies. In his reported reply St Constantine in effect gave priority to John 15:13 ("No one has greater love than this, to lay down one's life for one's friends"), arguing that as private people Christians can bear any offences, but when in company they defend each other and sacrifice their lives in battle for their neighbours. Accordingly, the martial feats of the "Christ-loving soldiers" in defence of their lands, the Holy Church and Christianity are interpreted through the prism of this precept in John as constituting paradigmatic Christian duties for which they should "fight to the last". After fulfilling these "precious pledges", the Church would qualify these Christian soldiers as martyrs and intercessors before God. But, unlike contemporary Catholicism, between the tenth and twelfth centuries this notion was not developed and affirmed systematically in Eastern Orthodoxy, and its rejection by Patriarch Polyeuktos during the aforementioned synod was an important precedent for its continuing negation by the Byzantine Church.

Despite becoming increasingly acquainted with crusading ideology in the era of the Crusades, Byzantine canonists who were critical of the severity of St Basil's 13th Canon still rejected the innovation attempted by Nikephoros Phokas to secure martyrdom for soldiers slain in battle. The one major exception, when an Ecumenical (Constantinople) patriarch altered this generally negative stance of the Byzantine Church towards the martyrdom of fallen soldiers, occurred during the patriarchate of Michael IV Autoreinaos (1208–1214) in the wake of the Fourth Crusade, the Latin conquest of Constantinople and the establishment of the Latin empire of Constantinople. The Orthodox patriarchate was compelled to go into exile in Nicaea as the Greek Nicaean empire was establishing its sway in the Byzantine heartlands in western Asia Minor, and beginning the struggle against the Latins in Constantinople aimed at reclaiming the ancient seat of the Byzantine empire. In these new and changing political circumstances, Patriarch Michael IV Autoreinaos took the radical step of promising remission of sins to Nicene soldiers who died in battle, a move that may have been influenced by contemporary Western crusading models and paradoxically may have been applied in the context of battles against Latin crusaders.[12]

The practice of promising such a reward, however, was not continued beyond his patriarchate. More than two centuries had to pass before his initiative was revived on one occasion during the first half of the fourteenth century when the last Byzantine strongholds and enclaves in western Anatolia found themselves under increasing pressure from the warlike Turkish emirates that emerged in the wake of the breakup of the Anatolian Seljuk sultanate. A contemporary Church calendar of saints and feasts bestowed military martyrdom on several Christian soldiers of Philadelphia in western Anatolia who fell in battle, this time against the Muslim forces of the feared Turkish warrior Umur Paşa Aydınoğlu, who was trying to extend the conquests of his coastal emirate of Aydın (on the western Anatolian littoral) further inland. Umur Paşa's political and military exploits included active and decisive involvement in the Byzantine civil war of 1341–1347, which provoked the formation of a Holy League (*Sacra Liga*) against him by the Latin powers in the Aegean, leading to the Crusade of Smyrna of 1344 when a joint Hospitaller, Venetian and Cypriot fleet re-conquered Smyrna from his forces.[13] Contemporary and later Muslim sources extol Umur Paşa as a model Islamic warrior for the faith who distinguished himself in the *ghazwa* warfare (originally "raid against the infidels"), which by that time had acquired increasingly religious overtones – the Turkoman *ghāzī* fighters in Anatolia could be praised as the "instruments" and "sword" of God, and their eventual martyrdom would bring them eternal life. It is intriguing, therefore, that this period of resumption of Latin crusading warfare in the Aegean (admittedly on a smaller scale) against the *ghazwa* campaigns of Umur Paşa witnessed a Byzantine Church attempt to honour as martyrs Byzantine Christians who fought Umur Paşa's warriors for the faith. Like the previous Byzantine initiative in the sphere of military martyrdom, however, this attempt remained isolated and, more significantly, did not succeed in gaining any recognition from the Constantinople patriarchate. During the Byzantine Church synod in Nikephoros Phokas' reign, moreover, certain priests and bishops were arraigned for having fought in battles in which they slew many adversaries and were accordingly defrocked by the synod that followed St Basil's 13th Canon.[14]

Finally, the prominent fourteenth-century Byzantine theologian and canonist Matthew Blastares confirms in his influential work on canon and civil law, *Syntagma kata stoicheon* (1355), the validity and relevance of the three-year penance of exclusion from communion "advised" in Basil's 13th Canon, rejecting the arguments of Balsamon and Zonaras on the basis of his own scriptural and theological exegesis.[15] At the same time, writing at a time when the Ottomans were establishing themselves in Gallipoli and Thrace and were to take Adrianople in 1365, Blastares states that, in essence, St Basil extolled the Christian soldiers who safeguarded Christianity and fought its enemies – a praiseworthy defence on behalf of chastity and piety.[16]

Apart from these regulations and debates striving to define the limits and various dimensions of Christian involvement in warfare in the sphere of canon law, speculation about what should be the correct, adequate or acceptable Christian response to the reality of war and affirmation of peace remained an important area in Eastern Orthodox theology, ethics and anthropology throughout the medieval period. In the context of the great theological disputes and schisms in the Church during the fourth century, which were especially divisive and dramatic in Eastern Christendom, the notion of religious peace was pre-eminent in the thought of most of the Greek Fathers of the period. It was clearly of primary importance for the Cappadocian Fathers, St Basil the Great, St Gregory of Nazianzus (330–389) and St Gregory of Nyssa (c.331–c.396), who vigorously fought the Arian movement. This accent on the quest for religious peace was closely related to aspirations for a unity of the Church, in the spheres of both doctrine and hierarchical organization.[17]

In the works of John Chrysostom, which remained extremely influential and popular throughout the Byzantine period, the theme of warfare and its legitimacy reappears in various theological and social contexts. In his *Fourteenth Homily to the Philippians*, he strongly condemns warfare, stating that "God is not a God of war and fighting", which are thus against God; therefore, the Christian ideal and virtue entail the cessation of warfare and fighting, as well as being in peace with all man. In his *First Homily on Corinthians I*, he explicitly declares that true peace can come only from God. He also clearly delineates the Eastern Orthodox "stratification of pacifism" in his work *On the Priesthood*, in which the priesthood is required to adhere to the highest Christian standards and, whenever needed, to serve as a corrective to the actions of the government and laity in the secular world spheres where the state holds sway, including the pursuit and challenge of warfare. Indeed, one of Chrysostom's well-known statements in his *Second Homily on Eutropius 4* – "Never be afraid of the sword if your conscience does not accuse you; never be afraid in war if your conscience is clear", which has been seen as affirming an Eastern Orthodox version of justifiable war – needs to be read in the context of his demarcation of the particular standards for the priesthood and the laity concerning their respective non-involvement/involvement in warfare.[18] Finally, in his *Seventh Homily on 1 Timothy 2:2–4*, Chrysostom provides a categorization of three types of warfare: those caused by attacking foreign armies, civil wars and the internal war of man against himself, the last being the most grievous because the first two cannot injure the soul, whereas the third disturbs the peace of the spirit, stirring up evil desires, anger and envy.

The peace of the spirit and its correlation to the divine peace, the mission of Christ and peace among humans remained important themes in Byzantine theology, mysticism and monastic spirituality throughout the history of the empire and found early expression in the thinking of Dionysius the pseudo-Areopagite (c. 500) and Maximus the Confessor

(580–662). Paradigmatic New Testament notions alluding to God as "not a God of disorder but of peace" (1 Corinthians 14:33); to Christ as "our peace" (Ephesians 2:14); to "the peace of God, which surpasses all understanding" (Philippians 4:7); to the Kingdom of God as "righteousness and peace and joy in the Holy Spirit" (Romans 14:17); to the gentle and quiet nature of "the hidden person of the heart" (1 Peter 3:4), had already undergone substantial theological embellishment in the patristic period. These patristic embellishments defined Christians as "sons of peace", a "peaceable race", "soldiers of peace", "workers for peace", etc. During the Byzantine period, along with the New Testament notions of peace, they became a constant source for new theological, ethical and mystical elaborations and reinterpretations of the presence of, cultivation of and fight for peace in the individual human, social, natural and divine spheres. At the same time, the notion of spiritual warfare against supernatural forces of evil (following on the influential pronouncements of St Paul in, for example, Romans 7:23, Ephesians 6:16–20 and 1 Thessalonians 5:6–8) remained central to Byzantine monastic spirituality, mysticism and asceticism. Accounts of such warfare in Byzantine hagiography and demonology can contain some striking and detailed imagery and terminology; hence monks could be defined as the true "soldiers of Christ", fighting on the front-line of this all-encompassing warfare.[19]

In the influential system of Dionysius the pseudo-Areopagite, for example, primordial peace has an archetypal cosmological dimension – without striving towards its restoration in human societies and within the individual himself, man could not embark on the spiritual path to *theosis* (deification or divinization) and universal salvation, leading to establishment of the ultimate eschatological peace. A similar overwhelming emphasis on the notion of peace in all these various dimensions developed in the Byzantine liturgical, hymnographic, homiletic and hagiographic traditions. However, the numerous invocations of and appeals for peace in Byzantine liturgical and hymnographic literature occasionally coexist with prayers and prayer services for the safety and well-being of Orthodox soldiers/troops and their victory in battle, sometimes alluding to the imperial God-aided victories over the empire's earlier adversaries and often accompanied with associated military imagery, symbolism and typologies.[20] Such prayers can be found in the various versions of the Divine Liturgy of St Basil, the Divine Liturgy of St John Chrysostom and the hymnic cycle for the Feast of the Exaltation of the Cross on 14 September. These prayers, prayer services and blessings reflect the tension between the normative Christian pacific ideal of the Eastern Orthodox Church and the political and military realities that the Byzantine empire faced after the period of expansionism and military triumphs in late antiquity. Forced to wage intermittently defensive warfare on nearly all fronts, the Byzantine imperial state felt compelled to cultivate inherited (and develop some new) religio-political mechanisms to legitimize and justify warfare against its numerous pagan, Muslim and Western (and, on occasions, Eastern) Christian adversaries.

Holy and just war in the Byzantine world (c.527 – c.1453)

Pacifistic and pacific currents in Eastern Orthodoxy may have maintained their currency in the medieval Byzantine world, but the existing rapprochement between state and Church in the late Roman and early Byzantine period meant that the Byzantine Church frequently found itself in situations in which its support for and justification of Byzantine military campaigns was seen as highly significant and necessary. With or without imperial pressure, the Byzantine Church could be involved in the mobilization of popular endorsement for Byzantine troops and inevitably was entrusted with ensuring that they observed their religious obligations properly and entered battle, to face danger and death, spiritually pure and in a pious frame of mind. As in Western Christendom, the involvement of Eastern Orthodoxy in the realm of medieval warfare found expression in military religious services, the early appearance in the field army of military chaplains (who could also serve in the fleet), the celebration of Eucharistic liturgies in the field, the use of Christian religious symbolism and relics for military purposes, the blessing of standards and weapons before battles, services for fallen soldiers after the cessation of fighting, and thanksgiving rituals to celebrate victory.[21] Focusing in great detail on the different aspects of warfare tactics and strategy, the various Byzantine military manuals such as the *Strategikon* attributed to Emperor Maurice (582–602) and the tract ascribed to Emperor Leo VI the Wise (886–912) also stipulate at some length the religious services that need to be performed in military camps and the religious duties of soldiers and priests.[22] Following on the paradigmatic use of the cross-shaped sign (the *labarum*) during Constantine the Great's victory over his rival Maxentius in the battle at Milvian Bridge in 312, crosses – either depicted on flags or carried instead of or alongside standards – were widely used during Byzantine military campaigns. A number of reports recount the use of relics and well-known icons before and during battles between the imperial troops and their adversaries. The widespread popularity and evolution of the cult of military saints such as St George, St Demetrius of Thessaloniki, St Theodore Teron and St Theodore Stratelates, and their adoption as patrons by the Byzantine military aristocracy, highlight another symptomatic dimension of the role of Eastern Orthodoxy in shaping the ethics and practice of warfare in the Byzantine empire.[23]

An interesting and (as far as the subject of this chapter is concerned) crucial debate has developed lately among Byzantinists focused on the religio-historical problem of whether Byzantium ever conceptualized and put into practice its own brand of wars fought for ostensibly religious purposes comparable to the contemporaneous jihad in Islam and the crusading warfare of Western Europe. This debate has brought to the attention of a wider audience some important but less well-known and often neglected evidence of the interrelations between Byzantine Orthodox Christianity, on the one hand, and Byzantine political and military ideology and warfare, on the other. Deriving from diverse secular and ecclesiastical records, this composite evidence highlights the various intricate ways in which Byzantine Orthodox Christianity permeated and contributed to important aspects of Byzantine military religious traditions. The continuing debates on the provenance, nature and implications of this evidence have demonstrated the simplistic nature and untenability of historical reconstructions of unremittingly pacific policies of Byzantium (or the monarchies/polities belonging to its contemporary or post-Byzantine Orthodox Commonwealth) advanced by some Orthodox theologians and popular works on Byzantine history.

The debate on whether Byzantium developed its own version of religious war or a crusading ideology, and the role of the Byzantine Church in this development, can be traced to the early stages of modern Byzantine studies – for instance, in the works of Gustave Schlumberger on tenth-century Byzantine history.[24] According to Schlumberger, the campaigns of Nikephoros Phokas and John I Tzimiskes (969–976) against the Arab Muslim powers in the Levant had a religious character and can be qualified as proto-crusades, especially as Tzimiskes aspired to re-conquer Jerusalem for Christendom. Schlumberger's views were followed by medievalists such as René Grousset[25] and George Ostrogorsky; the latter argued that Emperor Heraclius' famous campaign against Sassanid Persia in 622–630 can be identified as the actual forerunner of the Western Crusades, and some of Tzimiskes' anti-Arab campaigns betray a "veritable crusading spirit".[26] At the other extreme, in his influential publication on the idea of holy war and the Byzantine tradition, Vitalien Laurent argued that, in contrast to the medieval Islamic and West European versions of holy war, the Byzantines failed to develop a proper holy war tradition, owing to their inherent inertia and fatalistic attitudes, and thus, unlike Latin Europe, could not manage to find an active military response to Islamic expansionism.[27] The view that the notion of a "holy war", as developed in the Islamic and West European holy war ideologies, remained alien and incomprehensible to the Byzantines has since been upheld and supported with more arguments and evidence in a succession of important studies. However, the supporters of the position that when Byzantine ideology and practice of war are judged on their own terms and not just in the framework of Islamic and West European holy war models, they can exhibit on occasions the traits of a specifically Byzantine "holy war" tradition have also brought new valuable source material and methodological considerations into the debate.

The study of Byzantine and post-Byzantine versions of Christian warfare has been plagued for a long time by a number of influential inherited stereotypes (some of which derive from particular medieval West European perceptions of Byzantium), attributing to the Byzantines a distinct aversion to warfare and bloodshed, as well as passivity and compliance in the face of the Islamic menace from the East. Recent works on Byzantine military history, structures and strategy[28] have demonstrated again the unsustainability of such stereotypes. Most of these stereotypes owe their authority and currency to their repeated exploitation in eighteenth- and nineteenth-century European historiography of Byzantium and the Middle Ages and have survived the advance of modern Byzantine studies. This reassessment of Byzantine military religious traditions and ideology has also highlighted the need to re-visit the question of whether Byzantine policies, often seen as pacific and retreatist, derive from corresponding pacific traits in Eastern Orthodoxy (as frequently argued) or from the complex geopolitical situations in which the empire periodically found itself and the resultant strategic considerations.[29]

A number of distinguished historians and theologians have endorsed with varying degrees of certainty and emphasis different aspects of the thesis that Byzantium did not develop a holy war tradition and abhorred (or in the case of the crusading movement, also did not comprehend) the holy war ideologies that arose and matured in the contemporary Islamic Near East and Western Europe (with all the implications for the ethics and theology of war in the Orthodox Churches/polities in the post-Byzantine period). In many cases, the absence of a real Crusade ideology (in West European terms) in medieval Byzantium is attributed to the specific nature of Byzantine Orthodoxy, its institutions and approach to violence and warfare.[30] Proponents of this thesis,[31] a summary of which follows below, habitually approach Byzantine military history through the prism of contemporaneous Islamic and West European theories and practice of holy war and their shared features. These features include: the proclamation (and leadership) of the holy war by a "legitimate" religious authority – warfare is thus seen as decreed by God; the ostensible religious aims of the war, which needs to be seen as being waged against adversaries identified in a religious context as "infidel" or "heretic" – these aims can be thus virtually unlimited; and the promise of spiritual rewards to the warriors (remission of sins, martyrdom, eternal salvation, entrance into paradise). Since Byzantine military history only sporadically shows (at best only rudimentary) elements of these features, the inevitable conclusion is that Byzantium did not develop and put into practice an ideology of a Christian holy war. Even Byzantine wars that were characterized by a pronounced religious sentiment and rhetoric, such as those under Maurice and Heraclius against Sassanid Persia in the first three decades of the seventh century or the anti-Arab campaigns of Nikephoros Phokas and John Tzimiskes in the second half of the tenth century, do not possess, in this view, the core features of a Christian holy war. The Byzantines used the same religious services and the same Christian icons, relics and symbolism when confronting both non-Christian and Christian adversaries.

The different social and political conditions in the feudal world of Western Europe compared with the centralized imperial state of Byzantium conditioned the development of a very different military ethos among the corresponding aristocratic and military elites. The ethos cultivated among Latin knightly nobility was particularly conducive to enthusiastic support for and active participation in Christian holy wars. Unlike the medieval Catholic Church, the Byzantine Church did not promulgate war and did not indulge in the release of warlike and threatening declarations. The Byzantine Church entirely delegated the conceptualization and practice of warfare to the secular imperial government, trying on occasions to check what could be regarded as unwarranted imperial demands such as rewarding holy military martyrdom. Wars were declared, led and conducted by the emperor, a secular and public authority, entrusted to maintain the defence and unity of the imperial state. The conceptualization of Byzantine warfare overall was consequently in essence a continuation of the largely secular late Roman just war tradition; wars were, therefore, seen as intended to defend imperial territories or to regain lost territories and to protect imperial subjects. The late Roman just war tradition inevitably underwent Christianization in the Byzantine period and it was the divinely ordained mission of the Christian Romans (the new "chosen people") to safeguard Constantinople, seen as both the "New Rome" and the "New Jerusalem", and its single universal Christian empire the "New Israel", against the encroachments of the new "barbarians" – pagans, Muslims and, on occasion, West European Christians. This Christianized "just war" tradition became a fundamental part of Byzantine imperial ideology, closely interwoven with the reinterpreted and actualized Romano-Byzantine paradigms of God-guidedness in battle and imperial victory ("Victoria Augustorum").

Historians who argue that the study of the Byzantine version of Christian warfare needs to take into account to a much greater degree East Roman/Byzantine political and religious developments reach somewhat different conclusions,[32] which are summarized below. In their view, some of the criteria used to define holy war ideology in Islamic and West European contexts are not applicable to Eastern Christendom and Byzantium. Thus, the fact that it was the Byzantine emperor who declared and conducted the various Byzantine wars and military expeditions should not automatically lead to the conclusion that these wars were entirely secular, because Byzantine political and religious ideology could not be separated so easily. In Byzantine political theology, the emperor was extolled as Christ's vicar and God's chosen ruler to preside over and defend the God-elected Christian Roman empire, itself an earthly replica of the divine heavenly monarchy. As a defender of the True Faith, Orthodoxy, his God-granted mission was to lead his armies against those who threatened the integrity of the universal Christian empire and its providential mission – whose enemies thus were also enemies of Orthodoxy. Regaining lost imperial lands, therefore, also meant restoring and expanding Orthodox Christianity, a notion that could be used to justify offensive warfare. In reality, Byzantine wars were always seen as being waged in defence of the unity of the sole legitimate Christian empire and Orthodoxy, which attached a certain quality of "holiness" to these war efforts, regarded consequently as divinely ordained and supported. On occasions Byzantine imperial and military propaganda (during Heraclius' anti-Persian campaigns, for example) might define the adversary in religious terms as "infidel" and "impious", but these remained isolated instances and were definitely not a routine practice. The Byzantine Church tenaciously opposed the notion of sanctified military martyrdom for fallen soldiers, although the situation may have been somewhat different in the military religious ideology developed by the Byzantine military classes.[33]

There are indications that the idea of Christian warriors as martyrs for Orthodoxy, fighting for the salvation of their souls, became part of this evolving ideology and may have been encouraged more frequently by the imperial court than the only recorded case of such an imperial initiative during Nikephoros Phokas' reign would suggest. Such developments in the ethics and martyrology of Byzantine Christian warfare can be tracked down especially in the Anatolian frontier zones of the empire, where Byzantine troops and military formations continuously confronted the *ghazwa* warfare of the advancing Turkoman groups from around the mid-eleventh century onwards. Finally, revisiting some of the evidence of Byzantine campaigns in the Near East suggests that Byzantine aspirations regarding the re-conquest of Christian holy sites in Palestine were not that minimal, as usually accepted. Reassessed in this manner, some of the Byzantine military campaigns waged against non-Christian forces in Anatolia and the Near East may indeed be defined, in this view, as belonging to a certain degree to the category of holy war, to which the Islamic jihad and West European crusading warfare also belong as sub-categories.

The debate on the existence or non-existence of a Byzantine version of Christian holy war has undoubtedly opened new important venues for the exploration of Eastern Orthodox perspectives on the ethics and theology of warfare in the classical Byzantine and post-Byzantine periods. In some of the spheres of this debate and with the present state of published evidence and research, definitive conclusions cannot be reached as yet. Debating Byzantine military history in greater depth, however, has brought about a deeper understanding of some of the specifically Eastern Christian and Byzantine approaches to the ethics and conduct of warfare. In an important contrast with the medieval West, for example, in Eastern Christendom and Byzantium, ecclesiastical involvement and participation in warfare with some religious goals was important but not absolutely vital for its promulgation and legitimization. However, given the blending of imperial and religious ideology in Byzantine political theology, most Byzantine wars, even those without ostensibly religious objectives and waged primarily for geopolitical reasons, possess an aspect of "holiness" – at least in the specifically Byzantine context. All these wars were waged to defend the integrity of God's empire on earth and to recover formerly imperial and Christian lands – by extension they were fought for God and Orthodoxy. In this providential framework Byzantine military defeats and setbacks were interpreted as God's punishment for Byzantine sins – or, in the later history of Byzantium, as crucial stages in the unfolding of the God-guided eschatological drama determining the fortunes of the universal empire. Pleading for divine help and protection before and in the course of war was absolutely imperative and then God could be indeed invoked as the "mighty Lord of battles" and the "God of Righteousness" leading the Orthodox to a complete victory. Apart from being called upon to repel demonic hordes, in a succession of Orthodox hymnic cycles the victory-giving powers of the Holy Cross could be sought by summoning its influence as an "invincible weapon" of Godliness and peace, granting the Orthodox people and their rulers victory over their enemies.

The debates on and discussions of religious rhetoric and elements in Byzantine campaigns show, moreover, that some of them could have openly stated religious goals as part of their politico-military agenda. Such religious goals could include the recovery of the True Cross and its restoration to Jerusalem during Heraclius' anti-Persian campaigns[34] or the re-conquest of lost Christian lands and Holy Places in Palestine, including naturally Jerusalem, which were reportedly publicly declared as military objectives (along with the vanquishing of Islam) during the anti-Arab offensives of Nikephoros Phokas and John Tzimiskes.[35] Following the establishment of the Crusader states in the Levant, religious motives and sentiments arguably also played a prominent role in the successful Anatolian campaigns of Emperor John II Komnenos (1118–1143) against the Turkoman dynasty of the Danishmendids and Emperor Manuel I Komnenos' (1143–1180) ill-fated war against the Seljuk Sultan Kılıç Arslan.[36] These religious elements and the conducting of the campaigns are not sufficient to define the wars of Heraclius, Nikephoros Phokas and John Tzimiskes as "proto-Crusades" or those of John Komnenos and Manuel Komnenos as "Crusades" in the contemporaneous Western sense. But it would be difficult to deny that these campaigns possessed some elements of Christian holy war in the more general Christian medieval context. However, the heightened religious sentiments and elements in these Byzantine campaigns were not a result of a consistently and systematically developed theory of a Christian holy war, which was more or less the case in the Latin West between the eleventh and thirteenth centuries. They were largely conditioned by the specific religio-political conditions related to the separate Byzantine military operations. In the case of the Komnenian emperors' campaigns against the Danishmendids and Seljuks, exposure to the Islamic *ghazwa* of the Turkomans in Anatolia and West European crusading theory and practice during the eleventh century may also have played a role in enhancing their religious dimension.

Furthermore, what Western and Eastern Christian medieval military religious ideologies shared was their dependence on and exploitation of the Old Testament narratives and pronouncements of the God-commanded and -ordained wars of the Israelites against the "heathen" and "idolatrous" Canaanites. As the new "Chosen People", the Byzantines (and their Western Christian counterparts) could draw on these models to depict their wars as God-guided campaigns against the new "infidel" or "God-fighting" enemies. Accordingly, successful warrior-emperors and commanders could be compared to the kings of Israel or to paradigmatic figures in the Old Testament Israelite "holy" wars such as Moses, Aaron, Joshua and David. Thus, in Byzantine military religious ideology and art, Moses' crossing of the Red Sea could be interpreted as prefiguring Constantine the Great's victory at Milvian Bridge, and Joshua's military exploits and triumphs could be presented as alluding to Nikephoros Phokas' and John Tzimiskes' victories on the battlefield. The enemies of Byzantium could be "recognized" as new versions of the Old

Testament adversaries and oppressors of the Israelites such as the Assyrian king Sennacherib, acting again as instruments of God's punishment, provoked by the sins of the Byzantines.

The various Byzantine treatises on military strategy and tactics for combat shed further light on the distinct Byzantine attitudes towards the interrelationship of Christianity and warfare and its ethical implications. These tracts often draw heavily on earlier Hellenistic and Roman authorities, which highlights the continuity of the tradition of tactical and strategic manuals from Graeco-Roman antiquity to the Byzantine Middle Ages, but they inevitably contain much material and advice reflecting Byzantine Christian stances on warfare. The *Tactica* attributed to Emperor Leo VI states emphatically that fundamentally men are peaceful beings, but the devil incites them to indulge in violence and instigate warfare for his own insidious purposes. The origins of warfare are thus attributed to the devil and man should first and foremost prefer peace and avoid war. Accordingly, it was defensive warfare that was preferable and permissible in order to protect the imperial lands from invaders who have been essentially provoked by the devil to assail the territorial integrity of the empire. However, aggressive warfare and unnecessary bloodshed involving even potential enemies of the empire should be disallowed.[37] In an anonymous sixth-century Byzantine treatise on strategy, war is condemned as a "great evil", in fact the "worst of all evil", but, since the enemy has made the shedding of Byzantine blood a matter of honour and virtue, a study of military strategy is necessary so that the aggressor can be resisted and defeated.[38] This statement contains one of the core elements of the traditional just war theory (justifying war in self-defence) going back to antiquity and developed in detail in Western Christendom from the late fourth century onwards. The *Tactica* ascribed to Leo dwells on the need for a just cause for warfare in slightly more detail – again stating that, when enemies have initiated an unjust offensive war, a defensive war against them must be undertaken with courage and eagerness.

The provenance of these notions is clearly recognizable in the just war tradition that was crystallizing in the late Roman and early Byzantine period as a result of the merging of the inherited Roman political military ideology and post-Constantinian Christian political theology. But, apart from specifying in general the *jus ad bellum* regulations of this just war tradition, Byzantine military treatises do not develop in greater detail a theory or notions regarding more general questions raised by the need for a Christian justification of warfare. Their predominant focus remains the various practical and technical details concerning military strategy and tactics: campaign organization, siege warfare, skirmishing, guerrilla warfare, marching through mountainous terrain, setting up camps, etc. On occasions some *jus in bello* regulations may be specified in some detail; avoiding unnecessary loss of life in open combat is frequently recommended – a predilection related to both the Byzantine notion of philanthropy and the actual and well-attested strategic concerns of Byzantium to prevent or solve conflicts (when possible) through diplomacy, bribery and other non-military channels.[39] In the general ethics of war, touched on to a greater or lesser extent in the treatises, war largely appears a necessary or lesser evil – whether this is articulated explicitly or not. The need to plead for divine help and favour in warfare remains an important theme, and Christian rhetoric and polemic also occur on occasions; the *Tactica* ascribed to Leo, for instance, emphasizes that fighting the adversaries of Orthodoxy is spiritually meritorious for Christian warriors.

On the other hand, the study of the role of the Byzantine Church in the religious dimension of Byzantine warfare has as yet failed to uncover a systematic attempt at formulating a just (or indeed holy) war theory coming from within the Church. This applies also to the Orthodox churches that emerged in the Balkans and Russia following Byzantine missionary efforts in these areas from the late ninth century onwards. Thus the Orthodox churches in the Byzantine–Balkan world and Russia generally did not share the important transformation of Christian attitudes to warfare that occurred in medieval Western Christendom during the crusading period between the eleventh and thirteenth centuries. Apart from its continuing opposition to military martyrdom, Byzantine canon law remained static in this period and did not revise its traditional stance on regular, or what was perceived in the contemporary West as "holy", warfare. The abhorrence and criticism by Byzantine churchmen, and indeed historians, of the phenomenon of combatant Latin bishops and priests taking part in the Crusades are well attested. At the same time, despite telling changes in the widespread Byzantine veneration of military saints in which the early anti-warfare perspectives were softened or disappeared, apparently to be integrated more easily into Byzantine lay military piety, the Church was certainly not an enthusiastic supporter of all aspects of this piety. However, further research is needed to explore in greater detail the socio-religious dynamism underlying the emergence of a distinct Christian warrior culture in the Byzantine Anatolian frontier zones, which may reveal that the local church and hierarchs played some role in this process.

Attempts to uncover a coherent and continuous tradition of legitimizing "justifiable war" in the Eastern Orthodox Church, from the patristic through the medieval period, may not have been persuasive,[40] but individual medieval Orthodox churchmen did indeed on occasions articulate views that advanced or came close to such legitimization, or took some part in the organization of defensive warfare. For instance, during the great joint siege of Constantinople by the Persians and the Avars in 626, the Constantinople Patriarch Sergios I acted as regent in the absence of Emperor Heraclius and was in charge of defence. A contemporary homily reflects the patriarch's public statements during the siege, which carry the overtones of a religious war, proclaiming that God Himself will fight for Constantinople's citizens.[41] In an atmosphere permeated with religious enthusiasm, sustained with military religious rites and ceremonies, the patriarch used the image of the Virgin Mary to threaten the foreign and "devilish" armies with her supernatural martial protection of the city. Unsurprisingly, in her reported appearances during the siege she is in the guise of a warrior-maiden, fighting for her city and chasing away the Avar khagan, who concedes his inevitable defeat to the Mother of God.

The already quoted impressive and significant legitimization of Christian just war and the potential martyr status of the Christian warrior ascribed to St Constantine-Cyril the Philosopher can perhaps be best understood within the religio-political framework of his mission to the court of al-Mutawakkil.[42] As already indicated, this notion of sanctified military martyrdom did not find acceptance in the mainstream of Byzantine Church thought and practice. It is important, however, that it found such an emphatic and explicit formulation in a proclamation attributed to such an extraordinarily and enduringly influential figure in the Byzantine Commonwealth as St Constantine-Cyril the Philosopher. Owing to the continuing authority of his pronouncements in the Slavonic Orthodox world, this particular proclamation, as will be shown below, has been used as a basis for a more systematic formulation of Orthodox just war theory.

In the context of St Constantine's pronouncement concerning the sanctity embedded in the legitimate brand of Christian military endeavour, it is worthwhile noting the interesting and symptomatic proliferation of the canonization and widespread veneration of historical Orthodox warrior-princes in some of the late medieval cultures of the Byzantine Commonwealth, notably Russia, Ukraine and Serbia – for instance, St Alexander Nevsky, Grand Prince of Novgorod and Vladimir (1236–1263), St Dmitri Donskoi, Grand Prince of Moscow (1359–1389), St Stefan Lazar, Prince of Serbia (1371–1389), and St Stefan Lazarević, Prince of Serbia (1389–1427). These cults of saintly princes and rulers were evidently intended to develop a religio-political loyalty to a national dynastic line and, in the case of medieval Serbia, created a veritable genealogy of "holy kings". Some elements of the hagiographical biographies in the *vitae* of these saintly princes and rulers suggest that in these cultures the Orthodox churches were more prepared to foster and cultivate lay military piety than was the Byzantine mother church. The precise religio-political dynamism that determined such developments still awaits a systematic study. Characteristically, Byzantine political ideology, as reflected in a succession of Byzantine *Mirrors of Princes*, in general continued to adhere to and promote an image of an ideal ruler that goes back to Hellenistic and late Roman models of an ideal emperor, and did not accept or absorb the concept of a warrior-king even in the period when Western chivalric attitudes and stereotypes were exercising some impact in late medieval Byzantium.[43] At the same time, some of the hagiographic traditions surrounding Orthodox warrior-princes such as St Alexander Nevsky and St Stefan Lazar betray some remarkable continuity with Byzantine religio-political models. Furthermore, both South Slavonic and Russian Orthodox cultures offer some early paradigmatic examples of saintly princes who accepted martyrdom without resorting to violence or self-defence – for example, St John Vladimir, Prince of Duklja (d.1016), and Saints Boris and Gleb, Princes of Kievan Rus (d.1015).

The evidence of the presence and evolution of the notions of just and holy war in the medieval Byzantine world, notions that provided the underlying foundation of Eastern Orthodox attitudes to warfare in the early modern and modern periods, thus presents some important dissimilarities from the equivalent concepts and developments in the medieval Latin West. One may attempt a general explanation of these differences simply in the framework of the Christian tradition on the whole and the well-known trichotomy of Christian attitudes to war and peace proposed by Roland Bainton: pacifism, just war and Crusade.[44] But, for a deeper understanding of the provenance and fortunes of these notions in Byzantium and the Byzantine Commonwealth, one needs to take into account the specifics of their trajectories in Eastern Orthodoxy. The continuity of pacific and pacifistic currents in Eastern Orthodoxy from the pre-Constantinian into the Byzantine period and their interrelationship with the continuity and Christianization of Roman imperial ideology in Byzantium seem fundamental for gaining a more insightful perception of these distinct trajectories. Thus, with regard to changing Christian attitudes to warfare in the Early and High Middle Ages, the notable endurance of these continuities and their amalgamation in medieval Byzantium need to be seen in the context of the various factors creating discontinuity with the late Roman past in the contemporary Latin West and the early Islamic world in the Near East and Levant. These continuities and discontinuities also contributed significantly to the divergences of views on war and peace among these three cultures.[45]

The convergence of imperial and ecclesiastical ideology in Byzantium projected the formulas and images of Byzantine philanthropy in the spheres of political and military ideology, with the consequent use of pacific rhetoric and symbolism in diplomatic and political discourse (depending on the circumstances and the priorities of Byzantine pragmatism, this discourse could be also aggressive and militaristic). References to and images of Byzantine emperors as "peace-loving", "peace-protecting" and averting wars and violence acquired a ceremonial character and coexisted with forceful images of their military triumphs over the enemies of the empire. Ultimately, peace was supposed to be normative on both the religious and the imperial political level; the *Tactica* ascribed to Leo explicitly states that one should welcome peace not only for the Byzantine subject but also for the "barbarians". The resultant Byzantine synthesis between the inherited religious and political pacific models, the late Roman just war tradition and some innovations in the theory and practice of warfare conditioned by the changing strategic and political circumstances created an ambivalent and flexible system of nuanced attitudes to war in which various compromises were achieved to neutralize the inherent frictions between the various elements. Apparently, the elaboration of more systematic theories for the religious and philosophical justification of war was not seen as necessary; similarly, the *jus in bello* regulations in the Byzantine military treatises largely reproduce earlier Hellenistic and Roman models. Beyond military religious services, the Byzantine Church participated extremely rarely in the justification and legitimization of war, although individual churchmen on occasions ventured to speculate and communicate their views on Christian just war and military endeavour, which could amount to such justification.

This Byzantine synthesis was well suited to the religious and secular needs of an imperial state that viewed itself as an heir to the East Roman *imperium* and as the sole "holy and Orthodox universal empire"; it seemed appropriate also to the Orthodox monarchies and principalities that emerged in the Byzantine Commonwealth in South-Eastern Europe, Ukraine and Russia. Following the Ottoman conquests in Anatolia and the Balkans and the integration of these regions into the new Ottoman version of the Islamic caliphate, the Orthodox churches in these regions, along with the Ecumenical patriarchate, found themselves in completely new circumstances. In the wake of the fall of Constantinople to the Ottomans, an evolving Russian religio-political ideology came to claim the imperial leadership of the Orthodox Christian Commonwealth through the well-known doctrine of "Moscow the Third Rome". This imperial leadership extended to aspirations for the political and religious protection of the Orthodox communities and churches within the Ottoman empire, which in the nineteenth and early twentieth centuries went through dramatic periods of nationalistic anti-Ottoman uprisings and the formation of nation-states. Not long after these periods of painful and divisive nation-building, nearly all European Eastern Orthodox churches (apart from the Ecumenical patriarchate in Istanbul and the autocephalous Greek Orthodox Church) were forced to function and survive in the framework of the militantly secularist and repressive totalitarian regimes in Eastern Europe. During all these periods, including the current post-Communist phase, their adherence to and practice of the inherited New Testament, patristic and Byzantine attitudes to war and peace were every so often fiercely challenged and tested to their very limits.

Transformations of Eastern Orthodox attitudes to war and peace in the Ottoman and modern periods

The post-Byzantine/Ottoman period and the rise of nationalism

It is worth reiterating that, unlike the case of Western Christianity, the study of Eastern Orthodox approaches to the ethics and justification of warfare is still in its nascent stages. In the case of medieval Eastern Orthodoxy at least, the recent debates on and advances in the study of Byzantine military history and Byzantine political and religious attitudes to war and peace have made it possible to considerably update the state of the evidence and research summarized above. The same cannot be said about the study of the development of Eastern Orthodox stances on warfare and its legitimization in the post-Byzantine/Ottoman and modern periods. In this crucial area of the post-medieval and modern history of Eastern Orthodoxy, enormous quantities of wide-ranging and diverse material still need to be critically explored, first in the context of the various regional political and church historiographies, and then in the larger context of the respective developments in Catholic and Protestant just war traditions of thought during these periods. What can be offered in this chapter, therefore, will be a summary of the general tendencies and changes in the Eastern Orthodox discourses on the morality of war, as the various Eastern Orthodox churches struggled to adapt and respond in the post-Byzantine era to the changing religio-political circumstances in the regions previously belonging to the Byzantine Orthodox Common-wealth. Given the paucity of published archival material and research in this sphere of study, some of the conclusions in this summary will inevitably have a preliminary character. The summary will also aim to indicate important areas of research that could prove useful and rewarding in the pursuit of a better understanding of the occasionally puzzling changes in modern Eastern Orthodox perspectives on the ethics of armed conflict. Some better-researched cases of such changes or innovations will be highlighted that shed new light on the respective importance of tradition and innovation in modern Eastern Orthodox views regarding peace and war that can be considered normative and representative. This will also make it possible to gain a clearer perspective on the continuities and discontinuities between these views and their scriptural, patristic and medieval Byzantine foundations.

As a prelude to the discussion of these changes of perspective in modern Eastern Orthodoxy, one needs first to outline the process of the emergence of autocephalous churches and patriarchates in the medieval Byzantine Orthodox Commonwealth. In the early Byzantine period, the Orthodox Church followed the so-called pentarchy system, where the principal church authority lay with the foremost sees – the patriarchates of Constantinople, Alexandria, Antioch and Jerusalem, with honorary primacy granted to Rome. The early Arab conquests in the Levant brought the patriarchates of Alexandria, Antioch and Jerusalem under Islamic control, gradually decreasing their influence and significance. Byzantine missionary efforts in South-Eastern and Eastern Europe led not only to the Christianization of existing kingdoms, principalities and tribal unions in the region, but also to the eventual emergence of autocephalous churches and patriarchates in some of the newly Christianized Orthodox monarchies. The establishment of such patriarchates occurred as a rule in the framework of the political rivalries of these monarchies with Byzantium and their pursuit of aggressive policies towards Constantinople. Such was the case with the very early recognition of the Bulgarian patriarchate by Constantinople in 927 in the wake of the anti-Byzantine wars of the Bulgarian Tsar Symeon (893–926), during which he aggressively sought and received an imperial title, threatening to conquer and establish himself in Constantinople. The Bulgarian patriarchate was to remain the focus of intermittent Bulgarian–Byzantine political (not so much ecclesiastical) rivalries until the Ottoman conquest. The recognition of the autocephalous status of the Serbian Orthodox Church by Constantinople in 1219 proceeded in much more peaceful circumstances. But the establishment of an independent Serbian patriarchate in 1346 (with active Bulgarian ecclesiastical participation) again occurred in the context of the expansionist policy of the Serbian ruler Stefan Uroš IV Dušan (1331–1355) towards Constantinople, one year after he had proclaimed himself a *basileus* of the Serbs and Rhomaioi (Byzantine Greeks). Characteristically, the elevation of the metropolitan of Moscow in distant Russia to a patriarchal rank took place considerably later: it was acknowledged and presided over by a Constantinople patriarchate mission in 1589, 27 years after it had recognized the imperial title of the Russian ruler Ivan IV the Terrible (1530–1584). The formation of the Russian patriarchate was thus an event that again was conditioned by considerations of imperial ideology and status in the sixteenth-century Eastern Orthodox world.

In South-Eastern Europe, the establishment of the new patriarchates was intended to underscore the sovereignty of the new Orthodox monarch vis-à-vis Byzantine political ideology, with its central notion of Byzantine universal hegemony, specifically over Orthodox Christendom. Byzantine recognition of the new patriarchates can be seen also as a kind of concession to the political aspirations of the new Orthodox monarchs.[46] Encountering and being exposed to the distinctive Byzantine concepts of supranational "patriotism", the South Slavonic Orthodox cultures also developed traditions eulogizing their own people as being granted the status of the new "chosen people", entrusted with an exceptional mission to spread Orthodox Christianity further and act as its faithful guardians. As in Byzantium, in the South Slavonic Orthodox world these religio-political concepts could confer a providential dimension to the comprehension and rationalization of Christian warfare, especially in the period of the Ottoman conquest. The decline and shrinking of Byzantium in the fourteenth century made one of the principal themes of the Byzantine apocalyptic tradition – the final eschatological battles of the last Byzantine emperor with the forces of Islam prior to the advent of the Antichrist – more actual and influential than ever. With the spread of such eschatological expectations concerning the fate of Constantinople and Orthodox Christendom itself, in some Byzantine circles Orthodoxy developed into "surrogate patriotism", with strong anti-Latin/Catholic sentiments.[47] Features of such a development can be discerned in contemporaneous and later versions of South Slavonic Orthodox cultures, but its dynamics as well as links to the rise of national consciousness in the region and its religio-political elements have remained regrettably underexplored.[48]

Following the establishment of the Ottoman empire in the erstwhile Orthodox Anatolia and Balkan Europe, the Byzantine apocalyptic tradition enjoyed a continuation among nearly all strata of Orthodox cultures under Ottoman suzerainty, whether in the guise of post-Byzantine messianism or simple eschatological prophecies about the impending end of Ottoman rule.[49] This post-Byzantine messianism prophesied the advent of a liberator-emperor who would rout the "infidel" Islamic occupiers in "holy battles" at Constantinople and banish them forever to initiate the final events of the eschatological drama. In non-eschatological versions, such prophecies could simply predict the recreation of the Byzantine empire, ruling Orthodox Christendom again from its old capital, the Holy City of Constantinople. Elements of this Byzantine messianism undoubtedly reappear in a modernized and secularized form in the *Megali Idea* ("Great Idea") of Greek nationalism of the nineteenth and early twentieth centuries, aspiring to reinstate a Greek state for all the Greeks of the Mediterranean and the Balkans. Such concepts also find a parallel in the abortive "Greek Project" of the Russian Empress Catherine the Great (1762–1796), which was designed to force the dismemberment of the Ottoman realm and the establishment of a reconstituted "Russo-Byzantine" Orthodox empire in Constantinople. It is worth noting, however, that Catherine the Great's victorious campaigns and projects against the Ottoman empire were devoid of the rhetoric of religious war;[50] by that time the Russian patriarchate had already been abolished and the Tsarist administration was managing the Church largely as a state department.

By the time Russian imperial expansionism was beginning to make real headway into the Ottoman Balkans, the Russian Church and the Eastern Orthodox churches that had earlier found themselves under Ottoman dominion had developed different sets of state–church relations, which were to have far-reaching implications in the modern era of nationalism and nation-state-building. Following earlier precedents of the integration of the "Oriental" patriarchates of Alexandria, Antioch and Jerusalem into the Islamic system of governance, in the wake of the Ottoman conquest of Constantinople its patriarch was designated as the religious and administrative head of all Orthodox Christians under Ottoman sovereignty, regardless of their ethnicity. The implementation of these regulations, known as the *millet* system, assigned significant civil, educational and judicial roles to the Constantinople patriarchate, and the previously independent patriarchates now came under its authority (only the Serbian patriarchate was revived between 1557 and 1766). The *millet* system secured the survival and relative strength of Orthodox Christianity in the Ottoman empire, but it meant too that the ecclesiastical body of the Constantinople patriarchate, from its head to the diocesan metropolitans and the village priests, functioned as a secular administrative mechanism as well. Apart from his ecclesiastical role, the Constantinople patriarch was also the *etnarch*, the civil "leader" of the Orthodox Christians in the Ottoman empire. This substantial secularization of the role of the Church opened it to frequent lay interference in its internal affairs, whether by the Ottoman authorities or by influential lay figures such as lawyers and merchants, whom the Constantinople patriarchate had to employ in order to fulfil its function.

The *millet* system also led to frequent friction and hostility between the mostly Greek upper hierarchy of the patriarchate and the Serbian, Bulgarian, etc., local churchmen under its jurisdiction. With the rise of nationalism, in the wide-ranging and influential Greek communities and diaspora within and outside the Ottoman empire, "Hellenism" and Orthodoxy began to blend in a forceful nationalist ideology. Focused on the aspirations for the formation of a new Hellenic Commonwealth, this nationalist ideology further alienated the Serbian, Bulgarian and Romanian churches. Acting during the Ottoman era as a nationally and culturally unifying force, these churches inevitably played a crucial role in the formation of the respective national ideologies. Thus these national churches provided the religio-political source of the various eighteenth- and nineteenth-century Orthodox Christian identities, including the complicated process of the shaping of Romanian Orthodox culture in the principalities of Wallachia and Moldavia, which remained autonomous under Ottoman suzerainty until 1829.

The *millet* system, moreover, carried with it implicit dangers for the upper hierarchy of the Constantinople patriarchate. The outbreak of the Greek Revolution in 1821 (deemed to have been proclaimed by the metropolitan of Patras, Germanos) signified in the Ottoman reading of events that the patriarch and his senior prelates were guilty of high treason. Consequently the Christian *etnarch* was promptly executed, along with scores of other senior clerics in Istanbul, Edirne, Thessaloniki, Crete, Cyprus, etc. Similar, although less drastic, retributive measures are known to have been taken by the Ottomans in comparable circumstances against leading Bulgarian and Serbian churchmen. The event marked the beginning of the end for the old *millet* role of the Constantinople patriarchate, as its various functions and powers were eroded progressively. In the nineteenth century, the Orthodox churches in South-Eastern Europe, moreover, energetically sought and achieved autonomy from its jurisdiction, which was in some cases a divisive and arduous process. The consequent fragmentation of the ecclesiastical authority of the Ecumenical patriarchate of Constantinople in South-Eastern Europe was accompanied by bitter debates and a succession of ecclesiastical crises provoked by the secular factors that were determining the formation of the new autocephalous and national churches. Orthodox internal strife in the second half of the nineteenth century was further exacerbated by the attempts of Russian diplomacy in the Ottoman empire to use for its own political purposes the struggle of Bulgarian churchmen for ecclesiastical emancipation or indeed the increasing Arab–Greek rivalry for control of the bishoprics or the patriarchal posts in the old patriarchates of Antioch and, later, Jerusalem.

In the Ottoman period, the tradition of Byzantine messianism (in its original Greek or derivative Slavonic versions) often lay dormant but was kept alive and re-actualized mainly in clerical and monastic circles. The tradition maintained its principal focus – the violent end of the Ottoman Caliphate and a restoration of the Orthodox Christian empire at Constantinople (or the relevant Orthodox Christian kingdoms) in the wake of huge conflicts between Christianity and Islam – while allowing some innovations. These momentous events might be attributed, for example, to Russian military intervention. In the South Slavonic Orthodox world, these themes became interwoven with the rich epical traditions

commemorating and mythicizing military resistance to the Ottoman invasion. Greek or South Slavonic churchmen who became actively involved
in the actual armed struggle and uprisings against the Ottomans, especially from the late eighteenth century onwards, were as a rule aware of
and often under the influence of one of the versions or elements of the
tradition of this Orthodox *restoratio imperii*. Consequently, some of
them sought to add a providential and religious dimension to the military
conflicts with the Ottomans. Their pronouncements and agendas stood in
sharp contrast with the official position of the Constantinople patriarchate, which endeavoured to promote peaceful resolution to such conflicts
and reforms to improve the conditions of Orthodox Christians in the
Ottoman state. Such a stance was obviously affected by the precarious
position of the Constantinople patriarchate in the late Ottoman empire,
but also by its ostensible loyalty to the patristic, canonical and clerical
Byzantine views on war, organized violence and peace.

An especially instructive case in this context is the eighteenth-century
anti-Ottoman wars of the Orthodox Principality of Montenegro, which,
profiting from its inhospitable mountainous terrain, was never fully conquered by the Ottomans, and its heartlands remained de facto independent throughout the Ottoman period. In 1516, the secular power in the
principality was conferred on the bishop of the Montenegrin Cetinje diocese. This initiated the long era of the rule of the so-called prince-bishops
(1516–1697), a kind of Orthodox theocracy that continued after 1697
under the reign of bishops belonging to the charismatic Petrović-Njegoš
dynasty until one of them secularized Montenegrin rule in 1852. The
Montenegrin prince-bishops conducted and led a number of campaigns
against the Ottomans and maintained close links with the Russian imperial and ecclesiastic authorities; they were also able to gain an autocephalous status for their church. Perhaps it is not surprising that the
characteristic pre-battle speeches attributed to the influential Montenegrin theocrat Petar I Petrović (1784–1830), one of the four saints of the
Montenegrin Church, contain some of the notions of Christian religious
war, invoking divine support to crush the "devilish" enemies of Christianity.[51] Some of the pronouncements of his successor to Orthodox
theocratic rule, Petar II Petrović Njegoš (1831–1850), betray unmistake-
able echoes of these Christian religious war notions, which are graphi-
cally articulated in his dramatic poem "The Mountain Wreath".[52]

Imperial Russia and the Balkans

In the post-Byzantine period, Russian ecclesiastical views on war and
peace developed in markedly different religious and political circumstances from those in the Ottoman Balkans and Anatolia. During most of the

period of Tatar suzerainty over the Russian lands (1236–1452), the Russian Church continued to function as a metropolitanate of the Constantinople patriarchate and played the role of the pre-eminent carrier of the cultural heritage and evolving ethno-religious consciousness in Russia. The Tatar overlords did not intervene in the internal affairs of the Church and it was actually able to conduct some impressive missionary work to the north and east of the Russian heartlands. This era of Tatar suzerainty witnessed the military feats of the Russian warrior-prince saints St Alexander Nevsky and St Dmitri Donskoi, but the Russian Church, especially in the early stages of the era, remained generally pacific, in line with the prevalent Byzantine clerical attitudes in this period. It did not develop either the rhetoric or the approach of religious or holy war. In actual fact, most of Alexander Nevsky's major campaigns were directed against his Swedish, German and Lithuanian adversaries, while seeking peace and compromise with the Tatars. The Russian Church could on occasions promote non-resistance to the Tatars; however, before the great Russian–Tatar Battle of Kulikovo, Prince Dimitry Donskoi reportedly asked for the blessing of Russia's paradigmatic national saint, St Sergius of Radonezh (c.1314–1392), who not only encouraged him to "fight with faith" against the "heathen" with God on his side, but allowed two monks to fight in the Russian army.[53] Extolled as "the Builder of Russia" and as a close ally of the Grand Princes of Moscow, St Sergius of Radonezh was thus directly associated with the expansion of the principality and its reconquest designs and moves against the Mongols, not only in the actual political and military spheres but also in Russian national memory. As the Russian empire began to expand after the end of the Tatar dominion, certain later Russian campaigns, such as some of those conducted under Ivan the Terrible, were accompanied by heightened religious rhetoric, but they certainly cannot be qualified as religious wars – they were part of Russian imperial military expansionism.[54]

Generally, in the Russian post-Byzantine Christian worldview, "holy wars" to recover Constantinople for Orthodox Christendom would have seemed largely unnecessary. The "Second Rome" had been punished for its sins, and since its fall to the infidel it was Moscow, the "Third Rome", that, guided by the Holy Spirit, was entrusted to be the sole legitimate defender as well as the bastion of Orthodoxy. However, post-Byzantine Greek religious influence was reintroduced during the reign of Tsar Alexis I (1645–1676), himself known by the nickname "the most peaceful", through the divisive reforms of Patriarch Nikon, which aimed to harmonize Russian service books with contemporary Greek ones and ultimately provoked a schism within Russian Orthodoxy. With Greek influence back in fashion, some religious rhetoric from this period conjures up visions of the future deliverance of all Orthodox Christians from Ottoman subjugation by Tsar Alexis, ceremonially proclaimed by him in the re-consecrated Hagia Sophia in Constantinople in the presence of all five Eastern Orthodox patriarchs. This visionary convergence of the contemporary Orthodox sacred autocracy and its highest spiritual authority culminated in the celebration of the Eucharist for the first time since the fall of Constantinople in 1453.

Russian secular and religious concepts of just war began to crystallize early in the history of Orthodox Russia. Defensive war was seen as rule justified, as were military conflicts aimed at regaining territories unjustly lost to an invader – they could be seen accordingly as wars of liberation.[55] These notions of just war were intertwined with the belief in the inviolability of frontiers and war as the judgement of God. Thus the power of the Cross may be invoked to give victory to those whose war cause is just and to punish those who commit unjust military aggression. But, as elsewhere in the Orthodox world, these concepts were not systematically developed even in the period when Russian military thinking came under strong Western influence after the reforms of Peter the Great (1682–1725), which is clearly demonstrated by the first original Russian tract on international law written during his reign by the prominent diplomat Baron Petr Shafirov.[56]

Increasing Russian military involvement in Europe during the eighteenth and nineteenth centuries did not lead to any further major developments in Russian military thought of conceptual guidelines related to *casus belli* motives that could lead to military conflicts and to *jus in bello* means for conducting warfare. Napoleon's invasion of Russia in 1812 fortified Russian belief in the defence of the homeland as the highest form of just war and the ultimate patriotic duty. St Filaret, metropolitan of Moscow (1782–1867), made some interesting orations dwelling on the reasons for the Russian success, asserting that those who die for the faith and fatherland will be awarded with life and a crown in heaven and thus sanctifying patriotic armed defence.

The Russian Church's involvement in the wide-ranging Russian military campaigns in the eighteenth and nineteenth centuries was predominantly focused on performing the standard Orthodox military religious services. State control of the Church after Peter the Great's reign had obvious demoralizing effects on traditional Russian Orthodoxy. However, as the carrier of the established faith of the empire, the extensive missionary projects and operations of the Church, inspired by its self-entrusted mission to accomplish the Christianization of Asia, profited from Russian imperial expansionism. During these missionary campaigns and the establishment of its ecclesiastical structures in the newly conquered lands, the Russian Church inevitably became engaged in religious controversies and conflicts with local Muslim clerical and political elites, especially in the Volga-Kama region (modern-day Tatarstan), related mainly to Russian policies of Christianization in these areas. But such predictable confrontations did not lead to warlike religious rhetoric or a call for religious wars coming from within the mainstream of the Church.

The forceful rhetoric of Emperor Alexander I (1801–1825) during the confrontations with Napoleon in 1807 and 1812, castigating him as an enemy of the Orthodox faith, needs to be seen in the context of the religio-political climate in Europe and Russia during and after the French Revolution and the Napoleonic wars. In an atmosphere permeated with fears and trepidation about perceived increasing threats, not only to the European Old Order but to European Christianity (which led to the formation of the Holly Alliance in 1815), Alexander's increasing use of dramatic Christian rhetoric derived from his own belief that he had a divine mission as a defender of Christendom in general, as well as from the startling impact on the emperor of prophecy-oriented figures from contemporary European mystical pietism. This evangelical pietist dimension of Alexander's Christian worldview makes him an unlikely candidate for the role of a leader of an Orthodox "crusade" against the Ottoman empire sometimes ascribed to him, especially since Russian support for the Greek Revolution of 1821–1829 was initially non-existent and came only after Great Britain and France had already interfered on the side of the Greek rebels.

The treaty that followed the Ottoman defeat during the Russo-Ottoman War of 1768–1774 contained clauses that were seen in Russia as granting the Russian empire a mandate to protect the rights of Eastern Orthodox Christians within the Ottoman realm. These clauses were used constantly by Russia to intervene through diplomatic pressure or militarily in the turbulent processes that led to the formation of the post-Ottoman nation-states in South-Eastern Europe. The rise of European pan-Slavism and the Russian Slavophile movement in the nineteenth century made the aspirations for "liberation" of the various Slavonic peoples under foreign domination a popular and emotional topic in Russia. Debates and speculation on the ethics of war, justifiable rationales for resorting to violence and the Orthodox understanding of peace were rife in religiously oriented Russian cultural milieus in the nineteenth century, from the various doctrines and stances within the Slavophile movement to the influential pacifism of Lev Tolstoy or Vladimir Solovyov's literary rationalization of the Christian just tradition.[57] Whereas the Russian Slavophile movement had its liberal representatives, other trends considered the Russian version of "Byzantinism" as a religio-political antidote to what was seen as contemporary Western decadence and decline. More extreme Slavophile trends developed a Slavophile Orthodox messianism in which the Slavonic peoples were viewed as custodians of an authentic unpolluted Christianity and thus entrusted with a messianic role among the progressively degenerating European nations. Militant versions of this messianic Slavophilism, such as those developed by the polymath Nikolay Danilevsky (1822–1885), aspired to the unification of all the Slavonic Orthodox world in a realm ruled benignly by an Orthodox emperor residing in the old, re-conquered capital of Orthodox Christendom, Constantinople. It is still debatable how influential militant Slavophile doctrines were in shaping elements of Russian imperial ideology during the reigns of Alexander III (1881–1894) and Nicholas II (1894–1917). Opinions also vary as to whether the Russo-Ottoman War of 1877–1878 represented the martial peak of militant Slavophilism or whether its primary motive derived from Russia's old geopolitical goals of achieving access to the Dardanelles and the Mediterranean.

Orthodox churches in the East European nation-states and under Communism

Ultimately, the Russo-Ottoman War of 1877–1878 led to the Ottoman recognition of the full independence of Romania, Serbia and Montenegro and the autonomy of a Principality of Bulgaria. Inevitably, both in Russia and in the newly formed nation-states, this war was seen as a just war fought for the liberation and independence of the Orthodox Christian peoples, a *jus ad bellum* that was to be used by the new Balkan states in their forthcoming joint military aggression against the Ottoman empire in 1912. The Balkan allies of the first (anti-Ottoman) Balkan War of 1912 invariably viewed the war as a culmination of their struggle to achieve their respective "great" national ideas. Some of the subsequent disagreements and conflicts between them resulted from the fact that the ecclesiastical boundaries of the various churches' dioceses in the Ottoman period were different from the newly established and changing state borders. The role of some of the local churchmen, for instance, in the occasionally violent Greco-Bulgarian conflicts over the jurisdiction of Orthodox sanctuaries in Macedonia in the early twentieth century is one such symptom of the adoption of secular and nationalist agendas by Orthodox churches, leading in this case to bitter infighting.

The ecclesiastical, political and national spheres in the Orthodox world in South-Eastern Europe continued to merge and interact profoundly and unpredictably in the tense period preceding World War I. Not only did the various Orthodox churches provide the key elements of the re-inforced national identities of their people, but individual churchmen also took an active part in the political and even military struggles marking the protracted and frequently brutal dismemberment of the Ottoman empire. Inevitably they became and were to remain a crucial political force in the new, predominantly Orthodox, states – a Bulgarian bishop, for example, served twice as prime minister during the first 10 years following the establishment of the autonomous Principality of Bulgaria. But the Orthodox churches in these new nation-states were also subjected to constant secular interference, as government after government sought to exploit their influence and use them as a political tool, whether in internal or external state affairs.

Given the Balkan anti-Ottoman allies' just war rhetoric during the first Balkan War of 1912, a brief comparative analysis of the role of the various churches in the mobilization of public support for the war and the use of religious themes for its legitimization would have been extremely useful for the purpose of this chapter. Unfortunately, the religious dimension of this war is yet another unexplored chapter in the history of modern Orthodox churches' attitudes to warfare with non-Christian adversaries. Fortunately, the views and pronouncements of one of the most vocal churchmen and theologians of twentieth-century Balkan Orthodoxy, Bishop Nikolai Velimirović (1881–1956), on this war and on Islam in general are well known, accessible in the West and thus difficult to ignore.

Canonized as a saint of the Serbian Orthodox Church in 2003, Bishop Velimirović exercised substantial influence on twentieth-century Serbian Orthodox religious thought – he is often considered the greatest Serbian Orthodox theologian of the century and is praised by his adherents as Serbia's "New Chrysostom". His views (as well as those of his "school") can be seen as representative of the attitudes of very influential currents in the Serbian Orthodox Church during the interwar period and they enjoyed a far-reaching revival from the 1980s onwards, thus providing a useful basis for a brief case-study analysis.

In the tense period between the Balkan Wars and World War I, Bishop Velimirović published a book in which he resorted to an uncompromising "crusading" rhetoric to depict the Balkan anti-Ottoman war as the last stage of the earlier Crusades against Islam. He solemnly proclaimed that this Balkan Orthodox military effort was backed by Christ and culminated in victory despite the pro-Ottoman stance of the European Christian "pharisaic" powers.[58] In subsequent books published shortly afterwards in England (the first of them with a preface by the Archbishop of Canterbury), Bishop Velimirović kept his views and rhetoric similarly clear-cut and explicit: at the Battle of Kosovo in 1389, Serbian armies fought "for Cross and Freedom against Islam rushing over Europe".[59] He offered his own reading of the historical trajectory of the crusading movement. After passing through dramatic stages in Palestine, Spain and Russia, the Crusades of Christianity against Islam and its imperialism continue to this day and their most dramatic acts occurred in the Balkans and especially in Serbia.[60] Throughout this epic battle, Serbian political and military leaders served Christ as defenders of the Orthodox faith and "cross-bearing warriors against the infidels".[61]

Velimirović's religio-national ideology certainly lays great emphasis on the covenantal mythology that has evolved in Serbian Orthodox readings of the religious and spiritual dimensions of the Battle of Kosovo, which have some obvious links to earlier Byzantine apocalypticism and messianism. His own elaborations of this covenantal mythology led to a sanctification of the nation and its army. He saw the ultimate Serbian Orthodox ideal as aspiring towards a holy nation, holy church, holy dynasty and holy army – the holy army envisaged as defending the sacrosanctity of Christendom surrounded by a halo of sacredness.[62] One can also detect in this series of statements a new version of militant Slavophile ideology, which has now evolved into a national messianism,[63] manifested on occasions in the guise of "crusading" Orthodoxy. This national messianic ideology is articulated not in the abstract context of the rise and fall of civilizations (popular with Russian Slavophiles) but in the framework of a vision of an ongoing Orthodox Christian religious war against its perceived hereditary enemy – Islam.

The convergence of this updated Orthodox Christian warrior ethos with a warlike national ideology led Bishop Velimirović to a reassessment of the phenomenon of war, which he saw as the basis of art, human virtue and ability.[64] This represents a radical shift indeed from the fundamental Eastern Orthodox ecclesiastical approaches to war in the patristic and Byzantine period, when even a lay military strategist felt compelled to concede in his manual on the practice and tactics of warfare that it is the "worst of all evils".[65] It is worth mentioning in this context the declaration by the Serbian Orthodox Patriarch Gavrilo V Dožić-Medenica (1938–1950) in March 1941 in support of the military coup d'état against the regent of the kingdom, which poignantly blends epic warlike imagery with "just war" notions that ultimately ascribe to the war effort a religio-historic salvific quality.[66]

Apart from his crusading stance on Islam, Bishop Velimirović expounded strongly anti-Catholic and anti-ecumenical views that were also influential trends in the mainstream Serbian Orthodox Church in the interwar Yugoslav Kingdom. The Serbian Orthodox Church was thus ill equipped to develop a much needed inter-confessional dialogue in the multi-confessional kingdom with its competing identities when the Catholic Church in Croatia also began to undergo a process of ethnicization. The increasingly bitter conflict between the Orthodox and Catholic clerical elites in 1937–1939 was to lead to a virtual "mobilization" of the two churches in the prewar period and aggravated further the religious dimension of the Yugoslav civil war fought along religious/ethnic lines in

Axis-occupied Yugoslavia between 1941 and 1945. The severe blows that the Serbian Orthodox Church suffered in this period – a heavily depleted Church hierarchy and substantial destruction of Orthodox cult architecture in the western Balkans – contributed to the intensification and perpetuation of its general self-perception as a "suffering church" (a standard notion in Balkan Orthodoxy inherited from the Ottoman period), in dire need of securing its self-defence and survival in the region.

Paradoxically, World War II was to bring about a reinstatement of the Russian Orthodox Church after several cycles of massive Soviet repression of the Church, which began as early as the Russian civil war of 1918–1921 and progressively intensified in the 1920s and 1930s. In a successful attempt to boost national support and mobilization for the war effort against Nazi Germany as a just defensive war, Stalin revived the Russian Church and allowed a patriarchal election to be held in 1943. Earlier, during the Russian civil war, despite his various pronouncements and protests against the Bolsheviks, the Russian patriarch, Tikhon (1918–1925), did not officially "sanctify" the anti-Bolshevik war effort of the White Army, although a number of priests collaborated with it and were eventually executed by the Red Army and the Soviet authorities. Significantly, in one of his letters to the Bolshevik Council of People's Commissars in 1918, the patriarch accused them of ordering soldiers to abandon the battlefields and the defence of the motherland, extinguishing in their conscience the precept in John 15:13, "No one has greater love than this, to lay down one's life for one's friends".[67] The letter was written in the aftermath of the already collapsing Treaty of Brest Litovsk, whose terms were seen in Russia as humiliating and unfair. Accusing the Bolsheviks of sacrificing Russia's national interests for an unjust peace, the patriarch affirmed an Orthodox version of the just war tradition (national self-defence), using the same scriptural legitimization as St Constantine-Cyril the Philosopher in the ninth century. During the early cycles of Soviet anti-religious persecution the patriarch preached non-violent resistance to the suppression of Church institutions, hierarchy and religious life, repeatedly exhorting the faithful to abstain from vengeance and bloodshed, condemning anti-Jewish pogroms and pleading with the Bolshevik authorities to halt the cycle of bloodshed and destruction.[68] The patriarch condemned civil war as the worst kind of fratricidal violence.

During the same period, interesting debates developed in the émigré Russian Orthodox Church outside Russia between some bishops who strove to preach a kind of "crusade" against Godless Communism in Russia and those who argued that the Russian Orthodox response to Communism should be non-violent resistance and work on spiritual renewal. In 1929, the émigré metropolitan Anthony Khrapovitsky issued an epistle "To the Orthodox Population of the Far East", in which he argued more or less for a war against the "enemies of the Church". An essay entitled "The Sanctity of Military Endeavour", which appeared in a Russian publication in Paris in 1929,[69] is symptomatic of some of the attitudes to the Christian military ethos and war effort that enjoyed currency in some Russian émigré circles. The text eulogizes the historical and spiritual record of the Orthodox "Christ-loving army", its "cross-bearing spirit" and the "Christ-bearing and Christ-loving military endeavours" through which it defended the Church and the "Christian Fatherland" by the sword. Proceeding with the theme of military martyrdom and sainthood, the text proclaims that it was on account of these military struggles for the Holy Church and the Kingdom of God on Earth that emperors, nobles, military leaders and soldiers have been accepted into the host of Orthodox saints. In 1925, the Russian émigré religious and political philosopher Ivan Il'in (1883–1954) – often seen as belonging largely to the tradition of Slavophile thought – published *On Resistance of Evil by Force*,[70] in which he reaffirmed the necessity of war but questioned whether it can ever be defined as "just". The book provoked intense reactions and disputes in Russian émigré lay and clerical circles,[71] which have obvious relevance to the current debates on the historical constraints on the tradition of the justifiability of war in Eastern Orthodoxy.

The establishment of Communist regimes in Eastern Europe after World War II led to the institution of comparable patterns of initial oppression and persecution of the Orthodox churches in the various countries, followed by measures to secure their political subordination and subservience to the state. This new model of Church–state relations inevitably produced different variants of the immensely increased and usually hostile state control over Church institutions and differing patterns of passive and non-violent resistance to this aggressive and continuous secular interference at the various levels of the Church hierarchy.

After the first stages of anti-Church repression, Communist governments became aware of the potential of using the national Orthodox churches as a tool of their foreign policy through the existing ecclesiastical network of international Orthodoxy. The participation of these Orthodox churches in international ecclesiastical and lay peace initiatives during the Cold War period was largely supervised and controlled by the various governments. The Soviet efforts to use the Moscow patriarchate in this manner were particularly blatant and tensions and conflicts often arose between the patriarchates functioning within the sphere of the Eastern bloc, on the one hand, and the ancient "Eastern" patriarchates, as well as the Orthodox churches operating in non-Communist countries such as Greece and Cyprus, on the other.

Whereas Orthodox churches in the Communist countries were subjected to all these political and ideological pressures, the Orthodox Church in Cyprus continued to play a high-profile role in the political life of the state – a legacy of the ethnarch status of its archbishop in the Ottoman period, with its combination of civil and religious leadership duties. This inevitably brought the Church onto the centre stage of political and military developments on the island. In 1931, for instance, some of the Orthodox bishops took part in the organization of a riot against the heavy-handed British rule of the island. The election of Archbishop Makarios III in 1960 as president of the new Republic of Cyprus was another symptom of the interweaving of the ecclesiastical and political sphere in Cyprus, which in this case involved also dealing with the complex military political conditions provoked by the "Ecclesiastical Coup" of 1972 against Makarios, the military coup against him in 1974 (organized by the Greek military government) and the subsequent Turkish invasion of Cyprus. Such events showed that a modern Orthodox Church can embark politically on a direct collision course with state and military authorities when they encroach on the democratic process of statebuilding and its values.

The Yugoslav wars and Orthodoxy

The collapse of Communism in Eastern Europe in 1989 seemed to mark the beginning of a new period for the revitalization of Eastern Orthodoxy and the restoration of its traditional place in the social and religious life of the region. The military conflicts in Bosnia-Herzegovina and Kosovo in the 1990s, however, again put to the sternest possible test the model of state–Church relations established in the post-Ottoman Balkan nation-states and its implications for modern Eastern Orthodox approaches to warfare as well as its means and limits in multi-confessional and multi-ethnic regions and/or countries.

Initially, the state–Church model in socialist Yugoslavia after World War II was similar to the model in the East European countries. The trials of clerics and religious leaders for their actual or alleged collaboration with the Axis occupiers, extreme nationalists, etc. actually exceeded those in neighbouring Communist countries, which also reflects the nature of the inter-religious/ethnic conflicts in wartime Yugoslavia.

This model was altered in the 1950s and the 1960s following Tito's rift with Stalin and the Soviet Union in 1948. Religious organizations in Yugoslavia were able to take advantage of the various processes of liberalization in Yugoslavia, from the economic to the ideological spheres. In the 1960s, inter-faith dialogue between the Serbian Orthodox Church and the Catholic episcopate in Croatia made some, if uneven, progress;

both churches took part, again intermittently, in international ecumenical initiatives and meetings.

By the end of the 1980s, however, it was becoming increasingly apparent that relations between the Serbian Orthodox and Croat Catholic elites were deteriorating and approaching a crisis not dissimilar from the one in the late 1930s that preceded the inter-religious military conflicts in World War II Yugoslavia. It was also becoming increasingly clear that Orthodox and Catholic religious history, symbolism and practices were being subjected to a process of "nationalization" and politicization in the speedy formation of new national ideologies for the two communities. Elements of a similar process, but which began much later and was much less wide-ranging and influential as well as following a different socio-religious dynamic, could be observed in some circles of the Islamic community in Bosnia-Herzegovina. The impression that Orthodox and Catholic clerical circles were prepared to allow their religious institutions to be politically instrumentalized and used as an extension of the secular military sphere in an actual war situation was confirmed in the first political and military conflicts that triggered the disintegration of Yugoslavia in the 1990s. The obvious and multifaceted religious dimension of these conflicts has attracted much scholarly and general attention and many of its aspects are still under investigation.[72]

The accumulating evidence and critical analysis of the wartime post-Yugoslav national ideologies of the 1990s have led historians to apply terms such as "religious nationalism" or "ethno-clericalism" to define the processes that developed in some major spheres of Serbian Orthodox and Croat Catholic clerical and religiously oriented cultural circles in the 1980s and 1990s. In the case of Serbian Orthodox culture, the use of some of its traditional religious iconography and hagiography of principal national saints or religio-national pilgrimage rituals such as the Kosovo gatherings for the mobilization of what was viewed as a just national cause and the subsequent war effort is abundantly in evidence. What has become a focus of investigation and debate is whether the militarization of this Serbian Orthodox heritage was largely the outcome of its misappropriation by opportunist nationalist politicians and military leaders or did the Church or individual churchmen encourage this process?

The prominence of religious elements in the legitimization of Serbian war efforts and operations during the wars of the 1990s is clearly not sufficient to implicate the Church as an active conduit of this process. As in the case of other Balkan Orthodox nations, religious constructs played a central role in the formation of Serbian national identity and these could be invoked spontaneously in times of crises and conflicts. Furthermore, on one level the upper hierarchy of the Serbian Orthodox Church took part in regional and international religious initiatives and meetings for

peace and reconciliation during and after the Yugoslav wars of succession.[73] A number of observers, however, have questioned the sincerity
of the Serbian Orthodox clerical elite's participation in such initiatives,
pointing to cases in which senior Serbian Orthodox clerics publicly called
for campaigns of military vengeance for World War II crimes against
Orthodox Serbdom, endeavoured to provide religio-political justification
for the war in Bosnia-Herzegovina[74] or tried to use peace negotiations
and agreements for narrow ecclesiastical or political reasons (including
discussions of state and diocese borders).[75] Questions have been asked,
especially in Serbia, about whether senior Orthodox clerics who became
public figures in the 1990s used the build-up to and advance of the military conflicts to reclaim the political and social role of the Church in Serbia, which was strongly curbed in Tito's Yugoslavia.

Both Patriarch Pavle and some senior Christian clerics (Catholic and
Orthodox) in postwar Bosnia-Herzegovina tried to minimize the participation of religious institutions in the military conflict in the region, arguing that religious symbolism and discourse had been hijacked by all the
warring parties to strengthen and legitimize their war propaganda. There
is substantial evidence, however, that since the 1980s senior Serbian
Orthodox clerics and institutions have played a major role in the reinven-
tion of a religious national ideology grounded in intense Christian militaristic imagery and focused on the potent themes of heroic self-sacrifice as
personal and national redemption (as developed in the Kosovo covenantal mythology). This ultimately created an environment in which organized violence could be justifiable and even recommendable as the only
possible self-defence strategy for a perpetually beleaguered Christian
Orthodox nation and Church. It was this intensely emotional and aggressive religious rhetoric and imagery that entered the spheres of mass
media and mass politics (as well as, on occasions, Church media) rather
than the warning statements and views of Serbian liberal clerical figures
and religiously inclined cultural circles. During the armed conflicts this
religious rhetoric and symbolism was thoroughly militarized on all levels,
with the active participation of members of the higher and lower clergy,
from the use of traditional Orthodox insignia to allusions to Old and New
Testament passages to validate what was seen as a crucial martial stage of
national messianism in a time of fateful inter-religious confrontation.

The notion of Orthodox Serbdom as the avant-garde defender of
European Christendom from militant and expansive Islam, with its obvious "neo-crusading" overtones, enjoyed an understandable currency in
lay military and clerical circles. The resultant development of traditional
militarist Christian discourse, such as the "sacred" nature of the fight
against an "infidel" enemy of the faith, led some senior ecclesiastics to
heroicize (and even, on occasions, to sanctify) the war effort and some

of its protagonists to the extent that paramilitary leaders could perceive Patriarch Pavle as their supreme commander.[76] Some of these processes were further deepened by analogous developments in Croat wartime religio-national ideology and to a degree and somewhat later in some Bosnian Muslim ideological currents that sought to religionize the war effort. The simultaneous revival of the influence of Bishop Velimirović and his adherents in the Church, which was to culminate in his eventual canonization, meant also a revival of his militant anti-ecumenical, anti-Catholic and neo-crusading anti-Islamic discourse at all levels of the Church hierarchy.

Finally, the legacy of the wartime years and the Church's stance on the inter-religious conflicts has crucial implications for its current highly visible quest for a stronger political role in the new state–Church model that is evolving in the postwar years. In the unfolding debates on this process, Serbian liberal clerical and lay circles have expressed strong fears that senior churchmen continue to promote their vision of a politicized and exclusivist Orthodoxy, accompanied by reaffirmations of the tenets of the latest wartime religio-national ideology and elements of a rudimentary but growing "Orthodox fundamentalism".[77]

The role of senior Serbian Orthodox clerics in the politico-military instrumentalization of Orthodoxy during the Yugoslav military conflicts also explains the lack of a critical or any response by the higher echelons of the Serbian Orthodox Church to the methods of conducting war by Serbian regular army and paramilitary units throughout the conflicts, which repeatedly breached the codes of war established in the Geneva Conventions and which received wide-ranging international coverage and condemnation. But this ecclesiastical "indifference" to *jus in bello* norms during the Yugoslav wars of succession can be also related to the greater problem of the development of modern Eastern Orthodox stances on legitimate and illegitimate means of warfare, proportionality and discrimination, which lately have been the focus of growing international political, scholarly and inter-religious attention and debates.

As already indicated, even during the heyday of the Byzantine imperial era, on the whole the Eastern Orthodox tradition did not find it necessary to elaborate more systematic theories for the religious and philosophical justification of warfare and *jus in bello* regulations; the latter, as set out in Byzantine military treatises, largely reproduce inherited models from the Hellenistic and Roman antiquity. *Jus in bello* issues have received only occasional and cursory treatments in the later Russian just war tradition, a deficiency that certainly can be blamed to some extent for the absence of proportionality and discrimination that can frequently be observed in Russian combat practices.[78] The lack of a more detailed and systematic consideration of the *jus in bello* norms in modern Eastern Orthodox thought concerning the use of force and its limits, as well as its relevance to combat methods during military conflicts involving states or parties of the modern Eastern Orthodox world, deserves separate scrutiny. A major question to be addressed in this scrutiny should be how modern Eastern Orthodox thought can bridge the growing gap between its predominantly pacific legacy and the actual reality and conduct of modern warfare, especially when a warring party seeks an "Orthodox" legitimization of its war effort, as in the case of the Yugoslav wars of the 1990s.

Contemporary challenges

The Yugoslav military conflicts posed some obvious challenges, not to say theological and ethical crises of conscience, to international Orthodoxy, with its different Orthodox churches and patriarchates, which were also affected by their existing and increasing contacts with institutions related to the implementation of the League of Nations Covenant, the United Nations Charter, and so on. The Ecumenical patriarchates responded with the organization of a series of conferences and meetings that condemned aggressive nationalism and its exploitation to stir up inter-ethnic and inter-religious conflicts.[79] In effect, the Ecumenical patriarchate reiterated some of its earlier positions on religious nationalism and its dangers, referring also to more general issues in the ethics of war: the justification of humanitarian intervention, ethnic cleansing, nuclear weapons, etc. Both the Russian and the Greek Orthodox churches took part in regional and international peace-making initiatives and meetings during the armed conflicts, and in April 2004 the Russian patriarch, Alexei II, made a well-publicized visit to Belgrade during NATO's bombing campaign against Serbia and made a public peace appeal that also called for a peaceful reversal of the Serbian regime's policies in Kosovo. At the same time, some Russian and Greek Orthodox clerics sought to heroicize the Serbian war effort and its military/paramilitary leaders, or indulged (in the Russian case, in clerical circles associated with neo-Slavophilism) in anti-ecumenical and occidentophobic statements and discourse. These Greek and Russian clerical attempts at pan-Orthodox "solidarity" did little to support (and actually further isolated) the liberal circles and voices in the Serbian Orthodox Church.

The role of the Serbian Orthodox Church in the Yugoslav military conflicts provoked wide-ranging reactions in international Orthodox theological circles. As early as 1991, Paris-based Orthodox theologians accused Serbian Orthodox dignitaries of taking part (if unwittingly) in the regime's intensifying campaign to stir up inter-ethic hatred.[80] In 1995, the pacific Orthodox Peace Fellowship sent a written protest to Patriarch

Pavle that a service for the blessing of weapons in a Serbian edition of
the *Book of Needs* published in Kosovo in 1993 was being used in fratricidal war.[81] During a meeting of the Executive Committee of the World
Council of Churches in Bucharest in September 1994, the patriarch of
Alexandria, the pope/patriarch of the Coptic Orthodox Church and the
patriarch of the Romanian Orthodox Church issued a peace appeal (in
view of the military conflict in Bosnia-Herzegovina) in which they called
for an urgent inter-faith dialogue with Islam and condemned the political
expropriation of religious traditions on the basis of militaristic nationalistic agendas.[82]

Serbian Orthodox clerical approaches to the Yugoslav wars in the
1990s had implications beyond these military conflicts in the general context of contemporary Christian doctrines on the ethics of war. Accordingly the World Council of Churches and the ecumenical movements
often adopted critical stances towards the Serbian Orthodox Church in
this period. Consequently, the Syndesmos Declaration by the participants
in a "War and Peace in Europe" seminar, hosted by the Archdiocese of
Crete in 1994, appealed for inter-Orthodox solidarity in peace-making
efforts but also strongly criticized what they saw as a prejudicial bias of
the World Council of Churches against the Serbian Orthodox Church.[83]

These meetings, initiatives, statements and appeals made the debate on
contemporary challenges to Eastern Orthodox views on war and peace
an important theme in current theological and church history studies. In
2003, the Ecumenical patriarch of Constantinople, Bartholomew I, emphatically reiterated the traditional Eastern Orthodox patristic and Byzantine clerical precepts on warfare, declaring that in only a few specific
instances could the Orthodox Church "forgive armed defense against oppression and violence".[84] After a decade of redefining its new models of
relations with the state and indeed the military, in 2000 the Jubilee Council of Russian Bishops issued an extremely important statement of faith.[85]
This contains a section on "War and Peace" that advances a rare exposition of a more systematic Orthodox treatment of the Christian just war
tradition.[86] An earlier section of the statement, "Church and Nation",
alludes to cases in which national saints and churchmen have blessed defensive wars against invaders, including St Filaret of Moscow's declaration that defenders of the faith and fatherland will gain heavenly life and
crowns.[87]

The section on the Orthodox teaching of "War and Peace" begins with
an explicit restatement of the traditional Orthodox view of war as unconditionally evil, caused by fratricidal hatred and human abuse of God-
given freedom. But then the statement identifies the cases in which war,
although evil and undesirable, is necessary: national self-defence, defence
of neighbours and "restoration of trampled justice" (a near-secular for-

mulation that could easily provide rather wide-ranging options for the justification of warfare). To justify the resort to war in these instances, the statement reproduces the whole episode from the *Vita* of St Constantine-Cyril the Philosopher (as quoted above) and thus, like the "Apostle of the Slavs" and Patriarch Tikhon in 1918, bases its just war doctrine on John 15:13. This is given as a reason for the high respect of the Church for the Christian virtues of soldiers who follow the precepts of such a just war and rewards them by canonizing them as saints. Matthew 26:52 ("They that take the sword shall perish by the sword") is also used as a scriptural basis for this just war formulation, asserting that it should be impossible to serve one's country "by immoral means". Then the statement makes the important step of reproducing in detail the traditional *jus ad bellum* and *jus in bello* conditions of the Western Christian just war tradition, as based on St Augustine's teachings. Significantly, the document tries to redefine some of these conditions, using scriptural references to Sirach 8:8, 1 John 2:16 and Romans 12:21–22 to characterize the Orthodox teachings concerning *jus in bello* norms – a topic that, as already indicated, largely does not receive detailed attention in Eastern Orthodox thinking on justifiable warfare. The document articulates further the Russian Church's special concern for the Christian education of the military and the tasks of military chaplains. The "War and Peace" section concludes with a lengthy exposition of Eastern Orthodox conceptions of peace and ends by proclaiming the Russian Church's commitment to peace-making at national and international levels and its dedication to opposing any propaganda of war and violence.

It is difficult to overestimate the importance of this statement of faith for identifying the currently increasing religious, social and even political roles of the Russian Church in post-Soviet Russia. It has even been proposed that the document could be adopted as a basis for the state's religious policies. In the 1990s, the Russian Church had been involved in peace-making efforts such as Patriarch Alexei's forceful Moscow peace appeal during the Russian constitutional crisis in early October 1993 when Russia was on the brink of civil war, or the Russian Church's initiative to bring together the heads of the religious communities of Azerbaijan and Armenia for peace-rebuilding talks during their military confrontation in the same year.[88] At the same time, the Russian Church's clearly articulated doctrine of just war must be viewed in the framework of the visibly strengthening relations between the Church and the military and the various manifestations of this process (including some changes in the stances of Russian churchmen towards the war in Chechnya).[89] Finally, given the impact of neo-Slavophilism and/or anti-ecumenical and anti-Catholic discourse and campaigns in certain Russian clerical circles (related to issues such as relations between Orthodox and Uniate

communities in Ukraine), it is certainly significant that the official statement of this doctrine has incorporated Western Christian just war notions
in a non-polemical context.

These current reaffirmations and reformulations of Eastern Orthodox
stances on warfare have interesting implications for the application of
Bainton's trichotomy of historical Christian attitudes to warfare (pacifism,
just war and Crusade) to pre-modern and modern Eastern Orthodoxy.
Whereas the third component in Bainton's trichotomy (Crusade) is largely
absent from pre-modern Eastern Orthodox approaches to warfare, the
formation of religio-national ideologies in Orthodox Eastern Europe in
the nineteenth and twentieth centuries has led to the emergence of what
can be only defined as elements of "crusading" (or neo-crusading) discourse in some of their versions. Throughout this turbulent period the
historically prevalent pacific Eastern Orthodox ecclesiastical stance has
remained as influential as ever in higher-ranking Orthodox clerical circles
and "normative" Orthodox theology. It has been recently categorically
reiterated by Ecumenical Patriarch Bartholomew and a number of senior
Orthodox ecclesiastics and in statements issued at official Orthodox
meetings. At the same time, the Russian Church has attempted to sys-
tematize a new version of the Orthodox just war tradition (including
scripture-based reformulations of *jus in bello* norms), which previously
had been articulated in a fragmentary and inconsistent way.

There is little doubt that the successive military conflicts since the
1990s, both in the former Yugoslavia and in the Near East, have compelled Orthodox hierarchs and synods as well as Orthodox theologians
and Church historians to address more systematically the theological
and moral problems related to the justifiability and desirability of modern warfare – both within the Orthodox tradition and in Christianity in
general. The religio-historical model proposed in 2003 by Alexander
Webster symptomatically aims to revise the traditional thesis of a historical predominance of pacific and pacifistic attitudes in Eastern Orthodoxy.
Webster's alternative model instead reconstructs an unbroken and coherent Eastern Orthodox justifiable war tradition from the patristic period
onwards, recognizing war as a "lesser good" rather than a necessary evil
and adhering to a "teleology of justice".[90] Webster's reconstruction also
includes the presumption that the prevalence of pacific attitudes and the
rejection of just war thinking in modern Eastern Orthodoxy represent
misconceptions arising from ecumenical and theological contacts with
some trends in Catholic and Protestant religious thought in modern times
as well as the emergence of an Orthodox diaspora in the Western
world.[91] Webster's model and claims have met strong opposition and
counter-arguments[92] that the proposed reconstructions impose on Orthodox history and thought a just war conceptual framework similar to that

of Thomas Aquinas and ignore some crucial *jus in bello* issues related to the modern means of warfare.[93] The theory of the continuous existence of a justifiable war tradition in Eastern Orthodoxy, in which it is viewed as a moral good rather than a necessary evil, thus came to be seen by its critics as an attempt at a revision and modernization of Orthodox views on war and peace through the application of scholastic logic and a Thomistic conception of justice. The resultant symbiosis of Eastern and Western Christian concepts of war and justice can indeed be defined as a theological effort to initiate the conceptualization of an Orthodox just war theory adapted for modernity and its challenges. Perhaps it is significant that, after he more or less established the foundation for such a novel "Westernized" Orthodox just war theory, Alexander Webster co-authored a book intended to "reclaim" and harmonize the classic Eastern and Western traditions on war-making in view of the perceived need to justify an impending joint Eastern and Western Christian military response to militant Islam's increasing threat to Western civilization.[94]

At the same time, the traditional and widely held view that the quintessentially pacific teachings of Orthodoxy preclude the formulation of just war doctrines continues to be strongly reaffirmed not only by leading Orthodox ecclesiastics but also by Orthodox theologians, individually and as group statements.[95] In a public statement in 1991 in relation to the first Gulf War, the Holy Synod of Bishops of the Orthodox Church in America declared that just war theory does not reflect the Orthodox theological tradition, which maintains that war can never be theologically justified. Accordingly, questions have again been asked about whether Western Christian-style just war systems can really be appropriate for Orthodoxy and whether Orthodox theological and ethical thought should try "to bridge pacifism and just war theory through a re-conception of justice and peace-making".[96]

Modern Orthodox thought can certainly draw on a rich heritage of theological and ethical thought to stimulate such reconceptions. Meanwhile, the evolving debates on the coexistence of pacific and justifiable war trajectories in Orthodoxy can be only of great help to ecumenical and inter-Orthodox contacts and dialogue. It has been suggested that studying classical Eastern Orthodox and Byzantine views on war and peace could make it possible to consider the increasingly vital issues of war and peace through a "Byzantine" perspective – which remains little known in the Western Christian tradition but still furnishes sufficient "points of common reference" and may offer promising new directions.[97] Such studies and debates have become all the more needed given the current fundamentalization of mainstream Christian and Islamic traditions, with the resulting changes in their attitudes to the resort to violence and means of warfare. In this context, the study of the historical experience of the four ancient Eastern patriarchates of Orthodoxy, with their enduring tradition of inter-confessional dialogue and their search for a *modus vivendi* with Islam, as well as their non-alignment with national causes, may also provide some valuable new insights.

It is evident that further investigation and publication of the sources of patristic, medieval and modern Eastern Orthodox traditions on the use of force are certainly very much needed; some of these traditions have been greatly neglected to the detriment of the better understanding of the diversity of Christian attitudes to war- and peace-making. Such studies not only will enrich our knowledge of the historical transformation of stances towards war and peace in the monotheistic traditions on the whole but will have contemporary relevance in the quest for current religious answers to some vital problems in the ethics of war, ranging from the rise and misuse of aggressive religio-national ideologies to the legitimization of humanitarian intervention and pre-emptive war, as well as the impact of military conflicts and nuclear weapons on the environment.

Notes

1. An issue of *St Vladimir's Theological Quarterly* (47(1), 2003) was entirely devoted to these debates.
2. See, for example, the brief and cautious overview of this field in Timothy S. Miller, "Introduction", in Timothy S. Miller and John Nesbit (eds) *Peace and War in Byzantium. Essays in Honor of George T. Dennis.* Washington, DC: Catholic University of America Press, 1995, pp. 11–12; see also the comments in John Haldon, *Warfare, State and Society in the Byzantine World, 565–1204.* London: University College Press, 1999, pp. 2–7, passim.
3. On the attitudes of the early Christian Fathers to participation in warfare and military service, see the sources translated in Louis J. Swift, *Early Fathers on War and Military Service (Message of the Fathers of the Church).* Wilmington, DE: Michael Glazier, 1883. For studies of the problems raised by these attitudes, see A. Harnack, *Militia Christi: Die christliche Religion und der Soldatenstand in der ersten drei Jahrhunderten.* Tubingen: J. C. B. Mohr (Paul Siebeck), 1905; Cecil John Cadoux, *The Early Christian Attitude to War.* London: Headley, 1919; Roland H. Bainton, "The Early Church and War", *Harvard Theological Review*, 39, 1946: 189–213; Lester L. Field, *Liberty, Dominion, and the Two Swords: On the Origins of Western Political Theology (180–398).* Notre Dame, IN: University of Notre Dame Press, 1999.
4. Greek text in Georgios A. Ralles and Michael Potles (eds), *Syntagma Ton Theion kai Ieron Kanonon.* Athens: G. Chartophylax, 1852, vol. 4, p. 131.
5. Greek text in Ralles and Potles, *Syntagma Ton Theion kai Ieron Kanonon*, vol. 4, p. 69.
6. See, for example, Stanley S. Harakas, "The Teaching of Peace in the Fathers", in Stanley S. Harakas, *The Wholeness of Faith and Life: Orthodox Christian Ethics: Part One: Patristic Ethics.* Brookline, MA: Holy Orthodox Press, 1999, pp. 155–156; John McGuckin, "Non-Violence and Peace Traditions in Early and Eastern Christianity", in K. Kuriakose (ed.) *Religion, Terrorism and Globalisation: Non-Violence – A New Agenda.* New York: Nova Science Publishers, 2006, pp. 189–202.

7. This interpretation is still supported by the majority of scholars investigating Eastern Orthodox approaches to warfare; see, for example, Alexander F. C. Webster, "Justifiable War as a 'Lesser Good' in Eastern Orthodox Moral Tradition", *St Vladimir's Theological Quarterly*, 47(1), 2003: 3–59, pp. 25–27; Haldon, *Warfare, State and Society in the Byzantine World*, p. 26.

8. See the texts of some of the relevant canons in Swift, *Early Fathers on War and Military Service*, pp. 88, 92–93.

9. See the discussion of this approach in Stanley S. Harakas, "The Morality of War", in Joseph J. Allen (ed.) *Orthodox Synthesis. The Unity of Theological Thought*. Crestwood, NY: St Vladimir Seminar Press, 1981, pp. 85 ff.

10. Greek text of the Zonaras and Balsamon commentaries in Ralles and Potles, *Syntagma Ton Theion kai Ieron Kanonon*, vol. 4, pp. 132–133.

11. See the account of the emperor's request and the clerical hierarchy's reaction in John Skylitzes, *Synopsis Historiarum*, ed. Hans Thurn. New York and Berlin: Walter De Gruyter, 1973, pp. 273–275. This opposition between the emperor and the patriarch concerning the sanctification of soldiers fallen in battle was one of the high points of their power struggles during Nikephoros Phokas' reign.

12. See the publication and discussion of the relevant patriarchal acts in Nicholas Oikonomidès, "Cinq actes inédits du patriarche Michel Autôreianos", *Revue des Études Byzantines*, 25, 1967: 113–145, especially pp. 115–121 and 131–134.

13. On the "holy war" context of the fighting between Umur Paşa's *ghāzī* warriors, on the one hand, and the Byzantine and Latin forces in western Anatolia and the Aegean, on the other, see Elizabeth Zachariadou, "Holy War in the Aegean during the Fourteenth Century", in Benjamin Arbel, Bernard Hamilton and David Jacoby (eds) *Latins and Greeks in the Eastern Mediterranean after 1204*. London, Totowa, NJ: Frank Cass in association with the Society for the Promotion of Byzantine Studies and the Society for the Study of the Crusades and the Latin East, 1989, pp. 212–226.

14. See the accounts of the synod's decisions by Balsamon and Matthew Blastares in Ralles and Potles, *Syntagma Ton Theion kai Ieron Kanonon*, respectively, vol. 4, p. 133, and vol. 6, p. 492.

15. Greek text in Ralles and Potles, *Syntagma Ton Theion kai Ieron Kanonon*, vol. 6, p. 492. For a lucid discussion of Blastares' affirmation of St Basil's 13th Canon, see Patrick Viscuso, "Christian Participation in Warfare: A Byzantine View", in Timothy S. Miller and John Nesbit (eds) *Peace and War in Byzantium. Essays in Honor of George T. Dennis*. Washington, DC: Catholic University of America Press, 1995, pp. pp. 33–41.

16. Ralles and Potles, *Syntagma Ton Theion kai Ieron Kanonon*, vol. 6, p. 489.

17. On the significance of the concept of religious peace and harmony in the thought of the Cappadocian Fathers, see, for example, Gerardo Zampaglione, *The Idea of Peace in Antiquity*, trans. by Richard Dunn. Notre Dame, IN: University of Notre Dame Press, 1973, pp. 266 ff.

18. See, for example, the insightful analysis in David K. Goodin, "Just War Theory and Eastern Orthodox Christianity: A Theological Perspective on the Doctrinal Legacy of Chrysostom and Constantine-Cyril", *Theandros: An Online Journal of Orthodox Christian Theology and Philosophy*, 2(3), 2005; available at ⟨http://www.theandros.com/justwar.html⟩ (accessed 13 October 2008).

19. On the notion of spiritual warfare in Eastern Orthodoxy, see, for example, J. Chrysavgis, "The Monk and the Demon", *Nicolaus*, 13, 1986: 265–279; George T. Dennis, "Defenders of the Christian People: Holy War in Byzantium", in Angeliki E. Laiou and Roy Parviz Mottaheden (eds) *The Crusades from the Perspective of Byzantium and the Muslim World*. Washington, DC: Dumbarton Oaks Research Library and Collection, 2001, pp. 36–37; on Byzantine demonology in general, see the ground-breaking work of Ri-

chard P. H. Greenfield, *Traditions of Belief in Late Byzantine Demonology*. Amsterdam: Adolf M. Hakkert, 1988.

20. On these prayers, prayer services and blessings, see, for example, Robert F. Taft, "War and Peace in the Byzantine Divine Liturgy", in Timothy S. Miller and John Nesbit (eds) *Peace and War in Byzantium. Essays in Honor of George T. Dennis*. Washington, DC: Catholic University of America Press, 1995, pp. 28–31; Michael McCormick, *Eternal Victory: Triumphal Rulership in Late Antiquity, Byzantium and the Early Medieval West*. Cambridge: Cambridge University Press, 1986, pp. 239 ff.; Webster, "Justifiable War as a 'Lesser Good' ", pp. 37–42.

21. On the military religious services in the Byzantine army, see McCormick, *Eternal Victory*, pp. 238–251; George T. Dennis, "Religious Services in the Byzantine Army", in E. Carr et al. (eds) *Eulogēma: Studies in Honor of Robert Taft, S.J.* Rome: Pontificio Ateneo S. Anselmo, 1993, pp. 107–118; on the late Roman period, David S. Bachrach, *Religion and the Conduct of War, c. 300–1215*. Woodbridge, Suffolk: Boydell Press, 2003, pp. 13–19.

22. The *Strategikon* ascribed to Maurice is translated in George T. Dennis, *Maurice's Strategikon: Handbook of Byzantine Military Strategy*. Philadelphia: University of Pennsylvania Press, 1984; the tract attributed to Leo VI is edited in Rudolf Vári (ed.), *Leonis Imperatoris tactica*. Budapest: Sylloge Tacticorum Graecorum, III, 2 vols, 1917–1922; generally, on the religious practices prescribed in the Byzantine military tracts, see J.-R. Vieillefond, "Les pratiques religieuses dans l'armée byzantine d'après les traités militaires", *Revue des études anciennes*, 37, 1935: 322–330.

23. On the rise and evolution of the cult of military saints in Eastern Orthodoxy, see Hippolyte Delehaye, *Les légendes grecques des saints militaires*. Paris: Librairie A. Picard, 1909; Alexander F. C. Webster, "Varieties of Christian Military Saints: From Martyrs under Caesar to Warrior Princes", *St Vladimir's Theological Quarterly*, 24, 1980: 3–35.

24. Gustave Schlumberger, *Un empereur byzantin au dixième siècle: Nicéphore Phocas*. Paris: Firmin-Didot, 1890; Gustave Schlumberger, *L'épopée byzantine à la fin du dixième siècle: Guerres contre les Russes, les Arabes, les Allemands, les Bulgares; luttes civiles contre les deux Bardas. Jean Tzimiscés. Les jeunes années de Basile II, le tueur de Bulgares (969–989)*. Paris: Hachette, 3 vols, 1896–1905.

25. René Grousset, *Histoire des croisades et du royaume franc de Jérusalem*. Paris: Plon, vol. 1, 1934, p. 15.

26. George Ostrogorsky, *History of the Byzantine State*, trans. by Joan Hussey. New Brunswick, NJ: Rutgers University Press, 1957, pp. 90, 263.

27. Vitalien Laurent, "L'idée de guerre sainte et la tradition byzantine", *Revue historique du Sud-Est européen*, 23, 1946: 71–98.

28. See, for example, Walter Emil Kaegi, Jr, *Byzantine Military Unrest 471–843: An Interpretation*. Amsterdam: Hakkert, 1981; most of Kaegi's relevant articles on this subject are collected in Walter Emil Kaegi, Jr, *Army, Society and Religion in Byzantium*. London: Variorum Reprints, 1982; K. Tsiknakes (ed.), *Byzantium at War: 9th–12th Centuries*. Athens: Hidryma Goulandre-Chorn, 1997; John W. Birkenmeier, *The Development of the Komnenian army, 1081–1180*. Leiden: Brill, 2002; Haldon, *Warfare, State and Society in the Byzantine World*; John Haldon, *Byzantium at War AD 600–1453*. New York and London: Routledge, 2003.

29. See, for example, Haldon, *Warfare, State and Society in the Byzantine World*, chs 1–3.

30. This position is formulated lucidly by P. Lemerle, "Byzance et la croisade", in *Relazioni del X Congresso internazionale di scienze storiche, Roma, 4–11 settembre 1955*. Firenze: G. C. Sansoni, 1955, p. 617 ff.

31. See, for example, Nicholas Oikonomidès, "The Concept of 'Holy War' and Two Tenth-century Byzantine Ivories", in Timothy S. Miller and John Nesbit (eds) *Peace and War in Byzantium. Essays in Honor of George T. Dennis*. Washington, DC: Catholic University of America Press, 1995, pp. 62–87; Dennis, "Defenders of the Christian People"; G. Dagron, "Byzance entre le djihad et la croisade: Quelque remarques", in *Le concile de Clermont de 1095 et l'appel à la Croisade: Actes du Colloque universitaire international de Clermont-Ferrand (23–25 juin 1995)/organisé et publié avec le concours du Conseil régional d'Auvergne*. Rome: Ecole française de Rome, Palais Farnèse, 1997, pp. 325–337; Angeliki E. Laiou, "On Just War in Byzantium", in John Haldon et al. (eds) *To Hellenikon: Vol. 1, Hellenic Antiquity and Byzantium. Studies in Honor of Speros Vryonis Jr.* New Rochelle, NY: Aristide D. Caratzas, 1993, pp. 153–177; Angeliki E. Laiou, "The Just War of Eastern Christians and the Holy War of the Crusaders", in Richard Sorabji and David Rodin (eds) *The Ethics of War: Shared Problems in Different Traditions*. Aldershot, Hants: Ashgate, 2006, pp. 30–44.

32. See Athēna Kolia-Dermitzakē, *Ho vyzantinos "hieros polemos": hē ennoia kai hē provolē tou thrēskeutikou polemou sto Vyzantio*. Athens: Historikes Ekdoseis St. D. Basilopoulos, 1991 (and the critical review of the book by Walter Emil Kaegi, Jr, *Speculum*, 69, 1994: 518–520); Tia M. Kolbaba, "Fighting for Christianity: Holy War in the Byzantine Empire", *Byzantion*, 68, 1998: 194–221. See also John Haldon's reassessment of this thesis in Haldon, *Warfare, State and Society in the Byzantine World*, pp. 13–34 passim.

33. On these developments in the military religious ideology of the Byzantine troops positioned along the Anatolian frontiers, see G. Dagron and H. Mihaescu, *Le traité sur le guerilla (De velitatione) de l'empereur Nicéphore Phocas (963–969)*. Paris: CNRS, 1990, pp. 284–286; Kolbaba, "Fighting for Christianity", pp. 206–207; Haldon, *Warfare, State and Society in the Byzantine World*, pp. 28–32.

34. On the prominent use of religious rhetoric, ritual and symbolism during Heraclius' anti-Persian campaigns and its implications for the character of these campaigns, see Mary Whitby, "A New Image for a New Age: George of Pisidia on the Emperor Heraclius", in E. Dabrowa (ed.) *The Roman and Byzantine Army in the East: Proceedings of a Colloquium Held at the Jagiellonian University, Kraków, in September 1992*. Cracow: Uniwersytet Jagiellonski, Instytut Historii, 1994, pp. 197–225; Kolia-Dermitzakē, *Ho vyzantinos "hieros polemos"*, pp. 169–183; Kolbaba, "Fighting for Christianity", pp. 206–207; Dennis, "Defenders of the Christian People", pp. 34–35; Haldon, *Warfare, State and Society in the Byzantine World*, pp. 19–21. For an earlier case of Roman–Persian hostilities in which the religious dimension was especially noticeable, the war of 421–422, see K. H. Holum, "Pulcheria's Crusade A.D. 421–422 and the Ideology of Imperial Victory", *Greek, Roman and Byzantine Studies*, 18, 1977: 153–172.

35. On the evidence of Nikephoros Phokas' and John Tzimiskes' pronouncements concerning the recovery of former Christian lands and Holy Places in Palestine as military objectives of their anti-Arab wars, see Ostrogorsky, *History of the Byzantine State*, pp. 263 ff; 297; P. E. Walker, "The 'Crusade' of John Tzimisces in the Light of New Arabic Evidence", *Byzantion*, 47, 1977: 301–327; Mark Whittow, *The Making of Orthodox Byzantium 600–1025*. Basingstoke: Macmillan, 1996, pp. 356–357; Kolia-Dermitzakē, *Ho vyzantinos "hieros polemos"*, pp. 129–139, 220–240; Haldon, *Warfare, State and Society in the Byzantine World*, pp. 41–42; on the postulated Byzantine "holy war" aspirations towards Jerusalem and Palestine, see the arguments in Kolia-Dermitzakē, *Ho vyzantinos "hieros polemos"*, pp. 367 f, 403–404.

36. See, for example, Paul Magdalino, *The Empire of Manuel I Komnenos, 1143–1180*. Cambridge: Cambridge University Press, 1993, pp. 95–98; Kolia-Dermitzakē, *Ho vyzantinos "hieros polemos"*, pp. 251–290.

37. See Vári (ed.), *Leonis Imperatoris tactica*.

38. "The Anonymous Byzantine Treatise on Strategy", in George T. Dennis (ed. and trans.) *Three Byzantine Military Treatises*. Washington DC: Dumbarton Oaks, 1985, pp. 20–21.

39. On the coexistence in military treatises (and Byzantine political military ideology in general) of Byzantine philanthropic notions with the strategic and practical concerns of an empire that was intermittently on the defensive on one or more fronts, see Haldon, *Warfare, State and Society in the Byzantine World*, pp. 26 ff.

40. See the arguments for the existence of such a tradition in Webster, "Justifiable War as a 'Lesser Good' ", and the negative responses to his case published in *St Vladimir's Theological Quarterly*, 47(1), 2003: 59–65, 77–111.

41. On these episodes during the siege of Constantinople and the quoted homily of Theodore Synkellos, see Averil Cameron, "Images of Authority: Élites and Icons in Late Sixth-Century Byzantium", *Past and Present*, 84, 1979: 3–35, pp. 20–21.

42. On the religio-political circumstances of St Constantine's mission to the Abbasid court and their possible impact on his "just war" statement, see Goodin, "Just War Theory and Eastern Orthodox Christianity".

43. See the analysis in Joseph A. Munitiz, "War and Peace Reflected in Some Byzantine *Mirrors of Princes*", in Timothy S. Miller and John Nesbit (eds) *Peace and War in Byzantium. Essays in Honor of George T. Dennis*. Washington, DC: Catholic University of America Press, 1995, pp. 50–62.

44. Roland H. Bainton, *Christian Attitudes toward War and Peace: A Historical Survey and Critical Re-evaluation*. Nashville, TN: Abingdon Press, 1960.

45. See the brief analysis of the implications of these continuities and discontinuities in Haldon, *Warfare, State and Society in the Byzantine World*, pp. 32–33.

46. On this interdependence of ecclesiastical and secular politics, see the analysis in D. Obolensky, "Nationalism in Eastern Europe in the Middle Ages", *Transactions of the Royal Historical Society*, 5th series, 22, 1972: 1–16, pp. 15–16.

47. Michael McCormick, "Patriotism", in A. Kazhdan et al. (eds) *The Oxford Dictionary of Byzantium*. Oxford and New York: Oxford University Press, vol. 3, 1991, pp. 1600–1601.

48. On the need to integrate the study of the nation-building and ethnic self-determination processes in the Byzantine Commonwealth into modern mainstream attitudes to and narrative of European identities as well as the reasons for the general absence of Byzantium and the Byzantine Commonwealth from the predominantly "Eurocentric" reconstructions of the formation of Europe in European historiography, see Averil Cameron, *The Byzantines*. Oxford: Blackwell, 2006, pp. 163–179. This neglect of the nation-formation processes in Orthodox Eastern Europe is all the more puzzling since, as stated by Timothy Ware in his standard book on Orthodoxy, "Nationalism has been the bane of the Orthodox Church in the last ten centuries" (*The Orthodox Church*, London and New York, 1963, reprinted 1997, p. 77). It is worth noting in this context that, in the fourteenth century, the capital of the second Bulgarian empire, Tŭrnovo, came to claim for a time the imperial status and title of "New Constantinople"; for arguments that this notion of *translatio imperii* reached Russia through Bulgaria and not directly from Byzantium, see, for example, Baron Meyendorff and Norman H. Baynes, "The Byzantine Inheritance in Russia", in Norman H. Baynes and H. St. L. B. Moss (eds) *Byzantium*. Oxford: Oxford University Press, 1948, pp. 369–392.

49. On the transformation of Byzantine messianism in the post-Byzantine period, see, for example, Cyril Mango, "Byzantinism and Romantic Hellenism", *Journal of the Warburg and Courtauld Institute*, 28, 1965: 29–44, pp. 34–36; Cyril Mango, "The Phanariots and the Byzantine Tradition", in R. Clogg (ed.) *The Struggle for Greek Independence*. London: Macmillan, 1973, pp. 41–66, pp. 54–56.

50. Catherine the Great's regard for Islam is well attested and her policies towards the Muslim subjects of the Russian empire were far more benevolent than those of her predecessors; her reign witnessed the beginning of the little-explored process of integration of the Islamic communities in the Orthodox Russian empire. On this process and its long-term implications, see the ground-breaking work of Robert D. Crews, *For Prophet and Tsar. Islam and Empire in Russia and Central Asia*. Cambridge, MA: Harvard University Press, 2006.

51. English translations of these speeches ("Speech of Petar I Petrovic delivered to Montenegrins in July 1796 before departure in battle against Mahmud-pasha Busatlija on Martinici" and "Speech of Petar I Petrovic in September 1796 delivered to Montenegrins before departure in battle against Mahmud-pasha Busatlija on Krusa") are available at: ⟨http://www.rastko.org.yu/rastko-cg/povijest/sveti_petar-1796e.html#krus⟩ and ⟨http://www.rastko.org.yu/rastko-cg/povijest/sveti_petar-1796e.html#mart⟩ (accessed 13 October 2008).

52. Academic and general interest in "The Mountain Wreath" has lately increased owing to its perceived relevance to elements of Serbian ethno-religious discourse during the war in Bosnia-Herzegovina. See, for example, Michael Sells, "Religion, History and Genocide in Bosnia-Herzegovina", in G. Scott Davis (ed.) *Religion and Justice in the War over Bosnia*. London and New York: Routledge, 1996, pp. 28–31; Branimir Anzulovic, *Heavenly Serbia. From Myth to Genocide*. New York and London: New York University Press, 1999, pp. 51–68; see also the more cautious analysis of Ger Duijzings, *Religion and Politics of Identity in Kosovo*. New York: Columbia University Press, 2000, pp. 188–191.

53. See the English translation of St Sergius of Radonezh's blessing in S. A. Zenkovsky (ed. and trans.), *Medieval Russia's Epics, Chronicles, and Tales*, 2nd edn. New York: E. P. Dutton, 1974, p. 284.

54. See the analysis in Paul Robinson, "On Resistance to Evil by Force: Ivan Il'in and the Necessity of Evil", *Journal of Military Ethics*, 2(2), 2003: 145–159, pp. 147–148.

55. See the observations of A. Fedotov, *The Russian Religious Mind*. Cambridge, MA: Harvard University Press, vol. 2, 1966, pp. 175 ff.; Robinson, "On Resistance to Evil by Force", pp. 148–149.

56. Petr Pavlovich Shafirov, *A Discourse Concerning the Just Causes of the War between Sweden and Russia 1700–1720* [1717]. Dobbs Ferry: Oceania Publications, 1973. On the career and development of the views of Baron Shafirov, including those reflected in his tract, see S. I. V. Dudakov, *Petr Shafirov*. Jerusalem: Jews in World Culture, 1989.

57. Vladimir Solovyov presents his discussion of Christian pacifism and just war theory in a literary dialogue form in the first conversation of his famous *Three Conversations* written in 1899; see the new revised English translation, Vladimir Solovyov, *War, Progress and the End of History. Three Conversations*, trans. Alexander Bakshy. New York: Lindisfarne Press, [1899] 1990, pp. 27–66.

58. Nikolai Velimirović, *Iznad greha i smrti: Besede i misli*. Belgrade: Izd. S. B. Cvijanovića, 1914, p. 19.

59. Nikolai Velimirović, *Serbia in Light and Darkness*, with preface by the Archbishop of Canterbury. London: Longmans, Green, 1916, p. 40; available as an eBook at ⟨http://www.gutenberg.org/files/19871/19871-8.txt⟩ (accessed 13 October 2008).

60. Nikolai Velimirović, *Agony of the Church*. London: Student Christian Movement, 1917, pp. 64–65; available as an eBook at ⟨http://www.gutenberg.org/files/20206/20206-8.txt⟩ (accessed 13 October 2008).

61. Nikolai Velimirović, *The Serbian People as a Servant of God*, vol. 1, *A Treasury of Serbian Orthodox Spirituality*, trans. by T. Micka and S. Scott. Grayslake, IL: Free Serbian Orthodox Diocese of America and Canada, 1988, p. 40.

62. Nikolai Velimirović, *Dva Vidovdanska govora*. Kragujevac, 1939, p. 14 f; available at ⟨http://www.rastko.org.yu/kosovo/duhovnost/nvelimirovickosovo_c.html#_Toc44782063⟩ (accessed June 2007).

63. On the concepts of national messianism developed in the works of Nikolai Velimirović, see R. Chrysostomus Grill, *Serbischer Messianismus und Europa bei Bischof Velimirović*. St Ottilien: EOS Verlag, 1998.

64. Velimirović, *Iznad greha i smrti*, p. 14. Bishop Velimirović could on occasions also furnish elaborations on traditional Eastern Orthodox teachings on peace and its different dimensions; see, for example, his poetic "Prayers by the Lake", partial English translation available in Hildo Bos and Jim Forest (eds) *For the Peace from Above: An Orthodox Resource Book on War, Peace and Nationalism*. Bialystok, Poland: Syndesmos Books, 1999, Ch. 7, online version at ⟨http://incommunion.org/articles/for-the-peace-from-above/chapter-7⟩ (accessed 14 October 2008).

65. "The Anonymous Byzantine Treatise on Strategy".

66. In his declaration, Patriarch Gavrilo offered his passionate support to the bold military coup d'état against Prince Paul, the regent of the Kingdom of Yugoslavia, on account of his agreement to join the Axis powers' Tripartite Pact. Patriarch Gavrilo categorically proclaimed that all Serbian historical achievements had been won only and entirely "by the sword" – "in a sea of spilled blood" – and, without such war endeavours and their countless victims, no victory is possible – as no resurrection is possible without death. See the text of his declaration in "U čemu je značaj 27. marta", in Patriarch Gavrilo, *Memoari patrijarha srpskog Gavrila*. Belgrade: Sfarios, 1970, p. 270; English translation of the relevant paragraph in Anzulovic, *Heavenly Serbia*, p. 17.

67. English translation of the relevant paragraphs from Patriarch Tikhon's letter is available in Bos and Forest (eds), *For the Peace from Above*, Ch. 5, online at ⟨http://incommunion.org/articles/resources/for-the-peace-from-above/chapter-5⟩ (accessed 14 October 2008). For an analysis of Patriarch Tikhon's statement on justifiable Christian warfare, see David Pratt, "Dual Trajectories and Divided Rationales. A Reply to Alexander Webster on Justifiable War", *St Vladimir's Theological Quarterly*, 47(1), 2003: 83–97, pp. 86–88. The issues raised by the need to reconcile inherited Christian pacifism with the patriotic duty to defend one's fatherland by force had already been treated in a pamphlet issued at the beginning of World War I by Metropolitan Anthony Khrapovitsky (1863–1936): *Christian Faith and War*. Jordanville, NY: Holy Trinity Monastery, [1915] 1973; also available at ⟨http://www.portal-credo.ru/site/print.php?act=lib&id=173⟩ (accessed 14 October 2008).

68. English translations of relevant paragraphs from Patriarch Tikhon's pastoral letters, etc., are available in Bos and Forest (eds), *For the Peace from Above*, Ch. 5, online at ⟨http://incommunion.org/articles/resources/for-the-peace-from-above/chapter-5⟩ (accessed 14 October 2008).

69. Anton Kartachov, "The Sanctity of Military Endeavour", 1929, English translation in Bos and Forest (eds), *For the Peace from Above*, pp. 202–203; also available at ⟨http://incommunion.org/articles/resources/for-the-peace-from-above/the-sanctity-of-the-military-endeavour⟩ (accessed 14 October 2008).

70. Ivan A. Il'in, *O soprotivlenii zlu siloiu*. Berlin: V tip. O-va "Presse", 1925.

71. On the debates provoked by Il'in's book, see Nikolai P. Poltoratskii, *I. A. Il'in i polemika vokrug ego idei o soprotivlenii zlu siloiu*. London, Ontario: Izd-vo "Zaria", 1975; Robinson, "On Resistance to Evil by Force", pp. 155–157.

72. On the religious dimensions of the Yugoslav conflicts of the 1990s, see the occasionally differing approaches and conclusions in G. Scott Davis (ed.), *Religion and Justice in the War over Bosnia*. London and New York: Routledge, 1996; Michael Sells, *The Bridge Betrayed. Religion and Genocide in Bosnia*. Berkeley: University of California Press,

1996; M. Mojzes, *The Yugoslav Inferno: Ethnoreligious Warfare in the Balkans.* New York: Continuum, 1998; M. Mojzes (ed.), *Religion and the War in Bosnia.* Atlanta, GA: Scholar Press, 1998; Duijzings, *Religion and Politics of Identity in Kosovo;* Vjekoslav Perica, *Balkan Idols. Religion and Nationalism in Yugoslav States.* Oxford and New York: Oxford University Press, 2002; Sabrina P. Ramet, *Balkan Babel: The Disintegration of Yugoslavia from the Death of Tito to the War for Kosovo,* 4th edn. Boulder, CO: Westview Press, 2002, pp. 79–127; Mitja Velikonja, "In Hoc Signo Vinces: Religious Symbolism in the Balkan Wars 1991–1995", *International Journal of Politics, Culture, and Society,* 17(1), 2003: 25–40. The studies of Serbian researchers on the role of the Serbian Orthodox Church in the conflicts are of particular importance, since they have access to archival sources that can still be inaccessible for foreign scholars and journalists; see, for example, Radimlja Radić, "Crkva i srpsko pitanje", in Nebojša Popov (ed.) *Srpska strana rata. Trama i katarza i istorijskom pamećenju.* Belgrade: BIGZ, 1996, pp. 267–304; Milorad Tomanić, *Srpska crkva u ratu i ratovi u njoj.* Belgrade: Medijska knjižara Krug Commerce, 2001; Ivan Čolović, *Bordel ratnika,* 3rd edn. Belgrade: Biblioteka XX vek, 2000; Milan Vukomanović, *O čemu crkva (ne) može da se pita. SPC, država i društvo u Srbiji (2000–2005).* Belgrade: Helsinki Committee for Human Rights in Serbia, 2005 (English translation, "What the Church Can(not) Be Asked About – The Serbian Orthodox Church, State and Society in Serbia", available at ⟨http://www.helsinki.org.yu/doc/Studija-Vukomanovic-eng.pdf⟩, accessed 14 October 2008).

73. Regionally, such initiatives included two meetings with senior Croat Catholic clerics during the war in Croatia in 1991 (which resulted in general appeals for peace); an official appeal for peace and reconciliation in Bosnia-Herzegovina in 1992 (made jointly with the Catholic episcopate and the Islamic religious community); the peace "message" made during the Serbian Orthodox bishops' extraordinary meeting in Banja Luka, Bosnia-Herzegovina, in November 1994 (in Bos and Forest, eds, *For the Peace from Above,* Ch. 9, available online at ⟨http://incommunion.org/articles/resources/for-the-peace-from-above/chapter-9⟩); participation in various peace-making inter-faith programmes in postwar Bosnia-Herzegovina; involvement in the postwar Serbian governmental Commission for Truth and Reconciliation; and Serbian Orthodox Patriarch Pavle's overtures to Croat and Muslim communities and clerics from 1999 onwards. Internationally, such initiatives and pronouncements have included the statement of Patriarch Pavle to the World Council of Churches Central Committee meeting in Johannesburg, South Africa, 20 January 1994 (in Bos and Forest, eds, *For the Peace from Above,* Ch. 9, available online at ⟨http://incommunion.org/articles/resources/for-the-peace-from-above/chapter-9⟩); and the involvement of the Holy Synod of the Serbian Orthodox Church in the Vienna Declaration of 1999 on peace and tolerance in Kosovo (in Bos and Forest, eds, *For the Peace from Above,* Ch. 9, available online at ⟨http://incommunion.org/articles/resources/for-the-peace-from-above/chapter-9⟩). The Serbian Orthodox Church also integrated into the litanies at Vespers, Matins and the Divine Liturgy prayers for peace and protection against hostile persecution of and violent attacks on its Orthodox flock (English translation of the prayers in Bos and Forest, eds, *For the Peace from Above,* Ch. 7, available online at ⟨http://incommunion.org/articles/resources/for-the-peace-from-above/chapter-7⟩).

74. For quotes from and references to some relevant statements and writings of senior clerics such as Metropolitan Amfilohije Radović, Archimandrite Bishop Atanasje Jevtić and Bishop Filaret of Mileševa, see, for example, Radić, "Crkva i srpsko pitanje", passim; Anzulovic, *Heavenly Serbia,* pp. 5, 22–23, 121–122; Duijzings, *Religion and Politics of Identity in Kosovo,* pp. 180, 196–198; Tomanić, *Srpska crkva u ratu i ratovi u njoj,* pp. 126–128, 135–140, 146–149, 186–191 and passim; Perica, *Balkan Idols,* pp. 143–

145, 158, 161–162, 173–174; Tatjana Perić, "Facing the Past: Religious Communities, Truth and Reconciliation in Post-Milošević Serbia", paper presented to the 6th Annual Kokkalis Graduate Student Workshop, Cambridge, MA, February 2004, pp. 1–3, available at ⟨http://www.ksg.harvard.edu/kokkalis/GSW7/GSW%206/Peric.pdf⟩ (accessed 14 October 2008); Noreen Herzfeld, "Lessons from Srebrenica. The Danger of Religious Nationalism", *Journal of Religion & Society*, Suppl. Ser. 2, 2007, available at ⟨http://moses.creighton.edu/JRS/pdf/2007-8.pdf⟩ (accessed 14 October 2008).

75. See, for example, Perica, *Balkan Idols*, pp. 158–162; Vukomanović, *O čemu crkva (ne) može da se pita*, passim; Tomanić, *Srpska crkva u ratu i ratovi u njoj*, pp. 226–228.

76. See Perica, *Balkan Idols*, pp. 173–174.

77. See, for example, Lubiša Rajić, "Fundamentalizum cilj ili sredstvo", in Milan Vukomanović and Marinko Vučinić (eds) *Religijski dijalog: drama razumevanja*. Belgrade: Belgrade Open School, 2003, pp. 33–58; Vukomanović, *O čemu crkva (ne) može da se pita*; Radovan Kupres, *Srpska pravoslavna crkva i novi srpski identitet*. Belgrade: Helsinki Committee for Human Rights in Serbia, 2006 (English translation, "The Serbian Orthodox Church and the New Serbian Identity", available at ⟨http://www.helsinki.org.yu/doc/Studija-Kupres-eng.pdf⟩, accessed 14 October 2008).

78. Robinson, "On Resistance to Evil by Force", pp. 157–158.

79. In the 1980s, the Ecumenical patriarchate had organized a series of meetings and events at its Orthodox Centre in Chambésy, Geneva, with topics including the need for Christian–Muslim dialogue and the modern relevance of Orthodox teachings of peace. In the 1990s, the Ecumenical patriarchate repeatedly referred to its earlier condemnation of ecclesiastical nationalism/racism (or "ethnophyletism") during the Local Synod convened in 1872 in Constantinople to deal with the question of the establishment of an autonomous Bulgarian Exarchate, approved by the Ottoman authorities in 1870. See, for example, the address of Ecumenical Patriarch Bartholomew I to the Conference on Peace and Tolerance convened at Istanbul, Turkey, in February 1994 (with a number of references to the implications of nationalism and its religious variants in Eastern Europe), available at ⟨http://incommunion.org/articles/resources/for-the-peace-from-above/peace-and-tolerance⟩ (accessed 14 October 2008). The Bosporus Declaration issued by this conference (available at ⟨http://incommunion.org/articles/resources/for-the-peace-from-above/chapter-9⟩, accessed 14 October 2008) condemned the exploitation of religious symbols by aggressive nationalism in former Yugoslavia; it also reaffirmed the Berne Declaration of 26 November 1992, stating that "a crime committed in the name of religion is a crime against religion". More recent statements on peacemaking and religious bridge-building issued by the Ecumenical patriarch since the conference in 1994 are available at ⟨http://www.ecupatriarchate.org/making_peace/?index=9⟩ (accessed 14 October 2008).

80. "Appel aux évêques serbes", *Le Monde*, 27 November 1991, p. 2.

81. The relevant extracts from the letter of the Orthodox Peace Fellowship to Patriarch Pavle are available at ⟨http://incommunion.org/articles/resources/for-the-peace-from-above/chapter-7⟩ (accessed 14 October 2008).

82. The text of the peace appeal is available at ⟨http://incommunion.org/articles/resources/for-the-peace-from-above/chapter-9⟩ (accessed 14 October 2008).

83. The "Declaration of the Syndesmos War and Peace in Europe Seminar", which was hosted by the Metropolis of Kydonia and Apokoronos, Chania, Crete, in October 1994, is available at ⟨http://incommunion.org/articles/resources/for-the-peace-from-above/chapter-9⟩ (accessed 14 October 2008).

84. Patriarch Bartholomew I, *Cosmic Grace – Humble Prayer: The Ecological Vision of the Green Patriarch Bartholomew*, ed. John Chryssavgis. Grand Rapids, MI: William B. Eerdmans Publishing Company, 2003.

85. Sacred Bishops' Council of the Russian Orthodox Church, *The Basis of the Social Concept of the Russian Orthodox Church*, 2000, English translation available on the website of the Moscow patriarchate at ⟨http://www.mospat.ru/index.php?mid=90⟩ (not always accessible); edited edition prepared by St. Innocent/Firebird Videos, Audios & Books available at ⟨http://incommunion.org/articles/the-orthodox-church-and-society/introduction⟩ (accessed 14 October 2008).

86. English translation available at ⟨http://incommunion.org/articles/resources/the-orthodox-church-and-society/viii⟩ (accessed 14 October 2008).

87. English translation available at ⟨http://incommunion.org/articles/resources/the-orthodox-church-and-society/ii⟩ (accessed 14 October 2008). See, in this context, the extracts from an interesting sermon by St Filaret of Moscow on the consecration of a military church (envisioning the first church being established among hosts and armies), available at ⟨http://incommunion.org/articles/resources/for-the-peace-from-above/chapter-5⟩ (accessed 14 October 2008).

88. Patriarch Alexei's peace appeals and the joint statement on the situation in Armenia and Azerbaijan are available at ⟨http://incommunion.org/articles/resources/for-the-peace-from-above/chapter-9⟩ (accessed 14 October 2008).

89. On the relations between the Russian Orthodox Church and the military and their effect on the Russian churchmen's attitude to the war in Chechnya, see, for example, Zoe Knox, *Russian Society and the Orthodox Church. Religion and Russia after Communism*. London and New York: Routledge Curzon, 2005, pp. 123–125.

90. Webster, "Justifiable War as a 'Lesser Good' ", p. 51.

91. Ibid., pp. 54–57.

92. See note 40 above.

93. Pratt, "Dual Trajectories and Divided Rationales", pp. 90–93; Philip LeMasters, "Justifiable War: Response #4", *St Vladimir's Theological Quarterly*, 47(1), 2003: 77–82, pp. 80–81.

94. Alexander F. C. Webster and Darrell Cole, *The Virtue of War. Reclaiming the Classic Christian Tradition East and West*. Salisbury, MA: Regina Orthodox Press, 2004.

95. George Dragas, "Justice and Peace in the Orthodox Tradition", in G. Limouris (ed.) *Justice, Peace and Integrity of Creation: Insights from Orthodoxy*. Geneva: WCC Publications, 1992, p. 42; Harakas, *The Wholeness of Faith and Life*, pp. 155–157; Metropolitan Isaiah, Presiding Hierarch of the Diocese of Denver, "The Undeclared War Against Yugoslavia. A Christian Perspective", 6 May 1999, available at ⟨http://www.serfes.org/orthodox/waragainstyugoslavia.htm⟩ (accessed 14 October 2008). See also the statement affirming the absence of "just war theory" in the Orthodox Church resulting from the Minsk meeting of Orthodox theologians in 1989 in "Orthodox Perspectives on Justice and Peace", in G. Limouris (ed.) *Justice, Peace and Integrity of Creation: Insights from Orthodoxy*. Geneva: WCC Publications, 1992, pp. 17–18.

96. Pratt, "Dual Trajectories and Divided Rationales", pp. 93–94; see also Harakas, "The Morality of War", 1981, pp. 86–87.

97. Miller, "Introduction", pp. 1–3.

8

Norms of war in Protestant Christianity

Valerie Ona Morkevicius

Protestant just war thought has much in common with its Catholic counterpart. The fathers of the Reformation, Martin Luther and John Calvin, viewed political power conservatively, and largely appropriated Catholic just war thinking – especially Augustine and Aquinas – into their theological perspectives. True to the spirit of the Reformation, they also drew directly from the Old and New Testaments. Ultimately, most of the newly emerging Protestant churches, and their modern successors, would adopt just war theory.

Embracing just war theory was as political as it was theological. Luther and Calvin clung to the medieval conception of government as a divinely ordained gift, necessary for earthly order. At the same time, politically they relied on sympathetic princes for protection. Geneva even presented Calvin an opportunity to institute a Protestant theocracy. Over the last five hundred years, many Protestant denominations have been state churches, making the issue of legitimizing violence essential.

The panoply of denominations makes it difficult to systematically describe Protestant thought about war. These denominations, having evolved in the half millennium since the Reformation, developed in different historical and national situations and claim a variety of founding genealogies. To structure this discussion of Protestant just war thought, this chapter considers Protestants as five broad historically based groups: Lutheran, Calvinist, Anglican, Evangelical and Anabaptist. Within each of these divisions are numerous independent groups, which in practice may differ greatly (and may not even recognize each other as members of the

World religions and norms of war, Popovski, Reichberg and Turner (eds),
United Nations University Press, 2009, ISBN 978-92-808-1163-6

same family of denominations!). The first three – Lutherans, Calvinists and Anglicans, and their daughter churches – have often been state churches, or at least dominant social forces. These three Protestant families generally uphold just war theory, largely as it was inherited from the Catholic tradition. Evangelicals, a very loose grouping of denominations and sects, locate their historical roots in one or more of the first three traditions. Their beliefs about war are as highly varied as their origins. Anabaptists, with a few notable exceptions, encompass the "Peace Churches", which uphold pacifism.

This chapter examines three variants of Protestant thinking about war: the just war tradition, pacifism and crusading. The just war tradition receives the most attention – arguably, those claiming it have been the most dominant denominations, in political, social and demographic terms.

The Protestant just war tradition

The Lutheran, Calvinist and Anglican traditions, and many of their successors, uphold traditional just war theory, inherited from their Catholic predecessors. Several denominations within these three traditions have explicitly declared it to be part of Church doctrine.[1]

This section explores the most influential thinkers from these just war traditions, starting with Luther and Calvin in the sixteenth century, before considering the contributions of Grotius and Pufendorf in the seventeenth century and Tillich, Barth, Niebuhr and Ramsey in the twentieth. By focusing on these thinkers as individuals, rather than attempting to construct a systematic historical narrative, I follow Jean Bethke Elshtain's lead, treating the just war discourse "as an authoritative tradition dotted with its own sacred texts, offering a canonical alternative to realism as received truth".[2]

The foundations of Protestant just war thought

Martin Luther (1483–1546) was the most prominent reformer of his time, and had considerable influence on Protestantism. He was born in Saxony, and his father was prosperous enough to send him to university, to study law.[3] In 1505, however, after nearly being struck by lightening, Luther rather suddenly entered an Augustinian monastery. His Ninety-Five Theses, publicly calling for major reforms in the Catholic Church, appeared in 1517.

The rampant political instability in the Germany of his day clearly leaves Luther longing for peace and order. He likens a prince who engages in a just war to a surgeon who amputates a diseased limb, sacrificing some for the common good. If princes could not use force, "everything in the world would be ruined ... Therefore, such a war is only a very brief lack of peace that prevents an everlasting and immeasurable lack of peace."[4] The starting point for Luther's just war theory, as it had been for Aquinas, is therefore the question of just authority.[5]

Luther condemns rebellion in favour of submission to state power – even when unjustly exercised. Rebellion is intolerable, violating both Christian and natural law. On the eve of the 1525 Peasants' War, Luther implores the princes to consider the peasants' demands and to defuse their anger by rendering justice. He warns that the war's outcome is unpredictable: "Do not start a fight with them, for you do not know how it will end."[6] Yet despite sympathy for their cause, Luther warns the peasants against armed rebellion. Citing Paul, he reminds them of their duty to submit to authority.[7] Although they are suffering gross injustices, the peasants as Christians are obliged "not to strive against injustice, not to grasp the sword ... but to give up life and property".[8] After all, "a wicked tyrant is more tolerable than a bad war".[9] Rebellion, like "a great fire ... attacks and devastates a whole land ... it makes widows and orphans, and turns everything upside down, like the worst disaster".[10] A rebel is worse than a simple murderer, for he "attacks the head himself and interferes with the exercise of his word and his office".[11] Although punishment of a murderer may be left up to the prince, any good citizen can – and should – capture and punish a rebel to preserve public order.

Luther's definition of rebellion is quite specific. The Diet of Augsburg proclaimed in 1530 that all Reformation heresy should be removed from the empire. In this case, Luther counsels Protestants that self-defence is not rebellion, and urges soldiers not to obey the emperor if he orders them to suppress the movement forcibly.[12] So long as the Protestants did not first use violence, physical defence against the temporal authorities' intervention should not be counted as rebellion. The reasoning stems from Luther's belief that the "two kingdoms" were separate: the princes were overstepping their temporal authority by interfering in spiritual matters. Heresy could not be a legitimate cause for war.

Luther's principle of just authority applies equally to war and peace. Political leaders are granted their positions by God, and the right to use force to maintain order is not limited to Christians: "even a heathen ruler has the right and the authority to punish."[13] Punishment of tyrants should be left in God's hands.[14] In the case of the Peasants' Rebellion, Luther reminds the princes that they are God's servants, and that, if they fail to fulfil their duties by "punishing some and protecting others", they will themselves become "guilty of all the murder and evil these people commit".[15]

Luther's theology does not permit crusading. The issue here is also just authority. The spiritual powers are not to intervene in secular affairs, and vice versa. After the defeat of King Louis II of Hungary by the Turks in 1526, Europeans discussed the appropriate response. Luther felt that a war of self-defence against the Turks was not only justified but required by duty. However, he objected to the idea that the war's cause should be considered religious and that the war's aim should include eliminating Islam. Luther saw the war as God's punishment for Christendom's impiety, so military action had to be seen as a "secular struggle, not a religious crusade".[16] Furthermore, Luther strongly protested against calling the European army "Christian", for to do so would dishonour Christ's name, not only by associating it with violence but also because "there are scarcely five Christians in such an army, and perhaps there are worse people in the eyes of God in that army than are the Turks".[17] Additionally, it was wrong in Luther's eyes to make a temporal leader the defender of the gospel or the head of Christendom. Ultimately, the Turk should be allowed to "believe and live as he will", for, "if the emperor were supposed to destroy the unbelievers and non-Christians, he would have to begin with the pope, bishops, and clergy, and perhaps not spare us or himself".[18]

Luther's careful reading of the Scripture made him keenly aware of the tension between just war theory's conditional tolerance of violence and the Gospel's apparent pacifism. He therefore stresses personal nonviolence even while permitting the state to use violence to uphold order. In Luther's work, just war theory can be understood only in light of the "two kingdoms theory". This Augustinian idea holds that Christians simultaneously inhabit two realms: one spiritual and perfect, the other earthly and inherently sinful. Luther shares Augustine's view that our world is by nature corrupted, and thus the "coercive and violent" functions of the state are needed to protect the innocent.[19]

Rather than equating the ideal world with the end time, Luther imagined it as present in the private Christian life. Of course, as Luther constantly reminds his readers, the number of "true" Christians is very small indeed; thus, temporal authority is needed to preserve earthly peace.[20] Luther's politics is thus very realistic: "Certainly it is true that Christians ... are subject neither to law nor sword, and have need of neither. But take heed and first fill the world with real Christians before you attempt to rule it in a Christian ... manner."[21]

Applying the two kingdoms theory, Luther argues that it is possible to bear the sword over non-Christians "in a Christian manner", for the sake of justice and order.[22] Luther explains: "the Scripture passages which speak of mercy apply to the kingdom of God and to Christians, not to the kingdom of the world."[23] Although the "severity and the wrath of the world's kingdom seems unmerciful", it is actually "not the least of God's mercies", since it ensures justice for the innocent.[24] So, although "no Christian shall wield or invoke the sword for himself and his case, on behalf of another ... he may and should wield it ... to restrain wickedness and to defend godliness".[25]

Following Augustine, Luther distinguishes between the occupation of soldiering and the individual soldier. The soldier's work (or the judge's or hangman's) is in itself necessary, even "right and godly", but whether or not the soldier is a good man depends on him alone.[26] Luther's justification of the soldier's profession relies on his own interpretation of the New Testament. As neither Jesus nor John the Baptist explicitly forbade soldiering, it must be "certain and clear enough that it is God's will that the temporal sword and law be used for the punishment of the wicked and the protection of the upright".[27] Luther also highlights several New Testament incidents where the apostles had opportunities to forbid Christians from being soldiers, yet did not: John confirmed the soldiers' calling, telling them to be content with their wages, and Peter converted the centurion Cornelius, without telling him to abandon his profession.[28]

If temporal authority is a necessity – even a positive good – and if the military profession has not been condemned in the New Testament, then logically war itself must be justifiable. Luther cites Romans and I Peter to argue that "the very fact that the sword has been instituted by God to punish evil, protect the good, and preserve peace ... is powerful and sufficient proof that war and killing along with all the things that accompany wartime and martial law have been instituted by God".[29]

Implicitly, Luther limits just cause to state defence. War itself represents "the punishment of wrong and evil" for the sake of "peace and obedience".[30] Whoever starts a war is wrong, as is anyone who looks for cause to fight.[31] Princes are not to fight their feudal superiors, even if they have been wronged.[32] But they may defensively fight against equals, inferiors and foreign governments.

War should always be the last resort. Pointing to Mosaic law, Luther insists that the Christian prince should first offer the antagonist "justice and peace", before resorting to violence.[33] Therefore war must be fought only when an enemy "attacks and starts the war, and refuses to cooperate in settling the matter according to law or through arbitration and common agreement".[34]

Luther is not as interested in just means. If the cause is just, then the necessary means are justifiable. In a just war of self-defence, "it is both Christian and an act of love to kill the enemy without hesitation, to plunder and burn and injure him by every method of warfare until he is conquered".[35] The language Luther uses to exhort the nobles to suppress the Peasants' Rebellion reveals nearly any tactic to be acceptable: "Let no one have mercy on the obstinate, hardened, blinded peasants who refuse to listen to reason; but let everyone, as he is able, strike, hew, stab and slay, as though among mad dogs."[36]

Nonetheless, Luther does draw a distinction between legitimate tactics of war and other violent acts that often occur in wartime. Although the enemy may be killed in just about any fashion, the army should exercise self-control. Luther draws on Deuteronomy 20, where God commands the Israelites not to hew fruit trees for siege works, and deduces that such a God would "never have permitted them to rage against women and girls in debauchery, lust, and other violence after conquering the enemy, as happens nowadays in our barbarity".[37] After victory, restraint should be shown and peace and mercy offered to those who surrender.

There is also a possibility for conscientious objection. On the one hand, Luther argues against pacifists who, "because of tenderness of conscience", deny that Christians can ever participate in war, pointing to the passage in Luke in which John the Baptist tells the newly baptized soldiers to be content with their wages.[38] Subjects are bound to follow their lords into battle, so long as they are not convinced the cause is wrong. However, if it is unjust, they should neither "fight nor serve", despite the consequences.[39]

Ultimately, the Lutheran Augsburg Confession (1531), Article 16, enshrined just war theory as Church doctrine:

It is taught among us that all government in the world and all established rule were instituted and ordained by God for the sake of good order, and that Christians may without sin occupy civil offices or serve as princes and judges, render decisions and pass sentence according to imperial and other existing laws, punish evil doers with the sword, engage in just wars, serve as soldiers, etc.[40]

Lutheranism became the dominant religion of the Scandinavian countries and much of Germany, garnering a great deal of social and political importance in Europe.

John Calvin (1509–1564) shared many of Luther's ideals, and became an important leader of the Reformed Church. Born in France, Calvin was first sent to Paris to be educated toward a theological vocation; his father later withdrew him to study law instead. Ultimately, Calvin completed both degrees after his father's death. He does not seem to have been inspired by Protestant ideas before 1533, when he rather suddenly gave up his ecclesiastical benefices rather than taking orders in the Catholic Church.[41] His greatest opus, the *Institutes of the Christian Religion*, was published in 1535; a year later, he settled in Geneva to help implement the Reformation's ideals. Calvin remained in Geneva for most of his life, helping to "shape the life of the city as a community of believers, united in both the civil and religious orders under a shared commitment to Christ".[42]

Like Luther, Calvin was deeply troubled by the political insecurity of his time, making the threat of disorder one of the dominant themes in his works.[43] His justification for the use of force at home and abroad focuses on a fear of anarchy. This concern with maintaining peace and order leads him to criticize the Anabaptists, who encouraged their members to withdraw from public life and to be strictly non-violent.

Aquinas was of greater importance for Calvin than for Luther, possibly because of their shared affinity for the classics. Calvin draws freely from Socrates, Plato, Aristotle, Cicero, Seneca and others. He derives from them his concept of natural law, leading him to assert the decidedly Renaissance belief that "the law of God which we call the moral law is nothing else than a testimony of natural law and of that conscience which God has engraved upon the minds of men".[44]

In the *Institutes*, Calvin enters the discussion of the legitimacy of warfare from a similar starting point to Luther's: the importance of civil authority as a God-given office. Like Luther, Calvin makes it clear that Christians should not withdraw from public life: "no one ought to doubt that civil authority is a calling, not only holy and lawful before God, but also the most sacred and by far the most honourable of all callings in the whole life of mortal men."[45] Leaders' power is invested in them by God, creating a set of reciprocal duties. The magistrates owe their subjects protection, and should strive to uphold God's will; subjects owe their magistrates respect and obedience.

Magistrates must use force to fulfil their duty as "ordained protectors and vindicators of public innocence, modesty, decency, and tranquillity ... [providing] for the common safety and peace of all".[46] The magistrate's army "is not only an agent of the kingdom of the World, but of God".[47] Christian leaders may use their power "severely to coerce the open malefactors and criminals by whose wickedness the public peace is troubled or disturbed".[48] Like Augustine and Luther, Calvin asserts that the magistrate is not the actual actor judging and hanging criminals, but rather serves as God's tool, carrying out God's commandments on earth.[49] Mostly Calvin justifies the domestic use of force by reference to the Old Testament, although he does cite the apostle Paul (Romans 13) to argue that the sword has been given by God to earthly rulers.

Using the domestic analogy, Calvin asserts that leaders also have the right to wage wars to execute "public vengeance" and to "preserve the tranquillity of their dominion" by checking "the fury of one who disturbs both the repose of private individuals and the common tranquillity of all, who raises seditious tumults, and by whom violent oppressions and vile misdeeds are perpetrated".[50] However, war must always be a last resort. Citing Cicero, Calvin argues that "everything else ought to be tried before recourse is had to arms".[51] A ruler should not "lightly seek occasion" to fight, nor "accept the occasion when offered, unless ... driven to it by extreme necessity".[52]

Just cause for Calvin is primarily limited to self-defence. An invader – whether a king or a host of common criminals – is a robber and should be "punished accordingly".[53] Here, Calvin diverges from Luther. Intriguingly, although Calvin's legitimation of the sovereignty of kings and states is based heavily on both Old and New Testament sources, his discussion of war as a policy relies largely on natural law reasoning. Whereas Luther firmly based his justification of war on biblical sources, Calvin points to "natural equity and the nature of the office" as justifications.[54] Rather than teasing out a comprehensive doctrine justifying war from the New Testament's stories of soldiers' conversion, Calvin abruptly ends the section by stating: "and the Holy Spirit declares such wars to be lawful by many testimonies of Scripture."[55] Calvin justifies himself by arguing that "an express declaration of this matter is not to be sought in the writings of the apostles; for their purpose is not to fashion a civil government, but to establish the spiritual Kingdom of Christ".[56]

Like Luther, Calvin does not approve of rebellion. Subjects owe their rulers respect and obedience, regardless of their quality or justness.[57] He likewise counsels unhappy citizens to rely on God to avenge them in His own time, and "not at once think that it is entrusted to [them], to whom no command has been given except to obey and suffer".[58] Thus, although Calvin believed that constitutions and certain forms of representative government could be used to curtail kings' tyrannical tendencies (and repeatedly condemned abuse of power[59]), his political theory provided little room for subjects to create such institutions independently.[60]

Calvin also touches on the question of just means. Rulers should not "be carried away with headlong anger, or be seized with hatred, or burn with implacable severity".[61] Citing Augustine, he argues that they should instead "have pity on the common nature" present even in their enemy.[62] Enemies should be shown the same regard one would wish for one's self.

A form of conscientious objection is possible for Calvin, since obedience to earthly rulers must never lead to disobedience to God. Rulers derive authority from God, but, "if they command anything against him, let it go unesteemed".[63] Unlike Luther, who specifically discussed conscientious objection in wartime, Calvin's discussion of the subject is general and does not address soldiering directly.

Calvin's Reformed movement, which spread across northern Europe and later to North America, was the predecessor of several large Protestant groupings, including the Reformed, the Christian Reformed, the United Reformed, the Presbyterians, the Congregationalists (the United Churches of Christ) and some Baptist churches. These churches generally respect the just war tradition. The Presbyterian Church, for example, upholds the just war tradition as part of its doctrine. Article 23 of the 1648 Westminster Confession of the Presbyterian and Congregationalist traditions states:

> It is lawful for Christians to accept and execute the office of a magistrate (appointed or elected political office) when called there unto; in the managing whereof, as they ought to especially to maintain piety, justice and peace, according to the wholesome laws of each commonwealth, so, for that end, they may lawfully, now under the New Testament, wage war upon just and necessary occasions.[64]

The distinction between the Lutheran and Calvinist approaches to just war is subtle. A few key differences are notable. For Luther, the initial question as to whether Christians can justifiably use violence is more theologically and politically troubling. Luther carefully develops the two kingdoms theory to explain away the tension between New Testament calls for radical peace and the violence seemingly necessary for earthly stability and order. Luther does not deny the pacifist call; he simply sets it aside for some future time. Reinhold Niebuhr will explore this perpetual contradiction in the twentieth century.

For Calvin, the problem of justifying the Christian use of violence in the first place is not so significant. Influenced by natural law, Calvin views violent conflict as inevitable in human society. His focus, therefore, is on who may use violence, and how, in order to maintain a just order. Later, some aspects of Calvin's thought would be used to justify crusading-type violence, as for example during the English Civil War.

Like Lutheranism and Calvinism, the Anglican Church broke with Catholicism in the sixteenth century, for reasons as much political as religious. Ultimately, Queen Elizabeth I created an inclusive Calvinistic Protestantism, although the Church hierarchy remained highly conservative. The Thirty-Nine Articles of the Anglican Confession, dating to 1571, were influenced by the earlier Augsburg and Wurttemberg confessions. Article 37, dealing with civil magistrates, focuses on the temporal and spiritual role of the English monarch. Without theological discussion, it simply asserts that "it is lawful for Christian men, at the commandment of the Magistrate, to wear weapons, and serve in the wars".[65] This just war stance has been upheld by the Anglican Communion to the present, and by several of its daughter churches, including the Methodist and Wesleyan denominations.

Protestant just war thought and international law

Protestant just war thought is closely interwoven with international law. In the seventeenth century, Grotius and Pufendorf considered the ethics of warfare. It is important to note, however, that they framed their work not as contributions to Protestant just war thinking per se, but rather as projects of humanistic, international law.

Hugo Grotius (1583–1645), the Dutch legal scholar, published treatises on international law, ranging from the law of the sea to religious toleration. *Of the Laws of War and Peace*, published in 1625, is of central importance. Grotius unites theological and humanist perspectives in his discussion of whether war can ever be just, and in what circumstances. Grotius openly acknowledges his intellectual debt to Alberico Gentili, an Italian Protestant legal scholar whose *De Jure Belli* (1598) greatly influenced him. But Gentili's work, aimed at legitimizing English policy towards the Spanish armada, was later overshadowed by Grotius' more systematic approach. This section focuses on Grotius, who had the greater influence not only on other Protestant thinkers but on virtually all scholars of international law in the Western tradition.

Grotius asserts that war is a natural right. As Europeans explored Asia and the Americas in the sixteenth and seventeenth centuries, the idea of natural law – a universal set of principles observed by all peoples – came under fire from sceptics pointing to the vast array of cultures whose values seemed so irreconcilable. Grotius thus based his natural law system on the "one universal precept the sceptics did accept: the natural urge of all of us to self-preservation".[66]

Grotius does not treat natural law completely secularly. He posits that, "since the law of nature is perpetual and unchangeable, nothing contradictory to it could be commanded by God, who is never unjust".[67] Thus, although the Old Testament Mosaic laws are no longer binding for Christians, they serve as a good example for formulating modern laws of war. Furthermore, the New Testament also does not forbid war: "the laws of Christ do not impose duties ... above [those] ... required by the law of nature."[68] To justify his view, Grotius, like Luther and Calvin, points to the interaction between John the Baptist and the newly converted soldiers, arguing that, if Christians were obligated to give up the sword, an explicit command would have been given then. Grotius also agrees with Luther that true Christians would not need force: "if all people were Christians, and lived like Christians, there would be no wars."[69]

Grotius, like Luther, makes just authority the primary condition for establishing just cause. No war can be lawfully made except by the sovereign authority of a state. That authority lies explicitly in the political leaders, not in the people. Rebellion is not permissible, because subjects do not have a "right to restrain and punish kings for an abuse of their power".[70] War must be openly declared, not because secrecy is problematic ethically, but because it must be clearly demonstrated that the war is the will of the sovereign.[71]

Just cause for Grotius centres on self-defence. Aware that rulers could use "defence" to veil their pursuit of power and material gain, Grotius specifies that true self-defence arises only out of necessity, and must be based on actual knowledge of another's hostile intent, and not merely on fear or jealousy of the other's potential.[72] A war cannot be just simply because of its realist benefits, by providing territory or wealth. National honour is also not an acceptable cause, and Grotius is adamant that religious or moral causes cannot be justified – no doubt a critical response to the ongoing Thirty Years War between Protestant and Catholic states.[73] Lastly, Grotius explains that a leader must not simply act in a just way, but must have just intentions for doing so.[74]

Grotius' definition of self-defence is not as narrow and restrictive as it first seems. While cautioning that leaders should always act for the good of the entire country (and not their private interests), he argues that in some cases it may be just to intervene on behalf of others.[75] States may thus justly fight to protect allies and to uphold bonds of Common Nature. Grotius also permits war to recover an indemnity or to punish another state for some wrongdoing. Both of these can be subsumed by a broad definition of self-defence. Collecting an indemnity can be a form of territorial self-defence and, since the primary "crime" in the international system is a violation of sovereignty, punishment too can be seen as a subset of self-defence. The difference here is that, whereas self-defence implies simply staving off an invasion, punishment allows states to protect themselves further by preventing future crimes.

Grotius devotes more attention than his predecessors to the lawful conduct of war. Any means leading to a just end of the war are justifiable, but what is "right" in legal terms may not always be "moral".[76] Christians are called to restraint, especially regarding the lives of innocents. Grotius upholds Aquinas' principle of double effect: "it will be necessary to guard against things, which fall not within the original purpose of an action, and the happening of which might be foreseen: unless indeed the action has a tendency to produce advantages, that will far outweigh the consequences of any accidental calamity."[77] Although civilians may be injured or killed in the course of a legitimate military action, "yet humanity will require that the greatest precaution should be used against involving the innocent in danger, except in cases of extreme urgency and utility".[78] Grotius defines innocents as those who do not bear arms, such as women, children, priests, philosophers and merchants.[79] Such civilians may be killed in war, but not intentionally, unless their deaths are absolutely and inevitably necessary in military terms. His source for this is not a Christian one, but rather the Roman historian Seneca.

Even enemy soldiers should be shown some mercy, when they are not posing an active threat: "No one can be justly killed by design, except by way of legal punishment, or to defend our lives, and preserve our property, when it cannot be effected without his destruction."[80] Likewise, after surrender has been tendered, further bloodshed is no longer legitimate.[81] Alluding to his disgust over the violence between Christians during the Hundred Years War, Grotius urges conquerors to permit the continuance of the existing religion.[82]

Grotius even lays out principles for the respect of enemy property. The seizure or destruction of property may be legal, but yet not moral. Wanton destruction of property is unwarranted. Unnecessary violence and damage should be avoided, especially in capturing towns, where the lives and livelihoods of innocent residents are at risk. Grotius argues that, "besides being no way conducive to the termination of war, [such means] are totally repugnant to every principle of Christianity and justice".[83] Additionally, art, religious objects and tombs ought to be spared. Although the law of nations may give armies the legal right to destroy them, as a sign of respect it is better to forbear.[84]

Samuel Pufendorf (1632–1694) was Grotius' intellectual and historical successor. Born in Saxony, he entered the University of Leipzig to study Lutheran theology, developing an interest in natural law and moral philosophy. By 1659, he had moved to Holland, where Grotius' son recommended him to the Elector Palatinate. In 1673, *On the Duty of Man and Citizen According to Natural Law* was published.

Unlike his predecessors, who implicitly considered mankind as naturally sinful and tragically doomed to violence, Pufendorf declares that "it is most agreeable to natural law that men should live in peace ... [which] itself is a state peculiar to man, insofar as he is distinct from the beasts".[85] War, however, "is sometimes permitted, and occasionally necessary", when one's property or rights cannot be defended in any other way.[86]

Just cause is broader for Pufendorf, as it had been for Grotius, in the tradition of Aquinas who permitted war not only in self-defence but also for the righting of wrongs. One's fellow citizens have the highest claim to defence, followed by allies, friends and kin. Pufendorf legitimizes collective security, permitting fighting "on another's behalf", assuming that the other party "has a just cause and ... the party coming to aid has a reasonable ground for conducting hostilities on his behalf against the third party".[87]

War can be justly fought to collect "what is due to us from others but has been denied, or the procurement of reparations for wrong inflicted and of assurance for the future".[88] Although just cause can thus be claimed even in offensive wars, rulers must take care that war is always the last resort. Amicable settlement should always be sought first and, if there "remains some doubt about right or fact", one should avoid turning to arms.[89]

Just intent is also significant. Even a just cause can lead to an unjust war if the leader is motivated by "lust for wealth and lust for power".[90] Going to war on the basis of a false pretext, such as "fear of the wealth and power of a neighbour, unjustified aggrandizement, desire for better territory, refusal of something which is simply and straightforwardly owed ... or desire to extinguish another's legitimately acquired right", is unjust.[91]

Like Grotius, Pufendorf carefully describes rules for just means. He similarly distinguishes between the natural right to inflict unlimited suffering on one's enemy and the moral obligation to fight with moderation. A distinction must be made between "what an enemy may suffer without wrong and what we ourselves may inflict without loss of humanity".[92] The minimum of necessary force should be used, because "humanity ... requires that so far as the momentum of warfare permits, we should inflict no more suffering on an enemy than defence or vindication of our right ... requires".[93] The concern with moderation is thus two-fold: respect for the humanity of one's enemy and of one's self.

Pufendorf also discusses enemy people's property rights. Unlike Grotius, who liberally upheld their right to keep their property, Pufendorf simply refers to the common practice of warfare. By custom, property taken by soldiers is acquired for the state, but it is a "universal practice" that movable property is left to the soldiers, who take it as a reward or in lieu of pay.[94]

A century later, Swiss Protestant Emerich de Vattel would continue the conversation about international law in a decidedly secular tone in his *Law of Nations* (1758). This secularism is presaged in Grotius and Pufendorf, who carefully separate the roles of Church and state, as well as private and public morality. The integration of Protestant theologies of violence with modern secular international law suggests that, at least in the case of the mainstream denominations, there has been a willingness to accept and encourage the development of international law and institutions to limit and control violence.

Protestant just war theory: Facing the twentieth century and beyond

World War II's devastating destruction and genocide led to a resurgence in Protestant just war thought in Europe and the United States. Theologian Karl Barth (1886–1964) served as a pastor in his native Switzerland before becoming a professor of theology in Germany. On the eve of World War II, he attacked the German government as heretical in its attempt to nationalize the Church. Expelled from Germany in 1935, he volunteered for the Swiss army after the outbreak of war.[95] Although he vehemently opposed Nazi totalitarianism, Barth did not view Communism as an equal threat, and was the only prominent theologian of the era not to condemn the suppression of the 1956 Hungarian Revolution.[96]

The crux of Barth's critique of Nazism is that God ordains neither state nor nation. This differs from Luther, who claimed the state is created by God for mankind's sake. Barth argues that raising the nation to such a position is "heretical by the fact that it inevitably introduces a foreign deity, a national god".[97]

With the state no longer sacrosanct, the recourse to war becomes more complex. Even national self-defence cannot be a sufficient just cause. Barth even questions the defence of one's own person, arguing that such self-defence is "almost entirely excluded" by divine command.[98] Self-defence is not "natural", because it is not obvious why "force should be met by force, aggression by aggression, disorder by disorder", creating a cycle of violence resolving nothing.[99] Self-defence thus "degrades" the self, and perhaps more importantly violates the rights of the aggressor over whose life God "does not give us any authority".[100] Therefore, defence of our selves, our possessions and others' possessions should be prohibited.

However, "it is certainly not the case that God has abandoned ... the common life of man to the confusion which would inevitably result if ... individuals could assault others without restraint and at their own impulse".[101] Therefore, one *can* act to defend another's life. In that case, "it will not be a matter of his own conflict with the assailant, in which he tries to overpower and disarm him as an enemy, but of God's conflict with the disorder and disaster which devastate humanity".[102] Killing can be justified to defend others – especially one's community. There can be something in the life of the state that, if surrendered, would mean "[yielding] something which must not be betrayed, which is necessarily more important ... than the preservation of life itself, and which is thus more important than the preservation of the lives of those who unfortunately are trying to take it".[103]

Barth's definition of what is valuable enough to be thus defended is very limited. Concerns about the balance of power, honour, even the internal conditions of another state are all "too paltry to be worth the terrible price involved for their realization by war ... War for such reasons is an act of murder."[104] Even "the existence or non-existence of a state does not always constitute a valid reason for war", because sometimes a state's licence to exist has "expired" and it would be "thus better advised to yield and surrender".[105] A state has a right to self-defence only when it "has serious grounds for not being able to assume responsibility for the surrender of its independence" because the consequences would be so devastating for the life of its citizens as a people.[106]

Although war may sometimes be justified, the Church should always "start with the assumption that the inflexible negative of pacifism has almost infinite arguments in its favour and is almost overpoweringly strong".[107] War should not be accepted as a "normal, fixed and in some sense necessary part of ... the just state".[108] Instead, the Church should encourage states to fashion a just peace so war is no longer needed, urging states to observe "fidelity and faith in their mutual dealings as the responsible presupposition of a true foreign policy, for solid agreements and alliances and their honest observance, for international courts and conventions", and to disband their "standing armies in which the officers constitute *per se* a permanent danger to peace".[109]

Barth also upholds conscientious objection. In his view, "killing is a very personal act, and being killed a very personal experience. It is thus commensurate with the thing itself that even in the political form which killing assumes in war it should be the theme of supremely personal interrogation."[110] The burden of responsibility for killing in war lies squarely on the individuals involved – both as citizens and as soldiers. Thus, the state cannot command a man to serve, because "the state is not God".[111] But a conscientious objector must meet two conditions. First, this "act of insubordination" must be carried out in a way that does not deny the state but affirms it.[112] The individual's opposition must be a service to the political community, and not just a means of keeping his own hands clean. Second, the objector must accept the consequences of his objection without complaint. He cannot accept alternative service: if the war is not worthy of being fought with weapons, it should be resisted even in its non-military forms, such as civilian or ambulance service.

The views of German theologian Paul Tillich (1886–1965) on war would also be strongly influenced by the two world wars. A Lutheran minister in Berlin, Tillich was sent to the front in 1914 as a chaplain. In 1932, while teaching at Frankfurt University, he stood up against storm troopers who attacked students there, and was pressured to leave Germany. In 1935, he accepted an invitation from Reinhold Niebuhr to come to Union Theological Seminary in the United States. By the late

1950s, he had become the "foremost Protestant thinker" in the United States.[113]

Like Barth, Tillich argues that the totalitarian state is inherently in conflict with the Church. The Church should neither be subjected to state power, nor radically separated from it. In a 1934 essay, Tillich criticizes the traditional Lutheran position that the Church has the right to influence the state only indirectly, arguing that it leads to an "absence of public criticism of state activities" and a "separation between private and public morality".[114] If the state makes claims of an absolute and totalitarian character, it inevitably conflicts with the Church. Although the Church is not "absolute itself", it "gives evidence of the absolute", whereas the state has only "the task of regulating the finite and social sphere, and therefore has no right to a claim of an absolute or totalitarian character".[115] The Church must therefore demand that the state remain within its limits.

The difficulty, however, is that, even as the Protestant Church emerged to "challenge the totalitarianism of the Catholic church", the Reformation itself "propagated a nationalism of which culture as well as religion became its victims", and the "church's opposition to nationalistic ideology, with its unjust claims and untrue assertions, became weaker with every decade of modern history".[116] Between the "subjection of the churches to the national states" and the "liberal ideal of separation of church and state", the Church has been rendered "impotent" in modern times.[117] The Church must reclaim its independence and not allow itself to be pushed into a narrow corner of the social fabric. Otherwise, the Church loses "its radical otherness" and becomes no more than a "benevolent social club".[118]

For Tillich, international institutions can help foster more peaceful relations between nation-states, and even lead them towards greater (although never total) unity. "Despite all failures," Tillich writes in 1936, the League of Nations "has put into effect the idea of a ... sphere of power superior to individual sovereignty; the struggle for power of the national groups takes place at least partially in the arena of a legal order, which is democratic in form".[119] Institutions' capacity to create unity is limited by the competitive nature of human communities and by the fact that such institutions are "determined by a group of leading nations", namely the winners of the world wars.[120]

With this view of the international community in mind, Tillich lays out two conditions for a just war: when a higher unity must be created or defended. For the first case, Tillich provides the example of the American Civil War, when the nation had to be held together by force for some greater good (the expansion of civil rights); for the latter, Tillich points to the American Revolutionary War, when the colonies had to separate from Britain to acquire their legitimate political rights.[121] Just causes represent "creative justice" or "a justice whose final aim is the preservation or restitution of a community of social groups, subnational or supranational".[122] Creative justice is the only legitimate cause for war.

But there is "no way of saying with more than daring faith whether a war was or is a just war in this sense", for there are so many variables to consider and human reason is limited.[123] Nonetheless, this inescapable incertitude "does not justify the cynical type of realism which surrenders all criteria and judgements, nor does it justify the utopian idealism which believes in the possibility of removing the compulsory element of power from history".[124] Thus, the Church must encourage peace, but nonetheless should not deny this tool of statecraft to the body politic. After all, pacifism may end "in consequences which are opposite from those intended" in a world where "national as well as international peace depends on the power to restrain the violators of peace".[125]

Tillich also explicitly deals with the issue of nuclear weapons in the years after World War II. War cannot be just if it is "in reality universal suicide", and thus "one can never start an atomic war with the claim that it is a just war, because it cannot serve the unity which belongs in the Kingdom of God".[126] Furthermore, a nuclear war would be evil "if it could not serve the principle of creative justice", since it would be "[annihilating] what it is supposed to defend".[127] The "impotency of conventional weapons does not lift the prohibition against the use of atomic weaponry ... no first use of atomic weapons is permitted; and should this mean withdrawal from territory, this is a tolerable short term consequence".[128] However, "one must be ready to answer in kind, even with atomic weapons, if the other side uses them first", for the "threat itself could be a deterrent".[129]

In the United States, Reinhold Niebuhr (1892–1972) became one of the foremost Protestant just war theorists. The son of an immigrant Lutheran preacher, Niebuhr became a professor at New York's Union Theological Seminary. In 1932, Niebuhr and his younger brother (theologian H. Richard Niebuhr) engaged in a landmark debate within the pages of *The Christian Century*. Responding to the Manchurian crisis and the looming spectre of World War II, the younger Niebuhr believed that strict pacifism was the appropriate Christian response, penning the "Grace of Doing Nothing". He denied the usefulness of just war criteria, arguing that "war cannot be evaluated in terms of the rightness of particular causes, an exercise that results only in self-righteous hubris".[130]

But the elder Niebuhr argued that engagement was necessary, laying the foundations for Christian realism. Niebuhr pragmatically asserted that no specific norm could be taken absolutely, that "the thing for the moralist to keep in view historically is the social goal, and values must be wielded against each other to produce the pattern of activity that will result in the most egalitarian and inclusive social good".[131] For this reason, Niebuhr's work does not provide a systematic approach to just war theory, although it does outline a justification for violence and suggest some ways in which inter-state peace could be established.

Like Pufendorf, Niebuhr was moderately optimistic about the human potential to live in harmony. In his view, humankind is blessed with a "natural impulse", prompting him "to consider the needs of others, even when they conflict with his own".[132] But although education could encourage people to expand their range of benevolent impulse, "there are definite limits in the capacity of ordinary mortals", making it impossible for them to give others the same rights they grant themselves.[133]

As a result, coercion is a natural requirement for "all social co-operation on a larger scale than the most intimate social group".[134] Although states cannot rely on coercion alone to maintain unity, they would be lost without it. Realistic about the relationship between order, coercion and justice, Niebuhr admits that "power sacrifices justice to peace with the community and destroys peace between communities ... the power that prevents anarchy in intra-group relations encourages anarchy in inter-group relations".[135] Indeed, "the fact that the coercive factor in society is both necessary and dangerous seriously complicates the whole task of securing both peace and justice".[136] Humankind should not naïvely hope for an ideal society, but should instead concentrate on creating a society "in which there will be enough justice, and in which coercion will be sufficiently non-violent to prevent his common enterprise from issuing into complete disaster".[137] Ultimately, the "political order must be satisfied with relative peace and relative justice".[138]

Violence should not be blithely dismissed as a reasonable tool for achieving justice and social change. Although coercion undermines justice in some respects, "equality is a higher social goal than peace".[139] Without equality, "peace" is really nothing more than "an armistice within the existing disproportions of power".[140] Therefore, it is wrong to assume that "violence is intrinsically immoral".[141] Niebuhr unequivocally states: "Nothing is intrinsically immoral except ill-will and nothing is intrinsically good except goodwill."[142] Human motives are inevitably mixed, and a priori classifying certain means of achieving them as wrong or right is unjust. Typically, overt acts of violence (such as outright rebellion) are condemned, whereas covert acts of violence (such as systemic economic injustice) are tacitly permitted. So if coercion is ethically justified, although "always morally dangerous", we cannot "draw any absolute line of demarcation between violent and non-violent coercion".[143] Intent is difficult to determine, and our habits and laziness lead us to assume that non-violent acts are motivated by goodwill whereas violent ones are driven by ill will. In Niebuhr's view, this "traditionalized instrumental value" attached to all actions based on their violence or non-violence obscures the intents behind them, as well as their long-term effects.[144]

For Niebuhr, the question of whether the use of force is justifiable hinges on its intended results: "a political policy cannot be intrinsically evil if it can be proved to be an efficacious instrument for the achievement of a morally approved end."[145] Nonetheless, Niebuhr recognizes that violence as a political tool carries special moral risks and consequences. In the short term, "the destruction of life or the suppression of freedom result in the immediate destruction of moral values".[146] Whether this sacrifice could be justifiable depends on the circumstances.

Nations are, by nature, too selfish and hubristic "to make the attainment of international justice without the use of force possible".[147] The danger is that inter-state politics easily falls into an endless cycle of violence, as nations avenging wrongs against themselves engender new wrongs against others. Niebuhr therefore lays out several methods for overcoming this cycle and "making force morally redemptive".[148] One method is to place violence in the hands of a community or organization "which transcends the conflicts of interest between individual nations and has an impartial perspective upon them".[149] The League of Nations could have served such a role, but Niebuhr is sceptical about its potential for impartiality, given the broad differences in power between states. Furthermore, the international community itself neither carries enough "prestige" nor represents a "sufficiently unified" communal spirit to discipline violators.[150] Because of its institutional weakness, it would have difficulty proving itself in the one really important test of its efficacy: whether it would be "able to grant justice to those who have been worsted in battle without requiring them to engage in new wars to redress their wrongs".[151] Recognizing that human society will probably never completely escape social conflict, Niebuhr does not advocate abolishing coercion, but rather proposes limiting it by "counselling the use of such types of coercion as are most compatible with the moral and rational factors in human society and by discriminating between the purposes and ends for which coercion is used".[152] Realistically, the international community can reduce the occurrence of violence but cannot hope to banish it entirely.

Unlike Luther and Calvin, who unequivocally condemned rebellion, Niebuhr sees it as potentially leading to greater justice. The short-term upheaval of rebellion may be worth the long-term improvement in social justice: "if a season of violence can establish a just social system and can create the possibilities of its preservation, there is no purely ethical ground upon which violence and revolution can be ruled out."[153] If coercion is accepted as a necessary instrument of social cohesion, not only do violent and non-violent coercion have to be considered as a single category, but the distinction between coercion used by governments and that used by revolutionaries must also disappear.

Although Niebuhr justifies the use of force, he spends very little time on the question of just means. He does comment that, "if violence can be justified at all, its terror must have the tempo of a surgeon's skill and healing must follow quickly upon its wounds".[154] Logically, it seems that just means must therefore uphold the end goal of peace. Additionally, in his discussion of the possible injustices associated with non-violent coercion (i.e. boycotts and sanctions), Niebuhr points out that these tactics are no better than their violent counterparts at isolating the guilty from the innocent.[155] Implicitly, Niebuhr thus upholds the principle of non-combatant immunity. However, just as the validity of force as a legitimate political tool could be judged only against its ends, Niebuhr's lack of attention to just means suggests a similar relativist emphasis.

After the advent of the nuclear bomb, Niebuhr re-evaluated his thinking about just means. At first, he did not judge nuclear weapons to be significantly different from the conventional weapons already available, considering them an expansion of scale rather than a revolutionary technology threatening the very roots of just war thought.[156] When the massive US retaliation policy emerged, Niebuhr called it "reckless" and a violation of the principle of non-combatant immunity, yet came short of suggesting that the potential for nuclear war had really changed the nature of international politics.[157] Ultimately, Niebuhr's thought evolved towards a new "nuclear realism", recognizing that the risks involved in the new technology call for more than restraint, and perhaps even a policy of avoidance of war.[158]

Almost a generation after Niebuhr, Paul Ramsey (1913–1988) emerged as a significant Protestant just war thinker. A Methodist, Ramsey's theological roots lay in the Anglican tradition. Conservative both politically and religiously, Ramsey's work was a reaction against "the dominance of Niebuhrian political realism on the Protestant ethical scene – not because of its realism about coercion, but because of its political approach to morality".[159] For Ramsey, a Christian ethic could not be based on the political calculation of good ends. Instead, it must draw on a priori moral principles.

The most fundamental moral principle is love. In *Basic Christian Ethics*, Ramsey systematically presents his theological principles. Love functions in a distinctive way in Ramsey's theology, appropriating "much of the function of a Roman Catholic natural law ethic, without either its metaphysical or its teleological grounding".[160] Natural law is rejected on the Reformation grounds that it wrongly directs the "cultivation of virtue toward human fulfilment, rather than to ... obedience to God's commands".[161] For Ramsey, as for Augustine, love justifies the recourse to war (as opposed to concerns for justice, as in Niebuhr).

Ramsey was most occupied with the question of just war at the height of the Cold War, in the 1950s and 1960s, penning both *War and the Christian Conscience* (1961) and *The Just War* (1968). The latter text revises and reworks many ideas from the first, and so represents Ramsey's most refined ideas.

Like Luther, Ramsey holds that Church and state operate in separate spheres. Religious communities should be concerned with political doctrine, but "in politics the Church is only a *theoretician*", clarifying and laying out the legitimate options for choice.[162] Churches should not try to influence particular policy decisions, but should instead establish an ethical basis from which to evaluate them. In a sense, Churches can create *political doctrine* but not *policy*; they can say what may be done, but not what should or must be done.[163] Churches must submit to political authority, for political decision-making "is an image of the majesty of God".[164]

As for Luther and Calvin, Ramsey sees power as inherently involved in politics. Governments have the responsibility to uphold the national common good and, as far as they are able, the international common good.[165] The common good is based on order, without which achieving other goods becomes impossible. Order is "not a higher value in politics than justice, but neither is humanitarian justice a higher value than order"; instead, each is conditional upon the other.[166] Thus, there is always a certain degree of tragedy in politics, as it tries to negotiate between these often competing goals.

Ramsey traces the origins of just war not to natural justice but to "the interior of the ethics of Christian love".[167] Retelling the story of the Good Samaritan, Ramsey imagines what might have happened if the Samaritan had arrived while the robbers were still assaulting the man on the roadside. Should the Samaritan have just stood by, waiting for the altercation to end, before carrying the victim to the inn? Although Christ did teach that disciples should turn the other cheek, he did not counsel them to "lift up the face of another oppressed man for *him* to be struck again on *his* other cheek ... Instead, it is the work of love and mercy to deliver as many as possible of God's children from tyranny."[168] If forced to choose between the perpetrator of injustice and his victims, one must prefer the latter – they are deserving of love and protection. Thus, military force is justified out of "love for neighbours threatened by violence, by aggression or tyranny".[169]

The issue of right intention is clearly present in Ramsey's work. He argues that "it is never right to intend to do wrong that good may come of it".[170] This is especially true in a nuclear world. At the height of the Cold War, with the very real threat of mutually assured destruction, Ramsey counselled that "nuclear weapons have only added to this perennial truth a morally insignificant footnote: it can never do *any good* to intend or do wrong that good may come of it".[171] Whereas this interpretation led him in his earlier work to deny the justness of nuclear deterrence, in his later book he revises that position, arguing that deterrence does not really rest on the intent to murder.

Ramsey also upholds the traditional just means principles, especially non-combatant immunity. Although love for one's neighbour might justify the recourse to force, it could not justify a decision "to intend and directly to do the death of the aggressor's children as a means of dissuading him from his evil deeds".[172] The same love that permits violence limits its scope. Nonetheless, this restriction does not mean that non-combatants "were to be roped off like ladies at a medieval tournament";[173] they are immune "only from direct, intended attack".[174] Ramsey claims that the just war tradition "never supposed that non-combatants were morally immune from indirect injury or death on however colossal a scale, if there is proportionate grave reason for doing this".[175] One must make a prudential decision among good, evil and lesser evil consequences. Nonetheless, acts of murder and acts of war are not synonymous: "indiscriminate bombing or counter-people warfare stands indicted as intrinsically wrong."[176] Thus, counter-population nuclear targeting is unacceptable (because it directly and intentionally puts civilians in harm's way), but counter-force nuclear targeting may be acceptable, even if it causes large numbers of civilian casualties.[177]

Ramsey also addresses the issue of counter-insurgency warfare. Recognizing that the balance of nuclear terror had opened the world to a multiplication of small-scale conventional wars, Ramsey concentrates on the question of how a counter-insurgency war could be conducted justly. His discussion begins with a reminder that, in determining the justice of any war's conduct, the two most fundamental principles are those of discrimination and proportionality.[178] These principles apply equally to *both* sides in the conflict.

Unlike his predecessors, Ramsey does not discuss whether rebellion (or insurgency) itself is legitimate, assuming that sometimes insurgencies have justified causes. Nonetheless, Ramsey points out that insurgents often overstep the bounds of discrimination. An insurgency movement resorting to terror engages in "an inherently immoral plan of war, no matter how many benefits are supposed to accrue from it".[179]

The problem for the army involved in counter-insurgency warfare is that it risks involving itself in terror as well, owing to the intermixing of civilians and insurgents. Ramsey argues that modern war, "both at the highest nuclear level and at the sub-conventional level", has become "irremediably indiscriminate ... by an entire rejection of the moral immunity of non-combatants from direct attack".[180]

Ramsey suggests that a clearer principle of discrimination is needed, more clearly defining the nature of a combatant. A combatant "means anyone who is an actual bearer of the force one seeks to repress by resorting to arms", even if he or she does not wear a uniform.[181] Some surrendered soldiers fit this category, if it cannot be assured that they are completely disarmed, as do some apparent civilians, if they are evidently armed. Ultimately, Ramsey admits that it may be so difficult to sort out the combatants from the non-combatants that fighting a just war may become impossible. In that case, an alternative would be to combat the insurgency politically rather than militarily. Ultimately, "even if a revolution happens to be wholly unjustifiable because it uses means no end can warrant and seeks ends for which no political means are apt and is on balance evil in its worldwide consequences", that does not mean that it should be opposed militarily.[182] If a war is not winnable using just means, then justice may demand that it not be fought.

Protestant pacifism

Pacifism has always played a role within Protestantism as a counterbalance to just war thought. For the first four centuries, pacifist movements were limited to the smaller sects: the Anabaptists in the sixteenth century, the Quakers in the seventeenth, and the Brethren in the eighteenth.[183] These denominations, unlike the dominant Protestant state churches, were suspicious of state power, encouraging their members to remain separate from the world. Basing their politics on the "doctrine concerning the separation of the faithful from the world" and a "conception of the church as a suffering church", most Anabaptists historically embraced "the practices of persecution and oppression".[184] Thus, they would fight to defend neither themselves nor their state, and some would even go so far as to refuse to serve the state in any capacity. The relationship between Anabaptist groups and the state Protestant (and Catholic) churches was a troubled one. Several theological differences separated the Anabaptists from the mainline churches, of which the just war issue was one of the most significant. By refusing to serve the state in wartime, Anabaptists came to be seen as not only theologically heretical but politically dangerous.

The twentieth-century Mennonite theologian John Howard Yoder is the most dominant voice to arise from one of these traditional Peace Churches. Yoder's influence reaches far beyond the scope of traditional

Protestant pacifism, directly influencing theologian Stanley Hauerwas, who has become an outspoken advocate for pacifism from within mainstream Protestantism.

Yoder writes from outside the just war canon, yet his work encourages just war thinkers to take their own tradition more seriously.[185] His book *When War Is Unjust* directly engages both Catholic and Protestant just war thinkers, including critical responses from each of these traditions. Yoder argues that it is essential to engage those who uphold just war theories, because "it is still the case that every time just-war proponents exercise effective discipline and limit the harm they do, fewer lives and other values will be destroyed than if they had not applied that restraint".[186]

Yoder criticizes just war theory for employing a sliding scale of ethics. Once the proposition is accepted that the commandment against killing can occasionally be violated, it becomes necessary to make more and more exceptions in order to maintain the viability of the system.[187] The rules must evolve as military technology and tactics develop; otherwise they lose their efficacy. Furthermore, the laws of war unsurprisingly favour the interests of their crafters. Thus, they reflect the power disparity between states in the world, reinforcing structural injustice. Lastly, Yoder points out that just war theory's validity depends on its ability to distinguish between wars, permitting some while condemning others. Yet just war theory only very rarely accomplishes the latter: politically it is too difficult, and theoretically it raises an uncomfortable possibility. If a war cannot be waged justly, then a strict reading of just war theory implies that it should not be fought at all. But if the cause were just enough to legitimize violence, how is it that possible?

Much of Stanley Hauerwas' (1940–) advocacy of pacifism also directly confronts just war theory on its own terms. Hauerwas' first forays into the just war/pacifism debate came in response to the 1983 pastoral letter from the National Conference of Catholic Bishops of the United States condemning nuclear weapons.[188] In the pastoral letter, the bishops take on a near-pacifist (what Yoder would call a "nuclear pacifist") position,[189] arguing that, given the dangers inherent in nuclear weapons and the ever-present risk of escalation, warfare is less desirable now than ever. Yet they stop short of true pacifism, leaving open the possibility of Christian participation in war as a means of achieving earthly justice. Hauerwas also criticized the United Methodist Bishops' Pastoral (1985) on the question of nuclear war.

Hauerwas argues that the difficulty in maintaining a just war position is that tolerating war in certain circumstances gives war a moral status that then obscures our ability to judge it. To truly test the legitimacy of this status, an account of war must be made that would show "that if war were eliminated we would be morally the worse for it".[190] War is more than violence on a grand scale; it is an institution. This institution, clearly the product of human choices, is perceived as "an external agent ... an unsolicited yet unavoidable consequence of our shared activities".[191] Like any institution, war serves its creators' interests – in this case, states – enabling them "to perpetuate their own particular shared goods, to preserve their histories and moralities".[192] In other words, war protects not merely the existence of a people but, more importantly, "their interpretation of their existence".[193]

But the illogic of war as a positive good emerges out of the very attempt to demonstrate its positive side. How can just war be an exception to the general rule of non-violence, if war itself is an institution so determinative of our state system? Scepticism about the possibility of just war theory actually condemning a particular war leads Hauerwas to argue that "just war theory is not just a theory of exceptions, but an attempt to limit the destructive potential of war once it is recognized as a moral necessity ... [I]t does not attempt to make war impossible, but rather to make the moral necessity of war serve human purposes."[194] Thus, war theory "is a theory of statecraft", seeking not peace but "the maintenance of ordered justice through which the innocent are protected".[195]

Hauerwas argues that just war theorists' focus on the political "necessity" of violence fails to recognize that Christ has already created the possibility of peace on earth. Their condemnation of war reflects not theology but rather military reality: the existence of nuclear weapons threatens to turn any conflict nuclear, so therefore churches must reject war itself, to prevent mankind's destruction. But Hauerwas wonders whether this really has "anything to do with pacifism. If war is wrong, then nuclear war is clearly wrong, but no conclusions about how to keep war nonnuclear need to be drawn to reach that conclusion."[196]

Unlike Luther and Calvin, who conceived of two separate kingdoms, Hauerwas argues that the "kingdom has been made present fully in Jesus Christ".[197] The heavenly kingdom exists here and now, interwoven with the earthly one. Consequently, "the Christian commitment to non-violence is therefore not first of all an 'ethic' but a declaration of the reality of the new age".[198] Just war theory presumes a separation between these kingdoms; true pacifism denies it.

The use of war as a political tool is for Hauerwas a denial of God's power to act in shaping the course of human history. War is nothing but "the desire to be rid of God, to claim for ourselves the power to determine our meaning and destiny"; thus, "our desire to protect ourselves from our enemies, to eliminate our enemies in the name of protecting the common history we share with our friends, is but the manifestation of our hatred of God".[199]

However, giving up war as a tool should not be misconstrued as abdicating the responsibility to be active in the world. Pacifism is not easily "summed up as antiwarism or antiviolence".[200] Christians must be committed optimists, believing that war is not inevitable, and must make their message heard. This means changing the terms of the debate. The state is not an institution ordained by God to order human society; it is simply a fact of our existence in this time and place. Politics is not synonymous with power, but instead is an ongoing conversation.

Pacifism thus understood is about learning "to deal with conflicts through truth rather than violence".[201] If just war is "an account of politics that is nonutopian in the interest of keeping the political within humane limits", pacifists must offer a more hopeful view of politics.[202] Rather than denying the political nature of our common life, "nonviolence requires that we become political by forcing us to listen to the other rather than destroy them".[203] Most importantly, the Church must demonstrate its message of peace by *being* its message of peace. Its primary goal is not so much to "make the world more peaceable or just", as to manifest "the peaceable kingdom in the world".[204] Christians must be patient when faced with injustice, recognizing that they "cannot seek 'results' that require [them] to employ unjust means".[205]

Since the late twentieth century, some dominant Protestant denominations have also grown increasingly pacifistic in their views. The emergence of weapons of mass destruction has led some to declare that, in the modern world, a just war is no longer possible. These denominations, including the Federal Council of Churches, the United Church of Christ, and the United Methodists, have developed a "just peace" theory. This perspective begins with the assumption that war is unjust, rather than asking whether war could be justified or justly fought in certain circumstances. It also assumes that peace is possible, that war is not the obvious result of a fallen human nature. For this reason, this newly emerging tradition stresses cooperation and active peace-making, and applauds the efforts of the United Nations.

This theory claims that "the revolution in the destructiveness of conventional weapons (to say nothing of nuclear, biological or poison gas weaponry) is so massive that one cannot fight without an unacceptable amount of loss of innocent life".[206] The United Methodist Church, for example, declared in the 1972 edition of its *Book of Discipline* that "though coercion, violence and war are presently the ultimate sanctions in international relations, we reject them as incompatible with the gospel and spirit of Christ".[207] The Church's *Social Principles* declare its rejection of war "as an instrument of national foreign policy".[208] This position has been upheld in the subsequent editions.

Protestant crusading

At the opposite extreme, the crusading concept would be reinstated, to some extent, by the Reformed churches, especially those with Calvinist tendencies.[209] This choice reflects the denomination's early struggle for existence as a militant minority caught up in the wars of religion, as well as its theocratic conception of Church-led governance.[210] The earliest Protestant rhetoric of holy war dates to the Eighty Years War, not only on the Continent but within England as well.

Holy war differs from just war in three major ways.[211] First, in just war theory, the legitimate authority to declare war lies with the secular leader, acting on his own terms. By contrast, the authorization for a holy war comes from a religious authority, or from God himself, through a special revelation. Political leaders may be the recipients of such revelations, but they act under the explicit direction of a higher power, and not on their own terms. Secondly, holy wars not only use religious language rhetorically, but are fought for religious reasons, whereas just war theory denies the legitimacy of such causes. Lastly, just war theory holds open the possibility that there is some justice on both sides or, at the very least, the political and moral legitimacy of the other side's leaders are not irrevocably damaged by the mere fact of fighting for an unjust cause. Put simply, a good person could fight a bad war. Holy war, however, is understood as a struggle between good and evil, turning the other side into a "demonic and damned enemy committing sacrilege".[212] For this reason, it tends towards a self-righteousness that does not lend itself well to limiting the scale of the violence.

It is important to note, however, that Protestant crusading did not emerge explicitly as a third perspective on war, clearly separate from just war thought. Many theologians who use language reflective of a crusading or holy war position believe themselves to be speaking from within the just war tradition itself. Puritan theologians and ministers justifying England's Civil War, for example, did not abandon "the formal framework of just war theory", although they moved in the direction of holy war.[213] During World War I, most priests and ministers in Britain accepted that the "traditional teaching of the 'just war' theory was undeniably valid", despite using crusading language in sermons and pamphlets.[214]

The theological discussion of holy war and its justification re-emerges in the discourse each time there is a significant war. During the English

Civil War, the Puritans claimed God as their commander in war, passionately invoking the Bible to urge fellow Christians to violence, evidencing "a mentality not foreign to the crusades".[215] The Puritans found justification for their stance in Calvin, and also in a popular theological perspective of the time that "lessened the distance between old and new covenants, and, in fact, gave priority to the former in defining a normative pattern of Christian conduct in civil society".[216] Likewise, during the American Revolution, Congregationalist and Presbyterian ministers supported the colonists' cause with crusading language.[217] During World War I, some conservative Anglican priests argued that Germany should be showed little mercy, with the Bishop of London even calling for a "holy war".[218] In the United States, the language of Crusade re-emerged in the Protestant discourse during the Vietnam War and later during the first Gulf War in 1991.

Most recently, crusading language has appeared in the Evangelical Protestant discourse surrounding the war on terror and the Iraq War in the United States. This language has been used not only by certain fundamentalist and evangelical ministers, but also by key Republican Party leaders and even the President himself. (The President, having been raised Episcopalian, is a member of the United Methodist Church, neither of them an Evangelical denomination.) On the one hand, these politicians base much of their public justification for the recourse to war on just war theory, presumably to appeal to a broader range of voters. In his 2003 State of the Union address, President Bush asserted: "If war is forced upon us, we will fight in a just cause and by just means," language that he repeated numerous times throughout the year.[219] At the same time, the President has consistently used language more reflective of a holy war perspective. In addition to using enemy images in his rhetoric (that is, portraying the other as explicitly evil), Bush also explicitly painted the conflict itself as a struggle between good and evil: "Out of evil will come incredible good," he declared in October 2002.[220] A sympathetic chronicle of his years in the White House describes Bush as viewing the war on terror as a "religious war" between Christians and Muslims.[221]

Conclusion

Within Protestantism, the proper role for violence is still a matter of active consideration. The dominant Protestant churches have historically accepted just war theory, but, with the development of nuclear weapons and other weapons of mass destruction, several of these churches have begun to adopt positions that are nearly pacifist in nature. Their case is not that violence per se is unjust, but that modern weapons may make the just use of violence impossible. Nonetheless, none of these churches has officially forsaken the just war position, or cut it from its confessional statements.

Pacifism, once considered heretical by the dominant Protestant denominations, is the official position of only a few smaller denominations, and has remained vocal in its call for a radical transformation of politics. Its radical opposite, the crusading perspective, still exists, although not supported by the largest denominations. Nonetheless, the rhetoric of Crusade has reappeared in the Protestant tradition each time a major war looms, in the arguments made by theologians, ministers and politicians alike. Thus, Protestant just war theory remains at the crossroads between pacifism and Crusade, in a debate yet to be resolved.

Notes

1. Paul Ramsey, *The Just War: Force and Political Responsibility*. Lanham, MD: Rowman & Littlefield, 2002, p. xxi.
2. Jean Bethke Elshtain, "Epilogue: Continuing Implications of the Just War Tradition", in Jean Bethke Elshtain (ed.) *Just War Theory*. New York, NY: New York University Press, 1992. p. 323.
3. Lisa Sowle Cahill, *Love Your Enemies: Discipleship, Pacifism, and Just War Theory*. Minneapolis, MN: Augsburg Fortress, 1994, p. 101.
4. Martin Luther, "Whether Soldiers, Too, Can be Saved", trans. Charles M. Jacobs, in J. M. Porter (ed.) *Luther: Selected Political Writings*. Philadelphia, PA: Fortress Press, 1974, p. 103.
5. James Turner Johnson, "Aquinas and Luther on War and Peace: Sovereign Authority and the Use of Armed Force", *Journal of Religious Ethics*, 31(1), 2003: 16.
6. Martin Luther, "Admonition to Peace: A Reply to the Twelve Articles of the Peasants in Swabia", trans. Charles M. Jacobs, in Porter (ed.) *Luther: Selected Political Writings*, p. 72.
7. Ibid., p. 74.
8. Ibid., p. 78.
9. Luther, "Whether Soldiers, Too, Can be Saved", p. 109.
10. Martin Luther, "Against the Robbing and Murdering Hordes of Peasants", trans. Charles M. Jacobs, in Porter (ed.) *Luther: Selected Political Writings*, p. 86.
11. Martin Luther, "An Open Letter on the Harsh Book Against the Peasants", trans. Charles M. Jacobs, in Porter (ed.) *Luther: Selected Political Writings*, p. 97.
12. Martin Luther, "Dr. Martin Luther's Warning to His Dear German People", trans. Martin H. Bertram, in Porter (ed.) *Luther: Selected Political Writings*, pp. 136, 139.
13. Ibid., p. 87. See also, "An Open Letter on the Harsh Book Against the Peasants", pp. 97–98: "even if I served a Turk and saw my lord in danger, I would forget my spiritual office and stab and hew as long as my heart beat. If I were slain in so doing, I should go straight to heaven."

14. Luther, "Whether Soldiers, Too, Can be Saved", p. 109.
15. Luther, "Against the Robbing and Murdering Hoards of Peasants", p. 87.
16. Martin Marty, "Can Soldiers Be Saved?", *Christian Century*, 120(12), 14 June 2003, p. 47.
17. Martin Luther, "On War Against the Turk", trans. Charles M. Jacobs, in Porter (ed.) *Luther: Selected Political Writings*, p. 123.
18. Ibid., p. 129.
19. Cahill, *Love Your Enemies*, p. 108.
20. Martin Luther, "Temporal Authority: To What Extent It Should Be Obeyed", trans. J. J. Schindel, in Porter (ed.) *Luther: Selected Political Writings*, p. 54.
21. Ibid., p. 56.
22. Ibid., p. 57.
23. Luther, "An Open Letter on the Harsh Book Against the Peasants", pp. 92–93.
24. Ibid., p. 93.
25. Luther, "Temporal Authority", p. 59.
26. Luther, "Whether Soldiers, Too, Can be Saved", pp. 101–102.
27. Luther, "Temporal Authority", p. 52.
28. Ibid., p. 57.
29. Luther, "Whether Soldiers, Too, Can be Saved", p. 102.
30. Ibid.
31. Ibid., pp. 113–114.
32. Luther, "Temporal Authority", p. 65.
33. Ibid. See also, Martin Luther, "Lectures on Deuteronomy", in Jaroslav Pelikan (ed.) *Luther's Works, Volume 9*. St Louis, MO: Concordia Publishing House, 1960, p. 203. In regard to Deuteronomy 20, Luther points out that God commanded the Jews to "first offer peace to their enemies", a practice he claims was also observed by some Gentiles, citing Virgil.
34. Luther, "Whether Soldiers, Too, Can be Saved", p. 114.
35. Luther, "Temporal Authority", p. 66.
36. Luther, "An Open Letter on the Harsh Book Against the Peasants", p. 94.
37. Luther, "Lectures on Deuteronomy", p. 204. See also Luther, "Temporal Authority", p. 66: "one must beware of sin, and not violate wives and virgins."
38. Luther, "Whether Soldiers, Too, Can be Saved", p. 116.
39. Ibid., p. 117.
40. Augsburg Confession, Article XVI, "Civil Government", in *Augsburg Confession – A Confession of Faith Presented in Augsburg by Certain Princes and Cities to His Imperial Majesty Charles V in the Year 1530*, trans. Theodore G. Tappert. Minneapolis, MN: Fortress Press, 1980, p. 16.
41. Harold J. Grimm, *The Reformation Era: 1500–1650*. New York: Macmillan, 1967, p. 312.
42. Cahill, *Love Your Enemies*, pp. 109–110.
43. Derek S. Jeffreys, " 'It's a Miracle of God That There Is Any Common Weal Among Us': Unfaithfulness and Disorder in John Calvin's Political Thought", *Review of Politics*, 62(1), 2000: 107.
44. John Calvin, *Institutes of the Christian Religion* [1535], ed. John T. McNeill, Library of Christian Classics, vol. 21. Philadelphia, PA: Westminster Press, 1960, 4.20.16.
45. Ibid., 4.20.4, p. 1490.
46. Ibid., 4.20.9, p. 1496.
47. Paul Mundey, "John Calvin and Anabaptists on War", *Brethren Life and Thought*, 23, 1978: 244.

48. Calvin, *Institutes*, 4.20.9, p. 1496.
49. Ibid., 4.20.10, p. 1497.
50. Ibid., 4.20.11, p. 1499.
51. Ibid., 4.20.12, p. 1501.
52. Ibid., 4.20.12, p. 1500.
53. Ibid., 4.20.11, p. 1499.
54. Ibid., 4.20.11, p. 1499.
55. Ibid., 4.20.11, p. 1500.
56. Ibid., 4.20.12, p. 1500.
57. Ibid., 4.20.29, p. 1516.
58. Ibid., 4.20.31, p. 1518.
59. Jeffreys, " 'It's a Miracle of God That There Is Any Common Weal Among Us' ", p. 114.
60. Calvin, *Institutes*, 4.20.30. Here, Calvin uses Old Testament sources to show that "God raises up manifest avengers from among his own servants, and gives them his command to punish accursed tyranny". Uprising can thus be justified (only) in the case of a direct command from God.
61. Ibid., 4.20.12, p. 1500.
62. Ibid., 4.20.12, p. 1500.
63. Ibid., 4.20.32, p. 1520.
64. Article 23, "Of the Civil Magistrate", 6.128(2), *Constitution of the Presbyterian Church [USA], Part I: Book of Confessions*. Louisville, KY: The Office of The General Assembly, Presbyterian Church, USA, 1999, p. 147.
65. See ⟨http://anglicansonline.org/basics/thirty-nine_articles.html⟩ (accessed 4 November 2008).
66. Benedict Kingsbury, "Confronting Difference: The Puzzling Durability of Gentili's Combination of Pragmatic Pluralism and Normative Judgment", *American Journal of International Law*, 92(4), 1998: 717.
67. Hugo Grotius, *On the Law of War and Peace* [1625]. Kessinger Publishing, 2004, I.1.
68. Ibid., I.2.
69. Ibid., I.2.
70. Ibid., I.3.
71. Ibid., III.3.
72. Ibid., II.22.
73. Ibid., II.22.
74. Ibid., II.22.
75. Ibid., II.25.
76. Ibid., III.1.
77. Ibid., III.1.
78. Ibid., III.11.
79. Ibid., III.11.
80. Ibid., III.11.
81. Ibid., III.11.
82. Ibid., III.15.
83. Ibid., III.12.
84. Ibid., III.12.
85. Samuel Pufendorf, *On the Duty of Man and Citizen* [1673], trans. Michael Silverthorne, ed. James Tully. Cambridge: Cambridge University Press, 2000, 16.1, p. 168.
86. Ibid., 16.1, p. 168.
87. Ibid., 16.11, p. 170.

88. Ibid., 16.2, p. 168.
89. Ibid., 16.3, p. 168.
90. Ibid., 16.4, p. 168.
91. Ibid., 16.4, p. 169.
92. Ibid., 16.6, p. 169.
93. Ibid., 16.6, p. 169.
94. Ibid., 16.13, p. 171.
95. "Witness to an Ancient Truth", *Time Magazine*, 20 April 1962. See also Karl Barth, *How I Changed My Mind*. Richmond, VA: John Knox Press, 1966, p. 53.
96. Daniel Cornu, *Karl Barth et la Politique*. Geneva: Éditions Labor et Fides, 1967, p. 167. See also "Witness to an Ancient Truth". Barth "[regarded] anticommunism as a matter of principle an evil even greater than communism itself", finding such a knee-jerk reaction to be not only totalitarian but also naïve about the failings of Western capitalism (see Barth, *How I Changed My Mind*, pp. 57, 63).
97. Karl Barth, *Church Dogmatics*, vol. III, ed. G. W. Bromiley and T. F. Torrance. Edinburgh: T&T Clark, 1961, p. 305.
98. Ibid., p. 429.
99. Ibid., p. 430.
100. Ibid., p. 430.
101. Ibid., p. 434.
102. Ibid., p. 435.
103. Ibid., p. 462.
104. Ibid., p. 461.
105. Ibid., p. 461.
106. Ibid., p. 461.
107. Ibid., p. 455.
108. Ibid., p. 456.
109. Ibid., p. 460.
110. Ibid., p. 466.
111. Ibid., p. 467.
112. Ibid., p. 467.
113. "To Be or Not to Be", *Time Magazine*, 16 March 1959.
114. Paul Tillich, *Writings in Social Philosophy and Ethics*, vol. 3, ed. Erdmann Sturm. Berlin: De Gruyter – Evangelisches Verlagsweg, 1988, p. 434.
115. Ibid., p. 441.
116. Paul Tillich, *Systemic Theology: Three Volumes in One*. Chicago: University of Chicago Press, 1967, p. 216.
117. Ibid., p. 216.
118. Ibid., p. 216.
119. Paul Tillich, "The Problem of Power", in *The Interpretation of History*, 1936; available at ⟨http://www.religion-online.org/showchapter.asp?title=377&C=49⟩ (accessed 15 October 2008).
120. Ibid.
121. Tillich, *Systemic Theology*, p. 387.
122. Paul Tillich, "Seven Theses Concerning the Nuclear Dilemma", in *The Spiritual Situation in Our Technical Society*. Macon, GA: Mercer University Press, 1988, p. 197; cited in Matthew Lon Weaver, "Religious Internationalism: The Ethics of War and Peace in the Thought of Paul Tillich", dissertation, School of Arts and Sciences, University of Pittsburgh, 2006, p. 265.
123. Tillich, *Systemic Theology,* p. 387.

124. Ibid., p. 387.
125. Paul Tillich, *On the Boundary*. New York: Charles Scribner's Sons, 1966, p. 95.
126. Tillich, *Systemic Theology*, pp. 387–388.
127. Paul Tillich, "The Nuclear Dilemma – a Discussion", *Christianity and Crisis*, 13 November 1961, p. 204; cited in Robert W. Tucker, "Morality and Deterrence", *Ethics*, 95(3), 1985: 469.
128. Tillich, "Seven Theses Concerning the Nuclear Dilemma", p. 265.
129. Tillich, *Systemic Theology*, p. 388.
130. Cahill, *Love Your Enemies*, p. 192.
131. Ibid., p. 189.
132. Reinhold Niebuhr, *Moral Man and Immoral Society: A Study in Ethics and Politics*. Louisville, KY: Westminster John Knox Press, [1932] 2001, p. 2.
133. Ibid., p. 3.
134. Ibid., p. 3.
135. Ibid., p. 16.
136. Ibid., p. 20.
137. Ibid., p. 22.
138. Michael G. Thompson, "An Exception to Exceptionalism: A Reflection on Reinhold Niebuhr's Vision of 'Prophetic' Christianity and the Problem of Religion and U.S. Foreign Policy", *American Quarterly*, 59(3), 2007: 842.
139. Niebuhr, *Moral Man and Immoral Society*, p. 235.
140. Ibid., p. 235.
141. Ibid., p. 170.
142. Ibid., p. 170.
143. Ibid., p. 172.
144. Ibid., p. 173.
145. Ibid., p. 171.
146. Ibid., p. 171.
147. Ibid., p. 110.
148. Ibid., p. 110.
149. Ibid., p. 110.
150. Ibid., p. 110.
151. Ibid., p. 111.
152. Ibid., p. 234.
153. Ibid., p. 179.
154. Ibid., p. 220.
155. Ibid., p. 241.
156. Campbell Craig, "The New Meaning of Modern War in the Thought of Reinhold Niebuhr", *Journal of the History of Ideas*, 53(4), 1992: 689.
157. Ibid., p. 692.
158. Ibid., p. 694.
159. Cahill, *Love Your Enemies*, p. 198.
160. Ibid., p. 200.
161. Ibid., p. 200.
162. Ibid., p. 19.
163. Ibid., p. 20.
164. Ibid., p. 19.
165. Ramsey, *The Just War*, p. 9.
166. Ibid., p. 11.
167. Ibid., p. 142.

168. Ibid., p. 143.
169. Ibid., p. 144.
170. Ibid., p. 147.
171. Ibid., p. 147.
172. Ibid., p. 145.
173. Ibid., p. 145.
174. Ibid., p. 146.
175. Ibid., p. 153.
176. Ibid., p. 154.
177. Ibid., p. 156.
178. Ibid., p. 428.
179. Ibid., p. 433.
180. Ibid., p. 433.
181. Ibid., p. 435.
182. Ibid., p. 459.
183. Roland H. Bainton, *Christian Attitudes toward War and Peace: A Historical Survey and Critical Re-evaluation*. New York: Abingdon Press, 1960, p. 136.
184. Grimm, *The Reformation Era*, p. 267.
185. Charles P. Lutz, "Foreword to the First Edition", in John H. Yoder, *When War Is Unjust: Being Honest about Just War Thinking*. Maryknoll, NY: Orbis Books, 1996, p. xi.
186. Yoder, *When War Is Unjust*, p. 5.
187. Ibid., p. 50.
188. National Conference of Catholic Bishops, *The Challenge of Peace: God's Promise and Our Response*. Washington, DC: United States Conference of Catholic Bishops Inc., 3 May 1983.
189. John Howard Yoder, "How Many Ways Are There to Think Morally about War?", *Journal of Law and Religion*, 11(1), 1994–1995: 102. Neither Yoder nor Hauerwas recognizes "nuclear pacifism" as a truly pacifist position, instead classifying it as a variant of just war thought.
190. Stanley Hauerwas, "Should War Be Eliminated? A Thought Experiment", in John Berkman and Michael Cartwright (eds) *The Hauerwas Reader*. Durham, NC: Duke University Press, 2003, p. 395.
191. Ibid., p. 407.
192. Ibid., p. 409.
193. Ibid., p. 412.
194. Ibid., p. 417.
195. Stanley Hauerwas, "On Being a Church Capable of Addressing a World at War: A Pacifist Response to the United Methodist Bishops' Pastoral *In Defense of Creation*", in Berkman and Cartwright (eds) *The Hauerwas Reader*, p. 444.
196. Ibid., p. 433.
197. Hauerwas, "Should War be Eliminated?", p. 419.
198. Ibid., p. 420.
199. Ibid., p. 421.
200. Hauerwas, "On Being a Church Capable of Addressing a World at War", p. 442.
201. Ibid., p. 440.
202. Ibid., pp. 446–447.
203. Ibid., p. 454.
204. Stanley Hauerwas, "The Servant Community: Christian Social Ethics", in Berkman and Cartwright (eds), *The Hauerwas Reader*, p. 374.

205. Ibid., p. 380.
206. David R. Smock, *Religious Perspectives on War: Christian, Muslim and Jewish Attitudes toward Force*. Washington, DC: United States Institute of Peace Press, 2002, p. 33.
207. *United Methodist Book of Discipline*. Nashville, TN: United Methodist Publishing House, 1973, p. 95, para. 76D.
208. See United Methodist Church, *In Defense of Creation: The Nuclear Crisis and a Just Peace: Foundation Document*. Nashville, TN: Graded Press, 1986, p. 20.
209. Bainton, *Christian Attitudes toward War and Peace*, p. 136.
210. Ibid., p. 143.
211. Melvin B. Endy, Jr, "Just War, Holy War, and Millennialism in Revolutionary America", *William and Mary Quarterly*, 42(1), 1985: p. 8.
212. Ibid., p. 8.
213. Timothy George, "War and Peace in the Puritan Tradition", *Church History*, 53(4), 1984: 495, 502.
214. Charles E. Bailey, "The British Protestant Theologians in the First World War: Germanophobia Unleashed", *Harvard Theological Review*, 77(2), 1984: 211.
215. Cahill, *Love Your Enemies*, p. 143.
216. George, "War and Peace in the Puritan Tradition", p. 497.
217. Endy, "Just War, Holy War, and Millennialism in Revolutionary America", p. 10.
218. Bailey, "The British Protestant Theologians in the First World War", pp. 211, 214.
219. Valerie O. F. Morkevicius, "Faith-Based War? Religious Rhetoric and Foreign Policy in the Bush Administration", paper presented at the 2006 International Studies Annual Convention, San Diego, CA, 24 March 2006, p. 16.
220. George W. Bush, Unity Luncheon, Atlanta, GA, 17 October 2002.
221. Kevin Phillips, "Crusader", *Christian Century*, 13 July 2004, p. 9.

9

Norms of war in Shia Islam

Davood Feirahi

In Islam, as in many other civilizations, religious texts/principles define and set human behaviour. Religion and religious ideas have great importance in understanding the nature of war and military ethics in the Islamic world. If we define Islamic civilization through one of its major features, then we can say that it is a civilization based on religious jurisprudence (*fiqh*). As such, it is oriented around the Sharia, a comprehensive body of law that defines the values, rules and morality of Muslims in all areas of life (from birth to death), including war and military ethics.

Jurisprudence in Islamic society is the science that defines the historical life of Muslims in relation to the religious texts, in any time or place. Jurisprudence aims at creating harmony between religious commands and daily life within a given environment. In Islamic culture, religious text means the holy Qur'an and narrations from the Holy Prophet and the Infallible Imams in Shiism, all of which are closely interrelated. In Islamic terms, these are all referred to as *Sunna* (tradition). In other words, we may say that the Prophet's sayings (*Hadith*) and the narrations of the Infallible Imams of Shiism (*Akhbar*) are all interpretations of the holy Qur'an. The duty of jurisprudence is to interpret issues related to social life, such as war and peace, on the basis of the Qur'an and tradition, and to derive religious rules and laws from them, whose observance is obligatory for all members of the community. *Fiqh* (jurisprudence) also refers to two other sources, which are called "consensus" and "analogy" by followers of Sunnism, and "intellect" and "consensus" by the Shiites. Therefore, we may conclude that in Shiite Islam we have four sources of

World religions and norms of war, Popovski, Reichberg and Turner (eds),
United Nations University Press, 2009, ISBN 978-92-808-1163-6

interpretation: the Holy Qur'an, Tradition (*Sunna*), Intellect (*Aql*), and Unanimity (consensus).[1] These are the sources from which the rules for war and peace are derived; this is why we define religious jurisprudence as the deduction of religious rules from these four sources of interpretation.

In Islamic jurisprudence, war is equal to "jihad", which is one of the 10 secondary rules of Islam. However, it should be noted that one must necessarily distinguish between the Qur'anic and the jurisprudential usages of "jihad". In most cases in the Qur'an, jihad means "striving" in the way of God; in its jurisprudential usage, however, jihad refers to "war", which is a specific instance of striving in the way of God. Thus, in Islamic jurisprudence, jihad, whether offensive or defensive, is a term that always means "war". That is why one of the 10 chapters/topics of Islamic jurisprudence is entitled "The Book of Jihad" (*Kitab al-Jihad*).

This chapter aims to analyse the interpretation of jihad and military ethics in Shiite Islam, with reference to the Islamic texts that deal with jihad from the Shiite perspective.

The concept of jihad in traditional Shiite jurisprudence

Any proper study of the concept of jihad in Shiite Islam must be based on two principles:

1. differentiating the classical and the new interpretations of jihad in Islamic *fiqh*/jurisprudence;
2. understanding the basic difference between the Shiites and Sunnites in the concept of jihad.

Shia and Sunni are two major Islamic sects that in most theological and jurisprudential cases overlap. Their basic differences lie in the Caliphate and the imamate. In contrast to the Sunnites, the Shiites believe in the infallibility of the Twelve Imams. Since, in Shiite thought, offensive jihad is dependent on the Infallible Imam, the Shiite and Sunnite conceptions of offensive jihad are quite different.

Because the above principles are so essential, a thorough understanding of the issue of jihad is not possible without a proper understanding of the concept of jihad in Shiite Islam.

The classical Islamic jurisprudence, whether Shiite or Sunnite, classifies jihad on two levels: *offensive* and *defensive*. In this classical approach the main meaning of jihad is offensive jihad,[2] which is an obligatory act for any Muslim. Particularly among Sunnites, it is believed that the Qur'anic verses on jihad nullified (*nasikh*) the Qur'anic verses on peace,[3] and so it is believed that jihad is a permanent obligation, never to be suspended, for all Muslims up to the end of time.

Shams al-Din Abu-Bakr Mohammad bin Abi-Sahl al-Sarakhsi (d.1089), one of the Hanafi Sunni jurisprudents, has set the Qur'anic verses in such a way that the rules on relations between Muslims and non-Muslims start by abandoning any relation, then proceed to an invitation to convert to Islam through preaching, leading to defensive war in the event of any offence by the enemy, and ultimately to offensive attack on non-Muslims. The last step in this line of evolution is believed to be the final rule. He says:

> The Holy prophet of Allah (God) was first instructed to leave any relation with non-believers. Then He was instructed to preach to them, encouraging them to convert to Islam. Then, He was delegated to defensive war, but only if He was attacked first. Afterwards He was instructed to conduct an offensive war. This is how Jihad with non-believers is set as a religious duty, with its validity acknowledged until the Day of Judgement.[4]

Imam Mohammad Shafei (d.819), the founder of the Shafei sect (one of the four main Sunni schools of law), believes that the Qur'anic verses that deal with peace, non-violence and the prohibition of war during *haram* (forbidden) months, have all been abrogated by the Holy verse "fight with them until there is no persecution and religion should be only for Allah, but if they desist, then there should be no hostility except against the oppressors" (Qur'an 2:193; Shakir translation).[5]

Abu-Muhammad al-Maqdisi (d.1223), an eminent jurisprudent of the Hanbali Sunni school of law, believes that offensive jihad should be conducted at least once a year.[6] Abu-Omar Yousef bin Abdollah al-Qortobi (d.1070), one of the founders of the Maleki Sunni school of law, is of the same opinion.[7] Abu-Albarakat al-Maleki (d.1924) believes that Muslims are obligated to conduct jihad even under the rule of a tyrant or an illegitimate emir or governor.[8]

The idea of offensive jihad in the works of Hanafi is of the same nature as that in the other classical Sunni jurisprudence. The author of *Tabyin al-Hagha'igh* (Elucidation of the Truth) states that:

> It is our obligation to commence a war on them (non-believers), though they may not intend to commence a war on us. Because Allah has made it an obligation on us to kill the unbelievers, so nobody (Lawful or Unlawful Governors) would be in a position to suspend this rule, so that all the people would say that there is no god but Allah.[9]

In thus defining the obligatory nature of jihad, he refers to the consensus of the Muslims as one of the jurisprudential bases of such a deduction.

As quoted by Great Ayatollah Sayyid Hussain Boroujerdi (1875–1961), classical Shiite jurisprudence, in terms of methodology and method of reasoning, is somewhat like the Sunni version,[10] despite asserting a belief in the Infallible Imams. This theological difference led to Shiite jurisprudence considering "the narrations from the Imams of Shiite" (*akhbar*) as important sources of interpretation of the Holy Qur'an and the Prophet's narrations. Therefore, there is a significant difference in the definition of the concept of jurisprudence between the Sunnites and the Shiites, particularly concerning the nature of jihad.

The Shiite jurisprudents, like their Sunni counterparts, believe that jihad is one of the major religious obligations. However, from the Shiite perspective we have another important condition: jihad may not be conducted in the absence of an instruction issued by a just Imam, which has been interpreted in Shiite traditional jurisprudence as meaning an Infallible [Twelfth] Imam. Sheikh Al-Taefa Abu-Ja'far Mohammad al-Tousi (995–1075), who was a great Shiite jurisprudent, stated in his work *al-Nihayah* (The Ultimate):

> Jihad is a religious duty essential to be performed either by the person himself or by someone on his behalf. So it is an obligation for any one (except for women, old or sick people, children & insane). But, one of the conditions of Jihad is the presence of a just Imam, since he is the one and only to issue such command, so Jihad is only possible if such Imam is present or when he has appointed someone on his own behalf to take care of Muslim affairs. Therefore, Jihad is not a religious obligation when an infallible Imam is not present. If someone goes to Jihad upon the instruction of an unjust imam or an ordinary ruler, then one deserves punishment since he has committed a sin. Even if such Jihad would be performed with success, there would be no reward to that achievement. If one gets hurt or defeated in such unjustified Jihad, he is a sinner any way.

> But if Muslims are attacked by the enemy and the religion or lives of Muslims are in danger, in such a case Jihad and defence is a religious duty even under an unjust ruler, of course not as an offensive Jihad, but as one defending the lives of Islam and Muslims.[11]

These statements show the Shiite view of the nature of jihad in Islam, which is not in line with the Sunni ideas of jihad. Shiite offensive jihad belongs to the Infallible Imam. This position remained unchanged from the time of Sheikh Abu Ja'far al-Tousi in the eleventh century,[12] until Sheikh Mohammad Hasan al-Najafi al-Javahiri (d.1849), another important Shiite jurisprudent, compiled one of the most authoritative collections of Shiite jurisprudence, *Javahir al-Kalaam*.[13]

There are two main characteristics of Sheikh al-Tousi's statements:
1. he divides jihad (like the Sunnites) into two categories: offensive and defensive;

2. offensive jihad is dependent on the presence of the Infallible Imam or his appointed representative, either of whom can call for jihad; therefore, jihad is not permitted alongside, and by the order of, any ruler.

These two criteria are the determining conditions for jihad among Shiites. That is why jihad is the prerogative only of an Infallible Imam; i.e. the Twelfth Imam of Shiite, who is currently in a state of Greater Occultation (the period when there is no agent of the Hidden Imam on earth). In Shiite thinking, offensive jihad is not possible in his absence. Based on this fact, in classical Shiite jurisprudence, which it is also claimed has unanimous recognition by all Shiites (consensus), offensive jihad is suspended.

New trends

Contemporary critical interpretations of Islamic jurisprudence, both Shiite and Sunnite, have presented new approaches to understanding the Qur'anic verses on jihad. Among the Sunnite scholars we may refer to the ideas of Sheikh Mohammad Abdoh (1849–1905) in *Al-Minar*.[14] Among the Shiite scholars we may refer to Morteza Motahari (1920–1980)[15] and Salehi Najafabadi (1924–2006).[16] In contrast to the classical jurisprudents, who believed that the "absolute" (*mutlaq*) verses on jihad abrogated the "conditional" (*muqayad*) verses[17] and emphasized the legitimacy of offensive jihad, these modern scholars believe that the conditional verses in fact elaborate and interpret the absolute verses on jihad. Consequently, the maintenance of peace and the defensive nature of jihad in Islam remain the main valid concepts. Based on these new ideas, the classical classification of jihad into offensive and defensive forms is no longer acknowledged as valid, and jihad in Islam becomes a totally defensive measure.

I believe in the importance of these points since they show that in Shiite belief, in the absence of the Imam, jihad may be used only as a defensive measure. In other words, although there may be other new ideas on the subject, in the Shiite view jihad is of a defensive nature. This issue will be elaborated on here, followed by an examination of military ethics in Shiite Islam.

The principles of jihad and defence in Shiite jurisprudence

As previously noted, the system of Shiite jurisprudence *(fiqh)* is an imamate-based branch of Islam, whose major difference from Sunni Islam concerns the issue of the imamate.[18] The format and concepts of Shiite jurisprudence stand on the facts that the Prophet appointed 12 Infallible Imams by God's command, the last of whom is currently in Occultation.

Belief in the imamate also has a great impact on Shiites' conception of jihad.

As a criterion for reasoning, the "narrations" (*akhbar*) from the Infallible Imams are the main source for interpretation of the Qur'an and the *Sunna* (tradition) of the Prophet in Shiite jurisprudence.[19] Shiites believe that, although the Qur'an is an absolute and perfect text from Allah, we may interpret issues discussed in the Sacred Book in light of the Hadith of the Prophet and the narrations of the Imams. That is why in Shiism the sayings of the Imams occupy such a central position for interpreting and understanding the Qur'an. Jihad is also interpreted and defined in the same manner by Shiites.

Peace as a principle

There has been much discussion about the priority of war or peace in Islam. In the minds of many non-Muslims, and even in the minds of some Muslims, there is a belief that Islam is a religion of war and the sword.

This understanding may have two explanations. One is that traditional interpretations of Islam by the Sunnites resulted from the historical expansion of Islam by Muslim caliphs and rulers through wars. The other explanation is that the understanding of Islam in certain religio-political circles in the West results from Western contact with Sunnite Muslims during the medieval period, and more recently in light of the contemporary radicalism that prevails among many Muslims in the Sunnite world. Consequently, two important matters are neglected:

• the new interpretation of Sunnite Islam, which believes in peace as a fundamental principle in Islam;
• the voice of Shiites who emphasize that, in the absence of the Infallible Imam, only defensive war is valid and justified; this idea covers a vast geographical area in the Middle East.

I shall refer first to certain Qur'anic verses that emphasize that peace is fundamental, and then I consider the narrative ideas of Shiism (*Ravayah*).

The Qur'an and peace

There are two types of Qur'anic verse on war and peace: in conditional (*muqayad*/*mashrout*) verses, war against non-Muslims is contingent upon the enemy attacking first; the absolute (*mutlaq*) verses recommend jihad, no matter what the conditions might be.

As previously stated, classical Shiite jurisprudence accepts and interprets the *absolute* Qur'anic verses on jihad in the same manner as the Sunnite Muslims do, but then suspends jihad because the Infallible Imam is not present. The new Shiite interpretations emphasize that, according to legal/ jurisprudential rules, the *absolute* verses are interpreted by the *conditional* jihad verses, which make jihad subject to certain conditions. Salehi Najafabadi believes that this is a general rule, which must be observed in any sort of interpretation.[20] Morteza Motahari is of the same opinion: "The principle is that the *absolute* verses shall be interpreted by the *conditional* verses (*muqayad/mashrout*) and deduct that whatever is stated in *absolute* verses, meant the same as the concept presented in the *conditional* verses."[21]

Morteza Motahari says: "Religion shall be in favour of peace." The Qur'an also states that "Peace is better [than war]". But religion should also favour war when the other side does not want to coexist harmoniously, or when a tyrant disregards human dignity. To submit to such a tyrant would involve a great loss of human dignity. In such cases war becomes a legitimate alternative. Islam emphasizes peace if the other side also favours peace. But if the other side wants war, Islam commands war.[22] The old interpreters believed, in contrast, that the verses in which jihad is conditional are abrogated by the absolute verses, such as the chapter on *Toubah* (Repentance): "and fight the polytheists all together as they fight you all together; and know that Allah is with those who guard (against evil)" (Qur'an 9:36).[23]

In any case, the verses favouring peace as a principle state that war (jihad) is recommended only if the unbelievers start an attack on Muslims first. These verses are the guiding principles for contemporary Sunnite and Shiite interpreters, and lead them to believe that in these verses jihad is of defensive nature.

> Make prepare against them what force and horses tied at the frontier, to frighten thereby the enemy of Allah and your enemy and others besides them, whom you do not know. (but) Allah knows them; and whatever thing you will spend in Allah's way, it will be paid back to you fully and you shall not be dealt with unjustly. (Qur'an 8:60)

This verse says that to be prepared to defend is an obligation and the offenders are referred to as enemies of Allah and the Islamic community (*umma*). Then in the next verse the priority of peace is emphasized: "And if they incline to peace, then incline to it and trust in Allah; surely He is the Hearing, the Knowing" (Qur'an 8:61).

Some past Shiite scholars, such as Sayyid Ali al-Tabataba'ie (d.1814), emphasized that this peace (*selm*) verse and the verse cited above are not among the abrogated verses. Rather, they merely emphasize the consistency of peace.[24] Also, Allameh Mohammad Baqer al-Majlesi (d.1692), commenting on the peace verse (Qur'an 8:61), asserts that the Qur'an suggests that Muslims should accept peace if the enemy also desires it. Allah orders that Muslims trust Him, so the Islamic government need not worry about the enemy tricking them by accepting peace, because, if the enemy tricks Muslims and violates the peace, Allah is with them to bring them victory.[25]

Sayyid Mostafa al-Khomeini (d.1976) believes that the peace verse is not only a peace-centred rule for Islamic society but also a religious reason for establishing political relations between Islamic governments and foreign, non-Muslim governments, so as to recognize and respect these governments.[26] It is also stated in the Qur'an that;

> And fight [*waqatiloohum*] in the way of Allah with those who fight with you, and do not exceed the limits, surely Allah does not love those who exceed the limits. And kill them wherever you find them, and drive them out from whence they drove you out, and persecution is severer than slaughter, and do not fight with them at the Sacred Mosque [the Ka'ba in Mecca] until they fight with you in it, but if they do fight you, then slay them, such is the recompense of the unbelievers. But if they desist [fighting], then surely Allah is Forgiving, Merciful. (Qur'an 2:190–192)

In the same chapter, the Qur'an states that aggression is the same as endangering your own life, and recommends that you "spend in the way of Allah and cast not yourselves to perdition with your own hands" (Qur'an 2:195).

In a commentary on these verses from Chapter 2 of the Qur'an, Salehi Najafabadi draws our attention to an important point regarding the nature and limits of defensive war in Islam:

- "A war, though is an act of defense, but shall be for Allah's sake (in His way) with the intention to seek his satisfaction."
- "The condition to fight for Allah's sake is to make sure that the enemy has attacked first. So fight with the ones who have attacked you and are fighting with you."
- Since the war atmosphere is full of stress, the Qur'an strictly prohibits going beyond the limits of a just war (just to attack the militant enemy and not civilians). Furthermore, since going beyond the limits of a just war is known to all consciences and observable to all mankind, the Qur'an describes the word for aggression in very definite and absolute terms, and leaves the interpretation to the individual's conscience in any time or place. Islamic literature – as will also be discussed in this chapter – refers to these limits of legitimate defence, such as prohibiting violence against women, children, the elderly, clergy and scientists, who are neutral in war, in addition to refraining from burning crops, jungle, trees, rivers and houses.

- These verses emphasize that Allah does not accept aggression on the part of anybody or in any circumstances. Therefore, an attack by an enemy cannot be a reason for a full counterattack aimed at *teaching them a lesson* for their original aggression.[27]

Finally, in reference to the philosophy of defence, the Qur'an presents a general summary of the concept of defensive jihad in the following terms:

Permission (to fight) is given to those upon whom war is made because they are oppressed, and most surely Allah is well able to assist them. (22:39)

Those who have been expelled from their homes without a just cause except that they say: Our Lord is Allah. And had there not been Allah's repelling some people by others, certainly there would have been pulled down cloisters and churches and synagogues and mosques in which Allah's Name is much remembered; and surely Allah will help him who helps His cause; most surely Allah is Strong, Mighty. (22:40)

Shiite narrations and peace

In Shiite narrations (*akhbar*), peace is clearly respected as a fundamental principle. Imam Ali (martyred in 661), the first Infallible Imam of Shiism, states that "Peace is closer to salvation and is more beneficial up to the moment that Islam is not in peril".[28] In an order to his governor (emir) in Egypt, Malik Ashtar (d.659), Imam Ali says:

Never turn your back on peace, to which Allah has called you and your enemy. Because in peace there are lots of benefits, such as protecting the safety of your armed forces, giving them peace of mind, and bringing security to your homeland. But, never forget your enemy after making peace with them, because sometimes the enemy gets closer to you to make an ambush. So be quite careful and, while staying committed to peace, never be simple minded.[29]

Imam Ali further advises his governor that, "in order to keep the peace and peace of mind of people, listen to the advice of the scholars and wise men; because, peace would reveal the truth and the evil".[30]

Prophet Mohammad stated that if a person brought peace among people, even between two persons, the angels would continuously praise him.[31] Imam Ali also further emphasizes that "if someone calls for peace accept it and be patient because victory is the outcome of patience. Land belongs to Allah and He would grant it to the ones He wishes so and the future belongs to the believers."[32] In the same sermon he recommends that "if you face the enemy, never start the war".[33]

Imam Musa al-Kazim (743–798), the Seventh Shiite Imam, referred to the Bible when he addressed one of his close disciples, saying:

> Happy would be the ones who give alms, because they are forgiven on the Day of Judgment. Happy would be the peace seekers who are making peace among people, because they will be close to Allah on the Day of Judgment.[34]

The religious commands also emphasize the priority of peace and condemn corruption on Earth. In the story of Korah (Qarun) in the Qur'an, it is clearly stated that corruption is not acceptable and that Allah disapproves of those who engage in corruption: "seek by means of what Allah has given you the future abode, ... and do not seek to make mischief in the land" (Qur'an 28:77).

> We did not create the heaven and the earth and what is between them in vain; that is the opinion of those who disbelieve then woe to those who disbelieve on account of the fire. Shall We treat those who believe and do good like the mischief-makers in the earth? Or shall We make those who guard (against evil) like the wicked? (Qur'an 38:27–28)

The teachings of Islam provide further moral guidelines regarding corruption. As stated by Imam al-Sadeq (698–763), the Sixth Shiite Imam, outward corruption is an indication of inward corruption "in people's hearts".[35] The Qur'an says that Korah became corrupt because of his greed. Also, there are two concepts of corruption in Islamic jurisprudence literature: one refers to all unlawful acts, and the other parallels the Qur'anic words of *al-Fitnah* (sedition), oppression, pillage and prejudicial acts. Often the criteria of corruption are left undefined in the Qur'an. Thus, the exact features of corruption are left to be determined by social customs and rationality.

Jihad as defence, when the Imam is absent

As previously mentioned, jihad in traditional Shiite jurisprudence (like Sunnite) has two forms: offensive and defensive.[36] The guidelines established by the Shiite Imams and Shia jurisprudence set two main conditions for offensive jihad: (a) the presence of the Infallible Imam and (b) instruction by the Infallible Imam, alongside other objective conditions such as freedom, financial capabilities, being healthy enough to make such instruction, being a male Muslim, sane and mature or of adult age.[37]

In the absence of the Imam (or of his directly appointed representative when the Imam is available), offensive jihad with non-Muslims is not permitted.[38] Therefore, although jurisprudents are recognized as "representatives of the Imam in occultation", jihad remains the right solely of the Infallible Imam, not of his representatives in his Occultation. In this respect there seems to be a consensus amongst the Shiite jurisprudents.[39]

The Grand Ayatollah Imam Khomeini (d.1989), the religio-political leader of the Islamic Revolution of Iran (1979), in his book *Tahrir al-Wasilah*,[40] emphasizes that offensive jihad is the prerogative of the Infallible Imam only, and that jurisprudents do not share in this privilege. In addition, the Grand Ayatollah Sayyid Mohammad reza al-Golpaigani (d.1993) – a contemporary supreme source of Emulation (*marja'-i taqlid*) in Qom – believes that offensive jihad is the prerogative of the Infallible Imam only, and that no one else shares this privilege.[41] However, another authority, the Grand Ayatollah Sayyid abu-al-Qasim al-Kho'ei (d.1992) of Najaf, questions the validity of this statement.[42] He also points to the credibility among Shiite jurists of permission given by the Immaculate Imam or his special deputy in jihad. He provides two sources for this traditional and well-known position: (1) the narrations (*akhbar*) of the imams, and (2) the consensus of the jurisprudents. Kho'ei provides a critical analysis of these sources and maintains that, in spite of some narrations and the consensus among jurists on the prohibition of offensive jihad during times of occultation, jihad may nevertheless be conducted in the absence of the Infallible Imam.[43]

Grand Ayatollah Mirza abu-al-Qasim al-Qomi (d.1814) claims that the consensus on the suspension of offensive jihad in occultation is valid. Consequently, he also accepts the suspension of receiving tribute from the believers of other religions in the Muslim community.[44]

Some Shiite narrations emphasize the *theory of epochal dissimulation*; they consider the period of the absence of the Imam to be, in general, a period for dissimulation. On the basis of these narrations, most authorities focus only on the defensive aspects of jihad. Imam Sadeq states:

> He, who is killed next to his property, is a martyr. And, no non-Muslim shall be killed in Dar al-Taqeya (the dissimulation world), except those who are corrupt or are murderers. This restriction holds until there is no threat on you or your family's life.[45]

However, the prevailing consensus among Shiite jurisprudents is that offensive jihad is permissible only when the Infallible Imam or his special representative (on jihad) is present.[46] Therefore, offensive jihad in the absence of the Imam (i.e. in our time) is not permitted, although some past and present Shiite jurisprudents have expressed doubts over this position.[47]

Therefore, in the absence of the Infallible Imam of the Shiites, most Shiite jurisprudents believe in jihad as a defensive measure only, which does not require special permission or instruction from the Infallible Imam and is possible only if an enemy attacks Islamic lands first and intends to occupy or destroy them.[48] Defensive jihad does not have any of the restrictions of offensive jihad. Therefore, it is a duty for everyone – male, female, old or young – to defend Muslim land.[49] Shahid Sani, Zayn al-Din Ali ibn Mushrif al-Amili (d.1540) believes that, although such defence is a duty for all Muslims, it is more of a duty for those who are closer to the enemy and for those who are under direct attack from the enemy.[50]

In the absence of the Infallible Imam, Islamic society requires constant preparedness and protection of its borders as a primary defensive measure. As stated by Sheikh al-Tousi, unless war with an enemy is fought in defence of Islam and Muslims, it is not acceptable.[51] Imam Ali too says that Muslims should protect their borders but should never start a war, except in defence of Muslims and Islam.[52]

Prohibition on engaging in war

Shiite jurisprudents believe that defending the lives of Muslims and the borders of Islam is a duty and that a Muslim is never expected to surrender to an aggressor. Addressing his disciples, Imam Ali instructed, "If they impose a war on you and start war against you ... then go to war and accept death, since the real death is living in humiliation, oppression, and defeat, and eternal life is in going to war and dying or achieving victory."[53]

Imam Sadeq asserts that "To fight with the enemy is a duty for all the Islamic nations (*umma*), so obey it or you shall be punished".[54] He also narrates from the Holy Prophet: "Leaving Jihad would result in losing dignity, poverty, and collapse of religion ... and Allah would cover those who abandon the battlefield (Jihad) with the cloth of disgrace."[55]

Allameh Hasan bin Yousof al-Hilli (1250–1326) considers various stages of defence, from the most basic to the most advanced. The first stage seeks justice and demonstrates opposition towards war; the next stage requests assistance from others in order to deter the enemy; finally, if these measures prove unsuccessful, the next step would require arms – from the most rudimentary to the most sophisticated weaponry, in order to confront the enemy. These strategies should continue until the aggressive acts of the enemy have come to a halt. The defenders shall be considered martyrs if they are killed in this process.[56]

All these rules are valid only if the aggressor is not fleeing or ceasing aggression. If the aggressor stops attacking, any harm to the enemy shall be compensated through *al-Qisas*, the law of retaliation (for instance, an eye for an eye ...) or with the payment of blood money.[57] Even during such situations of war, the use of weapons other than those absolutely vital is not permissible. If heavy weaponry is used when there is no need, the user should receive punishment.[58]

Allameh Hilli refers in another book to the necessity of monitoring borders and emphasizes that offensive war (starting a war) against unbelievers is not permitted as long as the enemy stays away from Islamic lands. Hence, Muslims should be kept informed about the enemy's intention and situation. Muslims should never start a pre-emptive war but should only defend against the enemy's attack. Even then, such a war should not aim for jihad, only for the defence of Islam and Muslims.[59] Allameh Hilli also states that defending Islam and people's lives is a duty, and that defending property is permissible.[60] Imam Shafei considers escaping the homeland and migrating as a way of reacting to an enemy's attack, but Allameh Hilli rejects this idea in most situations, endorsing it only to save people's lives.[61]

Sheikh Mohammad Ali al-Ansari, in summarizing Shiite ideas on levels of defence, says:

> The first level of defense is requesting the assistance of others to stop an enemy. If the enemy (Muslim or non-Muslim) attacks a family, it is of course a duty to stop the aggressor and ask for help, and at the same time prepare to defend in any manner possible, even with bare hands. Other means of defense are not allowed unless when there is no help and lives of Muslims are threatened.

> Shaykh Tusi says: "If some one is attacked and his life or property is in danger, then he has the right to shout for help. That would be the best measure. If there is no help, he should use hands or cane/walking stick to defend himself and his property. If that is not sufficient, he could then use weapon to defend his life and property."[62]

These points are stated in other Shiite books, in more or less similar terms. Therefore, it becomes abundantly clear that, during the absence of the Imam, Shiite jurisprudence approves only of defensive – rather than offensive – jihad. It is clear that the strategy of defence also has its own rules and levels, from moderate measures to more extreme ones (from shouting for help, kicking, hurting and killing the aggressor).[63] In terms of defence, saving first of all life and then property are of great importance.[64] Towards that end, even cooperation with tyrannical rulers is permissible.[65] Shahid Avval, Mohammad bin Jamal al-Din Mecci (1336–1387) believes that, according to Shiite jurisprudence, if one is killed in defence of one's life and property, one is considered a martyr.[66]

Efforts to establish peace

The conditions described above show the basic position of Shiite Islam on the nature of defensive jihad. Such defensive measures must come to an end in the shortest time possible. Both sides in a war are then expected to return to the *status quo ante*. In other words, the necessities of defence shall not be a legitimate reason to prolong the war. Based on this reasoning, Shiite sources urge their followers to return to peace.

It has been said that Imam Ali called on his disciples to think and act in order to preserve peace. Instead of cursing the enemy, he asked them to recite the following prayer for their adversaries:

> Oh God, Save our blood and their blood and make peace among us and save them from misunderstandings that led to this animosity, and guide them to the right path.[67]

Attempting to bring peace is a religious duty in Islamic law, and deserves to be rewarded by God. That is the reason Shiite sources have discussed and emphasized the "objective outcomes" of peace. Islamic sources call for "seeking peace" (*istislah*) among adversaries engaged in war. Some Hadiths of the Holy Prophet show that there is a direct relation between ethics and peace. For instance, the Holy Prophet of Islam emphasized that "seeking peace and making efforts to bring it about is the sign of manliness and courage".[68] Other Shiite narrations deal with efforts to establish peace between enemies. The following are a few examples:[69]

- Imam Ali: "*seeking* peace with the enemy through friendly negotiation and proper actions is easier than meeting them on the Battlefield."
- "He, who tries to establish peace with the enemy, would gain more friends."
- "He who establishes peace between two enemies, certainly he will be granted what he wished for."
- Imam Hasan Askari, the Eleventh Imam (846–875), said:

> He who is pious in nature, observes ethics, and is virtuous in his character would be praised by his friends because through these measures he will be able to defeat the enemy.

All these sayings demonstrate the importance of seeking peace and making efforts towards the realization of peace. These sayings also show what types of behaviour and styles of negotiation lead to peace. Imam Ali says that "friendly negotiation" and "proper actions" are the prerequisites for reaching peace. Imam Hasan Askari also believes that "peace is not something optional, but is the outcome of observing the ethics of peace". He believes that proper behaviour in dealing with others is the sign of a sound mind that would be welcomed by public opinion, and such gestures would ultimately make the enemy retreat.

Peace in Islamic jurisprudence is a form of religious contract, which is made in order to end conflict between the two sides. One category of peace is peace between Muslims and non-believers. Allameh Hilli believes that such a peace contract is valid by itself without any other conditions, and is expected to be observed and enforced by both sides; it may not be cancelled except by mutual agreement.[70]

Condemning treason and the breaching of promises

Shiite jurisprudence condemns and forbids any act of treason or the breaching of promises or treaties in the defensive strategies of Shiites.

In "Majma'al-Bahrayn", the breaching of agreements or pacts is declared forbidden.[71] Saheb Javaher, Sheikh Mohammad Hasan al-Najafi al-Javahiri (d.1849), believes that all Shiite sources agree on this issue.[72] In all the sources we may find evidence to this effect. Treason or treachery is naturally abhorrent and may turn people against Islam. The Shiite jurisprudents present the following sayings and verdicts to substantiate this statement:[73]

- Imam Sadeq: "It is not proper that Muslims commit treason, order someone else to do so or even accommodate the ones who do not keep their promise."
- Imam Ali, delivering a sermon to the people in Kufa (a city in Iraq): "O people! I could be the smartest of all, if treachery and breaking the promises were not forbidden. Beware that breaking the promise is a terrible act that would lead to blasphemy. The one who breaks the promise would be labeled on Judgment Day to be recognized by every one."[74]

This demonstrates how treachery and the breaking of promises in agreements or bilateral relations are forbidden; they are naturally abhorrent and would harm Islam and Islamic society. Therefore, although treachery may be considered an act of war that helps to defend Islam against aggressors, any act of defence must be within the framework of the religion. No treaty or pact between an Islamic society or government and aggressors, nor any international treaty, must ever be broken or nullified unilaterally by an Islamic government.

In this respect, the role of the laws of treaties in Shiism must be highlighted, in setting the defensive strategy of the Shiites. Firstly, Islamic law allows Muslims to enter into bilateral or multilateral pacts and treaties. Secondly, since Shiite jurisprudence forbids breaking treaties, any international treaty signed by Islamic countries/governments is valid and must be respected by all sides.[75]

Military ethics in Shiite Islam

Military ethics covers all the values and norms that are expected to be observed under war conditions, and the sets of ethical values and rules to be implemented.

In Islam, the rules of ethics are obligatory. Therefore, observing them deserves reward and neglecting them requires punishment. There is a difference between laws and the rule of ethics, however. Islamic laws and legal injunctions must always be implemented, and there are means to ensure their implementation. Ethical rules, however, do not enjoy such measures and their implementation depends only on the conscience of the people. There are various rules of ethics for the military in Islam; a few examples will now be discussed.

Prohibition on cursing the enemy

Shiite sources categorically prohibit the cursing or scolding of the enemy. The Holy Qur'an instructs Muslims always to talk with "a recognised form of words" (2:235; Pickthall translation).[76] In Shiite jurisprudence, cursing is forbidden (*haram*).[77] In one of his prayers cited in *Sahifa Sajjadiyyah*, Imam Zayn al-'Abidin (the Fourth Shiite Imam, d.712) utters: "Praise belongs to God who gave me a chance not to scold, curse, make false testimony or backbite against any believer."[78] The Holy Prophet said, "Never curse the unbelievers."[79] On another occasion, Imam Sadeq said: "Abstaining from cursing one's opponents is a blessed act."[80] Imam Baqer (the Fifth Shiite Imam, d.732) said: "If you curse someone, you would make him your enemy. Therefore, never curse any one so that you would not make an enemy for yourself."[81] In comprehensive advice, the Holy Prophet of Islam said: "Do not curse even a camel for in case of an accident you must pay blood money of human or even from the dowry of your wife."[82] On another occasion the Holy Prophet said;

> Do not get angry with people. Seek the satisfaction of the people as if you are looking for your own satisfaction. Love people so they would love you. Smile to your brother and do not annoy him, so you would never get hurt in this world and the next.[83]

When Imam Ali heard his enemies were being cursed during the fight, he immediately ordered this practice to be stopped. Then his disciples asked him the reason. The Imam replied: "Being right does not mean that we have the right to curse. I do not like you cursing them. Just tell them of what they have done."[84]

Prohibition of terror

Although defensive jihad permits any kind of action against aggressors, in Shiism acts of terrorism are forbidden. In Shiite terminology, terror (*fatk*) refers to an unexpected attack on a civilian in a non-war situation. There is no verse referring to the concept of terror in the Qur'an. But other Shiite sources, for example narrations, denounce and condemn such acts. Therefore, from a Shiite perspective, terror or an unexpected attack as a defensive measure or for deterrence is forbidden.

Shiite scholars refer to the sayings of the Prophet as recorded by Imam Sadeq regarding the absolute prohibition on terror. These narrations refer to judging a person who cursed Imam Ali. Shiites believe that cursing Immaculate Imams is equivalent to cursing the Prophet. But Imam Sadeq prohibited terrorizing the accused person. In light of these sayings, Shiite jurisprudents absolutely prohibit acts of terrorism, because those narrations absolutely ban such acts.

Ayatollah Montazeri refers to a statement on terror and says: "It is truly narrated that Abu-Sabah al-Kafani told Imam Sadeq that he had a neighbour who was cursing Imam Ali and asked Imam's permission to catch him off-guard, and attack and kill him by his sword. Imam Sadeq replied that 'this would be an act of *terror* and is prohibited by Prophet of Allah. Beware Abu-Sabah that Islam prohibits terror'."[85]

Ayatollah Montazeri refers to another narration with the same concept. It is narrated by Muslim ibn-Aqil from the Holy Prophet who said:

After Muslim, the envoy of Imam Husayn (the Third Shiite Imam, d.681), prepared the city of Kufa for the arrival of the Imam (in 680), then Ibn Ziyad came to Kufa and captured the city by the force of his army. One day Ibn Ziyad went to meet Shoraik Bin-A'var, a wise man of Kufa. Bin-A'var was a Shiite and had hidden Muslim in his house. He told Muslim that when the time is right he will give Muslim a signal so that he can come out and kill Ibn Ziyad. In this way the condition would have changed in favor of the supporters of Imam Husayn. However, Muslim ibn-Aqil did not accept his suggestion. When Bin-A'var protested, Muslim cited a hadith of the Prophet who had said: "The faith forbids terror, a believer never terrorizes another."[86]

Prohibition of deceit

Not only does Shiite jurisprudence condemn terror, it also prohibits any kind of trickery and deceit, including any unexpected attack on the armed forces of the enemy at night. Sheikh al-Tousi emphasized that night ambush is not acceptable and all attacks must be made in daylight.[87]

Generally, anything related to deceit would not be approved by Shiite jurisprudence. Imam Sadeq said: "It is not proper for Muslims to do any deception or encourage deceit, or even fight along with cheaters."[88] Allameh Majlesi elaborated on the above narration in *Bihar al-Anwar*, which contains a vast number of Hadiths and sayings of the Imams. According to him: "It means that Muslims are not supposed to encourage the act of deception because deception is oppression and a hostile act.

They are both prohibited, even if the one who is deceived is an unbeliever."[89]

However, there is an exception in the general rule of prohibition of deceit, which in Shiite jurisprudence derives from the rule of *reciprocity*. It means that deceit is acceptable against those who are deceitful. In a statement attributed to Imam Ali, he says: "if we keep the promise with the ones who are deceiving us, then we are deceiving God and if we deceive them, it means that we kept our promise with God."[90]

Allameh Majlesi refers to various Qur'anic verses dealing with the question of reciprocity. In chapter 16:126 it is emphasized that: "And if you chastise, chastise even as you have been chastised and yet assuredly if you are patient, better it is for those who are patient." Also, in chapter 42:40 it instructs: "And the recompense of evil is evil the like of it but who so pardons and puts things right, his wage falls upon God; surely He loves not the evildoers." Imam Ali says: "Return the stone they have thrown. Fight fire with fire."[91]

Therefore, one can conclude that, although deceiving the enemy is an acceptable exception when the enemy uses deception, the Qur'an generally advises forgiveness and amnesty. In fact, the Holy Qur'an teaches forgiveness and amnesty rather than retaliation. In chapter 42:43, God says: "And whoever is patient and forgiving, these most surely are actions due to courage."

The reasoning behind this major exception is that an act of deceit is equivalent to a declaration of war; that is to say, by resorting to deceit, the enemy intends to fight. In such a war, deception is a means of war and therefore legitimate. The Prophet Mohammad said, "War is a kind of deceit".[92] Ali Bin al-Husayn Muhaqqiq al-Karaki (d.1533) refers to these religious arguments and concludes that:

> Deception is permitted in war because war is a kind of deception. However any deception, even against the unbelievers, is not allowed in no-war situation. No one may take the unbelievers' properties when there is no war.[93]

Prohibition of weapons of mass destruction

The Holy Prophet of Islam prohibited the use of any kind of poison against unbelievers.[94] This could include pouring poison in the water that the enemy uses or spreading it in the air that they breathe. This might cause the death of civilians. Allameh Hilli regards this as a terrible and detestable act, but suggests that one may resort to such an act if necessary in military circumstances. He also approves the exploitation of any kind of weapon, if necessary.[95] Sayyid Ali al-Tabataba'ie (d.1814) also refers to the prohibition on poisoning in many sources dealing with jurisprudence.[96] Sheikh al-Tousi says: "In war with non-Muslims any weapon is approved except poisons because if one uses poison one risks the death of women, children and the insane, whose killing is prohibited."[97]

Sheikh al-Tousi refers to a point that in jurisprudence is called *Manaat al-Ahkaam*, the foundation of the rules or religious command. The basis of the ruling is a general analogy; the religious prohibition on the use of poison is an instance of such an analogy. It means that it is not only the use of poison that is prohibited; the use of any weapons of mass destruction (WMD) would be prohibited because they endanger the lives of civilians. The following analogy explains this norm:

(a) The killing of children, women, the insane or any other innocent person (i.e. civilian) is prohibited.
(b) The use of any weapon that kills civilians is forbidden.
(c) Spreading poison would cause civilian casualties.
(d) Therefore, spreading poison in enemy lands is forbidden.

This is how religious reasoning on such issues (e.g. poisoning) is constructed. Based on a logical argument (the risk of civilian casualties) the use of WMD is prohibited.

Shiite jurisprudence also prohibits the disruption of the enemy's water supplies, or even surrounding the enemy in such a way that they do not have access to water.

Prohibition on aggression against civilians

In jurisprudence concerning jihad there is the term "*tatarros*", meaning to hide among civilians during war, so that civilians act as a human shield, protecting the armed forces. Shiite jurisprudence prohibits any aggression against civilians, except in cases of the enemy hiding behind civilians. The word "*tatarros*" in Arabic comes from the root "*tors*", which is a small metal shield on the handle of a sword, designed to protect the hands.[98]

Among civilians, children, women and elderly people are expected to be particularly protected. Ibn al-Baraj al-Tarablosi (d.1088) underlines that, if the aggressor hides behind children, shooting (releasing arrows) aimed at the enemy (not the children) is permitted. Once the war reverts to a conventional situation, children should once again be protected against any harm.[99]

In cases such as this, Islamic jurisprudence even allows the killing of Muslims.[100] Allameh Hilli and other Shiite authorities have explained this rule, arguing that, if the enemy hides behind women or elderly people, the enemy may be attacked.[101] However, Allameh Hilli adds that such an attack on an enemy who is hiding behind a civilian human shield is permitted only when there is a risk of defeat by this enemy.[102]

Among civilians to be protected during the war, men of science and religion who stay neutral are given special consideration. Shiite jurisprudents believe that their lives should be protected. When the Holy Prophet of Islam was sending troops to the Mouta war (in 629),[103] he recommended that the army not assault any scientist or any neutral representatives of religions.[104] On the basis of the Prophet's action, Shiite and Sunnite jurisprudents have upheld the same rule. Aggression against scholars, monks, specialists and masters of professions and industries is also forbidden, in their opinion.[105]

Preservation of the environment

The preservation and protection of the environment and the heritage of human civilization are also part of military ethics. Shiite jurisprudence refers to three major points in this respect.

Prohibition on damage to trees and farms
In numerous sources, the cutting of trees – especially fruit trees – and the burning of farms is prohibited.[106] In *Bihar al-Anwar*, it is stated that trees that do not bear fruit may be cut during war, if necessary.[107] These traditions are guidelines for Shiite reasoning in military ethics and describe the responsibility concerning the preservation and protection of the environment. In the same book, warlords are advised to protect the environment.

Shahid Sani, Zayn al-Din Ali ibn Mushrif al-Amili (d.1540), says that, except in special circumstances, the cutting or burning of trees, especially fruit trees, is prohibited.[108] However, there is no mention of what these exceptional or special circumstances are. Other religious sources have repeated the same rule; Sayyid Ali al-Tabataba'ie clearly stated that fruit trees and farms should not be burned.[109] Ayatollah al-Kho'ei explains the reasons for this, and adds that "all the narrations rule that such action is strictly prohibited. At any rate, it is not possible to give a verdict to this effect that can be applied to all circumstances; as such a verdict may cause other problems in managing the war. Therefore, each situation must be dealt with as it arises."[110]

Prohibition on the destruction of buildings and habitations
The Holy Prophet of Islam, in a command issued for troops, specifically ordered them "not to destroy buildings".[111]

Allameh Hilli believes that this command refers exclusively to civilian buildings. Military buildings or fortifications are subject to a different rule. They should not be destroyed if their destruction is not necessary for military considerations. However, if their destruction is important in military terms, they can be torn down even if there might be Muslim prisoners inside them.[112] Sheikh al-Tousi and some other jurisprudents believe that there should be convincing reasons for destroying military buildings, since destruction is generally prohibited.[113]

Ibn Edris al-Hilli (d.1201) prohibits any military attack resulting in the destruction of buildings and substructures, in the same manner as for WMD. He says: "In war many means may be taken, except for destruction of people's houses through flooding, burning or spreading poison."[114] Ibn Edris clearly prohibits the destruction of houses and other necessary substructures as well as the use of WMD.

Thus, it is clear that Islamic jurisprudence pays a great deal of attention to preserving the vital structures and facilities of society, especially water systems.

Although Shiite sources believe that when under siege by the enemy the destruction of buildings is allowed, they have qualms and special considerations regarding the water system – even if it belongs to the military. Although it is generally believed that restricting water is absolutely prohibited, some authorities believe that, as a last resort and under some conditions, it is permitted.[115]

It is also advised that Muslim warriors should not raid people's private water sources and justify this by being at war. In a narration by Imam Ali, he states: "Troops must not invade private water sources. They should ask for permission of the owner and then drink from their water sources. The properties and animals of the people must not be confiscated and usurped either."[116]

Prohibition on the harming of animals
The Holy Prophet of Islam prohibits the army from harming animals, and commands the army not to slaughter more *halal* animals than are necessary for the army's needs.[117] Imam al-Sadeq says:

> The Holy Prophet commanded the slaughtering of a sufficient number of animals to meet the army's needs. Like humans, animals must be respected and must not be killed randomly because of fighting with an enemy.[118]

Generally, in Islamic jurisprudence, several ethical points are expected to be observed by the military in times of war. For instance, there are prohibitions on burning farms, cutting fruit trees, killing animals, destroying houses and disrespecting the bodies of those who have been killed in battle.[119] This shows that preserving the environment and protecting animal rights along with human rights are important principles even during war.[120]

Summary and conclusion

In the Islamic world, the rules of war and military ethics are rooted in religious principles. This is why religious texts have defined the behaviour of Muslims regarding war and military ethics, from the earliest times in Islamic history up to the present day. In the modern world, in contrast, these issues and concepts are examined and observed from a secular viewpoint.

Islamic jurisprudence – both Shiite and Sunnite – is a system based on revelation, reason and intellect, and therefore establishes a logical relationship between religious laws and historical realities. The duty of jurisprudence is to provide answers to the questions that face Muslim societies. This explains how a close relation exists between jurisprudence and war, as one of the important issues in Islamic society – a subject that has been called "jihad jurisprudence".

Islamic jurisprudence pays special attention to the historical development and evolution of ideas regarding jihad. Notwithstanding Shiite and Sunnite differences in classification, this chapter has sought to show how traditional Islamic jurisprudence lends legitimacy to jihad. In particular, it has emphasized how the "absolute" (*mutlaq*) verses of the Qur'an on jihad abrogate the verses according to which jihad is dependent on certain conditions. That is the reason traditional jurisprudence considers those rules to be general rules that are everlasting and can never change or be abolished.

Conversely, the new jurisprudence gives priority to peace. In interpreting the jihad verses of the Holy Qur'an, it believes that the *muqayad* (dependent, conditional) verses elaborate on and interpret the *mutlaq* (absolute, definite) verses. In light of this approach, it becomes clear why jihad in Islam is defined as defensive war at all times. Moreover, modern jurisprudence rejects the classical Muslim idea of separating jihad into offensive and defensive forms.

It has also been mentioned that classical Shiite jurisprudence is related to Sunnite jurisprudence; hence both in principle accept the idea of offensive and defensive jihad. In Shiism, however, Infallible Imams and their sayings are the basis of action and interpretations, so Shiites come to a different definition of jihad. In the classical Shiite view, offensive jihad is permissible only when the Infallible Imam is present and orders Muslims to conduct jihad. Thus, since the Occultation of the Twelfth Imam began in 329/941, offensive jihad has not been permissible for Shiites and it would be illegitimate if it took place.

Regarding the nature of Shiite beliefs about the imamate and jihad, the classification of jihad as offensive or defensive is only a theory and is not of any practical use since the Imam is in occultation. Therefore, based on the same reasoning, both the old and the new Shiite jurisprudence emphasize that only defensive jihad is permissible when the Imam is not present.

This is the most important principle differentiating the Shiite from the Sunnite point of view on jihad and defence. Shiite jurisprudence asserts that, in the absence of the Infallible Imam, society is not sufficiently mature to perform offensive jihad and hence it is not permitted. In such an important matter as jihad, one may not rely on the fallibility and imperfect logic of humans or rulers who are subject to errors or mistakes. The duty of the Shiite is to coexist in a spirit of goodwill, not in a constant state of jihad in the military sense of the word. The obligation of the Shiite is to preserve and defend peace, not to promote war or acts of aggression. This chapter has attempted to demonstrate these principles in light of the sayings and interpretations of the imams and Shiite jurisprudents.

Notes

1. Sayyid abu-al-Qasim al-Kho'ei, *Mesbah al-Osoul*. Taghrir Mohammad Sarvar al-Vae'iz al-hoseini. Qom: Maktab al-Davari, 1996, vol. 2, p. 247.
2. Abu Abdellah Mohammad bin Abi-Alfath al-Hanbali al-Ba'li, *Al-Matl'a al-Abwab al-Fiqh: Al-Matl'a al-Abwab al-Almoqhn'a*, edited by Mohamab Bashir al-Adlabi. Beirut: Dar alnashr; al-Maktab al-Islami, 1981, p. 209.
3. Hebato Allah al-Moghri, *Al-Nasikh wa al-Mansoukh*, edited by Zahir al-Shawish and Mohammad Kan'an. Beirut: Dar al-Nashr; al-Maktab al-Islami, 1984, vol. 1, pp. 29–30. Ali bin Ahmad bin Hazm, *Al-Nasikh wa al-Mansoukh fi al-Qur'an al-Karim*, edited by Abd al-Ghafar Soleiman al-Bandari. Beirut: Dar al-Nashr; Dar al-Kotob al Ilmeyya, 1986, vol. 1, p. 27.
4. Shams al-Din Abu-Bakr Mohammad bin Abi-Sahl al-Sarakhsi, *Al-Mabsout*. Beirut: Dar al-Ma'refa, 1986, vol. 2, p. 2.
5. Mohamad bin Edris al-Shafei, *Kitaab al-Omm*. Beirut: Dar Almarefa, 1973. vol. 4, p. 161. An electronic version of the translation of the Qur'an by M. H. Shakir is available at ⟨http://www.usc.edu/dept/MSA/quran/⟩ (accessed 21 October 2008).
6. Abdollah bin Qodama al-Maqdasi, *Al-Kafi fi Fiqh bin Hanbal*. Beirut: Dar al-Nashr; al-Maktab al-Islami, vol. 4, pp. 252–254.
7. Abu-Omar Yousef bin Abdollah al-Qortobi, *Al-Kafi li bin abi-al-Barakat*. Beirut: Dar Alkotob al-Elmeya, 1987, p. 205.
8. Sayyid Ahmad al-Dardir Abu-Albarakat, *Al-Sharh al-kabir*, edited by Mohammad Alish. Beirut: Dar al-Fikr, 1991, vol. 2, p. 172.
9. Fakhr al-din Osman bin Ali al-Hanafi al-Zilai, *Tabyin al-Hagha'igh*. Al-qahera: Dar al-Kotob al-Islami, 1894, vol. 3, p. 241.
10. For more information about Boroujerdi's method of *ijtihad* (the process of making a legal decision by independent interpretation), see ⟨http://taghrib.ir/english/?pgid=43&scid=33&dcid=33092⟩ (accessed 28 October 2008).
11. Sheikh Abu-Ja'far Mohammad al-Tousi, *Al-Nihaya fi Mojarad al-Fiqh va al-Fatawi*. Beirut: Dar al-Andolus, 1986, pp. 289–290.
12. Nematollah Salehi Najafabadi, *Jihad dar Islam*. Tehran: Nei Publishing Co., 2003, p. 46.
13. Sheikh Mohammad Hasan al-Najafi al-Javahiri, *Javahir al-Kalaam*. Tehran: Dar al-Kotob al-Islameyah, 1983, vol. 21, p. 3.
14. From Salehi Najafabadi, *Jihad dar Islam*, pp. 23, 32; Sheikh Mohammad Abdoh, *Tafsir al-Minar*, edited by Mohammad Rashid Riza. Cairo: Alminar Publication, 1947, vol. 2, pp. 210–215.
15. Morteza Motahari, *Jihad*. Qom: Sadra, 1994, p. 7.
16. Salehi Najafabadi, *Jihad dar Islam*.

17. In Islamic jurisprudence, the Qur'anic verses related to jihad are classified into two groups: the conditional and the absolute. The conditional verses, revealed first, condition the legitimacy of jihad on attack by an enemy; however, the absolute verses, revealed after the conditional ones, do not limit the legitimacy of jihad to any prior attack by an enemy. Thus, in Islamic jurisprudence the jihad referred to in the conditional verses has been termed *defensive jihad* and the jihad in the absolute verses *offensive jihad*.

18. The main Shiite sects, i.e. the Ismailis, the Zaidis and the Imamis (also known as Twelvers), have a quite different conception of the imamate compared with the Sunnite sects. The Twelvers are the largest sect of Shiism, and are considered in this chapter as the main source wherever I mention Shiite. The different Shiite sects have differing opinions on the issue of the imamate. The Twelver Shiites live in Iran, Iraq and Lebanon.

19. Sheikh Abdolhadi al-Fazli has discussed the difference between the Akhbari and Osouli Shiite schools of jurisprudence. Osouli, whose ideas seem predominant among Shiites today, drew directly on the Qur'an for jurisprudential rules (*ayaat al-Ahkam*). Osoulis refer to Qur'anic ideas to make judgements. This has led to a logical interpretation of Islamic texts. Akhbaris, in contrast, refer to narrations from the Imams to interpret Qur'anic ideas. Akhbaris believe that narrations and sayings from the Imams are the basis for any rule or idea. Most significantly, both points of views accept the importance of the presence of the Imam. See Al-Sheikh Hadi al-Fazli, *Dorous fi Osoul Fiqh al-Imamiah*. Qum: Om al-Qora, 1999, pp. 143–146.

20. Salehi Najafabadi, *Jihad dar Islam*, pp. 30–32.

21. Motahari, *Jihad*, p. 7.

22. Ibid., p. 18.

23. Mohammad bin Jarir al-Tabari, *Tafsir al-Tabari*. Beirut: Dar al-fikr, 1984, vol. 10, p. 124.

24. Sayyid Ali al-Tabataba'ie, *Riaz al Masaa'el*. Qom: A'l al-beit Inst, 1991, vol. 1, pp. 487–495.

25. Mohammad Baqer al-Majlesi, *Bihar al-Anwar*. Beirut: Alvafa Inst, 1983, vol. 19, p. 137.

26. Sayyid Mostafa al-Khomeini, *Salaas Rasaael*. Qom: Imam Khomeini Pub. Co., 1997, p. 41.

27. Sahlehi Najafabadi, *Jihad dar Islam*, pp. 20–22.

28. Mohammad Mohammadi Reishahri, *Mizan al-hikmaht*. Qom: Daral-Hadis, 1996, vol. 2, p. 162.

29. Ibid., vol. 2, p. 162; Al-Majlesi, *Bihar al-Anwar*, vol. 97, p. 47.

30. Imam Ali, *Nahj al-Balaghah*, edited by Mohamad Abdoh. Beirut: Dar al-Ma'refa, 1991, vol. 3, p. 89.

31. Ali Namazi Shahroudi, *Mostadrak Safinaht al-Behar*, edited by Hasan Namazi. Qom: Islamic Inst, 1997, vol. 6, p. 308.

32. Al-Majlesi, *Bihar al-Anwar*, vol. 56, p. 32.

33. Ibid., pp. 32–33.

34. Namazi Shahroudi, *Mostadrak Safinaht al-Behar*, vol. 6, p. 309.

35. Ibid., vol. 8, p. 19.

36. Allameh Hasan bin Yousof al-Hilli, *Tahrir al-Ahkam*. Qom: Imam al-Sadeq Inst, 1999, vol. 2, p. 142.

37. Shahid Avval, Mohammad bin Jamal al-Din Mecci, *Al-Lom'aht al-Demashqieh*, edited by Ali al-kourani. Qom: Dar al-Fikr, 1989, p. 72.

38. Mohammad Ibn Edris al-Hilli, *Al-Saraer*. Qom: Jamea Modaresin, 1988, vol. 2, p. 4.

39. Al-Javahiri, *Javahir al-Kalaam*, vol. 21, p. 13.

40. Rouh Allah Al-Khomeini, *Tahrir al-Wasilah*. Najaf: Matba'ah al-Adab, 1969, vol. 1, p. 482.
41. Sayyid Mohammad reza al-Golpaigani, *Alhedaya Ela man laho al-velayaht*. Qom: Darol Ghoran alkarim, 1963, p. 46.
42. Sayyid abu-al-Qasim al-Kho'ei, *Menhaj al-Salehin*. Qom: Madinah al-Elm, 1975, vol. 1, pp. 361–365.
43. Ibid., vol. 1, p. 364.
44. Mirza abu-al-Qasim al-Qomi, *Jame al-shataat*, edited by Morteza Razavi. Tehran: Keyhan, 1992, vol. 1, p. 402.
45. Al-Majlesi, *Bihar al-Anwar*, p. 23.
46. In the Shiite jurisprudence, special representative is contrasted with general representative; jurisprudents are the general representatives of the Immaculate Imam in Shiite literature.
47. Mohammad Baqir al-Sabzevari, *Kifayat al-Ahkam*. Isfahan: Sadr Mahdavi School, 1999, p. 74.
48. Shahid Sani, Zayn al-Din Ali ibn Mushrif al-Amili, *Al-Masalik al-Afham*. Qom: Ma'aref Eslami Inst, 2000, vol. 3, p. 7.
49. Al-Hilli, *Tahrir al-Ahkam*, vol. 2, p. 142.
50. Zayn al-Din al-Amili, *Al-Masalik al-Afham*, vol. 3, p. 7.
51. Abu Ja'far Mohammad al-Tousi, *Al-Mabsout fi Fiqh al-Imamiah*, edited by Mohammad Taqi al-kashfi. Tehran: al-Maktab al-Mortazaviah, 1998, vol. 2, p. 8.
52. Al-Majlesi, *Bihar al-Anwar*, vol. 97, pp. 22–23.
53. Imam Ali, *Nahj al-Balaghah*, Sermon No. 51; Al-Majlesi, *Bihar al-Anwar*, pp. 441–442.
54. Al-Majlesi, *Bihar al-Anwar*, vol. 97, p. 23.
55. Ibid., vol. 97, pp. 7–9.
56. Allameh Hasan bin Yousof al-Hilli, *Qavaied al-Ahkam*. Qom: Al-Nashr al-Islami Inst., 1991, vol. 3, p. 571.
57. Ibid.
58. Ibid., p. 572.
59. Allameh Hasan bin Yousof al-Hilli, *Montaha al-Matlab*, edited by Hasan pishnamaz. Tabriz: Haj Ahmad, 1954, vol. 2, p. 903.
60. Allameh Hasan bin Yousof al-Hilli, *Tazkiraht al-Foqaha*. Maktab al-Razavieh, lithographic print, 1982, vol. 1, p. 457.
61. Ibid., vol. 9, p. 435.
62. Mohammad Ali al-Ansari, *Al-Movsou'aht al-Fiqheyah al-muyasarah*. Qom: Majma al-Fikr al-Islamiah, 1994, vol. 3, p. 22.
63. Al-Feiz al-Kashani, *Al-Tohfaht al-Saneyah*. Handwritten text, written by Abdollah Jazayeri, microfilm, Astan Ghods Library, Mashad, p. 202.
64. Mohammad bin Ali bin Ibrahim al Ehsa'ie Ibn abi Jomhur, *Al-Aqtab al-Fiqheyah Ala' Mazhab al-Imamiah*, edited by Mohammad al-Hason, Qom: Ayatollah Marashi Najafi pub., 1989, p. 105.
65. Shahid Avval, Mohammad bin Jamal al-Din Mecci, *Al-Dorous al-Shar'eyah*. Qom: al-Nashr al-Islamiah Inst., 1991, vol. 2, p. 30.
66. Shahid Avval, Mohammad bin Jamal al-Din Mecci, *Al-Bayan*. Qom: Lithographic print, p. 28.
67. Al-Majlesi, *Bihar al-Anwar*, vol. 32, p. 399.
68. Mohammadi Reishahri, *Mizan al-hikmaht*, vol. 4, p. 2984.
69. Ibid., vol. 3, p. 1849.
70. Al-Hilli, *Tahrir al-Ahkam*, vol. 3, p. 5.
71. Al-Javahiri, *Javahir al-Kalaam*, vol. 21, p. 78.
72. Ibid.

73. Mohamad bin Hasan al-Horr al-Amili, *Vasa'el al-Shi'a ela' Tahsil Masa'el al-Shariah.* Qom: A'l alBait Inst., 1995, vol. 15, pp. 69–70.

74. Imam Ali, *Nahj al-Balagha*, edited by Sobhi Saleh. Qom: Hejrat, 1971, p. 318.

75. Daviad Aaron Showartz, "International and Islamic Law", translation of Zahra Kasmati, in R. Tayeb (ed.) *Terrorism.* Tehran: Nei Pub., 2003, pp. 280–379.

76. An electronic version of the translation of the Qur'an by Marmaduke Mohammad Pickthall is available at ⟨http://www.usc.edu/dept/MSA/quran/⟩ (accessed 21 October 2008).

77. Al-Kho'ei, *Mesbah al-Osoul*, vol. 1, pp. 22, 353.

78. Imam Zayn al-'Abidin, *Al-Sahifa al-Sajjadiyyah.* Qom: Jame'a Modaresin Pub. Co., 1989, p. 106.

79. Sheikh Yousoef al-Bahrani, *Al-Hada'eq al-Nazerah*, edited by Mohamad Taqi al-Iravani. Qom: Jame'a Modaresin Pub. Co., 1985, vol. 18, p. 155.

80. Ibid.

81. Sayyid Mohammad Sadiq Al-Rohani, *Al-Fiqh alosadiq.* Qom: Dar al-Ketab, 1993, vol. 14, p. 293.

82. Al-Majlesi, *Bihar al-Anwar*, vol. 61, p. 110; Mirza Husayn Al-Nouri, *Mostadrak al-Vasa'el.* Beirut: A'l alBait Inst., 1987, vol. 8, p. 262.

83. Al-Majlesi, *Bihar al-Anwar*, vol. 74, p. 145.

84. Ibid., vol. 32, p. 399.

85. Ayatollah Husain Ali Montazeri, "Statement on Islam and Terrorism", 2005, available at ⟨http://www.bbc.co.uk/persian/iran/story/2005/07/050711_mj-montazeri-statement.shtml⟩ (accessed 22 October 2008).

86. Ibid.

87. Al-Tousi, *Al-Nihaya*, p. 298.

88. Al-Majlesi, *Bihar al-Anwar*, vol. 72, p. 289.

89. Ibid., vol. 72, p. 289–290.

90. Ibid., vol. 72, p. 97.

91. Ibid., vol. 72, p. 212.

92. Al-Hilli, *Montaha al-Matlab*, vol. 2, p. 913.

93. Ali Bin al-Husayn Muhaqqiq al-Karaki, *Jame' alMaqasid.* Qom: Al' al-Bait Inst., 1987, vol. 3, p. 388.

94. Al-Majlesi, *Bihar al-Anwar*, vol. 19, pp. 177–178.

95. Al-Hilli, *Tahrir al-Ahkam*, vol. 1, p. 135.

96. Sayyid Ali al-Tabataba'ie, *Riaz al-Masa'el.* Qom: Nashr al-Islami Inst., 1989, vol. 7, p. 504.

97. Abu-Ja'far Mohammad al-Tousi, *Al-Iqtisad al-Hadi ela Tariq al-Rashad.* Qom: al-Maktab Jame'ah Chehelsotun, 1982, p. 313.

98. Sheikh Morteza Al-Ansari, *Al-Makasib.* Qom: Alhadi Inst., 1996, vol. 2, p. 167.

99. Abd al-Aziz bin al-Baraj al-Tarablosi, *Javahir al-Fiqh*, edited by Ibrahim Bahadori. Qom: Jame'a al-Modaresin, 1990, p. 50.

100. Sheikh Ja'far al-Hilli, *Sharaye' al-Islam.* Beirut: al-Vafa' Inst., 1983, vol. 4, p. 971.

101. Al-Hilli, *Montaha al-Matlab*, vol. 2, p. 910.

102. Al-Hilli, *Tazkiraht al-Foqaha*, vol. 1, p. 413.

103. Jarir al-Din Mohammad al-Tabari, *Al-Tarikh al-Tabari.* Beirut: al-A'lami Inst., 1984, vol. 2, p. 321.

104. Al-Majlesi, *Bihar al-Anwar*, vol. 21, p. 60.

105. Based on the old tradition there is much divergence of ideas. For example, Allameh Hilli believes that if professionals and masters of industries, taking part in war, are an exception, the philosophy of war and defence would be meaningless. However, it seems that Allameh Hilli's viewpoint is not correct because the Prophet in this tradi-

tion refers to professionals not directly involved in war, not those directly taking part in war. Al-Hilli, *Tazkiraht al-Foqaha*, vol. 1, p. 412; Al-Javahiri, *Javahir al-Kalaam*, vol. 21, p. 76.

106. Al-Majlesi, *Bihar al-Anwar*, vol. 19, p. 179.
107. Ibid., vol. 97, p. 25.
108. Shahid Sani, Zayn al-Din Ali ibn Mushrif al-Amili, *Masalik al-Afham*. Qom: Ma'aref Islami Inst., 1993, vol. 3, p. 25.
109. Sayyid Ali al-Tabataba'ie, *Riaz al Masa'el*. Qom: Al-albait, 1984, vol. 1, p. 488.
110. Sayyid abu-al-Qasim al-Kho'ei, *Ketab al-Hajj*. Qom: Lotfi Pub. Co., 1987, vol. 5, p. 514.
111. Al-Majlesi, *Bihar al-Anwar*, vol. 21, p. 60.
112. Allameh Hasan al-Hilli, *Tahrir al-Ahkam*. Qom: Maktabat E'temad, 2001, vol. 1, p. 135.
113. Al-Tousi, *Al-Mabsout*, p. 11.
114. Ibn Edris Al-Hilli, *Al-Sara'er*. Qom: Al-Nashr al-Islami Inst., 1990, vol. 2, pp. 7–8.
115. Al-Tabataba'ie, *Riaz al Masa'el*, vol. 7, pp. 4–5.
116. Al-Majlesi, *Bihar al-Anwar*, vol. 34, pp. 13, 16–25.
117. Ibid., vol. 19, p. 179.
118. Al-Hilli, *Tazkiraht al-Foqaha*, vol. 1, p. 413.
119. Abu-al-Salah Al-Halabi, *Al-kafi Fe al-Fiqh*, edited by Reza Ostadi. Isfahan: Maktab Amir al Mo'menin, 1982, p. 256.
120. In this chapter, the issue of prisoners of war rights is not discussed, since it is a broad area that requires more focused research.

10

Norms of war in Sunni Islam

Amira Sonbol

Islamic communities, like other religious groups, over the centuries have developed laws and traditions pertaining to war and peace that can generally be referred to as ethics of war. Based primarily on the Qur'an, Islam's holy book, Hadith literature (oral traditions relating to the words and deeds of the Prophet Muhammad), *fiqh* (jurisprudence), politics and decisions necessitated by events with which these communities had to deal, and theological interpretations (*fatawi*) of religious and political leaders have all contributed to discourses on Islamic war ethics. As a body of collected wisdom, Islamic laws and traditions defining "just war" have received something of a consensus among Islamic scholars today and can be formulated into a classic interpretation of Islam's outlook on war and the handling of issues related to it. Still there have been and continue to be large disparities, historically and contemporarily, between various sects and between groups within the same sect. Put differently, although Islamic war ethics are generally presented as a finished product with principles set by the Qur'an and prophetic traditions, war ethics, like other discourses, are closely tied to the historical conditions that produce them. This does not mean that there are not consistent references and beliefs that represent essential points that appear in the writings of important thinkers over the ages. These principles exist and constitute the basic framework of war ethics and what is discussed today as just war theory. The point is that, notwithstanding the general acceptance among Muslims that principles of war were defined solely by God and the Prophet Muhammad, Islamic ethics have actually developed over history

World religions and norms of war, Popovski, Reichberg and Turner (eds),
United Nations University Press, 2009, ISBN 978-92-808-1163-6

and continue to be in process, and are developing today in various directions. But it is in this belief in the unchanging and absolutist framework of just war theory that various groups, including the most radical, find fertile ground to cultivate their movements.

This chapter considers the history and contemporary nature of the ethics of war in Islam, examining how they bear on war between Islamic and non-Islamic peoples. Hence the complex problems of civil war, or war among Muslims, are beyond the scope of the chapter, because to do justice to these questions would require a separate comprehensive study. The chapter not only takes into account historical sources, but also examines the views held by Muslims today on the question of war between Muslims and non-Muslims, with a necessary focus on non-Muslims in the West.

Deconstructing the discursive history of the ethics of just war in Islam is one way of explaining baffling contradictions between what Islam is purported to say and how various political groups act. Simply put, the problem can be located in the belief that there is a classic theory of war ethics that has been understood and accepted throughout Islamic history. One can make the general comment that, like other world religions, ethical discourses have developed with human history. There are basic principles and these principles are quite widespread among major religious groups, beginning with the protection of life and respect for human dignity. This joins Islam with Christianity, Judaism and Hinduism. Protecting human life, the body and soul that God has gifted us with, is a first lesson taught to a Muslim as he/she learns to walk. Considering life as a valuable gift from God and protecting the body from harm is a command in the Qur'an and in its dietary regimen, sexual ethics and communal relations. A close second is protecting the helpless; here the Qur'an and Hadith are expansive in their commands to feed orphans and take care of wayfarers, protecting them in every possible way, including going to war – as will be discussed later in this chapter. Protecting the wealth of orphans and the helpless is central to the Qur'anic text and this protection extends to pre-modern Sharia courts, where judges (*qadis*) take the child's welfare into consideration in any marital disputes, handing over the guardianship of children to mothers when it is to their benefit, notwithstanding what the different schools of Islamic law have to say about guardianship. Protection of the weak and helpless seems to have been the guiding principle rather than *fiqh* interpretations.[1] But it is not only the young who are to be protected; old people too are among those who need protection, particularly during war.

Included among those to be protected in war would be old people, children, the helpless and the handicapped, none of whom are subject to war. Among this group would be the *dhimmis* (non-Muslims), who paid the *jizyah* (a poll tax levied on non-Muslims) in place of participating in war. They were considered protected people and came into the group to be protected by the Muslim community. Perhaps it should also be pointed out that the wounded among enemy warriors also fit within the category of helpless, and extending medical care to the wounded among the enemy, even if they participated in battle, becomes an essential part of Islamic war ethics and fits with the ultimate purpose of protecting life. Similarly, Islam advocates humane treatment of prisoners who are un-armed and therefore rendered helpless. In the same vein, the poisoning of water-wells is completely forbidden, as are the poisoning of food sup-plies and the destruction of homes as methods of waging war. Such ac-tions jeopardize life and are therefore forbidden. Also forbidden are outright massacres and punitive punishment meted out to the kin and tribes of enemies, although punitive war to take back what has been usurped is not only acceptable in Islam but actually a duty. However, war cannot be outright war but must be limited, as precise as possible, and directed at an enemy who wages war against a community, which has the responsibility to retaliate.

Waging war

The following discussion about "waging war" makes a clear distinction between the word *jihad* and the word *qital* – or *qatilu* as it usually ap-pears in the Qur'an – and how the words are differently used in the Qur'an. "Jihad" has the meaning of "strive", which opens the door to generalizations and has therefore been the focus of historical interpreta-tions, particularly when Qur'anic support is sought. "*Qatilu*" is straight-forward in its meaning, which is "fight" or "go to war", and it is the actual word used in the Qur'an whenever the call to arms is made. The usual explanation for jihad is that it is a defensive mechanism, but actu-ally it is explicitly proactive, which makes it a better reference for those looking for legitimacy to go to war for various reasons, as long as the word "jihad" is narrowed down to mean "go to war for the sake of God". In fact, all the Qur'anic *ayas* (sentences) that use the word "jihad" use it with the meaning of to "strive" in the way of God and in a context and language that do not include actions pertaining to war or to killing, except if such action is warranted as part of "striving" in the way of God or in support of the Prophet Muhammad or the Muslim community. Good examples include:

> Those who believed and those who suffered exile and fought [*jahadu*] (and strove and struggled) in the path of God, they have the hope of the Mercy of God. And God is Oft-forgiving, Most Merciful. (Al-Baqara 2:218)[2]

Here the reference is to those who went on *hijra* (migration) from Mecca to Medina to escape persecution by the non-believers. They built a new Muslim community in Medina, making sacrifices in the process and fighting against those who would stop them.

> Did ye think that ye would enter Heaven without Allah testing those of you who fought hard (in His cause) and remained steadfast? (Al-Imran 3:142)

Here the Qur'an makes clear that Muslims are expected to strive for the sake of God and that will be the way to heaven. This type of general statement, because it does not give explicit or specific meaning to what is being referred to except that it is "His cause", opens the door to all sorts of speculation regarding what striving for "His cause" means. It could be internal striving to be a better Muslim, striving to create a strong believing community, or fighting for whatever His cause is determined to be – and that becomes open to place and time and the particular ideology.

> Not equal are those believers who sit (at home) and receive no hurt, and those who strive and fight in the cause of God with their goods and their persons. God hath granted a grade higher to those who strive and fight with their goods and persons than to those who sit (at home). Unto all (in Faith) Hath God promised good: But those who strive and fight Hath He distinguished above those who sit (at home) by a special reward. (Al-Nisa' 4:95)

Here the connection between those whom God favours and those who strive using their wealth and themselves (*jihad al-nafs wal-mal*) is made clearer in the Qur'an's comparison between those who stay put and do not become engaged in the way of God and those who are active in pursuing the way of God by giving of themselves and their wealth. Jihad, or striving, using one's wealth and person is mentioned many times in the Qur'an and the meaning is clear that Muslims have to work for the good and security of their community in every way possible and particularly in applying their own labour and in spending their money. Applying one's labour, i.e. striving with one's person, includes joining in the fight with the Prophet against Islam's enemies. This inclusivity is seen in the following lines:

> Those who believed, and adopted exile, and fought [*jahidu*] for the Faith, with their property and their persons, in the cause of Allah, as well as those who gave (them) asylum and aid, – these are (all) friends and protectors one of another. As to those who believed but came not into exile, ye owe no duty of protection to them until they come into exile; but if they seek your aid in religion, it is your duty to help them, except against a people with whom ye have a treaty of mutual alliance. And (remember) Allah seeth all that ye do. (Al-Anfal 8:72)

Here the lines are more explicit, speaking of the mutual protection that is due to those who migrate and put themselves in jeopardy in the cause of God. Here the Qur'an calls upon Muslims to help them, for they succour one another, and asks that help should be extended to them against any enemy except those who have entered into an alliance with the Muslim community. The meaning of "jihad" as fighting is clear here, although it still remains within the parameters of working for the good of the community and its security. The same meaning is conveyed, if with a different nuance, in 8:74, which points to asylum and assistance as forms of jihad, which gives a rounded meaning to the issue of protection and working towards the establishment of a community at a time when it was beleaguered, i.e. following the *hijra* of Muslims from Mecca to Medina in 622 to escape persecution.

> Those who believe, and adopt exile, and fight [*jahidu*] for the Faith, in the cause of Allah as well as those who give (them) asylum and aid, – these are (all) in very truth the Believers: for them is the forgiveness of sins and a provision most generous. (Al-Anfal 8:74)

The meaning changes perceptibly in other *ayas*, where the emphasis shifts away from physical defence or armed action.

> And if any strive (with might and main), they do so for their own souls: for Allah is free of all needs from all creation. (Al-'Ankabut 29:6)

> We have enjoined on man kindness to parents; but if they (either of them) strive (to force) thee to join with Me (in worship) anything of which thou hast no knowledge, obey them not. Ye have (all) to return to me, and I will tell you (the truth) of all that ye did. (Al-'Ankabut 29:8)

> And those who strive in Our (cause), – We will certainly guide them to Our Paths; For verily Allah is with those who do right. (Al-'Ankabut 29:69)

> But if they strive to make thee join in worship with Me things of which thou hast no knowledge, obey them not; yet bear them company in this life with justice (and consideration), and follow the way of those who turn to me (in love): in the end the return of you all is to Me, and I will tell you the truth (and meaning) of all that ye did. (Luqman 31:15)

> And We shall try you until We test those among you who strive their utmost and persevere in patience; and We shall try your reported (mettle). (Muhammad 47:31)

> O ye who believe! Take not my enemies and yours as friends (or protectors), – offering them (your) love, even though they have rejected the Truth that has

come to you, and have (on the contrary) driven out the Prophet and yourselves (from your homes), (simply) because ye believe in Allah your Lord! If ye have come out to strive in My Way and to seek My Good Pleasure, (take them not as friends), holding secret converse of love (and friendship) with them: for I know full well all that ye conceal and all that ye reveal. And any of you that does this has strayed from the Straight Path. (Mumtahinah 60:1)

These lines of the Qur'an speak of personal trials and the struggle to stay loyal to the faith in the face of temptations and pressures by friends and relatives who woo Muslims away from God's faith. They call upon Muslims to recognize Muslims as their friends and not to befriend those who are enemies of Islam, not to be hypocritical in dealing with enemies of Islam and always to follow the right path and the good of the community. In other words, Muslims should strive to work for the good of the community because that is the road to salvation by which the soul redeems itself. Ultimately it is the soul that follows the way of God that is saved through God's will. There is little about armed action here, even though the lines include various meanings of jihad as striving to do God's will, responding to the tests that God has placed in the way of Muslims, staying within the community and not befriending its enemies, and fighting for one's soul or salvation.

As for the term "qatilu", when it appears in the Qur'an it is always used in the context of some action dealing with war, fighting or killing. The language and context are quite explicit, involving taking up arms in the defence of the community.

Although this chapter deals with waging war in the Sunni tradition, there is a realization that, notwithstanding doctrinal and theological differences built primarily on the separate histories of the Sunni and Shia communities, there is today a strong rapprochement between them that can be dated back to the Iranian Revolution and the subsequent increased presence of the United States in the affairs of Arab countries and the aggression of first Israel and then the United States against Arab lands. The meeting of minds regarding the struggle for freedom among Muslims today and against whom this struggle is to be waged is eliminating the doctrinal differences between Shias and Sunnis, even while using sectarian differences to achieve political ends is becoming a greater threat to the stability of the Middle East region. I shall first discuss the classic Sunni approach to war ethics and then show how the ethics of war are closely connected with the historical process and the historical context during which new formulations of war and the handling of war were made. Since the issue is an important one in the current war against terrorism, the discussion will include war ethics formulated by major players in this drama today.

Why wage war?

In the Islamic tradition, war is waged only for a just reason. There are no early debates that one can categorize as "just war theory" because the presumption is that a war is waged only with justification and the justification is built on the experience of people regarding what is right or wrong (*halal* or *haram*). Basically war is waged against oppressors by those whom they oppress or those who are allied to them:

> Permission (to fight) is given to those upon whom war [*yuqatiluna*] is made because they are oppressed, and most surely Allah is well able to assist them. (Qur'an 22:39)[3]

Fighting those "who fight against you" has to be seen as the basic reason for Muslims to go to war and it is tied to the treatment of Muslims at the hands of the *kuffar* (non-believers) in Mecca during the early years of Islam when Muslims were persecuted for having accepted Islam as their religion and Muhammad as their Prophet. The order to "fight against those who fight against you" is not only seen as giving legitimacy to the waging of war in self-defence; it is actually a duty to undertake such a war. The Qur'an asks those who do not take up arms why they do not do so and calls on their chivalry and courage to fight back.

> And be not weak hearted in pursuit of the enemy; if you suffer pain, then surely they (too) suffer pain as you suffer pain, and you hope from Allah what they do not hope; and Allah is Knowing, Wise. (Qur'an 4:104)

Although the context for the verse may have been contemporary to the early Muslim community's experience, the Qur'anic lines do not differentiate between external and internal aggression, and thereby the door to just war is opened to fight against not only external enemies but also internal enemies who act wrongfully, making it the right of the oppressed to fight back.

Framing the meaning of aggression that makes it a requirement to wage war, the Qur'an is explicit about the necessity to go to war particularly against those who cause the expulsion of Muslims or other helpless people from their homes. This call has been central to the waging of war in Islamic history – from the need for Muslims to flee their homes in Mecca owing to the oppression by the Quraysh (the ruling tribe of Mecca at the time of the birth of the Prophet Muhammad), to the present-day expulsion and homelessness of Palestinians, whatever their religious affiliation.

Those who have been expelled from their homes without a just cause except that they say: Our Lord is Allah. And had there not been Allah's repelling some people by others, certainly there would have been pulled down cloisters and churches and synagogues and mosques in which Allah's name is much remembered; and surely Allah will help him who helps His cause; most surely Allah is Strong, Mighty. (Qur'an 22:40)

Two important principles are laid out in 22:40: one concerns "expulsion from their homes"; the second, "protecting places of worship" without which religion and worship of God would not survive. That expulsion from one's home is considered to be the greatest of harms is central to Islam's view of the right to fight back. This verse also makes it a duty to wage war to stop the destruction of places of worship, a great abomination in Islam that would mean God's name would not be "remembered".

But it is not only for home and faith that war is waged. Essential to Islam is support for the weak, the orphaned and the homeless. The Qur'an is full of exhortations to feed the poor and the homeless, to look after the orphan and his property, and to take care of the weak, the infirm and the old. The same support is extended to those who are helpless in the face of aggression. It is a duty of Muslims to fight for those who are unable to defend themselves.

And what reason have you that you should not fight [*la tuqatiluna*] in the way of Allah and of the weak among the men and the women and the children, (of) those who say: Our Lord! (Qur'an 4:75)

Fighting for the weak and the helpless is defined by the Qur'an from within the parameters of "fighting for the sake of God". This can be read in various ways and opens the door to waging offensive war for the purpose of protecting the oppressed among not only Muslims but all people of the book (Muslims, Christians and Jews).

Those who believe fight [*yuqatiluna*] in the way of Allah, and those who disbelieve fight in the way of the Shaitan. Fight therefore against the friends of the Shaitan; surely the strategy of the Shaitan is weak. (Qur'an 4:76)

In other words, according to the Qur'an, war is waged for self-defence, defence of one's faith, in support of those oppressed and who lose their homes, and to ward off evil, symbolized here by the Shaitan, an image often used to describe enemies of Islam.

The Qur'an also details what is forbidden in waging war:

And fight [*waqatiloohum*] in the way of Allah with those who fight with you, and do not exceed the limits, surely Allah does not love those who exceed the limits.

And kill them wherever you find them, and drive them out from whence they drove you out, and persecution [*al-Fitnah*] is severer than slaughter; and do not fight with them at the Sacred Mosque [al-Masjid al-Haram, in Mecca], until they fight with you in it, but if they do fight you, then slay them; such is the recompense of the unbelievers.

But if they desist [fighting], then surely Allah is Forgiving, Merciful. (Qur'an 2:190–192)

By "do not exceed the limits" is meant to wage what we can call limited war. Waging outright and comprehensive war appears to have no basis in Qur'anic text; on the contrary, conflicts were seen as having clear boundaries, waged to ward off aggression and undertaken in a humane way, sparing those who do not themselves participate in the war (Qur'an 60:8). The limits are further set in the demand to "drive them out from whence they drove you out" (2:191). Fighting back and regaining homes from which one has been expelled represent just reasons for going to war and for killing enemies "wherever you find them". There are, however, places where war is forbidden, but not when "they fight with you". Being attacked, expelled from the home or in danger justifies fighting back whatever the place or time. Fighting ends once the enemy stops attacking; those are clearly set limits.

The words used in the various *ayas* quoted above in reference to fighting or going to war derive from the word *qatilu*, or battling. I have included the exact word used in square brackets so as to differentiate it from the usage of the word "jihad" when it appears. As 47:4 illustrates, the use of the word *qatilu* or its derivatives is always used within a clear context, when actual war or another form of battling/fighting is actually taking place.

So when you meet in battle those who disbelieve, then smite the necks until when you have overcome them, then make (them) prisoners, and afterwards either set them free as a favor or let them ransom (themselves) until the war terminates. That (shall be so); and if Allah had pleased He would certainly have exacted what is due from them, but that He may try some of you by means of others; and (as for) those who are slain [*qutilu*] in the way of Allah, He will by no means allow their deeds to perish. (Qur'an 47:4)

The *aya* outlines the steps to be taken in battle. Believers are to fight hard until they are victorious, after which they should no longer kill the enemy but are ordered to take them as prisoners to be set free later or to be ransomed. Fighting only as long as you need to is urged, from which it is understood that war should be limited and restricted to achieving victory with minimum loss of life, and that continuing to slaughter after victory becomes an offence to God. From this can be understood Islam's approach to war as being wageable only when it becomes imperative for reasons focused on aggression and harm to self and to the helpless. War for revenge or for acquisitive reasons finds no place in this discourse.

As for peace, the Qur'an makes it clear that peace is preferable to waging war:

> Except those who reach a people between whom and you there is an alliance, or who come to you, their hearts shrinking from fighting you [*yuqatilukum*] or fighting [*yuqatiluna*] their own people; and if Allah had pleased, He would have given them power over you, so that they should have certainly fought you [*falaqatalukum*]; therefore if they withdraw from you and do not fight you and offer you peace, then Allah has not given you a way [to war] against them. (Qur'an 4:90)

The exhortation to work for peace when it is possible is very clearly stated here: "then Allah has not given you a way [to war] against them". It is repeated in 2:193: "And fight with them until there is no persecution, and religion should be only for Allah, but if they desist, then there should be no hostility except against the oppressors." Fighting oppressors and against only those who wage war first is made very clear, as is waging peace in preference to war.

> And if they incline to peace, then incline to it and trust in Allah; surely He is the Hearing, the Knowing. (Qur'an 8:61)

As to those who give support to enemies, the Qur'an is clear. Those who support your enemy become your enemy and you are to fight against them:

> Allah does not forbid you respecting those who have not made war against you on account of (your) religion, and have not driven you forth from your homes, that you show them kindness and deal with them justly; surely Allah loves the doers of justice. (Qur'an 60:8)

This *aya* is followed immediately by another making the parallel statement:

> Allah only forbids you respecting those who made war upon you on account of (your) religion, and drove you forth from your homes and backed up (others) in your expulsion, that you make friends with them, and whoever makes friends with them, these are the unjust. (Qur'an 60:9)

According to these two *ayas*, it would be forbidden to wage offensive war against those who had not acted as aggressors first, because there had to have been reasons to go to war against them and that would be the case if they had waged war or helped those who waged war against the believers or assisted others in dispossessing them of their homes. As 60:9 clarifies, God actually forbids Muslims from associating with those who have waged war against Muslims and driven Muslims from their homes or helped others in any of these activities. The *aya* also calls upon Muslims to stand against those who assist their enemy in fighting them. These lines are extremely important to Muslims' attitude towards those who disrespect Islam and to Muslims' response to those who attack Islam physically or vocally. There is almost a duty not only to end any alliance with Islam's enemies who fight against Muslim communities but also to stand against those who, by showing little respect for Muslims, become allies of Islam's enemies.

The significance of these lines to the contemporary situation cannot be lost, especially in regard to the Palestinians, their treatment by Israel and the unconditional support that the United States grants Israel. Members of extremist and terrorist groups need do very little to garner support among the Muslim masses in their fight against Israel and the United States. The same can be said in regard to the 2006 invasion by Israeli troops of southern Lebanon and the massive destruction meted out to its inhabitants – destruction of their homes and forced migration to the north. No matter how temporary this dispossession, it reminded Muslims of what happened to Palestinians in 1948 and their massive forced migration. Although Israel is the recognized enemy, there is some understanding regarding their position, which is clearly stated as acquiring land they claim from biblical times for the Jewish people. Understanding does not mean accepting, however, and particularly not accepting the total destruction of the Palestinian people or their daily suffering and destruction of life and home, exactly as described by the Qur'an as causes for waging war. The position of the United States becomes even more serious since, in the eyes of many Muslims, it has no reason to be so partial, particularly in light of the fact that the side it supports is overwhelmingly strong. Read literally and applied directly to the contemporary historical setting (by bin Laden and others like him), the exhortations of 60:9 appear to express a duty to fight the United States, a country now placed within the parameters of the Shaitan (4:76), an image popularized by Ayatollah Khomeini. This also explains the extreme reactions to Salman Rushdie, the Danish cartoon incident and Pope Benedict's Regensburg remarks about Islam, however academic and misunderstood they may have been.[4]

Caliph Abu Bakr, who followed immediately after the Prophet Muhammad in leading the young Muslim *umma* (community), summarized Islamic war ethics with the following words:

Do not commit treachery or deviate from the right path. You must not mutilate dead bodies. Neither kill a child, nor a woman, nor an aged man. Bring no harm to the trees, nor burn them with fire, especially those which are fruitful. Slay not any of the enemy's flock, save for your food. You are likely to pass by people who have devoted their lives to monastic services; leave them alone.[5]

The often-mentioned ideal of Muslim ethics in waging war is the example set by Salah al-Din al-Ayyubi, Sultan of Egypt and Syria, after he captured Jerusalem from the Crusaders in 1187. Even though the Crusaders were hardly the exemplary chivalrous knights depicted by the troubadour poets of medieval Europe (having committed atrocities against the inhabitants of the Holy Lands with no differentiation between Muslim, Christian or Jew), Salah al-Din prohibited any actions of vengeance against them, and those who wished to leave the city were allowed to leave, the rich among them being ransomed.

Discourses on war and ethics

The Qur'an's classic formulation of the reasons for waging war and how to wage war became the subject of interpretation as the Islamic *umma* expanded out of Arabia into the surrounding territories, bringing various cultures and peoples within its fold. As situations became more complex, there came a need to try to understand and interpret what had been set up during the time of the Prophet Muhammad through Qur'anic interpretation and following the Sunna (traditions) of the Prophet. This was not easy and, as might be expected, interpretations that may have followed a textual analysis fraught with pitfalls led to applications of war ethics far removed from the basic spirit of compassion, protection and conciliation that characterizes the lines of the Qur'an dealing with war. Problems arose almost immediately during the Ridda wars (wars of apostasy) of 632–664, fought in Arabia against tribes that had given their allegiance to the young Muslim *umma* at the time of the Prophet Muhammad but had reneged after his death. The Ridda wars made it clear that Jahiliya (the period before the rise of Islam) was still alive in Arabia as tribes and clans fought one another.

Perhaps one significant example may be used here to illustrate the type of situation that faced the new *umma* and led to interpretations of the Qur'an and the Prophet's Sunna by those who followed him as leaders of the Muslim *umma*. This example involves Khalid ibn al-Walid, the "sword of Islam", the man who led the Muslim armies in the Ridda wars and the conquest of Syria. During the Prophet's life, Khalid led a *ghazwa* (raid) against the Banu Jadhimah, who he persuaded to disarm and embrace Islam rather than face battle against him; then Khalid killed some of them. This was Jahili practice by which an enemy could become an ally or *mawla*. The Prophet had urged there should be no compulsion in Islam and here was a situation where compulsion could be said to have been used to create Medina's political hegemony over Arabia, if not necessarily religious hegemony. The Prophet's response on hearing what had taken place was to disown Khalid's actions, thereby setting the basis for the treatment of prisoners that forbade harming them. The Prophet died soon after and Khalid committed the same act, this time against Malik ibn Nuwayrah and his followers, who had committed *ridda* (breaking with Islam) by breaking with Medina and becoming its enemy after Muhammad's death. Khalid fought Malik and then imprisoned him after he and his companions surrendered their weapons. The day after this surrender took place, Malik and his companions were found dead and, on hearing about this, the Caliph Abu Bakr sent for Khalid to answer charges against him. Khalid justified what had taken place on the basis that he had given orders to his men to "warm them", meaning to keep the prisoners warm during the night, but that, owing to the different dialects spoken by Arabs, his men understood the words to mean "kill them". Here the essential condition that prisoners of war were to be treated with dignity was reconfirmed, even though Khalid's excuse was acceptable to Abu Bakr. Later, when 'Umar bin al-Khattab became Caliph he removed Khalid from leadership of the Muslim armies even though the conquest of Syria and Iraq was under way, a sign that 'Umar saw Khalid in a very different light than did Abu Bakr.

Discourses regarding waging war and confirming Islamic war ethics were further elaborated as the Islamic *umma* expanded outside of Arabia, bringing different cultures and peoples under its hegemony and becoming the leading world power of the medieval period. It was natural that the reasons for waging war and the actual conduct of war would change with the changing context in which Islam found itself. This continued to happen after the Islamic world succumbed to outside invasion and imperialism at the dawn of modernism, and continues today in a global world in which the clash between East and West is becoming a global phenomenon.

Very early on, Hadith literature expanded on the meaning of war and about the reasons to wage just war. It is here that we begin to see reference to the word "jihad" as meaning waging war, so that, even though the Qur'an uses "jihad" with a different meaning, less than 200 years later the term "jihad" became synonymous with waging war. This move is significant because the Qur'an urges jihad as almost a sixth pillar for Muslims and it is used as a duty in a proactive way, requiring a good believer to act in the indicated way. This is not the same as the actual word used in the Qur'an for waging battle, i.e. *qatilu*, which is used within a reactive context, requiring Muslims to undertake self-defence once attacked. that is, it is conditional on previous aggression against the Muslim community and its allies, and to protect and fight for those who have been driven out of their homes. As mentioned above, the word "jihad" is used in the Qur'an when it talks about a person "striving" in the way of God, as in spreading the message of Islam, trying to be a better Muslim, or working hard to protect the community against unbelievers, as the following quotes illustrate:

> Those who believed and fled (their homes), and strove hard in Allah's way with their property and their souls, are much higher in rank with Allah; and those are they who are the achievers (of their objects). (Qur'an 9:20; Shakir translation)

> And whoever strives hard [*jahada*], he strives only [*fa inama yujahid*] for his own soul; most surely Allah is Self-sufficient, above (needs of) the worlds. (Qur'an 29:6; Shakir translation)

> O Prophet, strive hard [*jahid*] against the unbelievers and the hypocrites, and be unyielding to them [*aghluth 'alayhim*]; and their abode is hell, and evil is the destination. (Qur'an 9:73; Shakir translation)

> Therefore listen not to the Unbelievers, but strive [*wajahidhum*] against them with the utmost strenuousness, with the (Qur'an). (Qur'an 25:52, Yusuf Ali translation)

> "Surely those who believed and those who fled (their home) and strove hard [*jahadu*] in the way of Allah these hope for the mercy of Allah and Allah is Forgiving, Merciful. (Qur'an 2:218; Shakir translation)

As explained earlier, in *ayas* that deal with the word "jihad" or its derivatives, the word means "strive" or "try hard" or "try to the best of your abilities", usually with the intention to work hard in the way of God, to become better Muslims, to serve the community, and so on. There is no mention of killing, "smite the necks" or doing "battle", as in the *ayas* that use the word *qatilu*. Rather, the meaning leads in another direction, such as "migration"[6] or "spending in God's way", i.e. spending your property and wealth to better the Muslim community. There are lines that are vague enough to open "jihad" up to mean the waging of war, for example: "They do not ask leave of you who believe in Allah and the latter day (to stay away) from striving hard with their property and their persons, and Allah knows those who guard (against evil)" (Qur'an 9:44). These lines have been used popularly as calling for fighting or waging war as a jihad, yet nowhere is there any reference to waging war, as in the case when the word *qatilu* or its derivatives is used.

This lack of differentiation can be traced back to Hadith literature, which uses the word "jihad" in many ways but usually in reference to war.

> Narrated by Ibn 'Umar ... Allah's Apostle said: "*I have been ordered (by Allah) to fight against the people until they testify that none has the right to be worshipped but Allah and that Muhammad is Allah's Apostle,* and offer the prayers perfectly and give the obligatory charity, so if they perform that, *then they save their lives and property from me* except for Islamic laws and then their reckoning (accounts) will be done by Allah."[7]

This Hadith conveys the message that jihad is to be waged against the unbelievers until they accept Islam. The Hadith is based on Prophetic Sunna as related through a Hadith that is clearly in contradiction to the *ayas* quoted above (which permit war only for the purpose of self-defence or to keep the houses of religious groups open), to Qur'anic demands for respect for people of the Book and forbidding the spread of evil in the world ("If anyone slew a person – unless it be for murder or for spreading mischief in the land – it would be as if he slew the whole people"; Qur'an 5:32, Yusuf Ali translation), and to Prophetic Hadiths that there is no compulsion in religion.

> Narrated Abdullah ibn Abbas:
>
> When the children of a woman (in pre-Islamic days) did not survive, she took a vow on herself that if her child survives, she would convert it a Jew. When Banu an-Nadir were expelled (from Arabia), there were some children of the Ansar (Helpers) among them. They said: We shall not leave our children. So Allah the Exalted revealed; "Let there be no compulsion in religion. Truth stands out clear from error."[8]

Even though Hadith literature is often contradictory, it seems to be the reference of choice among political and theological thinkers, particularly during periods of crisis in Islamic history when there was a greater need to develop a theology fitting the needs of the Muslim community. A good example here is the development of ideas regarding jihad into discussions by medieval Muslim thinkers differentiating between the abode of Islam (*dar al-Islam*) and the abode of war (*dar al-harb*) during the eighth to the tenth centuries. This occurred at a time when Islam was on the offensive and expanding into other territories. Medieval theologians saw Islam as God's way of establishing Muslim hegemony over the world, as a way of spreading Islam. *Dar al-Islam* (house/abode/land of Islam) was differentiated from *dar al-harb* (house/land of war or where war can be waged) in these medieval discourses by the establishment of Islamic law in one and its lack in the other. Considering their belief in the superiority of Islamic law, they saw it as striving in the way of God to spread Islamic law to those who lack it, through peaceful means if possible but with the use of force if necessary. Without Islamic law there could not be an equitable and just community, and chaos and immorality would reign. Therefore it became the duty of *dar al-Islam* to spread its word.

By the thirteenth century the discourse had changed, and discussions differentiated between two types, the "greater" jihad and the "lesser" jihad, in a discourse that is talked about by Muslim theologians today as the way jihad was always supposed to be. This discourse became particularly popular with the beginning of weakness experienced by the Abbasid empire (749–1250) and particularly after the mid-thirteenth-century Mongol invasion. This discourse was popularized into theory by Ahmad ibn Taymiyya (1263–1328), whose writings have had a deep influence on key thinkers in Islamic history such as Ibn Kathir and Muhammad ibn Abdal-Wahhab, the founder of Wahhabism. Ibn Taymiyya's ideas are central to Salafi movements (movements calling for a return to the practices of the early Muslim community during the lifetime of the Prophet Muhammad and his companions) and constitute an important source for radical movements today.

Before Ibn Taymiyya, Muslims, particularly Sufis, divided jihad into "greater jihad" – seen as a spiritual form of jihad of the self (*jihad-al-nafs*) in which the Muslim tried to cleanse his soul, find his way to God and follow the rightful path – and a "lesser jihad" – seen as a violent form of jihad in which holy war is waged on Islam's enemies. Ibn Taymiyya attacked this interpretation, declaring that the greater jihad was to carry arms in the cause of God by fighting the enemies of Islam. He saw that fighting against the unbelievers was the most honoured of deeds, and jihad was essential for Islam and a command for all Muslims. That does not mean that Ibn Taymiyya did not consider jihad of the self as a greater jihad; it is the weight that he gave to the two forms that is important and has had a deep and long-lasting influence. Both types were seen to be striving in the way of God, which is a reading that takes the Qur'anic meaning of jihad into the category of waging war which, as explained earlier, the Qur'an had been explicit about only as *qatilu*. The proactive or dynamic call for action that is presented by the *wa jahidu* and the later interpretation, according to which *jahidu* essentially means war against unbelievers, as presented by the Hadiths, have given the word "jihad" a radical meaning that is open to further interpretation in various directions contradictory to its original connotations. This was to be expected since, as this chapter emphasizes, historical context has been the moulder of these ideas. The case of Ibn Taymiyya is a clear example given the political situation of the Islamic world at the time in which he lived: the Mongols had invaded, destroyed and ruled over the world he knew. Ibn Taymiyya himself had participated in the battles waged against the Mongol invaders, and he saw at first hand how these non-Muslims showed no respect for Islam or its houses of worship.

The Mongol invasion and the establishment of the Ilkanid dynasty (1265–1335) as an Islamic dynasty were not the only problem facing the Islamic world during the lifetime of Ibn Taymiyya. Crusaders were another problem, and the connection with an aggressive West as *dar al-harb* remains important to those who follow his doctrines. But it is the internal threat to what Ibn Taymiyya saw as pure Islam that continues to have the greatest impact on concepts of jihad today. With external pressures from Crusaders and Mongols, and particularly with the settlement of Mongols within Islamic communities, conversion to Islam accelerated significantly throughout the thirteenth century in various parts of the Islamic world of that age. Conversion meant the entry of new peoples into Islam, peoples who brought with them new cultural baggage, including traditions, religious concepts, philosophical outlooks on life and creation, and laws. It was in these new cultures and traditions that Ibn Taymiyya found the greatest threat – what he calls *bid'a/bida'* (pl.) or innovations alien to Islam – to his ideas regarding the purity of Islam. In his hands, the concept of *dar al-harb* is extended to *dar al-Islam*, a concept that became critical to contemporary radical Muslim groups and was significantly expounded upon by Osama bin Laden.

The similarities between the age of Ibn Taymiyya and the age of bin Laden can be easily exaggerated. Nevertheless, during both periods the Islamic world was occupied by foreign troops and cultural diffusion from non-Islamic sources threatened the stability of Islamic states and societies' adherence to what was seen as a threat to Islam itself. This internal threat arose not only from alien rulers who did not follow the precepts of Islamic Sharia, but also from dangerous cultural mores (worship of "idols" – *shirk*), ideologies such as nationalism or capitalism, or the application of non-Islamic laws. As in the case of Ibn Taymiyya, modern fundamentalist Hanbali thinkers demand a return to pure Islam, which they interpret as a return to the practices of the *umma* of the Prophet during his lifetime and the *umma* that immediately followed him under the Sublime Caliphates (632–662) of Abu Bakr al-Siddiq, 'Umar ibn al-Khattab, 'Uthman ibn 'Affan and 'Ali ibn abi-Talib. This has been extended to include worthy Caliphs such as 'Umar ibn 'Abdal-'Aziz, who tried to stem changes in the Umayyad state by returning to a purer form of Islam using various methods, including separating Muslims from non-Muslim communities of the Umayyad empire.

A number of key words familiar to Islamic fundamentalists today are traceable back to Ibn Taymiyya. Words such as *Tawhid* (God's unity),

shirk (idolatry) and *bid'a* (innovations) have become central to fundamentalist discourses since that time. For Ibn Taymiyya, the state's primary purpose is to ensure that Muslims can practise their faith so as
to ensure salvation. To achieve this, the mosques have to be maintained,
Islamic law applied and morals upheld. Since absolute authority belongs
to God, with whom no other can compete nor any ideology be confused,
state and religion become inseparable in their purpose to institute God's
law, that being the only way to ensure human salvation. Under such conditions, the state's coercive power becomes essential for the establishment and maintenance of discipline and order, without which mosques
could not be opened and the practice of Islam carried out. The leader in
such a context becomes the shadow of God on earth, forbidding evil and
instituting good in the way God would have wanted him to. But a leader
cannot succeed on his own; he can do that only with the help of the
learned, who interpret the law. Here is born the symbiotic relationship
between the *ulama* class to which Ibn Taymiyya and later Muhammad
ibn 'Abdal-Wahhab belonged, and the political class, which had no legitimacy to rule except through the support of the *ulama*, who legitimated
this rulership if it fitted with the precepts of the Sharia, or at least what
they considered to be the demands of the Sharia. As protectors of God's
divine law, the *ulama* were made central to politics.

Conclusions

In a 1998 interview, Osama bin Laden was asked about his call to Muslims "to take up arms against America in particular". His answer went
as follows:

> The call to wage war against America was made because America has spear-
> headed the crusade against the Islamic nation, sending tens of thousands of its
> troops to the land of the two Holy Mosques [meaning the Hijaz in Saudi Ara-
> bia] over and above its meddling in its affairs and its politics, and its support of
> the oppressive, corrupt and tyrannical regime that is in control. These are the
> reasons behind the singling out of America as a target. And not exempt of re-
> sponsibility are those Western regimes whose presence in the region offers sup-
> port to the US troops there. We know at least one reason behind the symbolic
> participation of the Western forces and that is to support the Jewish and Zion-
> ist plans for expansion of what is called the Great Israel. Surely, their presence
> is not out of concern over their interests in the region.... Their presence has
> no meaning save one and that is to offer support to the Jews in Palestine who
> are in need of their Christian brothers to achieve full control over the Arab
> Peninsula which they intend to make an important part of the so called Greater
> Israel.[9]

In other words, even before the invasion of Afghanistan or Iraq, bin Laden was making his call for jihad in terms of self-defence, taking US influence in Islamic lands as a basis for going to war against the United States. Here was a new interpretation for waging war using Islamic principles, an interpretation clearly guided by a new global situation. The presence of US troops in Saudi Arabia at the invitation of its government exposed these troops to attack because they supported a regime considered by bin Laden to be an enemy of the Muslim community. The alliance with Israel added to the animosity towards the United States, given his conspiratorial belief in the intent of the United States and Israel to bring the Arabian Peninsula under their full control. Equally important was bin Laden's discussion of Israel's role vis-à-vis Lebanon and the Palestinian people, which he used directly in explaining the attacks of 11 September 2001.

> I say to you, Allah knows that it had never occurred to us to strike the towers. But after it became unbearable and we witnessed the oppression and tyranny of the American/Israeli coalition against our people in Palestine and Lebanon, it came to my mind.

> The events that affected my soul in a direct way started in 1982 when America permitted the Israelis to invade Lebanon and the American Sixth Fleet helped them in that. This bombardment began and many were killed and injured and others were terrorised and displaced.[10]

Bin-Laden, like other self-proclaimed Islamic jihadists today, claims to be speaking in the name of Islam, representing all Muslims and walking in the steps of the Prophet Muhammad: "As we have already said, our call is the call of Islam that was revealed to Mohammed. It is a call to all mankind. We have been entrusted with good cause to follow in the footsteps of the Messenger and to communicate his message to all nations."[11] This claim to speak for the Muslim masses is repeated in a message to George Bush from al-Qaeda's deputy leader Ayman al-Zawahiri: "Bush, do you know where I am? I am among the Muslim masses."[12] Similarly, Ahmed Ali Nejat, an Iranian Shia leader, speaks in almost the same terms as the Wahhabi bin Laden and the Sunni Ayman al-Zawahiri, calling the United States "the great Satan", the enemy of Islam waging a Crusader's war against the Islamic religion and the Muslim people, with the aim of destroying Islam and acquiring the oil wealth of its people. Nejat also points to the plight of the Palestinian people as central to Iran's stand vis-à-vis Israel and the United States. His call for the destruction of Israel is interlaced with Islamic references, although, like bin Laden and al-Zawahiri, he makes no claim to special theological competence.

The interpretation of Islam by al-Qaeda and other extremist groups has garnered support among young Muslims, many of whom face a bleak future. They see the war against a rich West and its Muslim ruling-class allies as a form of jihad that would correct wrongs perpetrated against Palestinians and Iraqis. Such a jihad would also be a way of reclaiming their heritage, in their belief that the oil wealth gifted by God to Muslim countries has been monopolized by a few supported by their US partners. Acceptance of this viewpoint by a broader spectrum of Muslims has not materialized if for no other reason than that their rhetoric does not fit with what Muslims know about Islamic war ethics – that there is an acceptable way to wage war, which does not include the killing of the innocent, decapitating prisoners, suicide bombing or the destruction of buildings and homes.

By contrast, the wide support received by Hezbollah and its leader Sheikh Hassan Nasrallah in the 2006 Lebanese war tells the story of how Muslims look on the question of jihad. Lebanon was once again invaded by Israel, many Lebanese citizens had wilfully and randomly been imprisoned, Lebanese territories continued to be held by Israel, and Lebanon's children were hurt daily by mines that Israel placed in Lebanon (refusing to indicate where they had been placed). Notwithstanding the provocation by Hezbollah in kidnapping two Israeli soldiers, the Muslim masses saw the latest Israeli invasion as yet another effort to occupy southern Lebanon. They saw Hezbollah waging a jihad in protection of Lebanese territories and in self-defence against the systematic destruction of village after village accompanied by a siege designed to stop food and medical supplies while Israeli planes pounded people into leaving their homes, fleeing to the north in repetition of what happened to Palestinians in 1948.

The differences between bin Laden and Nasrallah are obvious to the Arab masses, as is the difference between al-Qaeda and Hezbollah. One group manipulates jihad while the other practises jihad. As this chapter has shown:

1. Although there is a basic formula that one can call a classic theory for waging war in Islam, the reasons and methods of war ethics are connected to time and place.
2. Basic to Islamic war ethics is a set of universal concepts that can be found in other religions as well. These include a teaching about justifiable rationales for waging war (e.g. self-defence against aggression, protection of the innocent), as well as stipulations regarding the importance of treating prisoners humanely, respecting the life, limb and homes of the innocent, etc.
3. By the same token, however, even these well-established practices can be called into question when they are seen to be egregiously violated

by the enemy. Hence in recent years we have witnessed how the inhumane treatment of prisoners at Abu Ghraib and Guantanamo has led to the decapitation of Western prisoners and other atrocities. Similarly, in response to the helplessness of the Palestinians, suicide bombings have been used as a last resort, despite Islam's total prohibition on suicide and its emphasis on the sanctity of human life.

Notes

1. Amira Sonbol, "Living and Working Together: Negotiating and Disputing Marriage and Business in Early Modern Egypt and Palestine under the Ottoman Empire", *L'Homme. Zeitschrift für Feministische Geschichtswissenschaft*, 17(2), 2006: 37–60.
2. This and the following examples are from the Yusuf Ali translation of the Qur'an. A. Yusuf Ali, *The Holy Qur-an, Text, Translation and Commentary* [1938]. Lahore: Amana Publications, 2008; electronic version available at ⟨http://www.sacred-texts.com/isl/quran/index.htm⟩ (accessed 20 October 2008).
3. The quotations in this section are from *The Holy Qur'an*, translated by M. H. Shakir. New York: Tahrike Tarsile Qur'an, Inc., 1983; electronic version available at ⟨http://etext.virginia.edu/koran.html⟩ (accessed 20 October 2008).
4. John L. Allen, "Context Crucial in Vatican–Israel Uproar", *National Catholic Reporter*, 12 August 2005.
5. See Muslim Online at ⟨http://muslimonline.org/cgi-bin/hadith.cgi⟩ (accessed 6 November 2008).
6. In this context, "migration" (*hijra*) signifies the move from a place of iniquity to a setting where authentic Islam can be established. The paradigmatic case of this was the Prophet's *hijra* to Medina in 622, where he established the first Muslim *umma*.
7. Sahih al-Bukhari, *Al-Kutub al-Ilmiya*, 2004, Vol. 1, Book 2, No. 24.
8. *Sunan Abu Dawud*, Book 14, "Jihad (Kitab Al-Jihad)", No. 2676; University of Southern California Compendium of Muslim Texts, at ⟨http://www.usc.edu/dept/MSA/fundamentals/hadithsunnah/abudawud/014.sat.html⟩ (accessed 6 November 2008).
9. Frontline, Interview with Osama bin Laden, in "Hunting Bin-Laden", PBS, May 1998; available at ⟨http://www.pbs.org/wgbh/pages/frontline/shows/binladen/who/interview.html⟩ (accessed 20 October 2008).
10. "Full Transcript of Bin Laden's Speech", Aljazeera.net, 1 November 2004; available at ⟨http://english.aljazeera.net/archive/2004/11/200849163336457223.html⟩ (accessed 20 October 2008).
11. Frontline, Interview with Osama bin Laden.
12. "Terror Chief Calls Bush a 'Butcher': Al Qaeda's No. 2 Man Taunts U.S. President in Videotape", CBS News, 31 January 2006; available at ⟨http://www.cbsnews.com/stories/2006/01/30/terror/main1255755.shtml⟩ (accessed 20 October 2008).

11

Norms of war in cross-religious perspective

Gregory M. Reichberg, Nicholas Turner and Vesselin Popovski

The chapters in this volume explore how the world's leading religious traditions have dealt with the normative problems associated with war and armed conflict. Although non-violent strategies of conflict resolution have been considered in several of the chapters, the book's main focus has been on what Stephen Neff names "the just-war outlook in the generic sense of the term".[1] This is the idea that the use of armed force may be justifiable within determinable limits in order to uphold fundamental human values, such as protection of one's homeland from attack, defence of the innocent, preservation of the rule of law, or accountability for grave crimes such as genocide.

The reader may find this focus on "just war" unexpected in a volume that purports to study how religious traditions have assessed the normative dimensions of war. For many, the term "just war" has come to signify a secular Western discourse that is ill suited for describing religious attitudes towards the phenomenon in question. Moreover, on the theme of religion and war the reading public has grown accustomed to apparently contradictory attitudes. On the one hand, it is often assumed that "true" religion requires a renunciation of violence; on the other hand, it seems equally incontrovertible that, when individuals enter war with religious motivations, their use of force will know no limits. Hence the freighted term "holy war", long associated with historical excesses such as the medieval Crusades or the Reformation era wars of religion, has newly found application to a wide range of violent struggles in which religious identifications are taken to be a key factor. The discourse about

World religions and norms of war, Popovski, Reichberg and Turner (eds),
United Nations University Press, 2009, ISBN 978-92-808-1163-6

religion and war thus gyrates from principled pacifism to the most extreme realism (where it is thought that in war for religious reasons "anything goes"). The ground traditionally occupied by the world's great religious traditions – wherein over the centuries a network of overlapping distinctions has been drawn on the difference between justifiable and unjustifiable uses of force – has been neglected in favour of the more dramatic discourse that alternates between the opposing poles of non-violence and militant extremism.

If "just war" designates the search for a middle ground between "no violence whatsoever" and "anything goes", then it can be a useful term for designating the abundant literature that arose first in Hindu culture, then among the ancient Israelites, to a certain extent among followers of the Buddha, and finally with much explicit articulation by Christians and Muslims. The present book has been edited with the hope that careful study of this literature will yield insight into the influence – good and bad – that religious motivations can exercise in the tragic domain of war.

There can be much value in secular approaches to the norms of war, as found in philosophical treatises, policy statements and, not least, the growing body of legal statutes ("international law") that formulate when, how and by whom force may used in the public interest. This literature is largely about rules of restraint, with respect to both *jus ad bellum* (as may be found, for instance, in the UN Charter) and *jus in bello* (as, for example, in the Hague or the Geneva Conventions). Yet this literature also contains rules of empowerment,[2] which urge military action (a "responsibility to protect") when many human lives are at grave risk from violence. The legal statutes in particular are framed in a language that prescinds from any explicit mention of religious concerns. The aim by and large is not so much to exclude religion but rather to employ a language that will be understood across the boundaries of the world's many religious communities, and by non-believers as well.

Admirable as this secular universalism may be, it has a notable downside. In seeking a common denominator (a shared consensus on the rules of war), the religious springs of human motivation, which *in concreto* are founded upon the particularity of different religious traditions, go untapped. The result is a set of rules that may be compelling in their abstract clarity but that may fail to motivate in the concrete circumstances of action because they have but little resonance within the cultural matrix of ordinary moral agents. Since the cultural matrix for millions of people in the world today is infused with ideas, images and expectations that originate from their respective religious traditions, if rules of war are to have real traction, if they are to have a hold on the minds and hearts of believers, it is important that they be associated with longstanding norms of peace and war that can be found within each of these traditions.

People will continue to listen to preachers and follow the ethics of their religions, no less than they will continue to read the books of international law. One can find good use in secularizing the norms of war from the religious traditions and codifying them into inter-state agreements. This book is intended not only as a reminder of the religious origins of norms of war, but also to help us remember that religious convictions continue to shape our conduct today (both in a positive and in a negative direction) with respect to the onset and methods of war.

Gaining a better understanding of the norms articulated by the world's religious traditions provides an internal (in this sense privileged) standpoint from which to judge manipulations of religion by those political leaders and others who have not failed to appreciate how powerfully religious beliefs can motivate human beings to action. The instrumentalization of religion has been much in evidence in several recent conflicts, and it has not gone undocumented within the present volume.

The reasons that can justify behaviour leading to the elimination of human life are as religious and ethical as they are political or legal. All religious traditions have on at least some occasions been demonized and accused of provoking aggressions, wars and human suffering. The complexity goes even further, as not only individuals but entire societies have sometimes been blamed in this way. This book considers what religions say about going to war and methods of fighting, but it does not take up Samuel Huntington's contested claims about a "clash of civilizations" as an explanation for the persistence of war in the twenty-first century. Although historically it seems beyond doubt that religious teachings have been instrumental in motivating or justifying some wars, we see little evidence for an inherent animosity between religions. True enough, kings and politicians have made use of religious texts to justify warfare. Soldiers have been told to fight infidels and, if necessary, to die defending a faith, a holy place or a community. But throughout history, war, an inherently political activity, has needed religion much more than religion has needed war.

The newly revived discourse on "holy war"[3] has tended to obscure the complexity of traditional religious teachings about war and violence. The origins of this term merit close historical examination. One can speculate that it was first employed metaphorically in the Christian West to designate the arduous spiritual struggle in the face of sin, evil and temptation to remain faithfully on the path to God, much as Muslims speak of the "greater jihad" of the soul. However, after the sixteenth-century wars of religion in Western Europe, the term came to signify, often in writings by Enlightenment detractors of religion, narrow sectarian rationales for resorting to armed force. Used as a catch-phrase, "holy war" suggests that, applied within settings of violent conflict, the religious impulse is at its most intense and authentic when it serves to motivate action on behalf of one set of narrow "sectarian" religious interests, against a competing set of equally narrow interests.

Left out of the equation are what one might term "universalist" religious rationales for engaging in war. Such rationales (which express norms of both empowerment and restraint) are formulated within particular religious traditions and couched in a terminology proper to each tradition, but are not founded on reasons exclusively proper to any one religion. Thus we find a number of core ideas affirmed across a range of different traditions: for instance, that force may be used to protect innocent third parties from attack, that grievances should be openly aired before redress is sought through armed force, that non-combatants should not be directly targeted in war, that promises even to enemies should be kept, that prisoners should be treated humanely, or that especially cruel means of warfare should be banned. When these core ideas find expression in holy books, or are articulated by recognized religious authorities, they benefit from a kind of divine warrant that strengthens their credibility in the eyes of religious believers. Let us now summarize some aspects of what can be identified as common (or "universalist") causes and methods of war, based on the preceding chapters.

Jus ad bellum

The preceding chapters have shown that there is much overlap between the different religious traditions regarding what counts as a legitimate rationale for resorting to armed force. While revenge or purely acquisitive reasons for war are almost universally condemned, self-defence from attack is the rationale most often put forward for going to war. In Hinduism, Christianity and Islam, for instance, defence is not merely framed as an allowable course of action (a right or a justification); it is also promoted as an obligation incumbent upon the political leadership and citizenry alike.[4]

Despite this broad consensus, within the different religions there remain somewhat different assessments of what kinds of wrongdoing warrant defensive action. For instance, Islamic authors often view the expulsion of helpless people from their homes or attacks on holy places as among the greatest of harms; hence defence in this tradition will consist first and foremost in using force to protect against attacks of this kind. Likewise, within Islam there is a very strong condemnation of surprise attack as an especially perfidious form of aggression. Within Christianity, by contrast, although much is said about the protection of the innocent, the protection of holy places has typically not figured very prominently in discussions about legitimate defence. However, within this religion there may be found particularly rich discussions about whether or not the threat of future harm can legitimize defensive military action. Now referred to under the heading of "pre-emption", the consensus among leading authors (Catholic and Protestant) is that only immediate threats, based on demonstrable signs of imminent aggression, can warrant resort to armed force in the absence of any ongoing attack. More dubious is the legitimacy of defensive action in the face of a long-term plan to carry out future aggression. What is more, these authors are nearly unanimous in their rejection of preventive war, the strategy whereby nation x attacks nation y so as to prevent y from acquiring a capacity to cause x future harm. In this vein, the Dutch Protestant Hugo Grotius wrote that "[q]uite untenable is the position, which has been maintained by some, that according to the law of nations it is right to take up arms in order to weaken a growing power which may do harm, should it become too great.... [T]hat the possibility of being attacked confers the right to attack is abhorrent to every principle of equity."[5]

In several traditions, there may likewise be found a strong imperative to contemplate all possible alternatives before resorting to the use of force – the principle of last resort. Hence we find Christian and Muslim authors articulating the view that God has provided humans with means other than force by which to solve disputes, and a wronged party must declare its grievances to the perpetrator, allowing an opportunity for non-violent resolution before resorting to force. Similarly, Buddhist teachings, while rarely engaging in explicit discussion of war and its justification, do make clear that leaders are allowed to use limited force only when prior attempts at peaceful negotiation have met with failure.

It must be observed that the teachings of the major religious traditions regarding war are also strongly influenced by their respective conceptions of peace. The ethics of the transition between peace and war, which is the domain of *jus ad bellum*, will be construed very differently depending on how peace is conceptualized in relation to war. Some religious traditions define peace positively in relation to justice and friendship, rather than negatively as the absence of war. This is particularly salient in both Judaism and Christianity. With respect to the latter, for instance, the Eastern Orthodox tradition, while maintaining that war is unconditionally an evil, also acknowledges that there are times when war is necessary in order to restore a peace that has been disrupted or lost. Judaism similarly shares the conviction that war is not a natural condition, and adds to it the messianic ideal that universal peace will become a reality for the whole of humanity. In Islam, great value is attached to building and maintaining peace, to the extent that it is considered a duty for all Muslims, and, accordingly, those who bring peace are promised "continuous praise from the angels". However, in contrast to the normative centrality of peace in most traditions (including Buddhism, which traces war to human failings such as hatred and ignorance), Hindu teaching emphasizes the inevitability of inter-state war; its efforts are accordingly directed chiefly at limiting the harmful effects of violent conflict.

Several of the religions studied in this volume have on occasion held out the promise that heavenly rewards will be granted to individuals who conduct war in a manner consistent with the teachings of their tradition. This idea of "reward" is clearly vulnerable to political misuse and, notwithstanding certain biased portrayals, Islam does not find itself alone in this regard. Hence, in the *dharmayuddha* doctrine of Hindu religious thought, warriors who kill in the line of duty are assured a place in Heaven after death; similarly, in Eastern Orthodox and Roman Catholic Christianity, soldiers who fight justly for a worthy cause have sometimes been canonized as saints.[6]

It is true, however, that there can be found teachings on war and violence that are proper to specific religious traditions. Some of these teachings provide reasons for restraint, while others encourage resort to force. As an example of the former, one could cite the Shiite teaching that offensive war may be waged only at the command of an Infallible Imam. Since it is believed that no such Imam is present today (in light of the doctrine of "occultation"), the result is a general prohibition of offensive war and thus a special religious reason that narrows the *jus ad bellum* to strict defence. A related conception may be found within Judaism, in its teaching that "discretionary war" has no current validity and has not had such for well over 2,000 years, in the absence of a High Priest with access to an authorizing oracle (the Urim and Thummim). Similarly in Islam, although defensive war may be waged without the special permission of legitimate authority – under conditions of great urgency all citizens, including women and children, are expected to fight – offensive war is regulated much more strictly. It is stipulated, for instance, that grievances must be announced beforehand so that the offending party has an opportunity to make amends, and hostilities may be initiated only with an open declaration being made beforehand (surprise attack being strictly condemned) solely under the command of the highest authority in the land. Other religions, including Christianity, also distinguish between "defensive" and "offensive" war; with the proviso that significantly stricter requirements obtain for the latter than for the former. This framework has been adopted into international law, as evidenced for instance in Articles 51 and 42 of the UN Charter: although individual states retain the right of self-defence, the UN Security Council is alone permitted to authorize offensive war (termed "enforcement action").

The emerging contemporary norm of humanitarian intervention also has its roots in several religious traditions. In Islam, for instance, the faithful have been urged to fight in aid of those who are helpless to defend themselves, and in Christianity the ideal of fighting on behalf of the innocent has existed at least since St Ambrose in the fourth century, who famously wrote that "he who fails to ward off injury from an associate if he can do so, is quite as blamable as he who inflicts it".[7] The norm of humanitarian intervention has now achieved a strong basis in public consensus, in large respects owing to the duty of compassionate assistance that is affirmed in one way or another in all religious traditions. Applied historically in concrete circumstances, it goes without saying that religious justifications for the use of force have not always been altruistic. Acknowledgement of this fact should nevertheless not preclude us from recognizing that religious traditions have sometimes urged resort to force for humanitarian reasons, in ways that many of us would be willing to countenance today.

For examples of special religious reasons that encourage resort to armed force, one could point to the medieval Crusades in Western Christianity (premised on the belief that the Holy Land, having been "consecrated" by the birth and death of Jesus, was by right the property of Christians), or to the conviction, upheld by Ibn Taymiyya (thirteenth century) and some later Sunni authors, that Muslims have a positive duty to "strive in the way of God" by spreading Islamic law to those who lack it, "through peaceful means if possible but with the use of force if necessary". Other causes that have justified the resort to force include the Shinto belief in Japan as a "land of the Gods", which in the sixteenth century served to warrant the invasion of the Korean peninsula, ostensibly to spread the "benefits of civilization" to neighbouring states. In Hinduism, the realist doctrine of *kutayuddha* preaches the use of force to maintain power and protect territory, as advocated in Kautilya's *Arthasastra*. Closer to our own time, during the armed conflict in the Balkans, some Orthodox Serb theologians promoted a "Kosovo covenantal mythology" that helped create "an environment in which organized violence could be justifiable and even recommendable as the only possible self-defence strategy for a perpetually beleaguered Christian Orthodox nation and Church" (Chapter 7 in this volume).

There are many more examples of religious encouragement to violence. Although Islam has born the brunt of blame in recent years, it remains true that none of the world's religious traditions can claim immunity from such a tendency. There is much need for a systematic comparative exploration of the doctrinal factors that condition religious motivations for engagement in acts of violence. Such an exploration largely falls outside the scope of the present volume, but it can be noted, based on findings contained herein, that in ideological settings where there exists a tight fusion between state and religion a wide opening is created for the justification of religious violence. It is well documented, for instance, how in the "sacral" political order of the Christian Middle Ages heresy and other forms of religious dissidence were considered crimes against the state, akin to sedition, and on this ground would warrant armed suppression. This mindset has also promoted various forms of inter-civilizational conflict (say between Christians and Muslims) and inter-denominational wars of religion. In Islam, similarly, there have been times when the state's coercive power was viewed as "essential for the establishment and maintenance of discipline and order, without which mosques could not be opened and the practice of Islam carried out" (Chapter 10 in this volume). In either case (and here again examples could be multiplied with reference to other religions), when the very unity of the political community is constituted along religious lines and where, in addition, the political order is viewed as instrumental to religious ends, there will be increased pressure to use force in responding to religious threats. Inversely, doctrinal attempts at separating the cause of religion from that of the state have generally helped to bring about a de-legitimization of religiously inspired violence.[8]

Jus in bello

If we consider what the previous chapters have written about *jus in bello*, or proper conduct in war, it will become apparent that there is much overlap on this theme among the world's different religious traditions. One important case in point is the key norm of non-combatant immunity, a principle that has found expression in nearly all religious traditions. Although framed diversely in different settings, the idea that civilians, wounded soldiers, prisoners and even combatants who have lost their weapons should not be targeted with direct harm has found widespread affirmation in religious texts. True enough, some religious actors have preached the contrary, but it is difficult to find much support for this extreme view within the classical texts that have been discussed in this volume. Non-combatant immunity and related principles have been codified in international humanitarian law through treaties such as the Geneva Conventions (1949). The violation of such humanitarian norms regularly prompts widespread condemnation from figures of authority in the major religions, demonstrating how there exists much inter-religious agreement regarding these norms.

Despite the widespread support for non-combatant immunity, the implementation of this norm is anything but easy, particularly in settings that include the use of terrorist tactics and asymmetric warfare. In such contexts, normative discourse oscillates between inclusive and exclusive definitions of combatant status, which results in correspondingly different prescriptions for the use of force. Advocates of terrorism often claim that civilians are responsible for the actions and policies of their governments, and on this basis they are deemed legitimate targets of force. Asymmetric warfare likewise often involves a blurring of the line between combatants and non-combatants. When actors views themselves as unable to confront an opponent in conventional ways, but consider their cause just, they often feel justified in using unconventional tactics such as human shielding and kidnapping. The employment of "human shields" is now deemed a violation of international humanitarian law – accountability for the fate of these involuntary shields rests with the individuals who placed them in their precarious position. In responding to tactics such as these, some religious texts have emphasized the responsibilities of the active party, as for instance in Islamic jurisprudence, which permits the targeting of combatants who have taken shelter among women and children. The Israel Defense Forces (IDF) "purity of arms" code likewise maintains that minimizing the deaths of non-combatants is a priority, with however the qualification that, for a sovereign state, minimizing the deaths of one's own non-combatants takes priority over protecting non-combatants on the opposing side.[9]

Proportionality in the use of force is another concept that has found widespread acceptance among the world's leading religious traditions. Proportionality has proven to be especially hard to apply to unconventional weaponry, for instance nuclear arms. Within Christianity and Islam, strong condemnations regarding any possible battlefield use of such weapons have been enunciated, owing to the high number of casualties and the long-term harm that would inevitably result. On the other side of the spectrum, some Hindu authors allow for the use of these weapons in circumstances of last resort. In some religious traditions there has also been broad debate on the permissibility of designing and possessing nuclear weapons for purposes of deterrence. Whereas Roman Catholic teaching has allowed for a limited strategy of deterrence, as long as all nuclear states actively work toward the long-term goal of nuclear disarmament, in the Shia tradition any possession of nuclear weapons, for whatever reason (including deterrence), is considered incompatible with the teachings of Islam.[10] Indeed, consternation over the development of nuclear weapons prompted a reassessment in the Roman Catholic Church of the basic concept of just war, with Pope John XXIII maintaining (in 1963) that, "in this age which boasts of its atomic power, it no longer makes sense to maintain that war is a fit instrument with which to repair the violation of justice".[11] It must be said nonetheless that the "limited" wars of the post–Cold War era have reintroduced the just war idea into public (and religious) debate, since experience has shown that even states that possess a nuclear arsenal are able to fight without bringing (inherently) disproportionate force into the fray.

Evolution and interpretation

Most religious traditions, by their inherent dependence on historical texts, rarely offer detailed answers to emerging contemporary issues, including modern methods of warfare. Religious teachings are often taken to be universal truths that apply across time, irrespective of social, political or technological developments. Whereas religious texts do not readily change, the historical circumstances of human life are subject to profound transformations. Religion is not, therefore, about blindly following a set of rules, but more about considering how the principles contained in sacred texts and practices should apply to the emerging issues of the present day. Religious texts call for reflection on their meaning, and so it is natural that a variety of interpretations will be offered, adding to the rich diversity of opinions within each tradition. This highlights both the opportunities as well as the inevitable risks that accompany the interpretation and application of religious teachings. In the process of bringing religious teachings into the broader stream of public discourse, theologians and other scholars strive to show how their respective religions can maintain their core identity while allowing for diversity in their adaptation to the changing conditions of human existence.

In this fashion, from their origins in different times and different contexts, the world's great religious traditions have had to come to terms with the same changing world; they likewise have grappled with the same issues of war and violence. In doing so, they have reached many of the same conclusions. Although each tradition contains teachings that are unique to it alone – the role of the Urim and Thummim (the High Priest's oracle) in Judaism, or the occulted Twelfth Imam in Shia Islam, would be two such examples – this should not prevent us from seeing the many significant parallels and points of agreement on the norms of war among the different religions. This notwithstanding, it cannot be denied that religious discourse on war can also give rise to extremist interpretations, particularly when religious teachings are made to serve narrow political interests. One need only think of the use to which the concept of "holy war" has been put, not only by Christians (as recently as the Spanish

Civil War) and Muslims (al-Qaeda), but also by Buddhists (witness the ongoing conflict in Sri Lanka), Hindus (nationalist appeals vis-à-vis Kashmir) and Jews (the Settler movement), as justification for campaigns of violence. For political leaders engaged in war, there can be a strong temptation to deploy the rhetoric of religious justification, with all the increased support and protection from criticism this brings. Religious discourse can magnify and exacerbate pre-existing tensions; this effect is open to exploitation by leaders who use it to rally their troops, the public and other politicians. Religious calls to action can serve to reinforce the positive identity of "our" side, thereby demonizing the "other" side. For each potential soldier, if God is on his side he cannot easily refuse to fight, and his belief that the war will end in victory will be strengthened, thereby removing the fear of defeat and encouraging others to join the fight.

All religious texts contain internal tensions; passages calling for action often contradict those advocating restraint, and vice versa. Each exponent of a religion claims the validity of his or her interpretation, and herein resides the greatest problem: moderation is frequently seen as, at best, no more than one of many different interpretations. But this ignores the reinforcement that these moderate religious views receive from secular international law. In turn, it cannot be ignored that the core norms of international law originally took root in the religious thought of humanity, Christianity especially, but to some extent in other traditions as well.[12] The cross-cultural legitimacy of international norms in a range of areas, including the use of force, human rights and law, is based on, and continues to be enhanced by, the existence of shared religious principles. International norms "return the favour" by conferring cross-cultural validity back upon the moderate voices within each tradition that contributed to the formulation of these norms in the first place. In this way, the views of moderates, and therefore their readings of the core texts, are vindicated by international consensus. Extreme factions can never gain this validity. Here we need to be reminded of what Aristotle said about the mean of virtue: this is a mean of excellence, not of mediocrity; true moderation indicates great skill, akin to hitting the bull's eye on a target.

Inter-faith dialogue is an indispensable path toward building up a consensus on norms of war among people of different religions. This in turn contributes greatly to denying credibility to extremists who claim religious rationales for their violence. It is telling that, from the perspective of extremists, dialogue and mutual engagement are seen as unacceptable compromises, endangering the purity of their tradition's teaching and practice. Recent efforts to encourage dialogue between Muslims and Christians, including Pope Benedict XVI's meetings in 2007 with the Saudi king and with a group of Muslim scholars led by Jordanian Prince

Ghazi bin Mohammad bin Talal, have been criticized by the leaders of al-Qaeda, for whom inter-religious dialogue is viewed as a threat to the interests of "true religion". But Muslim hard-liners do not have a monopoly on this aversion to dialogue. Such aversion may be found, *inter alia*, among Christian advocates as well.[13]

The preceding chapters have shown how religious thinking contributes vitally to our understanding of norms of war. This said, much further research is necessary. In particular, a deeper knowledge of the ongoing internal tensions and developments within the different traditions would provide valuable insights not only about each religion in particular, but more generally about the processes by which religious teachings on peace and war develop. These insights, in turn, could throw light on the ways in which these teachings are interpreted and misinterpreted, as well as the nature and dynamics of their influence on the political sphere.

Notes

1. Stephen Neff, *War and the Law of Nations*. Cambridge: Cambridge University Press, 2005, p. 34.
2. On the contrast between rules of restraint and rules of empowerment, see Anthony Coates, "Is the Independent Application of *jus in bello* the Way to Limit War?", in David Rodin and Henry Shue (eds) *Just and Unjust Warriors: The Moral and Legal Status of Soldiers*. Oxford: Oxford University Press, 2008, pp. 176–192.
3. See, for instance, "The New Wars of Religion" in *The Economist*, 3–9 November 2007, and the CNN TV series "God's Warriors", 2007, available at ⟨http://edition.cnn.com/SPECIALS/2007/gods.warriors/index.html⟩ (accessed 22 October 2008).
4. This was summed up by the Swiss Protestant author Vattel, when he wrote that "[i]f a Nation is bound to preserve its existence it is not less bound to preserve carefully the lives of its members. It owes this duty to itself" (cited in Gregory Reichberg, Henrik Syse and Endre Begby (eds), *The Ethics of War: Classic and Contemporary Readings*. Oxford: Blackwell Publishing, 2006, p. 507).
5. Quoted in Reichberg et al., *The Ethics of War*, p. 405. A similar position was developed by the Catholic theologian Taparelli d'Azeglio; see *Essai théorique de droit naturel base sur les faits* [1840–1843], translated from the original Italian. Tournai: H. Casterman, 1875, vol. 2 (Book VI, chap. IV), pp. 45–48. For a survey of Christian writings on the theme of pre-emption, see Gregory M. Reichberg, "Preventive War in Classical Just War Theory", *Journal of the History of International Law*, 9, 2007: 5–33.
6. In Gratian's *Decretum* (c. 1140), one of the most influential works of Western Christianity, we read this invocation (attributed to Pope Leo IV): "Having relinquished all fright and terror, do combat with all your strength the enemies of the holy faith and the adversaries of all religions. For if any of you dies, the Almighty knows that he died for the truth of the faith, for the salvation of the country and the defense of the Christians, and he will therefore obtain celestial reward" (quoted in Reichberg et al., *The Ethics of War*, p. 124). For a study of military sainthood in Christianity, see André Corvisier, *Les Saints Militaires*. Paris: Editions Honoré Champion, 2006.

7. Citation from Gratian's *Decretum*, in Reichberg et al., *The Ethics of War*, p. 114.

8. As, for instance, in the Roman Catholic Church, which issued a Declaration on Religious Freedom (*Dignitatis Humanae*) in 1965. The text is available at ⟨http://www.vatican.va/archive/hist_councils/ii_vatican_council/documents/vat-ii_decl_19651207_dignitatis-humanae_en.html⟩ (accessed 22 October 2008).

9. For discussion of this topic, see *Journal of Military Ethics*, 4(1), 2005, special issue on "Israel and the Ethics of Fighting Terror".

10. This condemnation is reflected in the statement issued on 12 August 2005 by Ayatollah Ali Khamenei, Supreme Leader of the Islamic Republic of Iran, who declared that "the production, stockpiling and use of nuclear weapons are forbidden under Islam" (cited at ⟨http://www.mathaba.net/0_index.shtml?x=302258⟩, accessed 22 October 2008).

11. Pope John XXIII, "*Pacem in Terris*. Encyclical of Pope John XXIII on Establishing Universal Peace in Truth, Justice, Charity, and Liberty", 11 April 1963, §127; available at ⟨http://www.vatican.va/holy_father/john_xxiii/encyclicals/documents/hf_j-xxiii_enc_11041963_pacem_en.html⟩ (accessed 22 October 2008).

12. On this score, see Mostafa Mohaghegh Damad, *Protection of Individuals in Times of Armed Conflict under International and Islamic Laws*. New York: Global Scholarly Publications, 2005, pp. 52–55.

13. See, for instance, George Weigel, *Faith, Reason, and the War against Jihadism: A Call to Action*. New York: Doubleday, 2007.

Index